Confrontation

Encounters in Self and Interpersonal Awareness

Encounters in Self
and Interpersonal Awareness

Edited by
Leonard Blank
Gloria B. Gottsegen
Monroe G. Gottsegen

Confrontation

The Macmillan Company, New York

Collier-Macmillan Limited, London

The Macmillan Company
866 Third Avenue, New York, New York 10022

Collier-Macmillan Canada, Ltd., Toronto, Ontario

Library of Congress catalog card number: 70-139967

First Printing

ACKNOWLEDGMENTS

Chapter 9 © copyright by Daniel H. Casriel. Printed by permission of the author.

Chapter 17 © copyright by William Gellermann. Printed by permission of the author.

Chapter 21 © copyright by Morton A. Lieberman, Irvin D. Yalom, and Matthew B. Miles. Printed by permission of the authors.

This book is dedicated to the memory of three
leaders of the humanistic psychology movement

ABRAHAM H. MASLOW

FREDERICK H. PERLS

FREDERICK H. STOLLER

Preface

Alienation. Isolation. Search for intimacy. A craving for contact. A need to fill a void in our lives. Terms and phrases of this nature are common in describing the current scene. We seem to be groping beyond the stereotyped roles we assume with family, colleagues, and persons we deal with daily. We are confused about our identity, our status, and our very functions that are not structured by specific situations.

Something seems to happen, however, when we meet in a group under particular conditions. When stilted roles are loosened by permissiveness or changed expectations, and when frank interaction becomes the ground rule in lieu of the social amenities, a group phenomenon often occurs—a *confrontation*. People encounter each other and facets of their personalities that they were unaware of before. Put in another way, certain group processes generate an encounter with self and others. This confrontation or encounter may range along the spectrum of emotions but it transcends, in any event, an overemphasized intellectual interaction.

Encounter phenomena are not limited to psychotherapy patients, although they may most valuably benefit from encounters. The professional mental health specialist requires a continual feedback about his intrapersonal and interpersonal communication. Far more broadly, there are confrontations between youth and their elders, the advantaged and the disadvantaged, the powerless and the establishment, and so on. Student dissent, urban riots, protest movements, and strikes are all encounters that have burgeoned into expressions often beyond control. Would "controlled" encounters obviate frenzied attempts to be heard and recognized? Is not there a middle ground between the urge to radicalize and the pressure of conformity?

The existential stress on meaningfulness, involvement, and immediacy is a crucial feature of encounter phenomena. So too is the humanist emphasis on maximizing human potential, development, and communication and respect for other humans. Both the existential and humanist positions suggest that encounter phenomena are a reaction against a sense of mechanization and automation.

There is a wide variety of means of achieving these confrontations, which stress commitment, involvement, communication, and behavioral change—both verbally and nonverbally. The contributors to this book are pioneers and leaders in encounter theory and methodology. Each has been requested by the editors to make an original contribution that stresses the implications for encounter experience on intrapersonal and interpersonal behavior and for a variety of populations including patients, professionals, and other people. The contributors have been asked to relate encounter experiences to existential and humanistic theory and practice and to the social scene in general. And they have been requested to be generous in their use of case illustrations with the focus on the individual rather than the mechanics.

The book has been divided into five sections: "The Experience of Encounter," "Techniques," "Innovations," "Populations," and "Theory and Research." We begin the book with the account and rationale of marathons so as to confront you and, it is hoped, involve you with examples of intense encounters. And for the same reason, we leave theory for the last so that the reader's involvement and reading experience, at least, may serve as a foundation for the theoretic formulation.

L. B.
G. B. G.
M. G. G.

Contents

Part E
Theory and Research

Part A
The Experience of Encounter

Linda Hess

1 A Note on the Climate*

I had my belly massaged by a Catholic priest, groped through a ball-room full of 1,500 people with eyes shut, heard the latest research on out-of-body travel and the emotional life of plants, listened to a willowy brunette in underwear scream "NOOO!" while a psychiatrist pushed his finger down her throat, had conversations with hands, dialogues with eyes, embraces with strangers, fights with fresh acquaintances, discussions on new approaches to therapy, education, black-white encounter, transcendental experience, growth centers, communes . . . and that wasn't all. But the best thing was the way it ended, which wasn't on the program.

I was attending the seventh annual meeting of the American Association for Humanistic Psychology, an organization that represents a sprawling avant-garde in psychology and other interrelated disciplines. The chief guru-figures of the AAHP (I almost said father-figures, but that really wouldn't have been right) are Abraham Maslow and Carl Rogers, whose theories and practices point sharply away from the grim mechanism of behaviorist psychology and the grim pessimism of freudian psychology.

In the last five years or so the "human potentials movement," like

---

* Reprinted from *The Village Voice*, Sept. 4, 1969, by permission of The Village Voice, Inc.

the hippie mystique and the campus revolution, has burgeoned across the country. One of its most remarkable manifestations has been the phenomenon known as sensitivity training, which I won't try to explain here. We could say of the encounter group what was being said of LSD a few years ago: millions of people are fascinated by it, many readers of this article have tried it, almost everyone knows someone who has, and to find out what it really is you have to experience it.

The setting for the AAHP meeting, as for most conventions, was insipid: gray and orange plaster and plastic of the Sheraton in Silver Spring, Maryland, a drab suburb of Washington. It began Thursday evening with a mass encounter in the ballroom. The place was carpeted with 1,500 bodies—therapists, educators, community organizers, group leaders, students, gurus, and assorted truth-seekers. Everything seemed low: smoke hung like low cloud banks; heat pressed us into the floor. Even the crystal chandeliers were flat—there wasn't enough height for the dangling kind. Our President rose from among us and spoke: "I feel tremendously excited just looking at you. It has some of the feeling of that historic gathering at Woodstock, and before the weekend is over there may be much more of that sense of community and joy under stressful conditions."

I attended eight scheduled sessions in two days. But for each one I attended, there were six or eight others going on simultaneously. Some were called "experiential": if a person had developed certain growth-promoting techniques or workshop structures, you didn't just listen to him explain it. You got down on the floor with blocks and finger paints in "Adult Play Encounter," you experimented with new forms of behavior in "Creative Risk-Taking," you did sensitivity exercises amid a sensory bombardment in "Knowledge Transfer in the '70s: a Mixed-Media Experience."

The "theoretic" track included panels on developing humanistically based communities, the possibility of complete sexual freedom in mental institutions, current attacks on the encounter group movement, and the nude marathon as a way of combating alienation (too bad that one wasn't experiential).

Under "social action" were sessions devoted mainly to the use of small-group techniques to break through barriers among races, conflicting elements in schools, industry, and so on.

Finally there was "transpersonal," a new category for the conference. These sessions tended to point inward and eastward: Baba Ram Dass (Richard Alpert) on his odyssey from Jewish boyhood and Harvard through psychedelics and yoga in the Himalayas; a group of astrologers on Cosmic Humanism; researchers in the new science called Altered States of Consciousness.

In the ballroom there was a continuous series of meetings with the big names in the movement: William Schutz of Esalen in Big Sur, author of "Joy"; Fritz Perls, originator of Gestalt therapy; Alexander Lowen, the bioenergetic analyst who diagnoses and treats personality disorders through the body; Jack Gibb who demonstrates TORI (Trust, Openness, Realization, Interdependence) with groups up to a thousand strong; and more.

The atmosphere was convention and carnival, professional and curiosity-seeker. Arms and minds were reaching toward each other, toward intimacy, revolution, revelation, salvation. Permissions were broad, humor and pleasure were riding high, pain and fear flowed to the surface more freely than usual because the community accepted and supported the flow, and because some of the modes of experience being demonstrated were very powerful. Some scenes and sounds that flashed past me—

Lowen: "Ever notice how Charles Boyer walks like this, with his toes turned out? We call that a tightass walk."

The President: "What is the AAHP? Are we a bunch of oddballs?" (Roar of approval from the audience.)

Sign on the swimming pool door: "AAHP members *must* conform to the rules of the hotel and the Maryland state law."

Tableau with husky Paul Bindrim, practitioner of peak-oriented therapy, and John, his demonstration subject, skinny, frightened, large eyes protruding from narrow, diamond-shaped head. John has brought his favorite sensory stimuli: cashews to eat, roses to smell, fur to feel, the BeeGees to listen to, a romantic photograph to look at. Bindrim is leaning intently over him in a thick hypnotic atmosphere, waxy yellow light, holding a crimson rose to his nose while the BeeGees drum relentlessly, the same song over and over.

After the last session Saturday afternoon I felt keyed up, happy, nervous, hopeful, still responding to a mix of crisscrossing stimuli. It had been an exciting and unconventional gathering, laced with discoveries and surprises, but still pretty thoroughly programmed and scheduled. I didn't anticipate anything like the magnificent, totally improvised climax it reached that night.

I arrived late at that low-roofed ballroom where the official party was going on. A gooey band was pumping trombones, and a lady was selling tickets for drinks. After half an hour of aimless drifting, I heard someone whisper in my ear: "The real party's down on the mezzanine."

In a big closed-in sort of service porch with leaky pipes lining the ceiling, I found the real party. A bare bulb flashed on hundreds of sweaty bodies jumping, dancing, and singing to improvised percussion instruments. Sounds and forms kept flowing into new configurations.

Individuals differentiated themselves from the mass, then merged with it again.

Eventually an enormous clapping, vibrating circle formed around a wildly dancing couple. He looked to me like the spirit of Bacchus in the body of Apollo. She was May from Botticelli's "Primavera." They danced till they fell exhausted and the jubilant crowd converged on them, lifted them high, still locked together, the boy on top of the girl. They were carried triumphantly, then deposited gently with many communal caresses, in the center of the floor where they lay with arms around each other, looking dazed.

Meanwhile the crowd was swaying, all interlocked, humming and hymning in a chorus that swelled till you could almost see the vibrations ripple out through the solar system. It burst, subsided, was transformed into "Hare Krishna," then "Silent Night, Holy Night," then a rising chant of "Yes! Yes! YES!" which abruptly gave way to silence as a flute blew maroon velvet streams through the air.

The flutist had a full graying beard and wore black and white striped bells with a red silk poncho. He was probably a psychologist.

Another middle-aged man rose from the still bodies to undulate slowly with the flute. "The generation gap," I thought, "it's wiped out here tonight."

There were several more climaxes, crescendos of sound and movement, diminuendos of harmony and communion. Three young people stripped joyously and stayed that way for a long time without invasion from the uptight world. Hal Streitfeld, program chairman for the conference, was given a superdemonstration of a standard sensitivity exercise: lifted high by the community, rocked back and forth, slowly returned to earth to be stroked and caressed by dozens of anonymous hands.

Eventually it reached a final conclusion as if by unanimous tacit agreement. In the hotel lobby a last big circle formed, swaying and singing, then falling to the floor with bodies stretched out like spokes of a wheel, heads at the hub, eyes closed, arms around neighbors. By this time even the desk clerks were charmed: they stepped over the bodies as if it happened every day.

I had thought the golden age of the be-in was over. The last place I expected to retrieve it was in the lobby of a Sheraton Hotel among a practically drugless assembly spanning three generations and including many "established" professional people. It sprang spontaneously from a brief but intense shared experience of human community and expanded personal freedom. The spirit of it might be summed up by Fritz Perls's Gestalt prayer:

I do my thing, and you do your thing.
I am not in this world to live up to your expectations
And you are not in this world to live up to mine.
You are you and I am I,
And if by chance we find each other, it's beautiful.
If not, it can't be helped.

Figure 1-1. You are you and I am I. (Photos by Zev Guber and Gary Madderom.)

Elizabeth E. Mintz

 Marathon Groups:
Process and People

COMMENTARY

In this chapter, we are introduced to an intense form of confrontation, the marathon. The techniques described can be utilized in a variety of other basic encounters. The case illustrations set the tone for the experiential as well as didactic presentation of this book.

BIOGRAPHY

Elizabeth Mintz, Ph.D., has given well over 100 marathon groups, most of them in private practice but some in growth centers and industrial settings. The unusual facet to her practice is that she has combined physical encounter techniques and the Gestalt approach with a thorough background in psychoanalytic theory. She is a diplomate in clinical psychology of the American Board of Professional Psychology. She has taught psychoanalytic theory for the past ten years at the National Psychological Association for Psychoanalysis, an institute for the training of analysts. She has published many articles, principally in the field of group therapy.

People are beautiful, and for the first time in my life I hope for happiness.

Today feels like the real beginning of my life. Today is my real birthday.

Something wonderful happened, something to do with closeness and openness with others, taking off the armor, throwing away the shield.

I was inside my skin, tight and alone. I never thought I'd use such language, it sounds corny, but now I feel related to the stars.

Never before did I feel so loved and accepted.

For the first time I am a part of all humanity.

These ecstatic remarks, taken verbatim from letters sent to me immediately after their writers had participated in a marathon group, are not unusual. My files, now containing hundreds of letters from participants in approximately 100 marathon groups conducted over a five-year period, yield countless other passages that express a new and radiant awareness of selfhood, not solitary and isolated selfhood, but an enhanced selfhood that includes a joyous sense of closeness to family and friends, a feeling of participation in the mainstream of humanity, and in some instances even a feeling of being part of the cosmos—"related to the stars."

Nevertheless, it would hardly require a marked degree of cynicism to question the durability of these transcendental feelings. Religious conversions and drug-induced mystical experiences often induce temporary feelings of high elation, but do not necessarily bring about any lasting increase in personal effectiveness or happiness. In manic psychosis the patient often has a sense of omnipotence and may feel at one with a glorious universe; yet these conditions often lead to self-destructive behavior or swing back toward abysmal depression. Immediate subjective reports, however enthusiastic, clearly cannot in themselves be regarded as signs of basic personality improvement.

Yet there is also evidence that under some circumstances there may be fundamental personality changes as a result of religious conversion (James, 1902); or brief psychotherapy (Alexander and French, 1946); or unplanned life experiences (Worchel and Byrne, 1964). What these circumstances are and what constitutes readiness for such a change remain unknown; yet it is very clear that for certain people, participation in a marathon group may be a significant milestone in personal development; for others who at first are equally enthusiastic, it is little more than an exciting adventure; still others, comparatively few in number, remain unmoved.[1] The six quotations offered above

[1] In an earlier paper (Mintz, 1969) written feedback from marathon participants was tabulated, with these results:

were selected from former marathon participants still known to me three years or more after they wrote their exultant comments. Four of these people are still moving toward increasing self-fulfillment, perceive their lives as worthwhile, and look back upon their marathon experiences as uniquely valuable, though none retained the initial intense exhilaration. Two respondents were disappointed when their postmarathon euphoria disappeared within a few days, and even more disappointed when they found themselves still faced with the same inward and outward difficulties; one wrote: "Yes, the marathon was fun, but it was like an alcoholic binge. It didn't last." Research is indicated to explore what factors may be associated with such divergent results, but it seems likely that they are similar to characteristics generally associated with successful psychotherapeutic outcome—determination, vitality, the ability to become involved in the therapeutic situation (Mintz, "Prognosis, Outcome and the Therapist's Feelings," 1967), and probably also the ability to continue whatever efforts toward self-realization were stimulated by the marathon, as opposed to a wish to be the passive object of a magic cure.

What is a marathon? Essentially, it is simply a time-extended group, typically including from 8 to 20 participants and conducted by one or more leaders, remaining in continuous encounter for many hours. Its purpose may be primarily therapeutic: it may be utilized for a specific clinical problem, as with groups of drug addicts at Synanon and Daytop; or it may be an adjunct treatment for patients simultaneously undergoing more conventional types of therapy. It may be utilized to enhance sensitivity and stimulate personal growth by participants who would not be diagnosed as emotionally disturbed. It may be used to provide an atmosphere in which community problems can be approached in depth, as with black-and-white groups today. My own marathon groups, whether offered in private practice or under organizational auspices, are designed to offer participants as much leeway as possible in deciding whether to utilize the group to tackle a specific emotional problem or to seek a broad growth-enhancing experience.

Marathon leaders evolve their own individual formats. Some keep the group in session for 20 hours or more without interruption, assuming that fatigue aids in the relinquishment of defenses. Others, like myself, prefer to work for at least two days, with a seven-hour break

---

Self-Evaluation of Marathon Experience Immediately Afterward

Profited Greatly	*Profited Moderately*	*Profited Not at All*	*Total*
61	28	4	93

Self-Evaluation of Marathon Experience After Three Months or More

Profited Greatly	*Profited Moderately*	*Profited Not at All*	*Total*
37	33	10	80

for sleep, believing that sustained intimacy rather than fatigue is a crucial factor in the growth experience.

Style of leadership depends on the background, personality, and values of the leader; there is no orthodox approach to marathon therapy. My own approach, though based on training in the psychoanalytic approach to understanding human personality, utilizes techniques adapted from my own experiences with psychoanalytic group therapy, Gestalt therapy, psychodrama, and nonverbal encounter games (Schutz, 1967).

A continual effort is made to focus upon immediate feelings in the group, or else to translate emotional conflicts from the past or present lives of the participants into immediate, here-and-now experience. For instance, two participants (either men or women) who feel competitive toward one another may be asked to engage in arm-wrestling, in which usually they become intensely involved, and then to speak about their feelings. A participant who speaks about difficulty in making physical contact with others may be asked to go around the group and either touch or not touch each member of the circle, and with either choice try to express his feelings. A participant who speaks of difficulty in making a practical life decision may be asked to create a drama in which he or she acts out the alternatives, choosing the actors and setting the stage.

Strong anger is sometimes mobilized, either by direct, realistic confrontation between two participants or by the evocation of a childhood memory of being forbidden to express hostile feelings. In such cases an attempt is made to provide a chance for total expression of the anger, not only verbally but also physically, through pounding vigorously on a couch or on heavy pillows. Physical expression of this kind serves as catharsis, usually is followed by a sense of relief, and often leads to the liberating awareness that it is possible to experience intense, primitive rage without damaging anyone.

Always the aim is to elicit and express feeling at the most intense level possible, then to offer an opportunity for the participant to express these feelings in words, so that emotional catharsis and insight can both be experienced. These intense experiences, in which deep emotional conflicts are expressed on a symbolic level, are interspersed with group interaction, involving feedback among the participants about their reactions toward one another. Encounter techniques are used not routinely, but only when they seem called for by a situation in the group. Participants usually recognize rather quickly that they can be helpful to one another not by offering criticism and advice, but rather by expressing their own feelings and accepting the feelings of others.

Any comfortable, informal setting is appropriate. Gymnasium mattresses are desirable if activities such as wrestling and pushing are expected. Cushions are strewn about the floor. An adjoining room affords privacy for the rare occasions when someone needs emergency individual help. Except for such occurrences, the group remains in encounter at all times, even during meals, which are sent in. Liquor is not served, but coffee and snacks are continually available. Some marathon leaders require complete abstention from food; my own conviction is that the provision of food helps to create an underlying sense of security that facilitates the exploration of anxieties, and also that there is a primitive sense of communion in sharing food. Clothing is informal, and first names are used. Observers are not permitted. The weekend begins at an appointed time on Saturday and ends at an appointed time on Sunday, but the group decides when to break up for sleep. Most often, we separate around two o'clock on Sunday morning and reunite for breakfast around ten.

Who takes part in a marathon? For me, 12 people are an ideal number, and except for seeking an approximately equal number of men and women, no effort is made to bring together specific personality types. Ages may range from 19 to 60; diagnoses, which seem strikingly irrelevant to marathons, may range from borderline schizophrenia to clinical normality; and the occasional participant who seems below the group's general level of intelligence or sophistication may, before the group terminates, make outstanding contributions. All participants are present by their own choice; people who seek marathon seem to have the strength and stamina to meet its demands, although it is considered wise to undertake a brief screening interview with an unknown participant. Engaged or married couples are welcome, with the warning that they will probably not profit if they wish to keep secrets from each other. Professional psychotherapists, in my observation, work more spontaneously in a marathon of their own, not because of greater wisdom or intellectual superiority, but rather because the attitude of therapeutic responsibility is deeply ingrained after years of practice, and its temporary relinquishment seems easier in the company of colleagues. Some participants seek only one marathon; others take part in ten or more groups over a period of years. Many participants are concomitantly in individual treatment, and are referred by their therapists to help overcome resistance or to offer an opportunity for the patient to try out freer and more intimate ways of relating. If a marathon participant needs an individual therapeutic session after the group, to consolidate new insights or to work with unresolved anxiety, the name of a competent professional person is provided, but these emergency consultations are seldom necessary.

Every combination of personalities is different, and therefore every marathon is different. However, just as Freud has stated somewhere that psychoanalysis resembles a chess match in that the beginning and the end game can usually be described, but the principal middle portion varies indefinitely, so it can also be observed that in general marathons resemble one another in the beginning and at the end, with infinite variation between. The beginning is usually marked by superficiality, defensiveness, and sometimes even dullness; the ending nearly always brings the participants close together in a joyous acceptance of intimacy and spontaneity. Often, though by no means always, participants seem to regress first to a phase of hostility corresponding to the anal phase of psychosexual development as described by Freud; then proceed to the expression of unsatisfied dependency needs corresponding to the oral phase; and finally return to the mature acceptance of responsibility associated with the fully developed genital personality (Mintz, "Time-extended Marathon Groups," 1967).

During the initial period of defensiveness, my own policy is to be passive, except to make certain basic rules: that everything revealed must be kept confidential except from one's individual psychotherapist; that one-to-one conversations and social chatter destroy the value of the group; and that participants are requested to share their immediate feelings as openly as possible. Despite this request, most marathon participants begin by hiding behind their social masks, exchanging superficial information about jobs and family, and making intellectual observations about one another, which are often correct but rarely useful. Frequently doubt is expressed about the usefulness of the marathon and the competence of its leadership. Beneath this defensiveness, most participants, including those experienced in marathons, are frightened. Typical is the statement of a participant who wrote: "I did not know why I was so afraid—of my feelings? Of other people? Or just afraid they wouldn't like me? I had made up my mind to be myself, but wasn't sure just what myself might be. Perhaps this is what scared me." This initial apprehensiveness, in a situation designed specifically for authentic confrontation of the self and others, is probably an indication of how accustomed most people are to the safe familiarity of conventional, ritualized social contacts. Any experienced leader can avoid this period of dullness by introducing encounter games at the beginning, especially games involving physical contact. My own conviction, however, is that such a stratagem deprives the participants of an opportunity to face and express their individual anxieties. Encounter games, if introduced arbitrarily in order to diminish fearfulness and foster intimacy, seem to me merely one more method of providing people with a way to avoid experiencing their own deepest feelings in contact with others, just as in conventional situations we accept prescribed gestures and remarks as a substitute for authenticity. Therefore, tolerating my own anxiety as best as I can, my choice is to wait for spontaneous feelings to emerge.

Sometimes this occurs gradually, as group members begin to feel safe with one another. Sometimes a single member will take the first difficult plunge into self-revelation, either because of intolerable inner pressure or because of a courageous decision to risk embarrassment. Sometimes there will be a sudden flare of anger, sympathy, or identification between two members. The richness and variety of interaction, of emotional catharsis, and of self-discovery that follow this initial phase can hopefully be conveyed by a series of vignettes from several marathons.[2]

SARA

Sara was an attractive woman in her early fifties who had devoted her life to furthering her husband's career and to rearing children, and who was now suffering from a mild depression and a sense of worthlessness precipitated by difficulty in finding an identity other than the familiar wife-and-mother role. Because she could not see any value in herself outside this role, she was preoccupied with minor difficulties between herself and her family and was almost obsessively concerned with defending her point of view. Early in the marathon, she spent considerable time detailing some friction between herself and a grown daughter and exasperated the group by her need to be seen as wholly right. With a combination of friendliness and irritation, one of the other women challenged Sara to an arm-wrestling match, hoping to establish a more direct contact. Sara complied, and the two women began to wrestle. It seemed like an even match, and Sara showed the same painfully serious intensity as a wrestler that she had already displayed in conversation. Her face strained, her arm locked with the other woman's. Sara was so earnest and grim that it was difficult to believe she could possess a sense of humor.

"Cheat, Sara! Cheat, Sara, cheat!"

Sara heard. Suddenly, with shameless disregard of the accepted rules, she grabbed her opponent's hand with both of her own hands and brought down her opponent's arm. Then she began to laugh. She laughed harder and harder, with increasing abandon. The group laughed with her. She laughed, literally, until tears came to her eyes— and for the remainder of the marathon she was a different woman, warm, sparkling, with a sense of mischief. The group responded with appreciation and encouragement. In the ensuing two days, Sara was

---

[2] Quotations are taken from tape recordings or from notes made immediately after the marathon. Names and identifying data are altered.

able to use the group's support to begin seeing herself as someone whose value did not depend solely on being a perfect homemaker and was able to think of her future more optimistically.

Most psychotherapists in private practice are familiar with women who, like Sara, face an identity crisis at the end of the child-rearing years. Involuntional melancholia is its extreme manifestation; more often there are subclinical neurotic symptoms such as irritability and boredom. A series of marathon groups, combined with individual psychotherapy that usually need not be prolonged, is frequently the treatment of choice for such women, provided that there is enough latent ego strength for them to respond to this challenge. A new self-image, and a renewed interest in the world outside the circle of domesticity, often develop after the marathon experience, perhaps in part because usually it is completely different from any previous experience for women of this kind.

For Sara, the episode of cheating at arm wrestling was a fortunate and appropriate symbol. In trying to maintain her self-esteem, she had been compulsively perfectionistic about the details of her family life, but behind this defense she was still capable of spontaneity and enjoyment. When she at first accepted the arm wrestling as a serious task, then suddenly recognized that it could be treated as a joke, Sara on an unconscious level experienced a symbolic shift in her value system and began to understand that she did not really have to be trapped by the need to conform to such artificial standards as impeccable housekeeping. Simultaneously, through feedback from the group, Sara became aware that she could be perceived not as a dull, middle-aged housekeeper but as an interesting and appealing woman.

The person who shouted, "Cheat, Sara, cheat!" was myself, and the episode raises significant questions about the extent to which spontaneity is appropriate for the leader of a marathon. When I shouted, it did not enter my conscious mind that it might be symbolically useful for Sara to cheat at a game. Consciously I was aware only of an identification with Sara, as one middle-aged woman with another, and of a feeling that it would be fun if she could defeat her younger opponent. The felicitous quality of my unplanned intervention may, however, have resulted from a more basic identification with Sara, which I discovered in considering the episode in retrospect. With my own children grown and gone from the home, I have often been gratefully aware that my rewarding, challenging profession saves me from the kind of boredom and loss of self-esteem with which many women must struggle. Perhaps, therefore, there was some special resonance in me to Sara's needs.

Because of the long duration of the group, a marathon therapist faces special difficulties, even though his task is facilitated by the way in which participants become increasingly interested and skillful in working with one another. At one extreme, psychoanalytically oriented group therapists maintain that detachment and impersonality are necessary to create a transference situation that can then be analyzed with therapeutic profit. At the other extreme, experiential therapists maintain that the leader should express his own feelings with complete freedom, thus offering a model for authenticity and spontaneity. My own position is that, since after all I am collecting a fee from the participants, and have accepted responsibility for the group, it should not be used to help me with problems from my childhood or in my present life. In these years as a marathon therapist, there have been some occasions when personal preoccupations kept me from functioning well as a leader; and in these instances, if I could not overcome my distraction, it proved wise to tell the group about the situation. In no case was it necessary to ask the group to help me work it through. An open acknowledgment of the problem, along with a brief description of its nature, seemed enough to remove the block. In general, my policy is to share my own thoughts, feelings, and fantasies only if they seem directly related to what is happening in the room.

JOHN

John, referred by an out-of-town psychiatrist, had telephoned me to request a marathon. Since I had confidence in the psychiatrist, I thought it unnecessary to see John for a screening interview. When he appeared, on the day of the marathon, my heart sank. He seemed exactly like a back ward patient—waxy-pale, sunken-eyed, monosyllabic. He sat in a corner, arms folded, hunched over, hardly speaking, though he responded minimally whenever someone tried to draw him out. At that time marathons were regarded as a dangerous innovation, and colleagues had expressed anxiety that psychoses might be precipitated by the prolonged strain of a two-day group. It seemed to me that John was an excellent candidate to verify this prediction.

As tactfully as possible, I tried to draw John into the group, but my efforts only seemed to drive him further into his corner. The group went on without him. When food was brought, John ate by himself. Then, late in the evening, one of the other participants did what I had been unable to do.

Ann was in her middle twenties, untrained professionally. She went over and sat cross-legged in front of John. Almost casually she said "Play with me!" and began the child's game of pease-porridge-hot, in which the two pairs of hands are clapped together in a series of playful positions. John at first sat motionless and then, as she persisted, began to join the game.

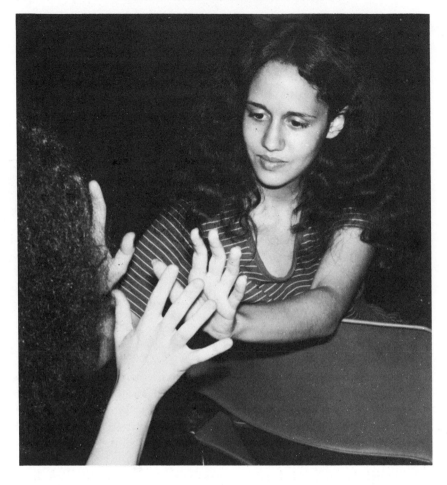

Figure 2-1. Pease-porridge-hot. (Photo by Gary Madderom.)

"Pease porridge hot, pease porridge cold, pease porridge in the pot . . ."

They were chanting together now. John's face was brightening slowly. He clapped lethargically, then more briskly. As the clapping and chanting went on, he finally laughed out loud. They ended the game, and Ann returned to her chair. With the extraordinary tactfulness often noted in the later phases of a marathon group, nobody threatened John by questioning him about the meaning of the game, but from time to time the members of the group took care to include him in whatever was going on. John responded. He never told the group his history, but he was emotionally present, still silent but alert and interested.

Later I received a letter from the psychiatrist who had sent John to me. It had been intended to reach me well before the marathon, but had been wrongly addressed and went astray in the mails. John was recently out of a mental hospital, wrote my colleague; now in individual treatment, he seemed unable to speak or to relate. In desperation, my colleague had referred John for a marathon in hopes of some kind of breakthrough. If I did not wish to work with such a sick patient, my colleague wrote that he would understand.

Some days after the marathon another letter arrived from John's psychiatrist. After the marathon, John had begun to talk—not much, but enough so that there now seemed some possibility of his responding to treatment. There was no miracle, but there was hope.

Anxiety is sometimes expressed by colleagues lest a marathon uncover unconscious material more quickly than it can be integrated and thus precipitate outright psychosis in such patients as John. My own observation is that this danger is speculative rather than actual; the real risk is rather that the patient will be unable to make contact with the group, become more and more depressed in his withdrawal, and be unable to handle the resultant depression with its concomitant fury. Ann's intuitive awareness of John's need for contact, and of the simple, childlike, playful level on which it would be possible to approach him, was an example of the sensitivity and concern for others that is a distinguishing feature of most marathons.

CLAIRE

In her mid-twenties, Claire came to her first marathon at the suggestion of her psychotherapist, who had worked with her for some years and who wished her to have an experience with a woman therapist. Claire had a childhood history of severe deprivation and parental psychosis, but she was functioning adequately as a teacher and had developed a meaningful, workable relationship with her therapist. She had dates, too, and there had been one important affair with a man. But, Claire told us despondently, she could attract men only with great difficulty. Men did ask her for dates, but she did not know how to act. She perceived herself as unfeminine, felt awkward, and was not often asked for a second date. Claire seemed unaware of her natural attractiveness, and made no effort to enhance it. Endowed with at least as much native good looks as most women, she saw herself as unappealing and clumsy.

When the group pointed this out, Claire agreed. Her mother (hospitalized several times, with a diagnosis of schizophrenia) had been the same way. Mother had never taken any interest in her own appearance, or in men—or, in fact, in Claire's father. They had been divorced when Claire was very young. It seemed to me that Claire needed the encouragement of a mother-figure to perceive herself as an attractive,

Figure 2-2. She touched his face. (Photo by Zev Guber.)

sexual woman. I suggested that she go around the group and speak in a seductive or flirtatious way to each of the men.

"I couldn't," Claire said.

"I'll go around with you. Come on."

Claire arose, and I put my arm around her shoulder. She was shaking violently. I stood embracing her while she spoke to the first two men.

"I like your necktie."

"You're getting bald, but that's all right. I like bald men."

Our progress around the circle was slow. After the first two encounters, Claire's trembling diminished. I took my arm away from her shoulder and held her hand as she continued.

"You'd probably be a good dancer."

"You've got such curly hair—I'd like to touch it." She reached out and touched the curly-haired man, and I relinquished her hand. For the next two encounters, I walked beside Claire but did not touch her.

"I know you're married. You have trouble with your wife, you told us, but I'll bet you're one great daddy to your kids."

"I'd love to date you if you weren't from out of town."

I returned to my chair. Claire went on by herself to the last two men in the circle.

"Hi." She touched the face of the man she was greeting. He took her hand, clasped it lightly, and let go.

"Hi to you." She looked at the last of the men in the group, and he reached out his arms, and Claire settled comfortably into his lap. She remained there for a few moments, then arose, her face glowing. She went back to her chair and said, with complete spontaneity and unconscious humor, "Oh, flirting's really fun, it's not so scary!"

Of all group techniques, this procedure of "going around," by which a group member relates in turn to each person in the circle, is perhaps the most useful, because it can be adapted to so many therapeutic needs. It was developed in the early stages of group therapy (Wolf, 1949) and was typically used as a method of obtaining feedback. As a simple example, a man who has been told that he creates an impression of extreme competitiveness but does not believe it may ask each group member in turn, "Do I impress you as competitive?" With Claire my purpose was to give her an opportunity to try out a different way of relating to men in a situation where she would be receiving the support and permission of a symbolic mother, a permission that normally is tacitly given in a healthy mother-daughter relationship, but that Claire had never experienced.

As Claire went around the circle, she became more confident and it grew easier for her to fulfill her task. This was more than a simple matter of increased confidence. The progression from pathology toward health is highly characteristic of "going around," perhaps because the series of encounters with group members affords an excellent opportunity to strengthen reality testing and to relate to others as real people rather than as frightening projections. My physical closeness to Claire in the beginning, and my gradual moving away until she was completely on her own, was a symbolic representation of what happens in a good mother-child relationship as the child grows older and more capable.

Claire attended several more marathons, in most of which I continued to function as an openly acknowledged mother-substitute for her. She continued to have occasional individual appointments with her male therapist and also with me. She used her sessions to increase her self-understanding and made no inappropriate demands on either therapist; yet it was clear that she was constructively using a father-figure and a mother-figure to replace her psychotic mother and indifferent father. Meanwhile, Claire began training for a new profession to which she was well suited, continued teaching, and became increasingly at home with her own femininity.

Claire's case exemplifies the value of the marathon group in offering time for a participant to integrate a reparative emotional experience, such as the symbolic mothering I offered Claire, and then to progress from accepting emotional nourishment to offering the same kind of nourishment to others. This progression may be especially noticeable if a participant attends several marathons. As Claire developed emotionally, other group members began to turn to her increasingly for warmth and understanding. An episode in her fourth marathon demonstrated strikingly how thoroughly she had assimilated her earlier experience.

DARLENE AND CLAIRE

In this marathon was Darlene, about the same age as Claire, but looking and acting like a girl in her teens. Darlene had never undergone psychotherapy, and appeared so withdrawn and shy that, although she did not seem endangered by a breakdown, it seemed dubious that she would benefit from the group. In an almost inaudible voice, she confided that she had occasional dates but was "petrified" with fear and sometimes could not even muster courage to answer the doorbell when a man came to call for her.

"That's just the way I used to be," said Claire. "You need practice in talking to fellows. Come on, practice here; I'll do it with you so you won't be scared." At first Darlene hung back, but Claire induced her to rise and make the rounds, walking beside her and clasping her hand, as I had done with Claire herself a year ago. Darlene was tongue-tied, and at their first pause, Claire had to give instructions.

"Don't panic. Look at him; look in his eyes. He's not so bad, is he? He doesn't bite. Well, is there anything you like about his looks? Then tell him so . . ."

Slowly Darlene grew less frightened and Claire became less directive, just as when Claire and I had circled the room. Claire, however, was by no means engaged in a blind imitation of me. She had listened to Darlene and her leadership was tuned to Darlene's particular problem.

"You said you lost your voice with fellows. Well, here's Jim. Say you're out with him; you've got to talk about something. Find out what he would like to talk about. Okay, now practice, have a conversation . . ." By the time the circle was completed, Darlene had gone through two "practice dates" and her voice had strengthened noticeably. Like Claire, she was able to make use of the time-extended group to try out new ways of relating, with the encouragement of a mother-surrogate. As for Claire herself, it seemed clear that, through the mechanisms of introjection and identification, Claire had assimilated me as a mother who accepted and encouraged her womanly sexuality, and that this attitude was now so thoroughly a part of her personality that she could utilize it not only for her own fulfillment, but in giving to others.

Marathon therapists are often asked whether the physical intimacy of these groups does not lead to promiscuous sexual behavior. My own belief is that the interpretation and enforcement of social mores is not

the proper responsibility of a group therapist, except when their violation constitutes an extremely self-destructive action; therefore, I set
up no taboos, although occasionally I warn the group that the exhilaration and glamor of the situation might lead to involvements that under
ordinary circumstances would seem inadvisable. The fact is, however,
that impulsive sexual behavior occurs very rarely in marathons—unless, perhaps, it is either deliberately fostered or provocatively forbidden by the therapist. The marathon atmosphere is not conducive to
the development of meaningless relationships, and people who are seeking ephemeral sexual adventures do not usually seek the intense self-
exploration and search for deep intimacy that mark the marathon
group.

Except with occasional cases of marathon participants who give evidence of a real phobia about physical contact, I do not formally encourage the physical expression of affection. Nonetheless, it occurs.
Certain techniques do exist that can quickly overcome our cultural
reluctance to touch one another; for example, pairs of group participants might be asked to clasp hands, stroke hair, or embrace one another. My own conviction is that such an artificial approach to intimacy
destroys its own purpose, substituting ritualized and superficial gestures
for true emotional contact. Nevertheless, spontaneous physical expressions of sympathy and warmth do become frequent in most marathons
after the first few hours. Very often, male participants speak of their
deep gratification at being in a setting where man-to-man affection is
accepted and is not labeled as effeminate, and men also are likely to
voice their pleasure that in the marathon group they can express
physical affection toward a woman without the implication of a sexual
overture.

Darlene

Although a marathon group is particularly well adapted to the use
of nonverbal encounter techniques and of special procedures such as
going around, an important part of its work is done by the simple
verbal sharing of feelings and opinions, just as in a conventional ongoing therapy group. An illustration is the case of Darlene.

After the episode in which Claire had helped her relate to men,
Darlene remained silent and in obvious distress for some time. At last
with great difficulty she told the group that, despite her shyness with
men, her usual behavior on a date was to invite and carry through
sexual intercourse. She was puzzled and frightened by this, especially
because she experienced little or no pleasure. In this way she had been
intimate with literally dozens of men and had never before been able to
discuss this with anyone. She had considered psychotherapy, but felt

that her problem was too unique and shameful to share. She was not entirely sure what the word "nymphomania" meant, but was obsessed with the fear that it might apply to her.

In many marathons, a participant shares a secret that is experienced as intensely shameful and has never been told before—in a few instances, not even to an individual psychotherapist. Invariably, even though the behavior described may not be approved, the group responds with support and reassurance to the participant's embarrassment and often displays a skill and tactfulness that could not be excelled by an experienced clinician.

To Darlene's intense relief, nobody seemed shocked. Sensing that she needed feminine support, two women in the group came to sit near her, and Claire took her hand. In a matter-of-fact way that seemed to alleviate Darlene's embarrassment, the group sought further information about how she felt with men. After a while there was a thoughtful silence.

"It seems to me you're more nervous holding a man's hand than being in bed with him."

"That's because it's really closer to hold hands, for you anyhow, Darlene."

"It sounds to me as if you go to bed because you get so nervous with a guy you just don't know what else to do."

As accurately as could have been done by any diagnostician, the group gradually formulated Darlene's unconscious terror of emotional intimacy and her paradoxical flight from intimacy by means of sexual intercourse, during which she successfully blocked off her feelings altogether. Nor could a seasoned therapist have done better at conveying this insight in an acceptable manner.

"It doesn't seemed so strange and awful any more, somehow," Darlene said slowly. Her voice was losing its odd, whispery quality, becoming clearer and deeper. She spoke further of her experiences and feelings, exploring herself and corroborating the group's interpretations. Reacting to her openness, some other participants began to share their sexual problems, particularly in regard to the culturally prevalent difficulty in integrating sexuality with affection. One man acknowledged that although he was always potent with women who meant little to him, his potency was often disturbed with a woman he cared for. Another man confided that, immediately after sexual intimacy, he felt antagonistic toward the woman and could not wait to get away. These were problems that none of the participants had ever spoken about before, except in one instance to an individual therapist, and that they had regarded as so abnormal that they must be kept secret.

Therapeutically speaking, the discussion of these interpersonal difficulties could hardly be expected to dissipate them. Yet every therapist knows that the recognition and open acknowledgment of a problem is a long first step toward its solution, and it was noteworthy that this first step was facilitated by the group's sense of mutual acceptance. In Darlene's case, the end result was gratifying. Her underlying conflict, of course, was deep enough so that a marathon group could only initiate its resolution, but a few weeks later she wrote me that as a result of the marathon, she no longer regarded her symptom as too horrifying to reveal, and had now been able to enter individual psychotherapy. A year later, she returned for a second marathon, using it to test out her growing ability to perceive and relate to men as human beings.

SAM

Burly, middle-aged, gruff, and matter-of-fact in manner, Sam was a successful businessman who, the first day of the marathon, confined his interaction with the group to an exchange of platitudes and disclaimed any "real" emotional problem. Late at night, however, Sam finally began to talk, and what he talked of was a dream, a recurrent dream. He was alone in a dark, old house, a place where to his knowledge he had never been in waking life. He walked through the house in the darkness, then somehow knew that confronting him was a creature.

"A creature, Sam?"

"Yes, some creature—just some kind of creature. I don't know. And then, to scare the creature, I just make a sound . . ."

It was the most appalling sound imaginable, said Sam. It was impossible that such a sound could ever exist in reality. It was like an animal or devil, yet many times worse. And the most ghastly thing of all was that in his sleep he actually made this sound. He woke himself up and could hear the end of the noise, and it was terrible. It wakened his wife, and she too was frightened. For a while he had been in individual psychotherapy, and his therapist had requested him to make the sound, but he had never been able to reproduce it while awake.

A sympathetic woman seated beside Sam took his hand, and a friendly man crossed the room to his other side. (Marathon participants frequently show an intuitive awareness that there is something particularly reassuring about simultaneous support from a man and a woman.)

"Now make the sound, Sam. Make it now. Here. For us, with us."

Sam breathed hard. His muscles strained as if making an enormous physical effort. His face darkened. At last he made a sound.

"That's it."

A prolonged silence, as everyone in the group experienced the drama of the moment. For there was nothing threatening about the sound. It was not ugly, not an animal or devil. It was a dreadful sound, but very human, the wail of a man in deep loneliness and pain.

"Sam, do you really hear that sound as horrible?"

"Yes."

"Sam, check it out with the group. Ask them how it sounded."

One by one, the group members responded to Sam's question. All of them had heard the same quality—pathos, loneliness, fear, but nothing horrible.

"But the noise sounds so awful—why, it even scares my wife!" Sam was puzzled.

"Sam, that creature in the dream, the creature you want to scare—what is it like?"

"I don't know."

"Play the creature, Sam. Be the creature. Go around the room and frighten us as if you were the creature." This technique, found useful by many group therapists (Corsini, 1966; Perls, 1969), is based on the assumption that each figure in a dream represents some aspect of the dreamer's personality that he is unable or unwilling to accept and integrate as part of himself. Verbal interpretations along these lines, however, are usually much less efficacious than asking the dreamer actually to demonstrate the walk, voice, gestures, and behavior of the dream figure, particularly in a group.

Once again, the going-around technique demonstrated a progression from pathology toward health. At the beginning of the circle, Sam's dramatization of the dream creature was a King Kong horror, malevolent, vicious. Gradually as Sam encountered other members of the circle, his manner became milder and more human. As he concluded, he was smiling.

"Oh, this seems silly—but somehow the creature doesn't seem so awful. Maybe it's just a human being after all. Like a man in wolf's clothing." Sam sat down, and I attempted to offer him a conceptual understanding of the episode, in accordance with my conviction that some verbalization, however minimal, is usually desirable if an emotional experience is to be fully integrated with the conscious personality. The "creature," Sam was told, was a part of himself, probably an angry part that he feared and rejected. The fear and anger were expressed in the way he himself perceived the "sound." Yet to our ears the sound was lonely and pitiful, perhaps because Sam felt that there was a part of him that other people could not accept; hence he must be essentially alone.

All this, it seemed to me, was more than Sam could assimilate in so short a time, and he was advised to return to individual therapy for at least a few sessions. He was advised also, after the group had ascertained that Sam had a reasonably good relationship with his wife, to tell her what he had found out about the sound and ask her if she could comfort him when he awakened from the nightmare. When the marathon broke up, Sam said that for the first time in many years he was no longer afraid of the nightmare.

SCENARIOS

Marathon groups are an ideal setting for the development and performance of miniature dramas, a procedure that is initially introduced by the therapist, but is quickly picked up by participants, who usually display great imagination and intuition in devising appropriate scenarios. This approach has something in common with psychodrama, but does not follow a prescribed format; the miniature dramas may be termed "games" but they are essentially serious and often bring out extremely deep, intense feelings; they can be termed "scenarios," but although they may begin with a histrionic quality, they soon become as real as the underlying feelings.

Terry was a college professor in his middle forties, whose life had been personally and professionally difficult, but who was just beginning to obtain professional recognition and who was, for the first time, emotionally satisfied in a second marriage. However, he had a deep self-destructive streak, which was manifest in his continuous heavy smoking, despite the fact that he had suffered two heart attacks and had been told by his physician that for him smoking was suicidal. The marathon participants, particularly concerned with Terry because of his likable and friendly personality, pleaded with him, reasoned with him, and shouted at him angrily, but he continued to smoke. Finally someone said, "Let's have a funeral." Terry was asked to recline on the couch and pretend to be dead, while someone placed a pack of cigarettes in his hands as a memorial, and the group filed by as if paying their last respects, most of them taking a rather facetious approach. But my cotherapist (Frank Rubenfeld), a man who is not afraid of his feelings, was so deeply stirred by the undoubted fact that Terry was endangering his life with each cigarette that he knelt by Terry's coffin and burst into unfeigned tears. Terry endured this for only a few moments and then cried out, "It's stupid to be dead!" He sat up abruptly, and did not light another cigarette for the two days of the marathon.

Tom was a young priest. In his late twenties, he was deeply involved in his vocation, which fulfilled him in both its social and its spiritual aspects. He had come to the marathon because of a sorrow that he expressed to the group very late at night—that despite his love for his work, he suffered deep regrets not so much because he had relinquished the gratifications of marriage but because he would always be deprived of the experience of fatherhood. He was given a pillow and was asked to pretend that this was the baby he would never have. Tom held the pillow tenderly, rocked it gently back and forth, and after a long silence began to speak, beginning, "Baby I will never have . . ." The words that followed were so deeply moving, in their love and longing, that several members of the group wept in silence as they listened. Then, as he continued, Tom began to tell the baby, as if he could understand, about the satisfactions of the priesthood and its importance to Tom and to his parish. At the end, he put the pillow gently aside, saying good-bye to the baby. In the morning, Tom rejoined the group with his face radiant, expressing a conviction that he had consecrated himself afresh to his vocation. Regardless of any individual opinion as to the value of celibacy for the priesthood, and as to the value of religious orthodoxy in general, there could be no doubt that Tom had faced an extremely deep conflict within himself and had resolved it in a way that strengthened his identification with his chosen values and enhanced his ability to function constructively in his chosen occupation.

Lars had for several years been dreading the death of his father, who at 78 was still alert but might die of a prolonged terminal illness at any time. Although in his boyhood he felt estranged and resentful toward his father, Lars had been fond of him for many years and dreaded the impending bereavement. In recent weeks, when his father was temporarily worse, Lars was apprehensive each time the telephone rang. One overly intellectual member of the group attempted to exploit the conventional psychoanalytic notion of an unconscious death wish on Lars's part (which, of course, may well have been part of Lars's total attitude), but his intervention was quickly dismissed because it seemed so unrelated to Lars's immediate feelings. Lars was then asked to imagine that his father had been dead for some months and to visit his grave. He complied. In complete silence, the group watched as Lars approached the "grave" and spoke in soliloquy as if to his father. Lars recalled the misunderstandings and bitterness of his childhood and also recalled happy and companionable occasions—walking together, a music lesson, a visit to a county fair. He spoke of remembering how touched his father had been by the birth of Lars's first child. "It was good knowing you, Dad," said Lars at last and moved away from the imaginary grave. Later, he told us that he was more nearly reconciled to his father's death, and also that he had made a decision to express affection and appreciation while his father still lived.

Meanwhile, in the group several people were in tears and were being comforted by whoever was sitting nearby. Eileen, one of the women, told us that her father had died when she was 15, and that she had never been able to cry for his death because she could remember only unpleasant episodes in their relationship. As she watched Lars, however, she had suddenly recalled for the first time an image of herself as a girl of five or six, walking along the sidewalk with her father, eating a strawberry ice-cream cone he had bought her. She told the group that now she "had the good part of her father back again" and could cry for him at last. Some months later, in response to an inquiry, Eileen wrote: "I still feel different about my father. He was a bastard but there were some nice things too and I'm glad I remembered them." She also reported that she seemed to be getting along better with her husband, and that she could particularly appreciate it that "he sometimes fusses over me if I'm blue or not very well, and this always used to bug me, but I'm getting to like it. Something to do with the marathon; I don't just know exactly what."

Such a case as Eileen's raises questions as to whether conscious cognitive understanding is invariably necessary for genuine personal growth. My own belief is that it is desirable, and whenever appropriate I do attempt to provide it, as in the episode of Sam; yet certainly there are instances in which lasting benefits are attained through an emotional experience without evidence of concomitant insight. Because Eileen was not in individual psychotherapy, it was impossible to explore the hypotheses, suggested by the data, that she had blocked off grief at her father's death because she was afraid of the intense dependent and oedipal needs symbolized by the memory of the strawberry ice-cream cone; that through identification and empathy with Lars she became able to recall happy moments with her father and thus experience her grief consciously; and that when she accepted the existence of dependency and sexual attraction in her feelings toward her father, she could accept these feelings toward her husband. Perhaps these same sexual and dependent feelings were unconsciously associated with a feminine sense of helplessness, and perhaps therefore she reached her repressed feelings more easily by identifying with a man. These speculations could not be verified, but Eileen's marathon experience certainly provides evidence that, at least under the special conditions of a marathon, a major emotional breakthrough can be initiated by identification with another group member.

As stated earlier, a marathon is only a time-extended group. Its special attributes vary, as do those of any other group, according to the individual participants, the methods chosen by the leader, the purpose, and the setting. Yet most people who undergo the marathon experience find that the extension of time not only offers a prolongation of the experiences that are valuable in conventional group therapy, but also intensifies these experiences to a point at which they become qualitatively unique.

Among the recognized values of an ongoing group is that it provides a situation in which participants can explore and discover the sources of their interpersonal difficulties and can then experiment with more honest, spontaneous, and rewarding ways of relating to other people. The marathon group offers these same opportunities, except that an opportunity to test out the newer, freer ways of relating to others can follow immediately upon the exploration of whatever anxiety has made relationships difficult. Moreover, the extension of time in itself makes possible a very wide range of situations in which a participant can explore and express new kinds of feelings toward others.

A marathon group is often regarded as a situation in which the pressure of prolonged intimacy, plus physical fatigue, breaks down defenses. This concept of the marathon situation has led some psychotherapists to fear that psychoses will be precipitated by the strain. My own conviction is that, on the contrary, the marathon group essentially provides more security than other therapeutic situations. There is time to regress, to yield to terrifying childhood feelings of dependency and panic and primitive rage, because there is then time to achieve maturity once again, hopefully with a new integration of the infantile feelings. Except on the basis of armchair logic, there is certainly no reason to assume that a two-day therapeutic experience, in which feelings can be discovered and expressed and worked through, should be less effective or more threatening than a 50-minute experience in which any feelings that are uncovered must be left in abeyance until the next 50-minute session.

Although intense anxiety and apprehensiveness are occasionally reported by marathon participants, reports of intensely joyful experiences, often termed "peak experiences," are far more common. In marathons it is possible to achieve intimacy and spontaneity to a degree unusual in our culture. We live in a world of role-playing, controlled and conventional behavior, socialized masks. There can be marvelous relief when the masks are dropped and great delight when people find that without the masks they are not only accepted but appreciated.

The therapeutic value of marathons remains to be explored through the use of control groups and statistical evaluation; however, these methods are notoriously difficult to apply in the evaluation of any form of psychotherapy. If marathon groups are to be regarded primarily as a therapeutic approach, in the sense of being directed toward the alleviation of pathology, they are probably most effective in combination with sustained individual or group psychotherapy that offers an opportunity to observe and analyze transference and resistance over a long period of time. It is possible to use the metaphor of a marathon group as a vertical cross-section of human experience, with intense emotional depths and heights, whereas ongoing therapy may be seen as a horizontal cross-section, less intense though probably eliciting a wider range of responses.

However, it is an open question whether the marathon group should be viewed primarily as a psychotherapeutic approach, or whether it can more appropriately be regarded as an experience in itself, which like any other human experience can sometimes expand the personal and interpersonal horizons of the participants.

BIBLIOGRAPHY

Alexander, F., and French, T. M. *Psychoanalytic Therapy*. New York: Ronald Press, 1946.

Corsini, R. J. *Roleplaying in Psychotherapy*. Chicago: Aldine, 1966.

James, W. *Varieties of Religious Experience*. New York: Random House, 1902.

Mintz, E. E. Prognosis, Outcome and the Therapist's Feelings. *J. Long Island Consultation Center*, **5**:2, 1967.

————. Time-Extended Marathon Groups. *Psychotherapy*, **4**:2, 1967.

————. Marathon Groups: A Preliminary Evaluation. *J. Contemp. Psychother.*, **1**:2, 1969.

Perls, F. *Gestalt Therapy Verbatim*. Lafayette, Calif.: Real People Press, 1969.

Schutz, W. *Joy*. New York: Grove Press, 1967.

Wolf, A. The Psychoanalysis of Groups. *Amer. J. Psychother.*, **13**:3, 1949.

Worchel, P., and Byrne, D. *Personality Change*. New York: Wiley, 1964.

Part B

Techniques

Daniel I. Malamud

The Second-Chance Family: A Medium for Self-Directed Growth

COMMENTARY

Dan Malamud makes two major contributions in his chapter. First, he describes a class program that has provided personal growth opportunities to a large number of students, of all ages and backgrounds, and that can be modified for a wide variety of educational offerings including extension and adult education classes. Second, he offers a spectrum of techniques that lend themselves to almost all basic encounter situations.

BIOGRAPHY

Dr. Malamud, a graduate of the William Alanson White Institute, devotes most of his professional time to the private practice of individual and group psychotherapy. In addition, he leads workshops in self-confrontation at New York University, serves as a group consultant at the Hunter College Educational Clinic, and is on the faculties of the Workshop Institute of Living-Learning and GROW. He is coauthor of the book, *Toward Self-Understanding: Group Techniques in Self-Confrontation*. His current work in the development of "second-chance families" reflects his conviction that the future holds a place for small "familial" groups in which the main ties will be based, not on birth or marital choice, but rather on the commitment of compatible individuals to search together for new means of personal growth.

Several years ago students in my Workshop in Self-Understanding at New York University told me that they felt a deep "family feeling" with other members in the group, that they often met after class to discuss the events of the session, and that some among them felt a greater trust and intimacy with each other than with most of their actual relatives. I had heard similar comments before, but on this particular evening the concept of a second-chance family took seed and began to sprout: What if I organized the workshop so that its members could create from among themselves families whose explicit aim would be to provide new opportunities for nourishment and self-expansion that they may not have had enough of in their actual childhood families? Could the very process of forming such families be a valuable learning experience, touching on each member's overconcern with others' reactions to him and with his difficulties in making choices and responsible commitments? Could I develop effective ways of training these families in working productively on their own? These questions fascinated me, and I began to revise the workshop along new lines to be described below.

The Workshop in Self-Understanding is offered at New York University's School of Continuing Education and Extension Services. The workshop is a noncredit course open to the public at large. It accommodates groups of about 30 adults who vary widely in age and educational background. We meet once a week for 15 weeks, and each session lasts for about two hours. Students also meet once a week without me. In response to numerous students' requests, an advanced course has been established. This second course follows the same general structure and aims, includes "graduates" of the first workshop, and may be repeated by students as often as they wish.

Self-confrontation exercises are the chief vehicles of movement in the workshop. These are structured activities in which I encourage members to involve themselves with a blend of playfulness, curiosity, and risk-taking. Some of these planned happenings are so novel that students' conventional responses are circumvented, and they have an opportunity to see themselves from unfamiliar or even surprising perspectives. Other exercises provide training and practice in new ways of experiencing, self-expressing, or relating to others.

Each exercise is followed by a period of group discussion. After such discussion I will sometimes suggest: "Let's repeat the exercise, but this time consider how you might participate in the situation differently, perhaps in a way that you might find more satisfying, even though it may involve taking some risk that you ordinarily avoid."

Self-confrontation exercises offer opportunities for learning in a personalized, firsthand way that expanded self-awareness is possible through focusing on what one is experiencing in the here-and-now, that the sharing of personal reactions can be more useful and less dangerous than is usually anticipated, and that the self can be an active, deliberate agent in its own growth and development.

I have been developing the workshop since 1950, and earlier versions of this course have been reported elsewhere (Malamud, 1955, 1958, 1960, 1969; Malamud and Machover, 1965). It may be useful at some future date to trace the development of the workshop from its inception, how my aims and methods have undergone successive modifications, and how my efforts at coping with various classroom situations were affected by inner struggles of my own. Suffice it to say at this point that my evolution as a group leader owes much to Rogers' views on self-discovered learning (Rogers, 1961, 1969; Rogers and Stevens, 1967), Assagioli's (Assagioli, 1965) emphasis on the use of imagination in furthering personal growth, and, most especially, my firsthand experiences with Perls (Perls, 1969; Perls, Hefferline, and Goodman, 1951) and his Gestalt therapy methods for catalyzing self-confrontation with dramatic aliveness and immediacy.

This paper outlines in compressed fashion the current status of the workshop with particular emphasis on the following aspects: my role as leader, the getting-acquainted process, the formation of second-chance families, methods of familyship training, the development of miniature growth actions, and descriptions of interpersonal and intrapersonal exercises for exploring the self. In offering this abbreviated progress report, I hope to convey the nature of the workshop's new directions sufficiently to stimulate others to try out some of its procedures.

LEADER'S ROLE

I usually begin the first session with a brief, orienting talk along the following lines, but in simpler, more colloquial language:

Welcome to the workshop. This course is a step-by-step training experience in self-discovery and personal growth. Workshop methods are going to be very different from those in the conventional classroom situation. Instead of lecturing, I will present group exercises that stimulate you to observe yourself in action, ponder on the personal significance of your reactions, and try out new ways of responding. I ask you simply to see what happens as you become involved in each situation. You need not press for anything in particular to happen, nor need you concern yourself with why you reacted as you did or with the rightness, wrongness, goodness, or badness of your reaction. Simply notice how you do react, the thoughts that occur to you, and what feelings you experience.

In a few weeks, after getting acquainted with each other, you will form three to five families of from six to ten members each, and you will work within your families throughout the course. These families can become your second chance at experiencing various kinds of personal learning that you may have missed in your childhood. These will not be groups with one member formally designated as a father, and another as a mother, and so forth. Rather each of you, while being yourself, will undertake the responsibility for doing all you can to create a good family atmosphere, one where you can feel free to experience yourself with minimum defensiveness, learn to give and take nourishment and challenge, expand beyond your usual boundaries, and try out new ways of relating. I know that this is a tall order for a 15-week period. Remember, though, that what is important is not the actual achievement of an ideal family, but the new possibilities you discover about yourself as you engage in the process.

During the early sessions I will introduce various structured experiences designed to facilitate your getting acquainted so that you can begin to form some basis for deciding whom you wish to choose or avoid in selecting your families. Then there will follow a series of preparatory exercises in which each of you will come to grips with the dilemmas involved in choosing whom you wish to be with in your family, inviting preferred people to join you, rejecting members who want to be with you but whom you do not want to be with, and being rejected by someone whom you prefer. These exercises will help lay the groundwork for the session in which the actual selection of family members will take place.

In the remaining sessions each family will focus on developing a good working atmosphere within which you can explore your relationships to yourselves and to each other with the objective of facilitating each other's growth. Each week you will meet with your family outside of class at a time and place of your own choice. From time to time I will introduce training exercises that focus on one or another aspect of how to be a good working family, for example, how to share feelings, confront without squashing, and give support without pampering. At some point in the middle of the course, each of you, with the assistance of your family, will explore these potentialities in yourself that you would like to develop further and then participate in miniature growth experiences of your own choosing.

Some of you may be concerned about being cut off from the rest of the class by virtue of working in your family. Let me assure you that you will have ample opportunities within the classroom sessions to interact with members from other families, for we will frequently engage in exercises as one large group. Also, each family can work out arrangements for visits with other families. Now, what questions do you have about anything that I've said?

I do all I can from the very beginning to create an atmosphere in which it is evident that members are not going to be criticized, ridiculed, or humiliated. I display an easygoing informality and listen to all comments in an interested, welcoming manner. I emphasize that each student has full freedom in deciding how far, if at all, he wishes to enter into any exercise. I assume constructive powers exist in every member, and I am on the alert for situations that can demonstrate convincingly that indeed he does have such unrecognized and/or unemployed strengths. My basic assumption is obvious: the more psychologic safety members experience, the greater their freedom to reveal, explore, and venture.

I try to maintain a supportive, personal relationship with each of my 30 students. I ask them to bring in one-page autobiographies with their photographs attached so that I can rapidly learn names, faces, and personal histories. During the last five minutes of each session, members write one-page letters to me. I take these letters home, write a brief response to each, and return them in the following session. In this fashion an ongoing dialogue develops between myself and each student throughout the course.

I come to each session prepared with several exercises and introduce each exercise with a tentative, experimental attitude. I am not wedded to any particular procedure or sequential pattern. When I feel that a discussion has been about as productive as it can be, I intervene and ask the group whether it is ready to move on to another experience. On the other hand, despite a preconceived syllabus and aims for the session, when I see that members are developing a momentum along fruitful, unforeseen lines, I recede into the background and allow them to go forward.

Just because people differ in terms of relative maturity, degree of psychologic sophistication, level of self-acceptance, and the pertinence of particular problems, it is virtually impossible to work out a fixed sequence of exercises that would be suitable for all workshop groups or for all individuals in any given workshop group. Some participants are more responsive to verbal techniques, and others find motoric experiments more meaningful. Some take easily to exploring their fantasies. Others respond more readily to here-and-now interpersonal situations. Thus far I have tended to take chief responsibility for deciding which exercises would be most appropriate for most members. However, I am becoming increasingly interested in developing "menus" listing a variety of choices from which each student or family could select those exercises deemed to be most related to the major concerns at the time.

Perhaps one of my chief traits as a leader is my readiness to participate in exercises along with the members and reveal my personal responses. As often as I am able, I acknowledge those occasions when my needs for a successful session, for admiration, or for a safe detachment from a "hot" group event may have interfered with my providing the kind of leadership that was necessary. Most students begin to question their stereotypes of authority (at least their stereotype of me) when they learn, much to their surprise, that I have my own personal hangups with people, that I get depressed, that I have a touchy, grandiose side, that I am sometimes unduly concerned about other people's approval and that I have my own troubles and dilemmas as a husband and as a father.

For many members who have had little or no experience with frank and honest sharing of feelings in their own childhood families, I offer myself as a person with whom they can practice unaccustomed equalitarian, frank, and direct ways of relating. From time to time, however, I take pains to caution the group against adopting patterns of sharing intimate feelings that may be as extreme and indiscriminate as were their former patterns of inhibition.

In leading a group discussion I am alert to the implicit, covert aspects of members' reactions, and I often try to bring these out into the open in order to sensitize the group to the rich background of unexpressed meaning that lies beyond the first observed, verbalized, or felt response. I ask eliciting questions such as the following: "You've been explaining Bill's motive, but can you tell us what you feel toward him?" "You say you feel so and so, but is it possible that you have other feelings as well?" "Can you recall situations outside the workshop that have aroused similar reactions?" "What do you think could account for your reactions to this exercise being different from those of other members?"

I sometimes adopt the following eliciting procedure as members report their reactions to an exercise. I listen carefully to a member's response, select some salient feature in it, and then throw out a question for him to think about. For example, during one exercise involving balloons a member reports some anxiety about "going too far" in blowing up his balloon. I say, "What happened when you went too far as a child? See if a specific memory occurs to you, and tell us about it later." I do not wait for any response to this suggestion; rather, I move from member to member getting their initial reactions and throwing out similar inquiries for each of them to consider. Only after all initial responses have been expressed do I invite members to report what if anything has occurred to them in relation to the questions that I raised earlier.

In every session spontaneous events occur containing possibilities for a brief, on-the-spot learning experience that can highlight something of value to the group as a whole. I capitalize on such potential opportunities by asking the student involved if he wishes to explore his reaction with me for a few minutes. Depending on the situation, I may invite him to role-play, create a fantasy, interact with another member, engage in a go-around with the group, or perform some physical action. These interventions on my part usually last no more than five minutes; I move on as soon as the student experiences something surprising, satisfying, or simply thought-provoking. I tend to be thrifty and careful in my use of interpretations, and when I give them, I do so to stimulate the group to think more deeply about what they have taken for granted rather than to resolve any particular problem. I express interpretations in a spirit of, "This could be. I really don't know. It's something to think about, if you wish."

I am at my best as a leader when I am most free of preconceptions, when my cognitive machinery is operating minimally at translating what is happening into this or that psychologic mechanism or dynamic, and when I am most able to assume the risk taking attitude I encourage my students to adopt. Above all, I need to be in an alert, confident, active mood. To the extent that I am not, I usually find that my efforts at on-the-spot interventions are sluggish, are poorly timed, or fall flat.

BECOMING ACQUAINTED

Members are naturally curious about each other. Will the "other one" be someone who satisfies or someone who frustrates, a friend or a foe? They become especially interested in each other's characteristics and reactions once they learn that the class group represents a pool from which they will be selecting family members. To facilitate the acquaintanceship process, I introduce a series of structured encounters, both verbal and nonverbal, that encourage each person to share of him-

Figure 3-1. Shifting subgroups. (Photo by Zev Guber.)

self or to interact with every other person in a variety of ways. These exercises are intriguing and yet, at the same time, relatively simple and nonthreatening. Below are some examples:

Shifting Subgroups. This exercise involves repeatedly breaking up the class into a series of subgroups whose memberships fluctuate depending on varying patterns of value choices. I read a set of three statements, values of one kind or another. Each member decides which one of the values he considers the most important in his life and which one the least important. The participants are then divided into smaller groups according to their patterns of choices. For example, the items might be: "To be generous toward other people." "To be my own boss." "To have understanding friends." All those who choose "To be generous toward other people" as most important and "To be my own boss" as least important gather together in one subgroup to talk over their choices. And similar subgroups are formed for every other combination of choices. After five minutes of discussion the class reunites to respond to another set of items, and we repeat this procedure for several sets, breaking up the group each time into new subgroupings. The last set of the series is: "To have a gourmet meal with a close friend." "To spend a beautiful day outdoors." "To have a good orgasm."

Subgroups can also be formed according to varying childhood patterns. For example, I group members according to their birth orders. Those who were the oldest children in their original families come together in one group, the youngest in another, the middles in a third, and the onlies in a fourth. These subgroups locate themselves in different parts of the classroom and then go on to explore the various experiences they had by virtue of their birth order position. After five minutes I bring all the groups together to be recombined into new subgroups, for example, a group whose fathers were the dominant parent, a mother-dominant group, and a group in which neither parent was seen as dominant.

As members find themselves in different groups not only do they have opportunities to become acquainted and to see each other from shifting and often novel angles, but they can also observe the fluctuating composition of subgroup memberships and come face to face with the diversity and complexity of the pattern interrelationships that define individual personalities.

Dyadic Belt Line. The large group is broken into pairs who position themselves in a circle. One member of each pair is designated A, and the other is B. A and B interact for two minutes around some theme (for example, "My first impression of you") or physical activity (for example, a thumb wrestle). Then at my signal all A's shift in a clockwise direction to the next B in the circle and repeat the theme or activity with this new partner. Such shifts are repeated every two minutes until all A's have interacted with all B's. I introduce new tasks or themes after every three shifts.

Who Stands Out? I say: "Let's mingle as relaxedly as possible and look each other over. Let's really inspect each other and see what we feel when we look at different people and how different members make us feel as they look at us. Feel free to touch members in any way that's comfortable for you, but do not talk to them. See if there is one member to whom you react in some unusually striking or intense way. When I give the signal, let's return to our seats and discuss who in this group stood out for each of you and how."

Me Too. Each member in turn shares in a sentence or two some thought, feeling, or event he experienced as a child, one he judges was experienced by all the other members in the group at one time or another. Upon hearing an individual's item all members who have ever had a similar experience raise their hands. Each individual's score equals the number of hands raised. There are two or three go-rounds, and each student strives for as high a total score as he can achieve. Examples of items that have been offered are as follows: "I felt scared when I had a bad nightmare one night." "I took money from my mother's pocketbook." "I had fun riding the Dodgems in Coney Island."

Ask Me a Question. I tell the group: "Write down a personal question, any at all, that you would like to put to me." After they have done this, I continue: "Close your eyes and imagine that you are walking up to me and, looking me squarely in the eye, ask me the question you thought of. Then listen and 'hear' my response. Once you've 'heard' my answer, open your eyes and write it down." When the group has completed this task, I ask for volunteers to ask me their questions, hear my real answers (as self-disclosing and truthful as I can comfortably make them), and then read aloud the answers they imagined I would give. The discussion centers on such topics as the following: how each person felt about the opportunity to ask a question, differences in the kinds of questions asked, how questions might reflect central issues in the life of the questioner, and how members reacted to my responses. After discussing this experience, I invite other members to volunteer one at a time to take my place, that is, to become the person toward whom others direct personal questions in the manner outlined above.

Say This to Me. I ask each member to close his eyes and to think of one sentence he would like to hear the group say to him: "This sentence will be addressed to you personally with your first name preceding the sentence itself. It can be any kind of sentence, one you have or have not actually heard. It can be a painful sentence or a pleasurable one. Tell us how many times you would like us to repeat the sentence, and how you wish us to say it—loudly, softly, scoldingly, caressingly, and so forth." I then demonstrate by giving such a sentence myself. In one group, for example, I ask the members to say to me three times in unison with loud vigor: "Dan, don't take things so seriously!" After my wish is granted, the group and I share our reactions. Other members then follow suit. One student has the group shout at him angrily, "John, fuck you!" so that he can "learn to handle it." Another member asks the group to whisper several times, "Bill, you're really not as bad as you think." These sentences almost invariably dramatize significant themes in members' lives in a succinct and transparent way.

Reversed-Name Definition. Name exercises rapidly acquaint members with each other's first names and at the same time provide significant stimuli to self-exploration. For example, I tell the group: "Spell out your first name in reverse. Look at your reversed name. Pretend that it spells some strange, new word that comes from a language of an alien species on the planet Mars. Roll this alien word over your tongue and decide how it is pronounced on Mars. Now write out a definition of the word as it would appear in a Martian dictionary." The group hears each person's definition of his reversed name and then later explores how these definitions might reflect some central dynamic or theme for each member. In one class I start the ball rolling by submitting my name, Nad, and defining it as "a state of anger covered by a layer of niceness." Bernice hates being a housewife; she defines her name Ecinreb (pronounced *Eki*nreb) as "a small household receptacle that is used for spitting in."

FORMING FAMILIES

The class is usually ready to undertake the formation of families after the third session. By this time they have become sufficiently acquainted to have some sense of their interpersonal preferences and aversions. This is, perhaps, the most critical phase of the course, and as yet I have no one sufficiently satisfactory way of proceeding. I am experimenting with different approaches, and these are still undergoing successive modifications as my experiences with different groups and situations accumulate.

Most members look forward to family formation with mixed feelings. On the one hand, they are eager to begin experiencing family closeness. On the other hand, they are apprehensive about the possible pain of the choosing process, for they sense that it is fraught with potential dilemma, and trauma: "Shall I pick someone whom I can help or who can help me, someone who resembles me or who is very different, someone I shall like easily or someone with whom I shall fight? Shall I take the initiative to invite, or wait to be invited? What if I don't want to be with someone who wants me? What if I'm rejected by someone whom I want?" To focus on these questions, and to minimize unnecessarily painful experiences, I lead up to the final choosing with a number of "immunizing" exercises selected from the following possibilities:

Accept All. Members mingle in the center of the room and extend invitations to each other nonverbally. The rule: "Every invitation has to be accepted. No one is rejected." People invite with a glance or a gesture, and as they accept each other's invitations, they clasp hands and move out of the center. The inviter briefly tells the invitee why he selected him. The invitee says simply, "Thank you for inviting me." They then return promptly to the center of the room to invite or to accept new invitations, pair off with someone new, move out again, return, and in this manner get repeated experiences in actively reaching out and in accepting or being accepted.

Reject All. A similar exercise gives members practice in rejecting each other. I say: "Your task is to invite and to be rejected, and to reject the invitation of others. Nobody moves out of the center of the room for nobody accepts anybody's invitation." So there is a kind of milling around in which people are nervously and sometimes laughingly going through this silent process of rejection. After a few minutes of this, about all that most members can take, we discuss our reactions.

First Aid for Rejectee. The participants close their eyes, and I invite them to experience the following in their imaginations: "You are now going to select your family. You are in the center of the room. You are moving up toward one person of your choice, and you are extending a hand to this person. And the person grimaces and turns his back on you and walks away. You feel surprised and disappointed. You swallow hard, pull yourself together, wander around the room, and pick out somebody else, a student whom you like very much, and who you believe likes you. You move toward this second person, and as you are about to extend your hand in invitation, the person deliberately snubs you and accepts the invitation of someone else. You feel like sinking through the floor. You feel awful. You can hardly believe this is happening to you. Without even thinking you turn to the person nearest you and make an inviting gesture, but this member rejects you too. You feel terrible. You hurry out of the room, go downstairs to the street,

Figure 3-2. I feel terrible. (Photo by Zev Guber.)

walk with unseeing eyes, and then finally enter a phone booth and call up your best friend."

Then I say, "Open your eyes, everybody, and break up into pairs." One person in the pair plays the one who has just been rejected, and the other person plays the part of the "best friend." For about five minutes the "best friend" does all he can to help the "rejectee" work through his feelings and gain some constructive perspective. At the end of five minutes new pairs are formed, and members who were previously "rejectees" now play "best friend." In the group discussion that follows we focus especially on what "rejectees" found most useful in the help offered them by "best friends."

What Do You Say to Yourself? In a variation[1] of the above exercise, after members imagine being rejected, I invite one third of the group to write a list of sentences they could say to themselves to make themselves feel worthless and suicidal with despair, another third to write down what they might say to themselves to make themselves feel furious with the rejectors, and the remaining students to write what they might say to take the rejection regretfully but without undue despair or fury. These different sets of statements are later aired and discussed.

Transmitting and Receiving Feelers. Each member writes his name at the top of a sheet of paper that is then passed around to every other member. As each member receives someone else's sheet, he jots down a few sentences as to how he would feel about being in a family with him and why, and then signs his first name. When each member's sheet is finally returned to him, he reviews it and obtains some over-all picture of how he stands with others in the group. I then invite members to "confer" with each other if they wish to learn more about what was written to them.

Want Ads. Each person composes two imaginary advertisements: one, a "Family Relative Wanted," in which he describes in 20 words or less the kind of person he wants, and a second one, "Family Relative Available," in which he describes what kind of a family relative he feels he could make. These ads are posted, discussed, and responded to either in person or in writing. Following are examples of such ads: "Family Relative Wanted: Honest person, neither wishy-washy nor rigid. Ready to criticize when necessary but in kindly fashion." "Family Relative Available: Bright male who loves self-exploring but sometimes gets scared and needs help in continuing the safari."

[1] Inspired by Ellis's approach (Ellis and Harper, 1961).

Members go through a series of dry-run family formations, engaging in one of the procedures to be described below, and aiming for families containing from six to ten members with as equal a distribution of sexes as possible. I encourage members to feel free to turn each other down: "We all need to cope with the problems of inviting and rejecting. You don't do your fellow classmates a favor if you hold yourself back from rejecting him when you really feel like rejecting." Each time a practice family is formed its members meet to explore how they got together, what feelings were stirred up, how satisfied or dissatisfied they were with their efforts, and what they might like to try doing differently in the next dry-run formation. Then the whole group gathers to give members an opportunity to air directly with the individuals involved the bases for their selections and what feelings they experienced in rejecting or being rejected. Through these preparatory experiences some members can try to overcome their timidity in extending invitations or their tendency to rush into inviting so quickly that they deprive themselves of the pleasure of being invited. Other members can practice how to reject with frankness and tact, or how to take rejection from others more matter-of-factly.

We do the final choosing of families when the majority of the class indicates its readiness. The following formation procedures have been the most useful thus far:

1. Members mill around in the center of the room silently. They send out nonverbal signals to each other of invitation, acceptance, or rejection. When two members communicate mutual acceptance, they clasp hands and move out of the center. After all members have been paired off, this process is repeated except that now the pairs come into the center of the room and silently send out signals to other pairs until mutually accepting quartets are formed. In a similar fashion quartets combine with quartets to form families of eight.

This procedure can be varied in numerous ways depending on how large the total group is and how many families are desired. For example, in one group of 25 members, five families of five each were formed as follows: First, members mingled among each other forming trios. As trios formed they left the mingling group. As soon as the fifth trio was formed, I instructed the remaining ten members to divide themselves into pairs. Then pairs combined with trios. The above procedures may also be carried out with verbal communication permitted.

2. In a group of 30, I pick six members at random to stand aside. Twelve of the remaining members line up as group A on one side of the room, and 12 as group B on the other. Six members in group A, each in turn, select a partner from group B. Then three of the remaining six members of group B, each in turn, select a partner from group A. The final three members in group A select partners from the re-

maining three members of group B. After these pairings are completed, I ask each of the six members who stood aside during this procedure to select a different pair they would like to join. There are now six trios and six pairs. Members in each pair and trio now discuss what determined their choices or how they felt about being chosen.

After five minutes I ask the trios to line up on the A side of the room and the pairs to line up on the B side. Three trios from group A, each in turn, select three pairs from group B. The remaining three pairs in group B choose three trios from group A. As groups unite they again discuss the determinants of and reactions to the choices made.

There are now six groups of five members each. I ask three groups to line up on the A side and three groups on the B side. A quintet from the A group then invites a quintet from the B group to join them. The B group may accept or reject the invitation, depending on majority vote. If the invitation is rejected, the inviting group must await its turn before inviting again. The next A quintet then invites a quintet from the B group, and so forth, until three groups of ten members each are formed. The above example can be modified appropriately for larger or smaller groups.

3. All members sit in a circle. Four students, A, B, C, and D, are selected by lot, each to be a "nucleus" of a family. Student A invites a member in the group to join his family and tells him why he selected him. The chosen student must accept the invitation, simply thanking the inviter. Students B, C, and D each in turn do the same. There are now four family cores consisting of two members each. A go-around begins in which each unaffiliated member chooses one of the four family cores and requests admission, stating his reasons for his prefer-ence. The chosen family polls its membership as to the acceptability of the prospective candidate for admission. Each one in the chosen family votes "yes" or "no" and gives his reasons directly to the candi-date. A student is accepted into the family of his choice if a majority of this family accepts him. When a family member objects to the ad-mission of a candidate, he states his objection as specifically as possible, and the candidate shares with the group his reactions to being rejected. When it is a student's turn to choose from among the four families, he may, if he does not feel ready to make a decision, "pass" and take his turn later. After the first go-around is completed, a family may decide to take the initiative and ask an unaffiliated person to join it. Two families may compete for the same person, each attempting to persuade him to join it. Any member may ask another member to reconsider his family membership and switch families.

Once final families are formed I assign each group to an area in the classroom that becomes its home base for the duration of the course. In their first meetings the families share their reactions to being together and bind the "wounds" of individuals still recovering from the stress of selection. Next, members in each family discuss the following questions: How do I want this family to be similar to or different from my actual childhood family? How do I want to be different with this family from the way I usually am with people? What kind of help turns me on and what kind turns me off? What should you avoid letting me get away with?

Family members exchange telephone numbers so that when one is absent the other members in the family can take the responsibility for calling him and inquiring about his absence. Each family holds at least one alternate meeting every week on its own, at a time and place of its own choosing. I usually suggest specific exercises for these out-of-class meetings.

The excerpts below from participants' diaries exemplify some of the individual and interpersonal events that unfold during this family formation period:

> I actually told several people that I would prefer not to be in a group with them. Including Bill. In the postsession he asked, and I told him, "Bill, you have separated yourself from the group. You have never been the least bit nervous, the least bit touched or distressed. You play Daddy. I do not want a Daddy in my group for I shall either have to play child or fight you for a role I don't want but don't want anyone else to assume either." My reasons for rejecting him are reasonable, and I was not at all afraid to talk it over with him.
>
> Why did so many people wish to have me in their group? Clearly, there is something very much awry in my notion of how I impress people. Perhaps instead of my goal of finding out why people dislike me, I should substitute the goal of finding out why they like me. Man, I am really confused now.
>
> Ruth then told Charlie that she was sorry she couldn't choose him. Both were visibly upset but were trying to find, and I think did, a common meeting ground for this difficult situation. Charles was trying to convince himself that just because he wasn't chosen he wasn't unworthy, which is sometimes very hard to do at gut level.
>
> I knew who I wanted to be with, and I wanted to make the selection in order to be with those people, rather than leave it to a chance as to which family I'd be in. On the other hand, it was difficult to name certain ones, because that meant, effectively, that I was rejecting the others. And then they wouldn't "like" me? Or they would reject me if given the chance? Why is it important to be seen as nice, which means never hurting anyone? I have to examine this.

Familyship Training

In my earlier and rather naive conception of the family I saw it as a medium that, no sooner formed, would facilitate its members' self-exploration and experimentation. I soon realized, however, that most students lack in varying degrees some of the most elementary skills in how to relate usefully to each other. For example, they need to learn how to talk more openly and directly, listen with minimal subjective static, become sensitized to body language, and respond supportively to another's expressions of feelings. They need orientation in how to participate responsibly in meetings in ways that make for productive group movement. They need some new and simple cognitive frames of reference for sharpening their understanding of themselves and others. Finding and developing ways of meeting these needs became a necessity if I were to fulfill my conception of the family as a unit that could become increasingly autonomous and self-directed.[2]

There are a variety of existing materials and procedures from which a training syllabus can be developed. These include Satir's systems and communication games (Satir, 1967), Lederer and Jackson's and Bach and Wyden's procedures for facilitating constructive marital conflict (Lederer and Jackson, 1968; Bach and Wyden, 1969), Berlin and Wyckoff's programmed courses in relationship improvement (Berlin and Wyckoff, 1964), Miles' group-training exercises (Miles, 1959), Berzon and Reisel's Encountertapes (Berzon and Reisel, 1968; Solomon and Berzon, 1969), the ground rules of Cohn's Theme-Centered Interactional Method (Cohn, 1970), and Gendlin and Beebe's instructions for groups (Gendlin and Beebe, 1968). Students can be introduced to various orientations to understanding people in a suggested-readings list that would include Ellis and Harper, 1961; Missildine, 1963; Coudert, 1965; Lowen, 1967; Rogers and Stevens, 1967; Schiffman, 1967; Shostrom, 1967; and Harris, 1969.

In addition to exploring the above possibilities, I am developing a number of training exercises that aim at stimulating members to recognize their habitual interactional patterns and/or practice new and potentially more useful responses to each other. Some of the examples below have been inspired by Ivey's ingenious microteaching of effective relationship behaviors (Ivey et al., 1968), an approach in which human relations skills to be taught are reduced to manageable units that are practiced one at a time:

[2] This conception is supported by mounting evidence that leaderless groups can be productive (Beach, 1968; Berzon and Reisel, 1968; Gibb and Gibb, 1968; Solomon and Berzon, 1969), and that nonprofessionals can be trained to be effective change agents (Guerney, 1969).

Here-and-Now Go-around.   We sit in a circle. Each person in turn says in a sentence or two what at that very moment he is noticing about or feeling toward another group member. We continue doing this for 15 to 30 minutes. This procedure is valuable not only in focusing members' attention on the here-and-now, but in providing silent members, in a relatively safe way, with opportunities to practice sharing with others what is going on in them.

Sharing Disturbances.   This exercise was inspired by Cohn's (Cohn, 1970) rule, "Disturbances take precedence." I tell members that it is important for them to become proficient in recognizing when they are disturbed in some way (for example, bored, hurt, or bothered by cigarette smoke) and to share these disturbances with the group as soon as possible. As practice in this kind of sharing, I invite them to close their eyes: "Imagine yourself in a family meeting. Visualize what is happening. There is a discussion going on. See what it's about and who is talking. In a few moments something will occur that will disturb you very much. See what it is . . .[3] Now fantasy yourself expressing your upset feelings as forthrightly as you can. Hear what reactions you get, and what develops next." Members later share their fantasies with special emphasis on practicing aloud the forthright expression of their disturbed feelings.

Get It Off Your Chest.   I divide the group into trios, and a circle of these trios is formed. One member in each trio is designated A; the second, B; and the third, C. I tell the A's to share with their B's something disturbing that they are experiencing in relation to the workshop, for example, an upsetting occurrence, some worry about what might happen in the workshop, or a negative reaction to a classmate or the leader. All B students are instructed to respond to the A's in ways that make A feel that he is really being listened to and that an effort is being made to understand how he feels. All C students are told to observe the interactions between A's and B's, with particular attention to evaluating the ways in which B's appear to fulfill their assignment. Student A and student B interact for five minutes, and then each trio takes five minutes to share its observations and reactions. Then all A's move in a clockwise direction, and all C's in a counterclockwise direction, to the next trio. In this fashion every member becomes part of a new trio. B's now share their disturbances with C's, and A's observe. Then, in a third shifting of trios, the A's express their disturbances. This exercise is useful in giving members practice in expressing disturbed feelings, and in providing training in some of the listening skills they will require in their family interactions.

[3] An ellipsis (. . .) denotes an interval of 5 to 15 seconds.

Sharing Feelings. I tell the group, "I have to present a paper at a professional meeting this Saturday, and I feel scared to death." I ask each member to respond to me with a single sentence. I reply to each sentence with either an "Ugh" or a "Thank you." For example, if somebody says to me, "You shouldn't be nervous. After all, you're a psychologist!" I answer, "Ugh! I don't want to talk to you anymore." But if, on the other hand, a student in the group says to me, "Gee, I have felt that way too," I say, "Thank you. I'd like to tell you more." So I go around in this way. It is a simple thing, but they get the point: Some ways of responding may turn people off, and other ways may encourage further self-disclosure. After I have modeled this exercise, I ask for a volunteer to take my place with a self-disclosure of his own.

In a variation of this exercise, I divide the group into two subgroups, A and B. I place myself in group A. I express a feeling; for example, "I don't know why, but I just don't like to be touched." I tell members in group A: "Each of you pretend that this is your feeling, and that you have just expressed it. Now each member in group B will respond in turn to this feeling of yours with a single sentence. See whether this sentence makes you feel closer to or more distant from the responding person. If closer, raise your hand. The number of raised hands constitutes the 'score' for each responder." For example, following are two B members' quite different responses to the above feeling with their scores in parentheses: "O.K., I won't touch you." (5) "You have a right not to like being touched, but perhaps talking about it might help." (12) After each member in group A has presented a feeling for response from group B, the two groups exchange roles, and people in the B group offer feelings to be responded to by the A group.

Dilemma Dialogue. This exercise can be useful in stimulating members to explore their patterns of helping each other. Each member in the family writes out on a separate sheet of paper (as many sheets as there are family members) a single sentence stating some difficulty, problem, or dilemma that he is experiencing in his class family. For example, a student may write: "I am having a difficult time telling all of you how I really feel." And if there are five other people in his family, he writes that same sentence on five other sheets, one sheet for each member of his family. When all members have prepared such sheets and have headed each of them, "From (the name of the author of the dilemma) to (the name of one of the other members)," these sheets are distributed to the appropriate family members. When a member receives a sheet, he reads the problem and writes a one-sentence response. He then returns the sheet to the original author of the problem, who then writes a one-sentence reply. With this ongoing back and forth exchange of sheets and of one-sentence responses, each member of the family develops a dialogue with every member around the same problem, as well as a dialogue with every member of the family about each of their dilemmas.

At the end of 30 to 45 minutes I stop the families and invite them to examine their written dialogues in terms of what happened in the exchange and what impasses may have developed or been broken through. I also ask each person to rate each of the responses on his dialogue sheets from 0 to 5, depending on how helpful he found them. We then compute helpfulness scores, which reflect the extent to which each member's way of responding was regarded as useful by the other members in his family. This exercise focuses members' attention on their ways of responding to others, what facilitates communication for some persons and not others, and similarly what interferes with it, and what dynamics might underlie these differences.

Expressing Feelings Directly.   I instruct members: "In a go-around each of you in turn will get in touch with some feeling you are experiencing toward one of your classmates. Express this feeling toward the person in the form of a question that gives the appearance of simply asking for information but that really expresses this feeling in disguised form. The member to whom you address your question will attempt to sense the hidden feeling and will ask, 'Are you trying to tell me such and such?' And if your answer to this is, 'Yes,' he will say, 'Why not say so?' You will then recast your question into a declarative sentence that openly states your feeling. For example, Joe asks Rachel, 'Why were you late tonight?' Rachel responds, 'Are you trying to tell me that you missed me?' Joe: 'Yes.' Rachel. 'Then, why not say so.' Joe: 'I missed you.' If the person to whom a question is addressed fails to sense the hidden feeling, he can ask for help from the class at large."

Tell Him, Not Me.   This exercise was designed to get members into the habit of talking to each other instead of about each other. Student A says a sentence to his neighbor B about student F. B says, "Don't tell me. Tell F directly." A does so. Then F says, "Thank you for telling me." Then F repeats the process, saying something to his neighbor G about another member in the room, and so forth.

Family Crisis.   I ask members to close their eyes: "Imagine that some person in your class family has just said something angry and hurtful to another member. You see this other member wincing. Look and see who specifically it is in your family who is saying something hurtful. See who winces. Notice what thoughts and feelings you are experiencing. Now let the scene develop by itself in any direction." Then after a minute or so I ask the members to open their eyes and to

Figure 3-3. Family crisis. (Photo by Gary Madderom.)

discuss their fantasies. Other "crises" that I ask families to imagine and develop include "a participant suddenly bursts into tears," "one member arrives extremely late for the third time in a row," and "a member monopolizes the discussion." Each fantasy is explored from different angles, but especially in terms of the constructive or destructive actions taken in coping with the "crisis."

Spitback. Spitback refers to the member's right to take as little or as much of another's feedback as he wishes, to taste what is presented, and to spit it out if it does not taste good. Members practice spitback in the following exercise: One member says to a second the first ritual sentence, "(First name), I wish you a good, long life, but I don't like the way you (here a criticism is expressed)." The criticized member replies with the second ritual sentence, "Thank you, (member's first name), for telling me. I'll think over what you say, but I wasn't put on earth to be the way you want me to be." He then selects a member in the group to criticize, and in this fashion the format of these two ritual sentences is repeated a number of times until each member has had at least one practice turn.

In a satiric variation of the above ritual, student A tells student C something he does not like about him or criticizes his behavior in some way. The dislike or criticism may be real or imagined. Student C responds with the ritual sentence, "Thank you, (member's first name), for telling me. I'll think over what you say, but I don't have to be as you want me to be." At this point the group choruses: "You *must* be. You *must* be!" Then C "criticizes" another member, and the ritual is repeated. Both the above exercises were designed to emphasize that it is up to each member to decide for himself what he wishes to value or change in himself, and that he must learn to accept this responsibility to himself in the face of pressure, whether from a single person or a group.

You Are You, Not Me. I give the following instructions: "In this game let's pretend that a new religion is sweeping the country. We will engage in one of its rituals. The family gets together on a given night and sits in a circle, as we are doing here. The father looks around, picks a member of the family, and says, for example, 'Jane, you are Jane, not Father.' Jane looks back at him and says, 'Yes, Father. I am Jane, not Father.' It is now Jane's turn to repeat the ritual. She looks over the family and picks a member, let us say, Peter, and says: 'Peter, you are Peter, not Jane.' And Peter replies. 'Yes, Jane, I am Peter, not Jane.' Then Peter repeats these ritual sentences with another member, and so forth. As a religious ritual this goes on into the wee hours of the morning, but here we are going to practice it only for about 15 minutes. You may choose whomever you wish as often as you wish, but we will always use the same two ritual sentences. We can introduce variations in our exchanges through changing our tones of voice, the emphasis we place on this or that word, how quickly or slowly we say the sentences, or the gestures we make as we say them." And then I begin the game by picking someone out.

In the second part of this exercise I instruct members to close their eyes: "Select a member of your real childhood family and imagine yourself saying to this person several times, 'Look, you are you, not me, and I am me, not you.' Notice the reaction in this person's face and listen to what he or she replies." After a few minutes the group opens its eyes and discusses its fantasies. These imagined confrontations are often extremely dramatic and focus on central interpersonal conflicts in the lives of the participants, usually involving parents. This exercise is designed to emphasize that each of us is an individual with our own ways of seeing, feeling, and doing, and that the existence of such individual differences needs to be recognized and respected. Sometimes there is such an impact on the group that members will return to the ritual statements as certain incidents arise in class. For example, when Steve says to Mike, "I just can't see why you would want to do that!"

Mike answers, "Look, Steve, you are Steve, not Mike!" and that clears the air.

MINIATURE GROWTH ACTIONS

I recently became interested in having students pinpoint their course goals as specifically as possible and share them with their families.[4] In response to my inquiry, members almost invariably expressed their change goals in rather broad, general terms; for example, "feel freer to express feelings." "take the initiative more," and "worry less about others' opinions." As I explored with them the possibilities for translating these goals into specific behavioral terms, I arrived at the concept of a miniature growth action: a challenging five-minute-or-less situation, usually involving one or more classmates, that a member undertakes to experience in front of the group. Thus far I have collected or devised over 200 actions falling into various thematic areas such as self-assertion, self-disclosure, body experience, anger, and affection. Below are some examples:

Tell the leader what you don't like about him.
Go around and have each person tell you something that they would like you to do. Then tell each one as forcefully as you can, "I don't want to do that."
Pick out a member of the group who scares you in some way. Talk to him about it.
Go around and have each person say to you, "I love you," or "I don't love you." Answer each person with a sentence.
Allow the group to lift and rock you.
Pick three people that you like and show your affection physically to each of them in three different ways.
Select three people and lead them in an activity.

I conceive of miniature growth actions as a pool of units that each member can draw upon in creating his own syllabus of living-learning experiences. He decides for himself which areas to concentrate on, selects and/or creates as many action items from these areas as he

[4] This interest was first inspired by Kolb, Winter, and Berlew's study on self-directed change (Kolb, Winter, and Berlew, 1968). Their students, as part of their participation in T groups, reflected on their own group-related behavior and selected change goals they wanted to achieve during the meetings. They kept a day-to-day record of their progress, usually in the form of graphs, and exchanged feedback on each other's improvement. The authors' findings supported the hypothesis that successful goal attainment is positively related to these self-research procedures.

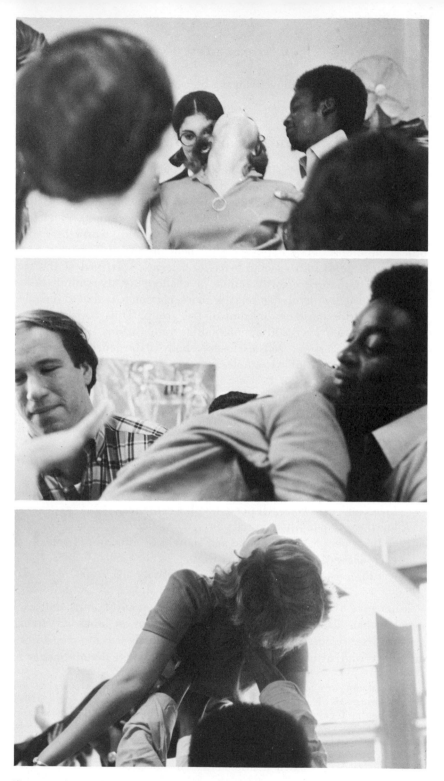

Figure 3-4. Allow the group to lift and rock you. (Photos by Zev Guber.)

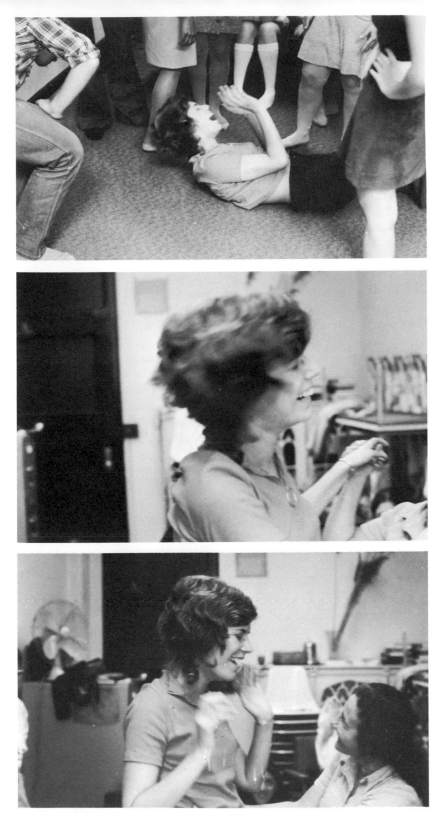

wishes to try out, and performs them in his family (or the class as a whole) in whatever sequence and timing makes sense to him. I am assuming that the student, in undertaking such sets of self-chosen activities, provides himself with a specific, concrete basis for both facilitating and measuring his own workshop progress.

I introduce the members to miniature growth actions through a game tentatively called action auction.[5] This game involves three phases. First, participants compete with each other to "purchase" activity items that strike their interest. Second, they participate in a barter and trading market. Third, they carry out one or more of their acquired growth actions. A more detailed description of action auction is presented below:

I tell the class: "We are going to have an auction. The items for sale are miniature growth actions, that is, specific experiences (each taking no more than one to five minutes) that might be beneficial for you to do in your family or in the group. Each of you will be given $1,000 in play money. You can bid for as many or as few growth actions as you choose until you have spent that amount. Successful bidders will be expected to actually perform their actions after the auction."

Before the auction begins, about 50 action items are exhibited for inspection, either by placing index cards (each containing a typewritten item) around the room, or by passing out mimeographed lists of the items. I tell the members: "Each of you knows within yourself what specific areas you wish to change and grow in, what kinds of satisfying experiences you've never had enough of, or what kinds of new situations you'd like to sample. So look over the items carefully and select those growth actions that would be most meaningful for you to do. Choose wisely and decide how much you would be willing to pay for each item. See how many valuable items you can acquire for your own growth in the next 45 minutes. Remember there are no returns at this auction, and each final bid must be paid."

Sometimes I refrain from exhibiting the items in advance or announcing a time limit, preferring to keep members in suspense as to what items are available and when the auction may end without notice. I tell him that, as often happens in real life, they will be faced with the repeated conflict of making an investment in what is available at the moment or waiting for something better to turn up.

I begin the auction by asking if someone has spotted an item on which he would like to place a bid, or I select an item at random. And very quickly the group falls into the spirit of the thing. The bidding is lively, and for many items, most competitive. I role-play auctioneer as

---

[5] This game was inspired by an identity auction of opinions and attitudes invented by Barbara Ellis Long as part of an ingenious course she is developing for elementary grade-school children (Long, 1969).

colorfully as I can; for instance, "The next item is number 12. 'Allow the group to hug you!' A beautiful item, ladies and gentlemen. Will anyone bid $100? I've got 100, 100, 200 now, now I have 250, 250, do I hear 300? 300? 300! I have 300, 300, do I hear $350? 350? 350! 400! 400! Going for 400! Going once, going twice, sold to Jim for 400!" As each member wins an item he pays for it, and then writes it out on an index card of his own.

Midway during the auction I sometimes call "time out" to give members an opportunity to discuss their patterns of bidding; these patterns frequently mirror real-life behavior with amazing fidelity. For example, one student reported: "My tendency to wait for the big things rather than to enjoy the little things showed. I was going to sink *all* my money into whatever 'clicked' in a big way. I missed opportunities as I waited. I became frightened by the prospects of getting nothing, and then I rushed headlong into anything just to have something, and later I didn't have the money to get what I really wanted. I must reconcile stagnant waiting with unthought-out impulsiveness." After the group has explored its midway reactions, I suggest: "Let's continue the auction, but now see if you can participate in new, more productive ways."

The discussion that follows the completion of the auction centers on the ease or difficulty members had in selecting items, changes in bidding behavior (if any), how members felt about winning or losing, and the appropriateness of any one person's choice of growth actions (as both he and the group perceive it).

Next the open-market phase of the game begins: I ask each member to create two original growth actions and to write each one out on a separate index card. I then invite members to exchange, buy, or sell items and vie with each other for the most advantageous trades they can negotiate, using their purchased items, their two originals, and whatever play money they have left.

In the final phase, members carry out their actions in the large group and/or in family meetings. After each item is performed, the student involved describes his subjective experience and receives in return the group's observations and reactions. Sometimes growth actions are repeated with modifications that emerge from this feedback.

Once members have been introduced to the possible values of miniature growth actions within the playful context of the auction game, I pass out a new and larger list of such items and suggest to the participants that they regard this list as a pool of units from which they can select as many as they wish to work on during the course. I also encourage them to create original growth actions custom-tailored to their own goals. I ask them to rank these items in order of difficulty and then proceed to work on one or more items in each family meeting, beginning with the easiest and gradually working up to the most difficult.

INTERPERSONAL RELATIONS

I have developed a number of exercises in which I ask members in each family to have an experience together or to work cooperatively on some task.[6] Some exercises confront workshop participants with their specific images of each other and their emotional reactions to these images. Other exercises have the additional aim of encouraging families to become more warmly cohesive. The building of a backlog of warm, mutual understanding facilitates later self-explorations into the more private and intimate regions of self and enables a more rapid and perceptive appreciation of subjective factors underlying overt conflicts between members. Examples of interpersonal exercises follow.

The Trip. I tell the class that each family will select one of its members to lead them on a trip: "On this trip, each of you will keep your eyes closed for the duration. Only your guide will have sight. You will line up in a row, holding onto the shoulders or waist of the person in front of you, and move as your leader instructs you. Those of you who become guides can lead your family on any kind of a 15-minute trip you wish. It can be in this classroom, in the hallways, up or down stairways, or outdoors. Make the trip as exciting as you can for your family by describing the fantasy places they are passing through, events that occur on the way, and the imaginary dangers and pleasures that lie ahead, and by instructing members on what actions (walking, remaining silent, running, crawling, and so on) they need to take to effect narrow escapes or experience satisfactions of one kind or another. Members, listen to your guides and imagine as vividly as you can the fantasy events your guides describe. You may talk to each other, unless your guide instructs you otherwise. Guides, remember that you are responsible for the safety and morale of every one of your members; so keep your eye on each of them and see that no one trips, falls, or gets hurt in any way. Talk to them. Lead them in song or chant to lift their spirits. Keep them informed. Reassure them when necessary. And if you tire of guiding, you can invite one of the members to take your place." Each family chooses its guide, lines up, and begins its

[6] The interested reader is referred to Bodin's review of the field of conjoint family assessment in which he describes several standardized procedures and games for studying communication and behavior patterns among actual family members (Bodin, "Conjoint Family Assessment: An Evolving Field," 1968). Some of these standard situations may be usefully modified for use in the workshop.

trip. (One guide took his family through a "jungle" and had them creeping silently past "a village of headhunters," then jumping over "a chasm with a 6,000-foot drop," and walking over "a board placed across a pool of quicksand.") Upon returning from these trips, members discuss such themes as their reactions to leading or following, being blind, and events on the trip. This experience can be usefully repeated with newly selected guides. In such a repetition of the experiment guides can plan joint maneuvers or unite all the families in one long line.

Family Reunion. I ask each family to form a standing circle. I instruct: "One family member at a time will stand in the center of the circle with his eyes closed. Then all the members in his family will touch him, memorize how he feels, and find some physical feature by means of which they could recognize him later in the dark. After all family members have memorized the participant in the center, he will return to the circle, and another member will take his place to be memorized."

When all family members have memorized each other, I give the following instructions: "You are about to begin an experience that you will probably find very meaningful and some of you even profoundly moving. To give yourself the opportunity of experiencing this as intensely as possible, I urge you to keep your eyes shut at all times. Opening your eyes even once, even for a moment, can detract significantly from the event. Also, do not talk to each other at all. This does not mean that you have to remain silent, but please do not exchange any words with each other. So again, let me underscore these two rules. Eyes shut throughout. No talking.

"Now, get into a huddle with your family, putting your arms around each other. Visualize each person in your family, one at a time, and say to yourself, 'Basically, he is a human being just as I am. He hurts and feels and hungers just as I do . . .' Now remind yourself that you and each member in your family, like all humans, are mortal. Think about being mortal and what it means . . . Show your family members how being aware of the mortality you share in common makes you feel toward them . . . Remember, none of us knows what tomorrow will bring. All you know right now is that you are here, and you are with each other. Now, without words, let each member of your family know what he or she means to you . . . In a few moments something new will happen. The lights will go out. See what it feels like to be with your family without anyone talking, with your eyes closed and the lights off.

"Families are together, and families separate. Soon you will experience separation. Perhaps you are ready to be by yourself, perhaps not. In any case, separation sooner or later is inevitable. So very, very slowly, in slow, slow motion begin to disengage from your family. Some of you may be reluctant to let others go, or to separate yourself. That's O.K. Express your resistance, and at the same time, very, very slowly, in slow, slow motion continue to disengage. Do this very, very slowly. Take your time. Give yourself a full opportunity to experience all the different feelings you have as you slowly, slowly separate . . . See what it feels like to have members in your family moving away from you, and you moving away from them, gradually becoming more and more separate and apart. Keep moving all the time, even when you've completed your disengagement. Move slowly, slowly away from your family, farther and farther away. You are entering an experience in apartness and aloneness, so avoid all other people, and if you bump into someone, move gently and slowly away . . . Slowly, slowly, keep moving, alone, avoiding contact with anyone, moving in very, very slow motion, taking your time.

"Now, scatter to the farthest ends of the universe, moving until you can move no farther. Then making sure that you are not too near anyone, stand still and let yourself experience full aloneness as much as you can. See what feelings, thoughts, and memories this separateness arouses in you . . .

"Now, slowly allow yourself to feel a growing longing to reunite with your family. Don't do anthing about it, but let yourself feel this yearning for your family grow in intensity. Now, moving very, very slowly, keeping your eyes closed and not talking, begin to find your family. Take your time . . . When you find someone from your family, show how good you feel to have found him. Then the two of you, hand in hand, or with arms around each other, hunt for a third member of your family. Each time you reunite with someone from your family, celebrate the reunion in some physical way. Let each other know how good it feels to find each other. When you all get together as a family, celebrate the event in some nonverbal way."

After all families are reunited: "Now, all the families are together, and a new stage unfolds. Each of you must now make a choice, perhaps a fateful one for you and your family. Let me outline the choices open to you. Listen carefully. If you feel like it, you may simply stay with your family and continue enjoying it. Or perhaps some of you would prefer to separate from your family and to move away and be all by yourself. That's O.K. Do so. Some members may try to hold you if they wish that you stay, but if you insist, they will let you go. Or, some of you may wish to separate from your family and temporarily visit another family. Or, perhaps some of you would like to move outside the family, simply circling it, occasionally touching members to reassure them and yourself that you are still with each other. Finally, your family may choose to merge with another family. Now, still keeping eyes closed and without any talking, let us see what dramas unfold as you make your decisions. In about ten minutes I will put on the lights, and we will discuss what we experienced."

This exercise is usually one of the most memorable events in the workshop. Students are often deeply moved at its conclusion, with most feeling that one or another central theme in their lives has been touched, for example, longings for closeness, the pain of loneliness, separation anxiety, the pleasure of privacy, the dilemmas of being free to choose, and the conflict between being with oneself and being with others.

Gifts. All family members write their names on slips of paper, fold them, and put them in a hat. Each member draws a name, making sure it is a name other than his own. I tell the group: "Bring in a gift next week for the person whose name you drew. This gift should be one that you make yourself out of materials costing no more than one dollar. It should be a constructive gift, one custom-tailored to fit the personality of the recipient. Include with the gift an appropriate note, poem, or greeting. Also gift-wrap your present in some fitting way." In the following session members exchange gifts and express their reactions to the task and how they dealt with it and to the gifts that they receive.

Advice. This exercise is best carried out in the group as a whole. I ask members to close their eyes and to "hear" a one-sentence piece of constructive advice from one of their parents, advice they wish this parent had given them when they were children but that, in fact, they had never received. I then ask them to imagine a single sentence of constructive advice they wish someone had given to one of their parents. These advices are written out and given to me. I read off a number of them one at a time. (Examples: "Don't be afraid to feel." "Remember, you can't please everyone.") After I read an advice, each member copies it on an index card, signs his first name, and, at my signal, gives it to the person he feels could make best use of it. After most or all of the advices have been distributed, we discuss the experience from various angles, including each member's reactions to receiving the advice he got, and to what extent he received the advices he himself had thought of.

Family Diagram. The following exercise, modified from one developed by Bodin (Bodin, "Family Life Space Diagrams in Therapy, Assessment, and Research," 1968), is very useful in drawing each family's attention to its network of relations as perceived by each member. I instruct the group: "Draw a diagram of the relationships in your family as you actually see or experience them. Show each member as a rectangle. Label each figure with the person's name. Include one with your name. The figures can be square, long, thin, or anything in between. They can be standing up on end the tall way, or lying down on edge the flat way, or tilted at any slanted angle. You can make them any size and any place on the paper. They can be separate, touching, or partly or completely overlapping." Members later compare and discuss their drawings. In a variation of this exercise, I ask members to develop a diagram in the form of a live tableau: "Each one of you in turn will express how you experience your family by placing yourself and the other members in some relationship to each other. You can have members standing, leaning, sitting, or lying down; you can place them in positions that are separate, touching, or overlapping, and in various expressive postures."

Who Reminds You?   Each member looks about his family and selects the one member, male or female, who reminds him most of his mother in some respect. This procedure is then repeated for father and siblings. These selections may be discussed as they are shared or after the rounds are made.

EXPLORING THE SELF THROUGH FANTASY

I introduce fantasy exercises toward the latter part of the course after most members have achieved a significant degree of security in their families. These exercises enter a realm of imagination characterized by varying degrees of freedom from considerations of reality, logic, and goal-directedness. Students often experience dramatic self-confrontations as they follow these new avenues into their private worlds. Such self-confrontations are convincing and moving to the extent that they are vivid, unexpected, and subjectively experienced as the member's own doing. Examples of these exercises follow:

Right-Hand–Left-Hand Dialogue.   This exercise was inspired by one of my learning experiences with Frederick Perls. I say to the members: "Pick up your pencil with your right hand and write a one-sentence statement to your left hand. When you have done this, shift the pencil from your right to your left hand and have your left hand write a one-sentence response to your right hand. Do this until you have written two or three interactions between your hands, that is, a total of four to six sentences." These dialogues are read aloud and explored in the family.

A person's relationship to himself often appears to be reflected with startling clarity in the exchanges between his two hands. I sometimes have members repeat this exercise at a later date in order to see what changes have occurred. Below are the dialogues of a student developed on two separate occasions about three months apart:

First Dialogue
RIGHT HAND: I guess you noticed how cool and sure I am of myself and my movements.
LEFT HAND: I envy you because I am awkward and heavy.
RIGHT HAND: I feel light and airy; maybe you don't feel this way because you haven't practiced or allowed yourself to be free.
LEFT HAND: I hate you, Right Hand.

Second Dialogue
RIGHT HAND: Hello, Left Hand. It's been a while since we have talked.
LEFT HAND: Yes, and we have come a long way since then.
RIGHT HAND: We! That's great!
LEFT HAND: I feel much more confident than I did before.

Secret Message. I tell members: "Let's pretend that each person has a wise, unconscious core that can guide him if he were but able to tune in.[7] Let's see if you can get a message from this wise core in you. Start by spelling your first name in reverse. Now pretend that each letter in your name, spelled backward, is the beginning of a word, and that all these words put together composed a secret message from your unconscious self communicating some piece of wisdom or profoundly important guidance. Concentrate very hard on each letter and see if you can receive this message. The words do not have to make immediate sense. The message may be in symbolic or cryptic form. You may need to stretch your imagination and experiment with punctuation, or even with the sequence of words; so don't discard something that comes to mind because it may seem trivial, childish, or far out. If you can't figure it out right away, get your family to help you. Mull it over before you go to bed tonight, and see if you can have a dream about it. Remember that if the message is valid, it should leave you with the satisfied feeling of having gained or learned something precious."

Following are examples of some easily grasped messages. James, who felt guilt about sexual urges: "Sex Emerges Meaningfully And Joyfully!" Esther, who felt oversensitive about feeling excluded by people: "Reverse Exclusion Hang-up. Tighten Self-Esteem." Margaret:

---

[7] This exercise and a number of those that follow reflect Assagioli's assumption (Assagioli, 1965) that each individual possesses such an inner source of guidance.

"Take! Everything Readily Available. Gamble! Releases Already Manifest."

Bird and Cage.　I instruct members to close their eyes and listen to me as I describe a fantasy for them to visualize. As I portray the situation, I leave silent gaps at critical points for their imaginations to fill in. The fantasy runs as follows:

"Experience as vividly as you can that you are in a room somewhere. Can you visualize details of the room? In the corner of the room there is a cage. There is a bird in the cage. Take a good look at both the bird and its cage . . . Now see the bird jumping up and down excitedly. The bird is saying something to the cage. Listen, and hear what the bird is saying . . . And now the cage is answering the bird, and a dialogue develops between the bird and its cage. Listen in, and hear what they say to each other . . . And now the bird is trying very hard to get out of the cage . . . It finally succeeds. See how it manages to get out . . . Now it flies into the room. Watch the bird and see what the bird does . . . And now the cage is saying something to the bird. Hear what the cage is saying . . . Look, a curious thing is happening! The bird is flying back into the cage. Hear yourself saying to the bird, 'Idiot! What are you doing? You just got out!' The bird, now in the cage, looks you directly in the eye and answers you. Listen . . . All right, open your eyes, and let's discuss your experience."

Responses to this fantasy vary tremendously, usually reflecting with considerable transparency members' current concerns, dilemmas, or status in living. Below is an example of a fantasy and the student's own interpretation:

> Cage was ordinary. Cage door was open. Bird flew around room searching for something, looking out windows, but didn't even attempt to fly out of room even though the thought arose. The cage said, "Come back. You need me." The bird said to me, "You don't know what a relief it is!" Interpretation: I know that I am free to become free of myself. There is nothing in my way but me. I've made some attempts at getting free but am easily discouraged when great changes don't occur as a result of my attempts. I am not yet able to accept that I am responsible for myself. I still feel like a child and want someone to protect me.

Headline.　I ask students to close their eyes and visualize the front page of a newspaper printed in the recent or distant past. When most members have raised their hands as a sign that they are "seeing" the paper, I ask them to focus on the headline. After a minute or two I ask members to open their eyes and share their headlines. I then invite each member to transform his headline into one that includes his first name: "For example, if Bill saw 'President Lincoln Inaugurated,' his revised headline might be 'President Bill Inaugurated.'" I then ask members to again close their eyes and visualize their personalized revisions and "read" the subheadlines and the first lines of the accompanying news stories. After a few minutes I ask them to turn to the editorial page and "read" the opening lines of the editorials on their headlined events. For example, one student, Henry, imagined the headline, "Pax Romana Begins." He changed it to "Henry's Peace Begins." His subheadline was "Nonaggression Pact Signed." The news story began: "Today Henry signed a pact within himself to cease personal hostilities and begin to implement constructive steps toward inner peace." His editorial was brief: "We heartily applaud this nonaggression pact and wish Henry every success toward the rocky road to peace."

The Flame. I put out the lights, and members close their eyes. I make a series of relaxation suggestions in a somewhat hypnotic tone of voice. When most members appear to be quite limp in their chairs, I ask them to imagine taking out a matchbook and striking one of the matches: "Look at the flame. See it as vividly as you can. As you watch it, hear yourself saying one sentence to it. Let the sentence come from within you without planning it. As soon as you've said your one sentence, blow out the match, and resume relaxing." When all have completed this task, I ask them to strike a real match: "Look at the flame in reality and 'hear' it reply to your statement with a single sentence of its own. Listen, and 'hear' what it says without planning it. Blow out the match as soon as you've 'heard' the flame, and resume relaxation."

After a quiet moment, I say to the group: "Pretend that this interaction between you and the flame is a significant one, that it can be understood in more than one way, and that contained in it is a surprising and constructive piece of guidance from your wise, subconscious core, your deeper, inner self. See how far you can get in arriving at these multiple meanings and at the surprising piece of guidance."

After a few minutes of silence, I say: "Allow me to interrupt and lead you in a chant. Let's murmur together softly three times, 'I am, I am, I am the flame. I am, I am, I am the flame. I am, I am, I am the flame.' O.K. Let's do it. (The group complies.) Again, but louder . . . Again, louder still . . . Again, as loud as you can! . . . Now let us be silent, and resume meditating on your interaction with the flame." A few minutes later I tell the group that I will count to five, at which time they will open their eyes feeling refreshed. Below are some students' reports describing their experiences:

I told the match: "I am afraid you will burn my fingers." Said the flame: "Don't worry so much about getting burned." I hesitate in doing things because to show my emotions to others, especially women, I might get burned. I'm afraid to let myself go, or I'll not live up to my image! That's silly, I should stop it.

I asked the flame, "Warm me." It answered, "Warm yourself." The message I got was not to be so concerned with getting from someone else but to develop my own feelings, to feel more, to be more warm, to take the initiative because it is there inside me.

I: "Your light is so light." Match: "And I last for such a short time." I feel that life goes very fast, and so many times my heart is not ready to let go of experiences, friends, loves after they move or die. I want to freeze all these people in a place somewhere. And this can be very unfreeing. But as I listened to the match say what it did, I felt an acceptance of this, an unscared feeling of letting go.

The Object's Problem.   I tell the group to close its eyes: "Visualize a commonplace, everyday object, the first that comes to mind. Become the object. Lose your human identity and flow into this object. Be this object and experience your everyday existence, the different situations you find yourself in . . . Now as you experience being this object and its daily existence, begin to feel some dilemma, conflict, dissatisfaction, or problem . . . Remember, not your problem, but the object's problem. Feel your distress, and long for some outside help. Now learn that there is a wise old object of your category in the neighborhood. If you are an orange, it is a wise old orange. If you are a table, it is a wise old table. This wise, old object is noted for his brief, pointed advice. Go to this wise old object now and tell him your problem . . . Now without forcing or making it up or deliberately pushing in any direction, 'hear' this wise old object respond to your problem in one or two sentences. See how you feel about his response . . . If you feel dissatisfied, don't settle for it. There is another wise old object belonging to quite another school of thought. Why not go to him and hear what he says? Do this . . . Now, continuing to keep your eyes closed, become your human self again and meditate on the meaningfulness of this experience in your personal life."

One student reported her experience as follows:

I am a candle in a candlestick on the dining-room table, and often when the wind blows in from the terrace I splatter wax all over the table. My counselor, who is a big, fat candle standing in a large floor holder, says, "Don't sweat it. " And that's fine. If I drip wax, it is easily cleaned off, and I decide to burn as gaily as possible and let the wax fall where it may. My "lighted-candle" dilemma means being unable many times to accept the inevitable fact of what *is*. What one can't easily change, I think, has to be faced and accepted. And for me that means that if or when I decide to marry again, I will just have to face the idea that my mother will have to live separate from me and my new husband.

Sales Copy. I ask members to pretend that they are advertising copywriters: "You have been assigned to promote a common, everyday object. See what object first comes to mind. Develop a full-page magazine ad to sell it from coast to coast. Make up a brand name and a slogan for the object and develop a few lines of advertising copy extolling its virtues." After members have created this ad on paper and shared their productions with each other, I tell them, "Look at this object, slogan, and ad from a new point of view. People's lives can often be understood as organized around some conscious or unconscious pursuit. For example, many people, without realizing it, keep looking for the good mother and/or the good father they feel they did not experience in their own parents. Others organize their lives around living up to or rebelling against what their parents expected of them. This exercise can illuminate what one of your central drives in life may be if you consider your ad in terms of how it might reflect your relationship to one or both of your parents. Mull this over for a few minutes, and then let's discuss what you recognize." Below are examples of some ads together with the students' own interpretations:

Kitchen sink. Spiffy is the brand name. The slogan: Wash your dishes quick as a wink in a lovely, new Spiffy sink! The copy: Spiffy sinks are made of a specially designed porcelain that won't scratch and dull, does not attract grease, and makes washing dishes sanitary again. Interpretation: I have always been pointed to by other people as the perfect daughter, and yet my parents never made me feel this at all. I never felt I was quite good enough, that I could ever quite measure up to their standards. I was and still am an overachiever and a perfectionist.

Christmas tree ball. Duraball is the trade name. The slogan: The finest of its kind! The copy: Duraballs on your tree will make it glisten for years. No more worries about broken ornaments. No more dullness or lusterless trees. Just gleaming durability. Interpretation: The ornament and trade name are related to my father who angered me for not being durable and independent. He had "balls" for a short time, but they were fragile. I think durability also stresses my need to carry all the weight, all responsibility, to exaggerate my strength, which I feel my father gave up too early.

Concluding Notes

I have thus far presented very little about the effects of the workshop on its membership. I could quote enthusiastic testimonials, as is often done, expressing members' judgments that their second-chance family experiences have been deeply meaningful, and that they have achieved positive changes in insight, self-esteem, and interpersonal relations, but the fact is that, in the absence of rigorously controlled studies, the validity, depth, or permanence of such subjective claims is unknown. Unfortunately, I do not have the time and energy to both develop methods and evaluate them statistically, and so for the time being I guide myself in my efforts at revision and improvement of the workshop by what I see and hear and feel, and by the participants' own reports of their experiences.

Within this phenomenologic frame of reference I plan to study more intensively such questions as the following: How do the self-exploratory styles of different students differ, and how can these best be taken into account by workshop methods? How can the family formation process be improved so that maximum experiential learning occurs with minimal obstructive pain? What dynamics characterize the group life of different second-chance families? What makes for family growth or stagnation? How do members help or hinder each other? What family crises occur, and how do members cope with them? What unanticipated risk and harm might be associated with second-chance family experiences? To what extent do families continue to meet productively after the workshop is over?

The search for effective approaches to the problems of treatment, prevention, and personal growth has produced many varied and imaginative methods that could be adapted for use in the workshop. One pioneering contribution is the course in self-development described by Perls, Hefferline, and Goodman, 1951, as part of their exposition of Gestalt therapy. The course is a self-administered one in which the reader engages in a series of tasks and notices what inner factors interfere. Assagioli's psychosynthesis approach (Assagioli, 1965) to therapy and education is noteworthy in its emphasis on teaching people specific training techniques that they can use on their own and on the use of imagination involving images and guided visualizations. Huxley, 1963; Schutz, 1967; Otto, 1967; Otto and Mann, 1968; Gunther, 1968; and Pfeiffer and Jones, 1969, have each presented a variety of intriguing individual and group techniques for increased self-realization. Recently I have become acquainted with Pesso's psychomotor approach to therapy (Pesso, 1969), an original, carefully conceptualized, and comprehensive set of techniques for the emotional re-education of an individual.

In summary, I have described a still evolving Workshop in Self-Understanding that centers on the formation and training of second-chance families dedicated to the personal growth of their members. With the support of his family, each participant engages in training and self-confrontation exercises that aim at stirring his realization that he has the power to discover hidden and undeveloped aspects of himself, that the self-directed cultivation of new and more satisfying ways of behavior is possible, and that he can evolve wise guidelines for his own life.

BIBLIOGRAPHY

Assagioli, Roberto. *Psychosynthesis: A Manual of Principles and Techniques.* New York: Hobbs, Dorman, 1965.

Bach, George R., and Wyden, Peter. *The Intimate Enemy.* New York: William Morrow, 1969.

Beach, Leslie R. *Learning and Student Interaction in Small Self-directed College Groups.* Final Report, Project No. 7E-020, Grant, U.S. Department of Health, Education, and Welfare. Holland, Mich.: Hope College, 1968.

Berlin, Jerome I., and Wyckoff, L. Benjamin. *General Relationship Improvement Program.* Atlanta: Human Development Institute, 34 Old Ivy Road, N.E., 1964.

Berzon, Betty, Solomon, L. N., and Reisel, Jerome I. Self-directed Small Group Programs: A New Resource in Rehabilitation. Final Narrative Report on Vocational Rehabilitation Administration Project RD-1748. La Jolla, Calif.: Western Behavioral Sciences Institute, 1968.

Bodin, Arthur M. Conjoint Family Assessment: An Evolving Field. In Paul McReynolds (ed.), *Advances in Psychological Assessment.* Palo Alto, Calif.: Science and Behavior Books, 1968, pp. 223–43.

———. Family Life Space Diagrams in Therapy, Assessment, and Research. Paper Read at Western Psychological Association, San Diego, March, 1968.

Cohn, Ruth C. Group Therapists as Group Educators. *J. Group Psychoanal. Proc.,* in press, 1970.

Coudert, Jo. *Advice from a Failure.* New York: Stein and Day, 1965.

Ellis, Albert, and Harper, Robert A. *A Guide to Rational Living.* Englewood Cliffs, N.J.: Prentice-Hall, 1961.

Gendlin, Eugene T., and Beebe, John. Experimental Groups: Instructions for Groups. In George M. Gazda (ed.), *Innovations to Group Psychotherapy.* Springfield, Ill.: Charles C Thomas, 1968, pp. 190–206.

Gibb, Jack R., and Gibb, Lorraine M. Leaderless Groups: Growth-centered

Values and Potentialities. In Herbert Otto and John Mann (eds.), *Ways of Growth*. New York: Grossman, 1968.

Guerney, Bernard G., Jr. *Psychotherapeutic Agents: New Roles for Non-professionals, Parents, and Teachers*. New York: Holt, Rinehart and Winston, 1969.

Gunther, Bernard. *Sense Relaxation*. New York: Collier Books, 1968.

Harris, Thomas A. *I'm OK—You're OK: A Practical Guide to Transactional Analysis*. New York: Harper & Row, 1969.

Huxley, Laura A. *You Are Not the Target*. New York: Farrar, Straus, 1963.

Ivey, Allen, Normington, Cheryl J., Miller, C. Dean, Morrill, Weston H., and Haase, Richard G. Microcounseling and Attending Behavior: An Approach to Prepracticum Counselor Training. *J. Counsel. Psychol.*, Monog. Suppl., **15**: no. 5, Sept., 1968.

Kolb, David A., Winter, Sara K., and Berlew, David E. Self-directed Change: Two Studies. *J. Appl. Behavioral Sci.*, **4**:453–73, 1968.

Lederer, William J., and Jackson, Don D. *The Mirages of Marriage*. New York: W. W. Norton, 1968.

Long, Barbara Ellis. Where Do You Learn to Be People Now—in Schools? *Amer. J. Orthopsychiat.*, **39** (2):291–93, 1969.

Lowen, Alexander. *The Betrayal of the Body*. New York: Macmillan, 1967.

Malamud, Daniel I. *A Participant-Observer Approach to the Teaching of Human Relations*. Chicago: Center for the Study of Liberal Education for Adults, 1955.

———. A Workshop in Self-Understanding Designed to Prepare Patients for Psychotherapy. *Amer. J. Psychother.*, **12**:771–86, 1958.

———. Educating Adults in Self-Understanding. *Ment. Hyg.*, **44**:115–24, 1960.

———. The Workshop in Self-Understanding: Group Techniques in Self-Confrontation. In Hendrik M. Ruitenbeek (ed.), *Group Therapy Today: Styles, Methods, and Techniques*. New York: Atherton Press, 1969, pp. 245–55.

Malamud, Daniel I., and Machover, Solomon. *Toward Self-Understanding: Group Techniques in Self-Confrontation*. Springfield, Ill.: Charles C Thomas, 1965.

Miles, Matthew B. *Learning to Work in Groups*. New York: Teachers College, Columbia University, 1959.

Missildine, W. Hugh. *Your Inner Child of the Past*. New York: Simon & Schuster, 1963.

Otto, Herbert A. *Guide to Developing Your Potential*. New York: Scribner, 1967.

Otto, Herbert A., and Mann, John (eds.). *Ways of Growth*. New York: Grossman, 1968.

Perls, Frederick S. *Gestalt Therapy Verbatim*. Lafayette, Calif.: Real People Press, 1969.

Perls, Frederick S., Hefferline, Ralph F., and Goodman, Paul. *Gestalt Therapy*. New York: Julian Press, 1951.

Pesso, Albert. *Movement in Psychotherapy: Psychomotor Techniques and Training*. New York: New York University Press, 1969.

Pfeiffer, J. William, and Jones, John E. *A Handbook of Structured Experiences for Human Relations Training.* Iowa City, Iowa: University Associates Press, 1969.

Rogers, Carl R. *On Becoming a Person.* Boston: Houghton Mifflin, 1961.

Rogers, Carl R. *Freedom to Learn.* Columbus, Ohio: Charles E. Merrill, 1969.

Rogers, Carl R., and Stevens, Barry. *Person to Person.* Walnut Creek, Calif.: Real People Press, 1967.

Satir, Virginia. *Conjoint Family Therapy* (revised ed.). Palo Alto, Calif.: Science and Behavior Books, 1967.

Schiffman, Muriel. *Self Therapy: Techniques for Personal Growth.* Menlo Park, Calif.: Author, 1967.

Schutz, William C. *Joy.* New York: Grove Press, 1967.

Shostrom, Everett L. *Man, the Manipulator.* Nashville: Abingdon Press, 1967.

Solomon, Lawrence N., and Berzon, Betty. The Self-directed Group: A New Direction in Personal Growth Learning. In J. T. Hart and T. M. Tomlinson (eds.), *New Directions in Client-centered Psychotherapy.* Boston: Houghton Mifflin, 1969.

Robert W. Siroka
Ellen K. Siroka

 Psychodrama and the
Therapeutic Community

COMMENTARY

The Sirokas describe and illustrate the use of psychodrama and its extension to sociodrama and the therapeutic community. The Siroka concept and application of the therapeutic community are innovative and exciting in the possibilities of utilizing encounter techniques continuously in the lives of participants.

BIOGRAPHIES

Robert W. Siroka, Ph.D., is codirector of the Institute for Sociotherapy, New York City; director of training and evaluation, New Jersey Society for Crippled Children and Adults; and director of psychodrama, Moreno Institute, New York City. Dr. Siroka was formerly associate director of the Ruth M. Knight Counseling Service, Manhattan School of Music, where he taught psychology and sociology. He was director of training for the Domestic Peace Corp in Harlem and conducted a therapeutic recreation program for emotionally disturbed blind children. Dr. Siroka has taught at Hunter College and was associate professor of special education at Jersey

City State College and visiting professor of education at New York University.

Ellen K. Siroka, M.A., is codirector of the Institute for Sociotherapy, New York City, and acting director of Psychodrama at the Moreno Institute, New York City. Mrs. Siroka formerly was the speech clinician at Hudson County New Jersey Speech and Hearing Center. She has led many interaction workshops in psychodrama for community and professional groups. Mrs. Siroka was formerly on the faculty of Iona College, New Rochelle, New York, where she taught speech and conducted psychodrama workshops.

> "In the beginning was the word," said St. John of the Gospel. "In the beginning was the deed," exclaimed Goethe's Faust. Let us go further. "In the beginning was the doer, the actor, in the beginning was I, the Creator of the Universe."[1]

I, THE CREATOR

Psychodrama places each man at the center of his world, showing him how he can more truly become its author. Yet to become "the Creator" man must also know himself and turn his insides outward so the world can see him. Psychodrama combines the pain of seeing our weaknesses with the excitement of feeling our depth and strength. It demands nothing more or less than honesty with self and others, and honesty is often a cutting edge rather than a magic wand. We offer no miracles and do not believe that any technique works better than the people who use it. Learning to use psychodrama means learning about oneself and learning the different roles it involves, such as the chief actor or protagonist, the spectator who shares his experiences, and other people who assist in the drama. All these roles, which will be described later in detail, are natural extensions of the helping or sharing role, which is a model for relationships with others. We believe that our therapeutic community, the Institute for Sociotherapy, which we develop later in this article, is the embodiment and fulfilment of the best aspects of the psychodrama. Through it a person learns himself and others.

First it is important to supply a more philosophic orientation toward psychodrama, so that its historical development as an idea can be traced. The originator of psychodrama is J. L. Moreno, and his basic theories about it are contained in four volumes—*The Theatre of Spontaneity* and *Psychodrama*, Volumes 1 through 3 (Moreno, 1947;

---

[1] Moreno, J. L. *The Theatre of Spontaneity.* New York: Beacon House, 1947, p. 13.

Moreno, *Psychodrama*, 1934; Moreno, *Who Shall Survive*, 1953). These amply demonstrate practical and technical ideas together with philosophic speculations. Moreno also links his concept of psychodrama to religion, existentialism, and the encounter movement. We shall be concerned with the encounter group at a later point. The existentialist aspect of psychodrama is its stress on action, on *doing*, rather than *thinking about* or describing. The particular skill involved in it is creation, not via materials, but via the act. Man must be, not the student of that which has taken place, but the creator of experience, the "locus of freedom."[2]

Psychodrama is man's need to create, to make and authorize his own play. In the delight of discovering his creative self he may learn to see better who he is in relation to others, and what he might wish to become. It provides both gratification and learning.

Psychodrama represents a turning away from what would normally be considered fundamentals of theater, such as trained actors, plot, script, rehearsal, scenery, and, most important, audience. In psychodrama the audience has come up onto the stage, pushed aside the artificial mimetic conventions of the play, and staged its own. It is its own protagonist: it plays no one but itself and its own reality, and there is no esthetic distance between life and art. It celebrates its own creativeness in the moment of creation, not that of a playwright disguising his self by expressing it though masks. Psychodrama not only bases itself on particular acts of spontaneity, but is also a means of training oneself to discover and to use it. We need spontaneity or creativity of the self, not only to work, but also to interact with others.

According to Moreno, man feels fundamentally superior to the laws of nature that seem to confine him. However, since it is hard to express this urge in his everyday environment, he needs to consciously make for himself a place in which to exercise this freedom, where he can practice his own selectiveness toward reality. He is also free in psychodrama to make his own script, saying and doing things that he might not say and do elsewhere, even if he wanted to. The psychodramatic act is not an imitation of another act, but a playing out of whatever is within the protagonist. Time and space are not conceived as forces conditioning man in psychodrama. The protagonist, the chief actor of the drama, is able to live scenes from the past and the future, moving them into the present tense in which he is realizing whatever is within him.

What is the continuity, the process in time, whereby a person develops the ability to change inside by participating in psychodrama? Moreno sees psychodrama as a cathartic process whereby the protagonist vents or exhales his sickness. Several factors are significant

2 See "metapraxie," *Moreno*, 1947, p. 110.

here in contrast with analysis as practiced by analyst upon analysand. First, the protagonist is active not passive. On the couch he defines himself mainly through words, but on the stage he must also do. Second, and connected with this, the arena is an environment that can be used expressively by the protagonist. The psychodrama provides free space, whereas an office, with desk, chair, and couch, limits through its structure what can take place between its occupants. (Moreno points out that the couch for Freud was a carry-over from the period of his use of hypnotism [Moreno, *Psychodrama*, 1934, Vol. II, p. 91].) Third, and most important, the protagonist essentially performs therapy on himself and maintains responsibility for himself at all times. "The patient drives his disease out himself" (Moreno, 1947, p. 83).

The function of the director is to protect rather than control the self-actualizing nature of what transpires on stage. The protagonist needs this sense of protection because he must magnify the disease and is vulnerable to rejection: ". . . the intention is to make the disease visible. Paradoxically speaking, the purpose of spontaneous treatment is not to get well but to get sick" (Moreno, 1947, p. 83). This cathartic process takes place because of the depth at which the protagonist produces. If catharsis implies purging of the past, it does not contradict the idea of spontaneity or creation in the present. Catharsis means not only deep involvement in something past, which suggests a reliving or repetition onstage, but also means creative representation or "doing" of inner feelings. The second time brings the first time into focus with other experiences: ". . . One gains towards his own life, towards all one has done and does, the *point of view of the creator*" (Moreno, 1947, p. 91).

To re-experience something we should become its master not slave, and this is assured in that a sickness has become what it is through suppression and hiding, whereas it can only exist psychodramatically by being exposed and laid open. "In order that they may be driven out from their cages, they (the demons of the past) tear up their deepest and most secret wounds, and now they bleed externally before all the eyes of the people" (Moreno, 1947, p. 91).

Cartharsis is thus the chief means by which psychodrama is therapeutic. As part of its therapeutic nature, however, there are other elements of technique developed by Moreno through trial and error. He staged the first psychodrama not in a theater but in a public park, where children came to hear and act in stories. In his model psychodramatic theater, the ideal stage is a circle surrounded by concentric circles progressing outward to the circle of the horizon, and thus open on all sides (Moreno, 1947, pp. 3–4). This open structure is expressive of the relationships between participants in the psychodrama, whether or not they move onto the inner circle of the stage. All are sharers to a greater or lesser extent: "The psychodrama cannot begin unless the last inhabitant of the town is present" (Moreno, 1947, p. 91).

Just as the traditional actor-spectator barrier has been lowered, so has the concept of therapy as something flowing from therapist into therapee been altered. Such phenomena as "transference" and "countertransference" are viewed basically as interpersonal exchanges, and the role of the unconscious is not sharply distinguished. All interpersonal phenomena involve a two-way rather than one-way process, which is called "tele." The deeper interactions between people, whether they are on the stage to play a role or as themselves, are not merely verbal, nor are they created by the methods of the director. They involve "tele," the I-in-you and the you-in-I. The self is thus not circumscribed by insurmountable barriers, but sends and receives messages to and from others. Ideally it is as open as the stage, accessible from all sides.

The unique dimension in which psychodrama takes place is based on what Moreno calls "surplus reality" (Moreno, *Psychodrama*, 1934, Vol. III, pp. 15–19). This differs from the everyday reality of life, the world at large, in that the latter is hard to control as we might wish to control it. In order to experience a simulated reality where we can try out something new, we need a therapeutic environment to practice in. This environment needs to be susceptible to the widest range of possibilities, and not to be implicitly or explicitly structured by an agent other than the protagonist—hence the use of the theater and stage. The reality of the psychodrama is "surplus" because it belongs in another dimension. It is not simply reality, or an exact repetition of phenomena that have already occurred. When the protagonist plays out something of himself postulated in the future, he is well aware that his real future may be different, and that in surplus reality the laws of pastness and futurity are abrogated. In surplus reality a man may become an object such as a chair or desk, yet still talk and feel. He may choose to be a room or house and talk about how he feels toward his occupants, of whom he may be one himself. He can choose any age, nationality, profession, or sex he wishes. He may also become another person who is on the stage with him, and the other may play him. Through surplus reality the personality, defined as a cluster of roles, can expand itself by trying out new ones, rejecting or incorporating them in the process. Thus the psychodrama stage offers a way for the individual to learn through his own process of experimentation, without books or teachers. He can do this in a dimension that provides experience, yet is safe and protected from unforeseen or undesirable consequences. The protagonist must also make the decision to become involved in this dimension. This involvement, the "fact of *embodiment*" (Moreno, *Psychodrama*, 1934, Vol. III, p. 21), makes him the creator of his world rather than its artifact.

ENCOUNTER

> *A meeting of two: eye to eye, face to face.*
> *And when you are near I will tear your eyes out*
> *and place them instead of mine,*
> *and you will tear my eyes out*
> *and will place them instead of yours,*
> *then I will look at you with your eyes*
> *and you will look at me with mine.*[3]

We have many interactions with people during the course of a day, but do not always "encounter" them in the sense that we see them and let them see us. We sometimes feel that as children we had strong feelings and impressions about others, but have since then lost them and do not know how to feel close with another. The above poem by Moreno succinctly expresses the idea of encounter as meeting, as "seeing" the other, and also conveys the intense effort involved in the act. Exploring relationships with another is an important part of the self-exploration of psychodrama: the protagonist fills in his world on the stage by including some individual or individuals who play significant roles in it. At one or more places in his psychodrama he will be bound to meet them. In such a meeting he will be free, as he is not off the stage, to express his real feelings, to say and do things that social and/or family patterns would not permit. They might range from intense love to intense anger. This is how the concept of surplus reality applies to psychodramatic encounter. It frees whatever is within the protagonist in his emotional life that specifically concerns an important relationship with another. Of course, the other person may be from the past, or even dead: here again surplus reality permits the protagonist to catch up with himself, because the results of a long-dead relationship may be surviving inside him. Alternatively, the protagonist may choose to encounter a person in a future or hypothetic relationship, a spouse or child that he does not actually have in the present. In the same way he may meet a person he does not know, such as a historical or political figure, and interact with him. Usually in one psychodrama there will be a series of encounters, as relationships in the present are shown to duplicate elements of those of the past. In the achronologic sequence of the psychodrama, past and present may be juxtaposed; so the protagonist can encounter not only the flesh and blood of people he sees in the present, but the spirit of past figures he may have impressed onto them.

[3] As quoted in Moreno, J. L. *Who Shall Survive*. Beacon, N.Y.: Beacon House, 1953, p. xxxi.

The most important meeting that takes place in psychodrama is that of protagonist and spectator. This perhaps most completely fulfills the images of the poem, seeing "me" through "you" and "you" through "me." Although the actual drama of psychodrama centers around a single individual, he is also representative of everyone. It is natural to allow the experiences of others to affect us; this is the basic principle of the theater, although it extends beyond it into the whole sense of community. However, we often find we have built up a strong resistance to this impulse, so that for some people there is an initial struggle to drop defenses and become involved in the protagonist's drama. Through this involvement the spectator becomes more truly a sharer, and when the drama is over, he may also be able to give back to the protagonist some of the self that the spectator recognized in him. Thus the spectators encounter themselves in the protagonist, and through their sharing of this fact after he has finished, he comes to feel that he is one among many rather than one alone. The whole process of a psychodrama, which develops spontaneously but is also a carefully worked-out method, is designed to create this encounter, this bond between different individuals based on self-recognition in the other. To have any deep experience through a psychodrama it is only necessary to feel something toward or through others. Its appeal is not based on other "theatrical" values, such as moralism or sentimentality; it is not a lecture, a display, a means of breaking someone down, or a method of practicing crowd manipulation. Without proper training in its techniques, would-be directors may be attracted toward it as a substitute for theater, with therapeutically useless or destructive results.

Psychodrama is thus based around the concept of encounter, and as we describe its parts in more detail, this will become clearer. However, we should distinguish it from what is generally called the encounter group, which operates on different principles from the psychodrama. The aim of the encounter group is, of course, to learn to "encounter" others, but its techniques are usually based on socially unconventional interpersonal behavior. Thus there is often an emphasis on physical and sensory awareness of others as a way of getting closer, penetrating barriers imposed by words and custom. The encounter group basically teaches the total psychic involvement of man in his life. The group itself becomes the model, and members are often encouraged to develop relationships among each other of an emotional or even sexual nature. The group leader may be directive about behavior, but usually the emphasis is on throwing off artificial restraints. The goal is to express feelings, to seek confrontation, to plunge oneself into an interpersonal experience, and to learn from the concrete situation. In an encounter group the "acting out" does not involve a surplus reality and is confined to the terms of the actual confrontation.

Although the encounter group can be a vehicle for new and exciting experiences, its weakness from the point of view of changing behavior is that acting out is not valuable without a stress on looking in. Reflection and consciousness of experiential patterns have too little place in a process that relies on actualizing impulses of the moment. Members of such groups may be angry with themselves, or with people (such as parents) who bear in their eyes the responsibility for these feelings. However, this anger goes unexamined, even though it may be transferred to other relationships, and may even be implicitly taken for granted in some of the confrontation-oriented techniques. Stock encounter group practices tend to have an unconsciously hostile element, especially in appealing to "shock" value, with the shock being aimed at parental figures. The same is true of the emphasis on positive feelings: physical intimacy, for example, may in this climate cater to the need to do something unconventional, to hit back rather than grow inside. Feelings about other members may develop in a solipsistic climate in which there is no examination of what underlies a projection. Acts of physical intimacy such as body exploration, hugging, and kissing may be manipulative rather than expressive of spontaneous warmth, a kind of "instant" love. Spontaneity dies if the individual does not feel safe to express his feelings (whatever they are), and he may be tempted to cover them if they are not in harmony with those of a group where he must relate to survive.

We are not just attacking encounter group techniques, of course; we are stressing that alone they cannot provide the essentially therapeutic encounter that psychodrama is designed to provide. We use some of these techniques at a particular place during the psychodrama. Before a protagonist has been selected, there is always a need for the audience members to participate in a form of group process to become sensitized to their feelings, and to warm up to what is to follow. This stage itself is not the psychodramatic encounter, but a preparation for it. There is no "encounter" of therapeutic significance unless those involved can see each other, and can see themselves too. Encounter presupposes some sense of self, and the protagonist can work on his identity through self-encounter: he needs the security provided by surplus reality. Figures in his emotional past may be too entwined with his perception of others for him to have meaningful contact with them, but the encounter group does not deal sufficiently with this, and is, in fact, not designed to. Psychodramatic emphasis on the here-and-now is more important than that of the encounter group, because the present tense of the latter is limited to the particular moment in which something happens. In surplus reality, on the other hand, the present is an immensely expanded dimension, embracing all that is within the individual, including much from the past. It requires only minimal honesty to acknowledge something occurring before a group of witnesses, but much deeper honesty to expose painful feelings about what has been hidden, which no one else could see without the protagonist's willingness to create his psychodrama.

Getting into the Act

What follows is a description of how we conduct psychodrama, rather than a prescription for others. All directors have, or should have, their own style, as well as techniques that they prefer. Inasmuch as we may differ consciously from some things we learned or inherited through our training, we expect others to differ with us. No vital discipline (if that is not a misleading word) should be expected to stand still, and something as concrete as psychodrama must reflect much of the living qualities of its practitioners, who are all different people. Indeed, it might be said that proof of the authentic value of psychodrama lies in its ability to outlive its originators, and to outgrow its original molds, in the same way as the drama, the novel, and the silent movie have changed beyond anything envisioned by their first, great exponents. We also recognize that our methods may change, as our own insights develop, and as we accumulate and absorb new experiences, and these are interwoven with our work. The style of a director should reflect, not simply a learned methodology to be applied cold to every situation, but the spontaneity of knowledge that comes from life itself. "Warmth," which we think of as the attribute of a person, may justly be applied to a therapeutic style, because it implies care for the person it deals with. Of course it goes without saying that some of the "coldest" therapeutic styles are the ones most superficially jazzed-up with sentimentality.

We think of psychodrama as a single unified process in three movements. The first is the warm-up, for which we use some encounter techniques. The second is the drama itself, based on the world of a particular individual, the protagonist. The third is the sharing period, which involves the whole audience. In the first movement the audience members begin to feel part of a group, and in the third they feel as individuals, but are brought into harmony by the experiences of the protagonist. The first flow is toward the group, the second wave brings out an individual but one who is still part of a group, and the last allows the rest of the group to reach out to the exposed individual by sharing comparable aspects of their lives. In the last part the protagonist is the focus for the group's exploring of itself. These three steps should be made as smoothly as possible and seem to flow naturally. Although the psychodrama follows a method, it fails if it appears to be a series of isolated techniques.

In warming up, the director should bear in mind the kinds of warm-up that he responds to. We as codirectors need to warm up to the group as much as it needs to warm up to itself. We also try and sense the vibrations in the room: an audience is a surprisingly individual entity, and audiences vary in what they respond to. Usually, however, people are tense before an open psychodrama session. Some people may feel alone, afraid they will be unable to get involved even if they want to, whereas others may be equally afraid that the people they came with will not like them if they reveal themselves on the stage. All of us have this feeling at many social functions, and perhaps never entirely get rid of it with friends. The group of people that has assembled must first become an audience, a unit, by warming up to other people. We use several techniques at this point, several of which are nonverbal and involve physical contact. Some of these, such as touching a stranger without speaking to him, seem to violate cultural taboos, and in this way they stir up reactions that help the individual to feel "where he is at." Sometimes there is a sense of conflict within the person: physical contact with others, strangers or friends, fulfills a need all have for feeling closer. On the other hand, in this situation an individual may feel a need to protect himself and may judge this adversely without realizing that others may feel the same way.

Another good reason for this kind of warm-up, especially of the nonverbal variety, is the passive role people play in most public places. We sit back and watch plays, movies, and television, listen to recorded music controlled by a few knobs, and consequently need to be jolted out of the expectations and demands that go with this kind of event. For example, it is in this passive frame of mind that the audience is most likely to judge the protagonist in terms of whether he provides an interesting "show." Also, in this role, where our active self remains dormant, we retain illusions as to what we could have done, either as protagonist or as director, and do not have to put these fantasies to the test. In order to profit from psychodrama as an audience-member, one has to be a potential protagonist, someone who has tried, or is prepared to try, to expose himself before a group. These preliminaries are thus a good way to put the individual audience-members in touch with their feelings and jolt them out of the defensive role of passive, intellectual critic.

What follows here is an imaginary scene involving a member going through the warm-up.

> *Scene.* A group of approximately 30 people is seated around an oval stage raised about one foot from the floor. There are two rows of empty chairs at each end of the long room, farthest from the stage at the center. There is a lot of talking. Although a fairly large

proportion of the audience is young, perhaps in college, there are people of all ages and both sexes. Except for those who have come as a group or with friends, they are unknown to each other. They are waiting for the director to enter and begin a psychodrama.

Place. The Moreno Institute at Broadway and 78th Street, New York City. It could be anywhere.

Time. 8:30 P.M.

Codirectors. Bob and Ellen Siroka.

A large room with seats around a stage. People look smaller and hard to know. Lights make everything dimmer. I'm not sure why I came; perhaps I want to stand up on the stage and do something, but I don't want anyone to see. These people I came with (I don't feel I'm with them any more) wouldn't know me. I wouldn't know them. I think I'll stay out of it. How boring it would be not to do something. I don't want to miss anything. I could be great up on the stage.

I'm on the stage; so is everyone else. This isn't how I imagined it. Everyone is talking. I'm talking to *someone you don't know.* I'm asking her a lot of questions in case she asks me one. She asks me why I'm here. I guess we're both here for the same thing, but I can't really say what. People look about the right size up here on the stage, and there's a lot of laughing. The guy I'm talking to now is CRAZY. He's reading Ellis on "rational therapy." He says he tells himself there's no reason to be uptight in these things, so he isn't uptight. I guess it's the heat that makes him sweat.

Now we're making two circles around the stage. There's a girl I used to date over there. I'm getting in the same circle so I don't have to *get to know her without words.* The two circles face each other, like having partners. I feel like we're going to dance. *Communicate without words.* It's hard to communicate without words. The noises are mostly growls and it's easier to smother them. Difference between throat noises and stomach noises. Stomach noises change the facial expression; throat noises are more polite and tentative. *Move on to the next person,* around.

This time *communicate without words but eyes closed.* Are you supposed to touch? I touch a shoulder, an arm, maybe a face or hand. I'm glad my eyes are closed. I feel rather embarrassed, yet happy. There is a hand on my neck, I can feel it shaking a little. Maybe this person likes it; I don't know. We open our eyes. Now it's harder. It's over, and the circles break.

Look for a family among the people here on the stage. I don't need a family. It's a horrible word; I don't feel part of anyone, anything. Maybe I should find one anyway. I could find an attractive girl. Perhaps I'll let someone else pick me. But I want to be the father (a big lie). Other people don't seem to mind. There's a lot of families in the world. O.K. I made it, I'm the father. I have children—the kid wants to be the son, that's his problem. Two good-looking daughters. A grandmother. Something missing? A wife, "mother," but only for the others. Anyway she seems to be running the whole show. I'll steal it from her later. Let her hang herself. *Instant sociometry.* She points her finger at me: she feels *least comfortable with* me. I feel *least comfortable with* her too. Actually I feel *most comfortable* with the guy. He's younger than me, at least on top. I wonder if he knows what's going on. He seems shy.

The other families are talking about their relationships. Everybody enjoys it so much. It is fun, though why? It's fun if you are shy and have to do something; you like the feeling of having "gone for your turn." My voice sounds strange to me. I can make everyone laugh. I laugh, I feel better."

When the group is ready we find a protagonist. Often there is more than one individual thinking of becoming protagonist, and we have them introduce themselves and talk briefly about what they want to explore. After this, if there is still more than one volunteer, we ask the audience to make the decision.

The first thing a protagonist should understand when he begins a psychodrama is that it is his psychodrama, his world as he perceives it. Philosophically and therapeutically, it is wrong to let him feel he is being subjected to an alien process, like Joseph K. in *The Trial,* which is operated and controlled by others. The particular scenes in which he plays should be the results of his suggestions: ideally, there should be a technique applicable to each feeling and problem as it arises. We do not approach him with a previously selected strategy; the same tools do not work for every person and situation. We begin by having him fill in some parts of his life-space through narration or, preferably, action. In this way we warm up to him as an individual, and he warms up to the director. The relationship between director and protagonist is crucial and should be established as soon as possible. Since he is going to share important parts of his world through the agency of the director, the protagonist needs to feel trust for him and a sense of acceptance from him. He should feel the director on his side even if the going becomes rough and should never have the feeling he is being experimented upon, or placed on display before an audience. The director ought to make the protagonist feel he understands him and will not reject him if he becomes stuck or overwhelmed by something. Thus the director acts as a part of the protagonist in the sense that he enters his world and assists in bringing it into the open.

A protagonist may not always know what he wants to explore. Frequently the problems he brings up at first are only symptomatic, with deeper ones lying beneath. At first we have him do action scenes as much as possible, which help fill in the outlines of his self and the world he lives in. If he says he "feels good" when, say, scuba diving, we might have him show this in action by having him move around the stage "underwater," expressing some of the feelings he has in this new and different element. He himself may decide what to do "down there," whether to be more himself, to speak to a particular fish, or just to think more freely about certain things. The value of this lies in stimulating him to feel free in the psychodrama, as well as enabling him to throw out more leads for the action to follow.

After this he may be ready to move into a scene presenting what he conceives of as a problematic area. Again we try to have him "do" the scene as much as possible, preventing him from talking away the feelings. At least in the early stages, it is important to be concrete, and we will probably have him set up on the stage an environment that approximates the appropriate setting. For the same reason we sometimes allow him to select from the audience a person who reminds him of someone involved in the forthcoming scene. It may be worth sacrificing a more competent auxiliary for the sake of letting the protagonist choose his way of doing things. The setting up of environmental props, whether real or imagined, is important insofar as it supports the role the protagonist will be in. The same table and chairs will serve for kitchen, office, or bedroom. The purpose is not to produce an exact replica of an original, but to activate an image in the protagonist (and audience) of a place about which the protagonist has thoughts and feelings. Most fantasies or memories have some appropriate setting, and to bring about a serious construction of the setting localizes and concretizes the inner thought, making it less possible to evade its implications. It is like letting something "out" that once embodied can no longer be hidden or swallowed back. Thus, paying attention to a particular layout on the stage is not only a matter of realism, giving the participants the feeling that this can be a home or an office, but involves the protagonist in an action. Once he has created the environment of a part of his life, he assumes some responsibility toward it, whether he really wishes to or not. Only he can initiate it, and, in the end, only he can resolve what it represents.

However, the protagonist's world is not just a matter of environment: it is largely people. There are people in it at the moment he is onstage, and there are people going all the way back to his earliest moments.

Figure 4-1. Protagonist, double or auxiliary ego, director. (Photo by Jacqueline Paul.)

Sooner or later he confronts some of these in the psychodrama, and he thus introduces a role, or several roles, into his play. These roles are not played by us when we direct. The director should remain free to guide and protect the protagonist, to help him bring forth what is inside him. There may be considerable transference toward those in the roles, and it is important not to disturb the director-protagonist relationship by beclouding it with feelings about other figures. Since transference takes place toward a role rather than an individual, role-playing by *auxiliaries* provides a good way to work with it. There may be many deep or painful associations involved here, so that effective role-playing is important for these relationships to be expressed out loud or in action. Two important techniques involving individuals other than director and protagonist are *role reversal* and *doubling*.

At its simplest level role reversal is A playing B and B playing A. It is as natural as the child playing the mailman or policeman, with the proviso that the latter also plays the child. This technique may be used in a relationship between two people who are on the stage together, though it is more likely in psychodrama that the other person, B, will be an auxiliary playing the role of someone in the protagonist's life. We almost always have him reverse roles with the main figures in his drama, especially at the beginning. Role reversal can accomplish several things. If A is the protagonist and B the other person, from the way A acts in B's role it becomes clear to the director, and perhaps to A as well, how he perceives B. It also shows the other person, B, probably an auxiliary, how A sees him and hence how he should be played. Verbal description is a poor substitute for showing concretely how a person looks to someone else. Role reversal is therapeutically effective because it gives someone the opportunity to put himself in another's position, to feel that he too is human, and perhaps to understand that that position is more difficult than he could have realized from his own vantage point. It also gives A the unique opportunity to be B as it feels to be interacting with A: problems inherent in that interaction, which he may not see as A, could be perceptible to A-as-B. The same things apply to B, whether he really is the person involved with the protagonist, or whether he is an auxiliary standing in in a role.

The technique of doubling consists in giving the protagonist an auxiliary unconscious who gets on the stage with him and voices feelings he may be afraid to express. The person who plays the double thus acts as a fairly intimate part of the protagonist and may be closer to him than the director, who is concerned with the whole psychodrama. On the other hand, the double is not independent of the director, and part of the double's function is to let the director know how the protagonist is feeling. It is the choice of the director whether the double is to reflect back to the protagonist the feelings he presents as he talks, or whether he is to be more interpretive, expressing deeper hidden feelings he perceives within the protagonist's unconscious. In either case the double has to be aware of what lies beyond the protagonist's words, and he should not project his own reactions over those of the person for whom he is doubling. In general he waits for the protagonist to react first to something, because his role is to support not to act as leader. He also has to be careful not to extend any interpretive doubling to a point at which, even if true, it is too threatening to the protagonist to apply to himself at that particular moment. He must respect the protagonist's humanity at all times and never betray irritation or mockery, even if he feels impatient with what the protagonist is doing and saying. He should help the protagonist in difficult encounters and not desert him by becoming silent if the going gets rough. Sometimes in an encounter on stage we give both sides a double: an auxiliary playing a role in the protagonist's life may have a double as well as the protagonist. In this case the auxiliary's double would react as the unconscious not of the individual in the role, but of the person who emerges in the role itself. He would be double to the role rather than the actor.

Two other techniques that may be used are the *soliloquy* and the *mirror*. The soliloquy involves the protagonist talking out loud about his feelings, partly to help him integrate feelings about what just happened or is about to happen, and partly to clue in the auxiliaries as to his perceptions. It is a situational rather than associational technique, thus different from having the patient lie on a couch verbalizing his thought associations. The psychodramatic soliloquy is usually directed toward something specific that has either emerged already or is about to emerge. Often a double may help in a soliloquy, either by supporting from behind the protagonist, or by placing himself beside him and speaking in the first person plural as another part of him. Even so, the soliloquy is not a private dialogue between the two, but a dramatic expression before an audience that ideally shares in his expression of what is happening within him in a particular situation.

The mirror technique reflects back to the protagonist what another person sees of him in a situation (Hollander, 1967). Audience members may be asked to convey, by verbal, physical, or interpersonal means, a "mirror" of how they see the protagonist's behavior. The protagonist may thus learn something about the way others see him. This is more or less an imitation of something seen or given and differs from more interpretive doubling in that it does not go beyond observation. It is not necessarily supportive, and may indeed present the pro-

Figure 4-2. Protagonist (left) wrestling with part of himself. (Photo by Jacqueline Paul.)

tagonist with an image of himself that he does not like, or that at least does not confirm all he thinks of himself.

We also use certain scenes, performed with the aid of an auxiliary who has practiced them, designed to help the protagonist with particular common problems. We do not use them for every psychodrama, but as they apply to the individual's drama. Among these are the *future projection*, the *magic island*, the *height elevation technique*, *death and/or trial* scenes, and a *diabolic* scene (Moreno, 1965; Siroka and Schloss, 1968; and "magic island," a variant of the "magic shop," a technique developed by Hannah B. Weiner, Director of Psychodrama, The Moreno Institute, New York).

In the future projection the protagonist steps into the future as he sees it and describes it in the present tense. This has several results; one is that he is confronted with the fact that how he lives now leads

Figure 4-3. Height elevation techniques —feeling higher and better. (Photo by Jacqueline Paul.)

toward something, and he must decide what it is he really wants from his life. Sometimes the protagonist allows the problems he is evading to emerge in the "now" of the future: for instance, he may project an ultimate confrontation with his parents some time in the future and take a position in regard to them he would like to adopt in the present. At other times he may discover that he has nothing projected for his future, and that he is passively waiting for it to come to him. In any case, it is valuable for the protagonist to step out of the present for a while so as to gain perspective. On the magic island, as in the *magic-shop* scene, the protagonist makes wishes for himself that are to be granted, and we explore what he is willing to give up or exchange in return for getting something he wants. This confronts him with making decisions as to what he aims at in life, what he must do to fulfill these aims, and why he may not yet have done it. In the death scene he also makes an important self-confrontation, because he steps right out of his life and reviews it. We usually emphasize this by staging a funeral or other event at which people discuss him aloud, perhaps in an uncomplimentary way. If there is also a trial scene, he will be asked to judge himself, probably by reversing roles with the judge, applying standards to his life as he might to another's. A related function of death and trial scenes is to make the protagonist think about his responsibility for his life. In the death scene he may feel as if he has to choose between remaining in a passive, "dead" role and living the kind of existence he wants. Likewise in the trial scene he may feel he has to act on the judgments he passes on himself. In another scene we use, the protagonist is tempted by the devil, who offers to hurt anyone against whom the protagonist has a grudge. This scene may help him reveal hostility toward others that he would normally hide, and that has made it difficult for him to confront them. Also it may help him accept that he has the right to be angry.

The third and final part of psychodrama is the *sharing*. The protagonist remains on the stage, but it is his turn to listen to others. He is now the focus for individual members of the audience to share experiences with him, and these should be related to parts of his life as it unfolded on the stage. Until this point the audience, when it identifies with something revealed by the protagonist, sees itself through the actions and thoughts of another. The complementary step must also be taken, in which the protagonist is permitted to see parts of himself in the narrated experience of others. This creates the encounter, the "meeting of two," we spoke of earlier.

Sharing in this context is different from, say, the question period after a lecture, or the analysis and criticism we all do on the way home from the theater or concert hall. This period of time is designed for a specific purpose, and no analysis of the protagonist or judgments of his

Figure 4-4. Audience sharing experience with protagonist. (Photo by Jacqueline Paul.)

behavior (favorable or unfavorable) have a place in it. Also, it is inappropriate for audience members to do their psychodrama here, and there should not be an atmosphere of "revivalist" hysteria. The concern is for the part of each person he has seen in the protagonist; it is not the time to save his soul, unless there is salvation through sharing. We always protect the protagonist from people who try to denigrate him, either explicitly in a lecture, or implicitly by making him feel that they have bigger problems or more powerful feelings. An important aspect of the discipline of psychodrama is learning to relate to another person, finding mutual grounds for meeting each other, and not imposing our particular values or preoccupation of the moment onto the interaction. This can happen only if there is a mutual willingness to expose parts of the self while respecting and seeing the self-exposure of the other. The protagonist of a psychodrama has exposed a great deal of himself on the stage; so it is now up to the individual audience members to respond to what he has opened up.

The other purpose of the sharing period is for the benefit of the protagonist himself. He has no way of knowing whether his problems or feelings are burdensome to him alone, and he should not leave with the idea that he is the only person in the world in a particular situation.

His need at this moment is for support, rather than insights given by others. He derives this support, not from mere benevolence, but from sensing that others are like him, and that his ordeal of self-exploration, whether arduous or not, has resulted in increased possibility for contact with others, rather than in ostracism.

THE THERAPEUTIC COMMUNITY

The psychiatric hospital can be seen as a microcosm of society outside, and its social structure and culture can be changed with relative ease, compared to the world outside. For this reason "therapeutic communities" to date have been largely confined to psychiatric institutions. They represent a useful plot run preliminary to the much more difficult task of trying to establish a therapeutic community for psychiatric purposes in society at large.[4]

We have taken the crucial step outside the psychiatric institution. Our therapeutic community, the Institute for Sociotherapy, is nonresidential and does not function within another institution. It consists of 40 to 50 members, who are functioning members of society, economically solvent, and self-supporting.[5] They are in it because they chose us as therapists and we chose them as clients.

Our concept of the therapeutic community has evolved through psychodrama, group interaction, and our experience with the neo-analytic therapy of Sidney Levy, as well as the kind of community described by Maxwell Jones (Jones, 1953; Jones, 1962; Jones, 1968; List, 1961; Clark, 1964; and Levy, 1958). It arose as the most natural environment for our over-all view of man as a biosocial animal, whose self is formed by the socially learned modes through which he fills his various needs. These needs are basically biologic, but take on social character as he becomes adult. This socialization is healthy if man's emotional, animal drives are satisfied. We should be able to feel our aggressiveness and our desire for physical contact, sex, and so forth, and also know what to do with them. Often, however, becoming physically adult has meant blocking or stifling emotional needs, the social self having little contact with the nature of the individual.

Through therapy the individual can understand or relearn this

---

[4] Jones, Maxwell. *Beyond the Therapeutic Community*. New Haven, Conn., and London: Yale University Press, 1968, p. xii.

[5] See "Demographic Information on the Therapeutic Community" at the end of this chapter.

process of growing up. First he needs, through transference to parental figures, to break out of the warped social mold and regain contact with what lies beneath, where the emotions may be still very young. Through the corrective "mothering" of therapy a person becomes more conscious of these feelings, and they begin to play a more active role in his life, so that he is less frustrated and angry. The experience of interacting with others, which he has in a therapeutic community, helps him resocialize this newly contacted part of him. He learns how to meet his needs in a personally constructive way, growing in awareness and autonomy. In the therapeutic community each client's interpersonal patterns are exposed and seen. Change in these patterns is supported and guided in the communal context. The community offers social reinforcement, which modifies the destructive and rewards the desirable patterns of behavior unique to the individual.

Our community (set in an urban environment) is not so much a place as something that exists in the interpersonal network of relations among its members. The physical or structural focus is in the offices of the institute, but people may meet in many different places for different reasons: for tutoring, to have a party, to play football in Central Park, to plan something, or simply to talk and be together. Although we firmly encourage people to help each other and live through as many things as possible together, we do not plan anyone's daily life. A group of individuals is a group inasmuch as it interacts spontaneously, and most of this organic phenomenon, "community life," is entirely spontaneous. Its spontaneity gives it the quality of being *real*, a quality missing in many community-style functions where togetherness is forced. The reason is at once paradoxic and fundamental: people must expose themselves to each other, especially the parts not normally considered "likable," before they can enjoy, and learn from, one another. Each must be the protagonist, perhaps many times, before the barriers are sufficiently lowered between the individual "I" and the "they" outside. Self-confrontation becomes the means to interact positively with others.

These are the kinds of groups available to each member of the institute. First, everyone attends a small weekly group run by both of us together, called the *ensemble*. This group, in which the maximum number of people is six, is designed to give each individual enough time to discuss what is going on in his life, whether or not it is connected with anything else brought up by the group. Thus, the focus is not so much on group interaction (as with the other, larger groups) but on the individual per se. The experience of ensemble combines the individuality of the "private session" with seeing others open up their emotional patterns and problems. This creates a feeling of closeness within it, though the group does not necessarily act as the sole therapeutic agent for its members. In a questionnaire we gave to community members in November, 1969, we asked them to express their feelings about the groups with adjectives, and in regard to the ensemble the recurring theme was closeness and warmth. Adjectives such as "sharing," "safe," "close," and "intimate" were common, though there were others like "probing," "exposing," and, on a different theme, "competitive," "sharp," "angry," and "scared."

In addition to the ensemble there are other, larger therapy groups that function according to different norms. In a large group it is the group itself that plays a role comparable to that of the therapist, especially because problems that come up may involve peer relationships. There are two basic large-group sessions: the *men's* and *women's* groups for members of the same sex, and the *open* group, attended by everyone in the community. A third large group is the *couples'* group, attended together by people who are married or dating. Each of these, like the ensemble, is a weekly group: a minimum therapeutic requirement for every member is regular attendance in an ensemble and one large group.

In a group like the weekly men's group the topics will probably center not around an individual, but around feelings stirred up by events within the community. Something as "simple" as a game of football in Central Park, in which the male therapist played too, can serve as a starting point for feelings about father-and-son relations, which members bring into the community with them from their family experience. As well as father-son relationships, there are other common themes in the men's group, such as competition between males, friendship, sexual feelings, and male identity. There are comparable themes in the women's group, where women can explore all facets of female identity—maternal, sexual, sibling, competitive, "masculine," aggressive—much of which they would be less likely to expose in a mixed group. The men's group is led by a male therapist, and the women's group by a female therapist. Working on problems related to the identity of one's sex is a vital part of the resocialization process for men and women. In the questionnaire both sexes indicated that men's and women's groups were important to them, though the women selected it more often as the group they felt was most important to them. All the women who chose the women's group in this context indicated that they felt most comfortable discussing "certain matters in a group of my sex." This accounts in part for the frequency of such adjectives as: "safe," "warm," "caring," "beautiful." Men applied what would seem conventionally more masculine adjectives to the men's group, such as "tough," "hard," "exciting," "powerful," "intense," and "black." They did not indicate such a strong preference for a group of their sex in which to feel comfortable. There was less emphasis on emotional involvement in the men's adjectives, probably because it may be a masculine trait to play down warm feelings toward other men.

The weekly open group, led by both of us together and open to the whole community, functions in part as a town meeting. There is often a good deal of information to be exchanged and passed around about numerous activities. As in the men's and women's groups, there is emphasis on feelings between people, friends and "competitors," which have been brought up in the context of community life. Because of the three-hour length and the physical size of the group, it can attain considerable power and intensity. We use psychodramatic techniques in all the groups, but this is the most psychodramatically oriented because individuals relate to the experiences brought up by the group rather than vice versa. The group meets in a room with a stage in the center, and the members sit around it on four sides. Problems that involve a face-to-face confrontation can be handled by having people step up onto the stage. The therapeutic community is an ongoing warm-up, and we can shift immediately into psychodrama. Relationships within the community may serve as material, but group members may also perform as auxiliaries and doubles if we are moving into something in an individual's life from the past. Even though it is also an audience, in such a group as this, the community is involved more than in traditional psychodrama, because of the close identification built up between fellow members, and because all have become sensitized to the process. For similar reasons we have people act as auxiliaries and doubles spontaneously as the need arises in other groups.

Finally, of the large therapy groups, there is the couples' group. The purpose of this is to help people examine their feelings and behavior with a member of the opposite sex, and to learn to see their partner as a person without the distortions of male-female relationships acquired from home and society: hence the significance of both members of the couple being present, and encountering each other directly with the guidance of a male and a female therapist, also a couple. It is important that group members let each other see how they feel and confront each other openly.

An important aspect of learning to grow within the community is the ability to contribute and acquire skills. We have many peer-led groups that function in the institute, created because someone has something valuable enough to be passed on to others who want it. Activities on which such groups are based include learning disability, research in social science, dance and movement, computer programming, writing and editing, and creation of a library at the institute. As well as these, many informal group activities spring up constantly, centering around such things as planning social events or helping confirmed cigarette smokers kick the habit. Thus many of the important activities are client-led, and they exist primarily because of people's need to build into their lives a range of things that enhance their creativity. The other value is that within the community both teacher and pupil are on equal terms, and each can confront the other at any time with feelings about the group, either on the spot or in a therapy group. Thus there is a relationship between members' talents as practiced and recognized in their life outside the community and their activities within it.

How does the community see itself? Members interact on many levels, and those most involved in it indicated in the questionnaire that it functioned as a model for life in a total sense, for example:

> In our meetings we have the opportunity to examine our lives and the way we live with others.

This is particularly true in the area of relating to others, as indicated in statements like these:

> I was amazed to learn that underneath all those glaring differences we are very much the same, with the same emotional needs . . . These people . . . practice how to be with other people.

The question of other people goes hand in hand with that role, of learning to be oneself, so that many members indicated that the community was a place to learn:

> The therapeutic community is like a second chance at life . . . Somehow for me, too, it's like a new family or school.

The community represents to its members, not simply a sum of activities, but a unified way of seeing and relating. Learning to confront oneself, to acknowledge painful feelings, to let others see into us is not just practiced in a group session, but lived as a basis for relating to others. This was expressed by several writers in the questionnaire, as for instance:

> It's the only place I can go where I don't feel alone and all my deepest feelings of love, hate, etc., come out for an airing. I feel refreshed after a group, and when I meet someone on the street from the community it always makes me feel good. I know I'm making it sound like a bed of roses, but it isn't always that way, because finding out you're a big phony isn't too good for the ego. But once you give it up, believe it or not, you feel more comfortable.

Here is another example, placing emphasis on feeling as a touchstone in the community:

You can go there (wherever there's another community member but more intensely in the groups) and feel and learn to accept feeling and how to live. If you accept these feelings you can progress in the community, can be open to accept others and accept yourself without any labels.

This is probably one of the biggest differences between the therapeutic community and what most of us experience in society at large, where emotional dishonesty is so prevalent.

The dynamic of the community is self-exploration with the aid of others' sharing and support, and this is a paradigm of the psychodrama. But the community also provides the essential "follow-through" that traditional psychodrama often lacks. There is no growth in an emotional breakthrough that is not translated into new behavior, and the community gives the needed support for this. The concept of therapeutic community both embraces and surpasses psychodrama. Psychodramatic warm-up is equivalent to the encounter of different people and relationships in the community. The psychodrama itself takes place in the groups, where a therapeutic experience is shared by spontaneous "auxiliary" group members. Finally, the community provides support for new learning and reintegation that isolated psychodrama does not.

It is one of the basic values of the community that it writes its own script of encounters and psychodramatic experiences. A group is not simply a certain number of individuals who do not see each other outside the allotted time and space of the session. A member who brings up a problem in group is a protagonist, much of whose life-space is already there in the room with him. What happens in the large groups is usually a working out of something triggered by the life of the community, and this in turn brings out the deeply embedded emotional patterns that everyone brings with him into the community. If a significant part of the client's world is there with him, he has a good way to work on relating to it. Most problems are ones of relating, and in such a community the growth of the individual is accelerated because the objects of his relationships can be worked on as well as he. Through the community people learn how to build their own environment within a particular, common process. Thus the protagonist acts his psychodramas in a world of other protagonists and shares with others who share.

This community then is stage, warm-up, protagonist, and sharing

Table 4-1 Demographic Information on the Therapeutic Community

Location of Birth		Background Setting		Religion		Education	
East	34	Urban	26	Protestant	11	Ph.D. degrees	3
West	3	Suburban	15	Catholic	10	Master's degrees	13
Midwest	3	Rural	2	Jewish	22	Bachelor's degrees	11
South	1					Some college	14
England	1					High school	2
Canada	1						

Students	
Undergraduate	6
Graduate	11
Nurses' training	1
Premed	1

Age Range		
Ages	Men	Women
15–20	1	1
21–25	8	9
26–30	5	8
31–35	0	1
36–40	2	0
41–45	2	0
45+	2	3

Length of Time in Community		
Time	Men	Women
0–1 yr	6	8
1–2 yr	4	9
2–3 yr	5	1
3–4 yr	6	4

Helping Professions

Psychotherapist psychologist
Psychodramatist
Music therapist
Dance therapist
Poetry therapist
Social worker
Child-care worker
Psychiatric hospital attendant
Sensitivity trainer
Training consultant

Business and Commerce

Computer programmer
Secretary
Typist
Modeling agent
Cab driver
Restaurant hostess
Beautician

Teachers

College professor in English, psychology, social work, and music
High school instructor in English and music
Music teacher with the mentally retarded
Private music teacher

Researchers

Sociological and anthropological researcher
Ethnomusicologist

The Arts

Professional musician
Jewelry designer
Jewelry crafter
Organ builder
Cabinet finisher
Sculptor

audience, all in one. Each member goes through a series of psycho-dramatic experiences in groups and, building on them successively, becomes stronger as he learns to expose his insides to others. Through the sharing and support (which may also be critical if his patterns are harmful), he becomes stronger in being his own guide, dealing with behavior that undermines him. He also learns to use his own strength and creativity rather than rely on the "divine" guidance of a therapist, because he receives no direct benefit in a group session without making the choice of opening up before others and risking the honest reactions of peers and "siblings." Group process represents a nurturance and weaning that is hard, but strengthening and healthful; each member is protagonist and, sometimes, therapist, not a sick patient. This is why we call the institute's activity "sociother-apy," because it involves therapy through the group, through resocial-ization. But this society is not faceless or mechanized. It understands how to play, how to be a part in another's existence, and how to be personal.

This is our therapeutic community as it stands now. It may not work for everyone; it is not the only form of therapy that we believe to be effective. It is probably far more involving than can be con-veyed on paper, and we are not following a pre-established model. Not only does it change of itself as its members grow, but we learn through it and make changes of our own. We do not prophesy what form the community will take in the future, but we are sure it will not stand still.

BIBLIOGRAPHY

Clark, David H. *Administrative Therapy*. London: Tavistock Publications, 1964.

Hollander, Carl. The Mirror Technique as a Psychodramatic Encounter. *Group Psychother.*, **20**:25–38, 1967.

Jones, Maxwell. *The Therapeutic Community*. New York: Basic Books, 1953.

Jones, Maxwell. *Social Psychiatry in the Community, in Hospitals, and in Prisons*. Springfield, Ill.: Charles C Thomas, 1962.

Jones, Maxwell. *Beyond the Therapeutic Community*. New Haven, Conn., and London: Yale University Press, 1968.

Levy, Sidney. Case Study of an Adult: The Case of Mr. P. In Emanuel F. Hammer (ed.). *Application of Projective Drawings*. Springfield, Ill.: Charles C Thomas, 1958.

List, Jacob S. *Education for Living*. New York: Philosophical Library, 1961.

Moreno, J. L. *Psychodrama*, vols. 1–3. New York: Beacon House, 1934.

Moreno, J. L. *The Theatre of Spontaneity*. New York: Beacon House, 1947.

Moreno, J. L. *Who Shall Survive*. New York: Beacon House, 1953.

Moreno, Zerka T. Psychodramatic Rules, Techniques and Adjunctive Methods. *Group Psychother.*, **18**:73–86, 1965.

Siroka, Robert W., and Schloss, Gilbert A. The Death Scene in Psychodrama. *Group Psychother.*, **21**:202–5, 1968.

Sidney M. Jourard

5 A Way to Encounter

COMMENTARY

"A Way to Encounter" is Sidney Jourard's personal way of escorting
the reader through his views and experiences, both positive and negative. What is to be accomplished by the leader? What are one's responsibilities toward members of the group? How active a participant
should one be? How close does one have to be to one's own feelings
while leading encounters? The author takes us with him and shares
personal feelings about his work. And in this way, we begin to have a
sense of what one encounter group is about, through the inner perspectives of its leader.

BIOGRAPHY

Sidney M. Jourard was born in Toronto, Canada, obtaining his bachelor's and master of arts degrees from the University of Toronto in
1947 and 1948, respectively. He continued his training in clinical psychology at the University of Buffalo and obtained his Ph.D. from there in
1953. He has taught at Emory University and the University of Alabama
Medical College and since 1958 has been at the University of Florida, where
he holds the position of professor of psychology.

He has been active in individual psychotherapy since 1951, at which time he began a part-time private practice, which continues up to the present. He is a member of the American Academy of Psychotherapists, is a past president of the Association for Humanistic Psychology, and has served on the Council of Representatives of A.P.A., as well as on the Executive Council of the A.P.A. Division of Psychotherapy.

As Sidney Jourard points out, he received training in group psychotherapy and began encounter group work in 1958 with the faculty of a nursing college. Since 1965, he has been conducting encounter groups at various growth centers around the country and is himself a cofounder and director of the Center of Man in Florida.

He is the author of several books and recommends that readers of this chapter might well consult three of these: *Personal Adjustment, an Approach Through the Study of Healthy Personality* (Macmillan, 1963) ; *The Transparent Self* (Van Nostrand, 1964) ; and *Disclosing Man to Himself* (Van Nostrand, 1968). These volumes provide the theoretic background for the present chapter.

Gimmicks, gadgets, and techniques, the genius of America. What have these to do with a person's growth, which *happens* as he struggles to reinvent his world, encountering obstacles and helpers along the way. Are encounter groups "gimmicks and techniques"?

I first heard about "encounter groups" as something special when I went to Esalen Institute, shortly after returning from a year in England. I was to conduct an informal seminar advertised, ambiguously enough, as "A Weekend with Sidney Jourard," to discuss *The Transparent Self* and anything else I was up to (Jourard, 1964). About 150 people jammed into the meeting room at the main lodge of Esalen, and I began to talk about self-disclosure, thinking that was appropriate. Every few minutes someone would interrupt my brilliant oratory and say something like: "But Dr. Jourard (or Sid), you've written *about* self-disclosure in *The Transparent Self,* and you're not telling *us* anything about *you.* Disclose yourself to us!" I ignored several of these comments, but one person (I forget whether man or woman) was persistent. I said: "Damn it! You're not asking for self-disclosure, which I'm doing! You seem to want a strip-tease! Would you like me to undress?" I continued: "Look, if you want to sit with me, and really talk, I'm ready. But I'm a private person. Respect this as much as I respect your right to disclose or withhold." This was a brief encounter between the other and me and an invitation to continuing encounter, which the other person declined. Esalen Institute, I learned, was a place where many "encounter groups" were conducted.

I knew about group dynamics and sensitivity training, and I had had some training in group therapy. But as my research in self-disclosure progressed, I came to think of individual and group therapy, not so much as "treatment," but as an invitation to authentic disclosure and self-reinvention. For four years, I had conducted what the dean called "Faculty Training Group" with my colleagues in a college of nursing. I thought of it as a "disclosure group"; the nursing faculty seemed to view it as a therapy group. My aim was to invite the nursing instructors to be less bitchy, defensive, game-playing, one-up women, hoping they would then serve as more human and humane role-models for their students. I think I succeeded to a modest extent. Perhaps more important, I left the college of nursing after four years, feeling no less a man, no less vital, and more grown than I felt on first joining the faculty.

I have been conducting something like encounter groups since 1965, and I had been "in" them (through my association with the American Academy of Psychotherapists) before that date. My feelings about the encounter group phenomenon are mixed. I'm delighted that people have begun to gather in small groups to *try* really to address one another in the spirit of good will. It's reminiscent of the early Christian church. And I am somewhat suspicious about the growing technology of "group process" and encounter groups that are "led." There are manuals for group leaders available, giving opening gambits, nonverbal games, touching exercises, group gropes, and the like—like rainy-day suggestions, the boon for all who direct summer camps for children. I have created one or two such games myself and intend to develop more. But everything depends on the projects, the purposes for which people enter into or lead an encounter group. I run them, when asked, with the aim of encouraging personal growth in myself and the others through encounter with one's situation and the other people in it. And I invite encounter in my individual counseling, my teaching, and my personal life, for the same reason.

What is personal growth? One's situation? And encounter? I have grown when I perceive the changes that occur in my embodied self and my world—my situation—decide how I next want to be in this world and how I want the world to be for me, and then act. Change in my world happens continuously as process—the result of agency other than my own. And change is consequent upon praxis, that is, my own acts, acts that affect the world as well as me, the actor. I discover change when I pause from my projects and take a fresh look at me and my world. And change discloses itself to me as I go about my business and find that the people and things are not as I believed. At these moments my situation becomes a question, an invitation, and a challenge. The question is: "Do I want the present situation to endure?" Whether my answer is yes or no, my situation challenges me to *act,* to preserve it, or to let it drift as it will. If I choose to change it, I must envision, however dimly, a better situation for me, a better way for me to be (and be seen) in the world. And I must envision a better way for the world to be for me. Given the image, I must then act, to "actualize" it. My situation is "factical." It is the facts of my condition and the condition of my world that are disclosed to me when I survey my situation. It is man's lot in this world to acknowledge the change of the world and himself, change that follows the "process" of the world and change that follows his own acts. And it is every man's lot to face the changed situation—change that has occurred behind his dim perception of the world until he peers through the veil—and answer the question, "What will I do in, with, and to this changed situation that I confront, the situation that encounters me?" Without such true perception and challenge in a situation, there is no encounter, and there is no growth. And if you are part of my situation, and I am part of yours, there can be no encounter and no growth unless we disclose ourselves to each other in truth. Then I encounter you, and you encounter me. Our worlds merge into a shared realm of "between."

The difference between my encounter with some nonhuman part of my world and an encounter between you and me is this: I encounter a tree when I perceive it as it now is. The tree does not know it is perceived. When you and I disclose ourselves to one another in dialogue, I perceive you and am perceived in return, and I know that you perceive me, and you know I perceive you, because I tell you what of you I perceive. We both have the chance to grow through our encounter, if we dare be and disclose who we *are* just then. Because that is our ground, our situation.

I do not encounter my situation. I can only offer encounter, and that only to another person. Encounter *happens* to me when I let my situation speak to me, touch me, blast my preconceptions, and let me know what is there. Because what is there is not what I assumed, presumed, or imagined. The encounter is fulfilled when I acknowledge my situation and respond with the truth of my being, including my vision of a better situation.

My situation and yours are complex. Mine includes what I perceive and misperceive of my body and the world beyond my body, through my several sensory systems ("receivers" of the disclosure of the world). And it includes my recollections and feelings and imaginings and fantasies and thoughts, as these exist for me right now. In fact, my memories, thoughts, and imaginings "turn off" my perception, so that I no longer receive the disclosures transmitted by my body and the world. To think, imagine, or remember with full attentiveness is to be functionally blind, deaf, anesthesic, shut off from the world. When I am "in my head," I am out of my situation and I do not perceive it as it is. I cannot change my situation until I know it, let it encounter me in the intense immediacy of perception. Everyone is a specialist at some kind of "blindness." This person cannot see, that one cannot smell, the other has not felt, tasted, or heard what his situation is saying. Everyone's perceptual grasp of his situation is partial. If a group of people share a situation, each can disclose his perspective to the others, thus inviting them to see, hear, smell, and feel what he does, but which they do not; but they can. Thus, the shared disclosures of how it is with me that a group-for-encounter affords can turn a person's perception on and enlarge his awareness of his situation. If people likewise share their memories, inventiveness, and ways of construing situations, they likewise grant an invitation to others to experience in comparable ways. And if they show one another how they act, and cope, they afford the others an opportunity to copy or adapt these ways for themselves. My disclosure in words and actions is thus a precious gift to those who receive it. When I am in your situation, and let myself be *perceived,* I have truly helped you to awaken and grow, because I may have shown you a part of your world—me—that is not as you expected.

But I have met (or, better, *not* encountered) numerous people whom I think of as "T-group bums," or encounter-group bloodhounds—who can enter a town or neighborhood, sniff the air, and say, "There's an encounter group going on somewhere," and they track it down. Once in, they cry, swear, touch, and insist people stop the bullshit intellectualizing and get down to the nitty gritty, the gut level, the here-and-now, and then go home with pleasant memories to a routine, cosmetic existence. There is nothing wrong with following the groups and developing expertise, comparing Schutz with Perls with Rogers, and so on. Fun is hard to find, and I'm all for it wherever it can happen. Moreover, watching a master do his thing in a group is a much less bloody spectator sport than boxing. And there are the equivalent of fan clubs developing. "I like the way Schutz handles body contact better than Bindrim does," one buff might say to another.

In fact, as America enters the age of leisure, people have to learn to play with their own possibilities, to delight in human variety and in one another's company or else we shall all go mad. Encounter groups at their best can be places to go to play and to grow.

I see groups in which I take part as an opportunity to present to those attending who I am, where I am in any spheres of my life I feel comfortable talking about, and how I struggle against the barriers that get in the way of my projects and my growth. Someone present always reacts to me, and we are off! Where we go from there and what happens for the next hours or days depend on all of us. I don't take responsibility for everyone participating, everyone having a good time, everyone touching somebody or being touched, though, at a given moment, I may ask someone to join me in a headstand or a dance. The only thing I really *try* for, while I am in a group where encounter may happen, is to be *available,* in touch with my own state of being, and to disclose my state of being, my feelings, wishes, fantasies, my action whenever it is relevant in a dialogue between myself and whomever I am personally *with* just then. At the time I am in dialogue with another, everyone else is part of the background, as a spectator. Whenever two others have commenced to encounter one another, letting dialogue unfold in words, feelings, and actions, I become part of the audience, and sometimes I will tell others who try to interfere to leave the two alone. But I always hope that the pair who are "at it" will themselves ask the intruder to stay out, or invite him into an effort at a triad.

I am anxious at the start of every group meeting because I have no plan, no routine, and I intend for it always to be that way for me. I do not practice techniques of "good group leading" because that implies trying to "have it made," to be a competent practitioner of someone's

Figure 5-1. Dialogue unfolding in feelings and actions. (Photo by Zev Guber.)

techniques that are appropriate for Us to practice on Them. I don't believe in Them. "Them," "Him," or "Her" is a way for me to experience a You, who properly is one of Us. When I am in a group-for-encounter, and find I am thinking about you others as Them, I immediately speak out and say, "I'm out of this scene right now. I wonder why?" But I also feel free to leave the group scene, either by getting up and walking out for awhile or by retreating into my own experience, to think, to tune in on myself. And if someone intrudes, I say, "You are intruding just now. I'd like to sit here in silence for awhile."

If someone in the group talks to me about somebody else in the group, I invite him to speak directly to the one he is discussing, so that encountering may happen. I don't know how to *make* encounter come into being. I can only be open and ready for it to happen and committed to respond in honest spontaneity to the one with whom I have engaged.

I am vulnerable to Berneish games, to being conned and manipulated, until I discover that that is what is going on. Then I tell what my experience is and withdraw from the game, unless it is fun. I don't take pride in being expert at interpreting games, transference phenomena, defenses, and so on, though I am pretty good at it when it seems meaningful to pull back and be a critical diagnostician.

I inevitably find, in leading a group-for-encounter, that someone present is trying to write my autobiography. When I appear different from what they expected, they become angry or disappointed and try to invite me to be the one they imagine I am. I decline the invitation. But often I awaken to myself and find that, for the last few minutes, I was being someone else, not myself. And I go back to being me, and tell what had happened.

I usually decline others' invitations to invent myself to their design. I feel pretty good about myself, in spite of assorted hang-ups, inconsistencies, and the like. I don't hesitate, however, to disclose my view of how the other person might be. I encourage him to reinvent himself and his world in any way that makes sense to him.

This gives me an opportunity in the group (as well as in these pages) to expound my view of the human situation. I am a psychologist, and I see part of my job as that of forming an image, or "model," of man in his situation that makes him intelligible but does not warp or diminish him to fit the image. I'm not satisfied with conceptual models that regard man as an analogue of a rat, pigeon, monkey, or computer—though much of what we learn about those beings does throw some light on how you and I function. I am a "humanistic," not an animalistic or mechanistic, psychologist. I am committed to a view of man as a *person*—a being like *me,* and like you, when I experience you as a person. So I believe that anything I learn about me is your possibility, as your way is mine. When you trust me enough to let me experience you, your "insides" as well as your behavioral shell, you are augmenting this emerging image or theory of man as possible person in possible worlds. The best analogies I can think of for man are *artist* and mimic. Man is like the parrot—he has no native song, no God-given essence that he unfolds like a tape. He has to copy or invent his speech and his being. Here I agree with Rank in the choice of conceptual models. But not in terminology, necessarily.

One of my projects, then, is seeing how far I can rewrite psychology in the light of an image of man as artist and mimic, as opposed to man as organism, as animal, or as machine. A mimic, after all, is an artist of a sort. I see no contradiction among research, practice, teaching, and writing when I proceed from the assumption that every man, woman, and child is more like me and you than he is like a machine or animal, and that we are all artists. I don't have a special "researcher" self, a "therapist" self, a "teacher" self, and a "personal" self. These are names for places to do my thing.

Now, seeing man as mimic or artist, I have to correct the image and say that all men like me are artists *manqués*. We are embodied, situated consciousness of being, and we have no choice but to invent and reinvent our personal worlds, our situations. We are in the world exactly as is the artist or sculptor facing his clay or canvas. To leave the canvas blank, the clay unshaped is a choice, an artistic act. To add form and color, or produce a shape, is another creative act. To copy another's example is apprenticeship in authentic artistry. The artist is limited in his creations only by the vitality of his imagination, his proficiency with tools and hands, his courage and resolution, and the plasticity or resistance of his materials.

I view the world as plastic—not synthetic plastic, but plastic like plasticine. Everything has its "plasticity quotient"—its amenability to change before it is destroyed or changed into something else. I *am* my world, and I can change it in many particulars without destroying it or me. Everything has its plasticity quotient, whether it be my appearance, my behavior, my relationships with others, the landscape, the arrangement of furniture in my room, the behavior of others in my world. Each moment of existence is an invitation or challenge to me to let the arrangement of my situation be as it now is, or to change it, reinvent it, or invite it to change. Every project of mine projects an image of a possible me in a possible world, in my imaginative consciousness. My action is the work of a skilled or unskilled artist-craftsman, aimed at transmuting the image into actuality. Most often, I invent and reinvent me and my situation according to the same template, day after day, year after year. That's why I say I am an artist *manqué*.

It is not necessary to change one's personal world radically daily. But sometimes, the situation in which a person finds himself—including his way of being in that situation—is unlivable. The other people in it may be inviting him to die, or to live in ways that are sickening him, though these ways are pleasing to the others; and he has accepted their invitations. He may view himself and his world as unchangeable, and grit his teeth, enduring daily existence with no hope of escape.

If you regard yourself as unchangeable, as the victim of your past and your heredity, I respect this as your view, *but I disagree with it.* My view of you is more scientifically informed—you and your situation embody incredible possibilities for change. So I don't hesitate to confront you with my view of your possibilities. If I say, "You can change your way of being," you may reply, "I cannot." I regard your statement, not as a matter of scientific fact, but as a stubbornly held commitment to keep your situation the same. You and I may then argue. If you win the argument, you lose much of your life. If you lose the argument, you win. I used to call this argument "psychotherapy," whether it went on in my consulting room or in the encounter group setting.

In a group-for-encounter, I assume that spontaneous encounter is a good thing and that when it happens, people's views of themselves and the other are challenged, upended, and they attain a larger perspective on their own worlds. With an enlarged view of an enlarged world, there is more room for them to move, change, and grow. And so I invite people to encounter me or anyone else in the spontaneous flow of group interaction.

But if I am charged with "leading" the group, I take certain responsibilities. I assign ground rules—no "ganging up" on anyone, however hung-up he is on some way of being, so he will then conform to some emerging group norm. That is brainwashing, not encounter, and I oppose it. In encounter, both parties are changed. I am committed to a view of society and our group as a place where eccentricity and one's own pace are respected, and one's privacy. I "lead" by example. I don't cast myself into the role of facilitator, or interpreter of group process, or interpreter of psychodynamics. Not in an encounter group. I participate with the group and risk as much of myself as I have freely available. I may lecture for awhile. Tell a joke. Tell someone who asks me what I think of him. I may ask him to tell me (and the group) about his situation at home and explore with him ways in which he might commence the project of reinventing his world.

If someone complains that I and another, or some other pair, monopolizes the time, I invite him to dive in, participate more fully, or shout. The time "up front" is available to all, usually in pairs, but sometimes three, four, or five people will get some honest interchange going.

Figure 5-2. Encounter is more than exchanging words. (Photo by Gary Madderom.)

I view encounter as more than exchanging words. Hugging, holding, occasionally wrestling, shouting, dancing, showing off—whatever is someone's "thing" just then may happen, and I or the others reply in ways that express our being. At least I do. The purpose in all this is to afford myself and the others the chance to discover and reveal more of ourselves than we usually do "back home," to shatter our concepts of ourselves, our situations, and each other. But I am keenly aware that the aim is not just to "have" an experience in the group, which, at home, becomes a happy or frightening memory; it is to encourage a person to be and to disclose more of his possibilities here *and* back home. I see my groups as settings for the experience of authentic being-with-others and of beginning the project of reinventing oneself and one's situation wherever one is—so one can be free to live, move, and grow.

Though I participate in encounter groups somewhat as I've described, I always feel a certain artificiality prevails. My most common experience is with week-end encounter groups, or workshops, at various "growth centers." I don't see any magic in these "happenings," though sometimes a participant or I will undergo a realization, a confirmation, or a challenge that carries over back home. I like best to be with people who have committed themselves to a continuous project of growth and self-renewal, and who share with each other their ways of overcoming obstacles, because we can begin being artists of our situations by copying one another—if we show, and show off, ourselves to one another.

If I or the other participants leave the group experience with a heightened and confirmed sense of our identity, and the recollection of some intense and meaningful encounters with others, and with our courage and imaginations enlivened, I count it a "successful" group. I am suspicious of sudden conversions and more impressed by quiet resolve to change one's world so it is more fit for an eccentric human like you or me to live in.

I have no systematic follow-up of the persons who have been in groups with me. Some have written me of changes they began in the group and resolutely carried over into the rest of their lives. I have not heard from persons for whom the week end, or series of meetings, or the "marathon" might have been unrewarding. We need more data on this.

I see groups-for-encounter as places and times for each who is present to disclose himself as he now is, and for each to respond, truly respond, to what has thus been revealed. In such interplay, encounter might happen; someone may experience himself as truly addressed or truly answered. Sometimes I feel truly asked to be a teacher or discloser of something I know or am. It is at these times that I may invite one other, or several others, or all in the group to play a game, for the experience that it may afford them. One game is the "dialogue game." I list a number of topics on a blackboard or ask people to write them down on a slip of paper: "my favorite foods"; "my hobbies"; "my work"; "my past life with my family"; "my marriage"; and so on. I pair the people at random and ask them to take turns disclosing themselves to their partner on each topic. The only rules for the game are to speak truth; to respect one's own and the other's reluctance or embarrassment; and to let it be known when one does not wish to disclose. Players of the game often find that, under the protective mantle of being "told" to disclose themselves, they commence a dialogue that lasts up to eight hours, or a lifetime. When the "players" are done, we reconvene as a group and often find that disclosure within the group is less reserved, as if the game has enabled the players to take off masks and armor. But just as important to me as a teacher is to give the players a chance to discover their limits to dialogue—threat, embarrassment—to respect these, and to explore their possibilities of gently pressing against them toward fuller unreserve with a partner. Sometimes, instead of a disclosure game, I will suggest a physical-contact game, where partners will, in full respect for their own and their partner's feelings, give a back rub, foot rub, belly rub, or buttocks rub, and, moreover, do this in silence. Again, the aim is as much for each person to discover his embarrassment or shyness, and to disclose this, as it is to enable physical contact to happen. Such games, or experiments, are intended as didactic experiences as well as ways for inviting encounter between the players.

Often, in a group, members will begin to talk of their weaknesses, hang-ups, problems, peccadilloes, and the like. I find that such "confessing" is harmless if it helps the people present to realize that everyone has this dimension to his existence. But I don't hesitate to disclose my own excellences, to show off, as an invitation and challenge to the others to explore and to demonstrate what is magnificent about themselves. In fact, group members may help a person recognize some realms of magnificence that he never acknowledged before, but that we all have as our possibilities, buried under habit, faint-heartedness, and lack of imagination or insight.

There are many ways for a person to be. I see myself as engaged in this world, trying with no guarantee of success to make it fit for me to live and grow in. I cannot pursue this goal for long if I am chronically open, in the way of *I and Thou*. Nor will I move far if I am chronically cunning, self-concealing, and self-protective. Nor will I get anywhere without courage, resolve, and, above all, inventiveness. This is the "self" with which I "lead" the other persons in groups I conduct. I lead, if at all, by showing, or showing off. There is nothing, that is, *no thing*, to show—just a way of being, and being with, here. I can enter your world, as one who invites your growth or as a strangler of your possibilities, a prophet of stasis. I try to be the former.

BIBLIOGRAPHY

Jourard, Sidney M. *Personal Adjustment, An Approach Through the Study of Healthy Personality.* New York: Macmillan, 1963.

Jourard, Sidney M. *The Transparent Self.* Princeton, N.J.: Van Nostrand, 1964.

Jourard, Sidney M. *Disclosing Man to Himself.* Princeton, N.J.: Van Nostrand, 1968.

Herbert A. Otto

6 · The Peak-Joy Method and the Death-in-Life Experience

COMMENTARY

Herbert Otto presents methods for confrontation of peak experiences, from joy to death. Such encounters with one's inner life in the context of group process, he believes, can lead to meaningful personal growth.

BIOGRAPHY

Herbert A. Otto received his bachelor of arts from the University of Michigan, master of social work from Tulane University, master of science (specialization in Community Mental Health) from Harvard University, and doctor of philosophy from Florida State University. He was director of the Mental Health in Education Program, University of Georgia, and then associate professor, Graduate School of Social Work, and director, Human Potentialities Research Project, University of Utah. Among his recent books are *Group Methods to Actualize Human Potential: A Hand-*

Reprinted from *Group Methods to Actualize Human Potential: A Handbook*, by Herbert A. Otto, © copyright 1970 by the Holistic Press, 329 El Camino Drive, Beverly Hills, Calif. Used by permission of the publisher and author.

121

book (Beverly Hills, Calif.: Holistic Press, 1970), and *More Joy in Your Marriage* (New York: Hawthorne, 1969). He was editor of *Explorations in Human Potentialities* (Springfield, Ill.: Charles C Thomas, 1967), *Human Potentialities: The Challenge and the Promise* (St. Louis: Green, 1968), and *The American Family: In Search of a Future* (New York: Appleton-Century-Crofts, 1970).

As a result of over a decade's work with small groups, beginning with the Human Potentialities Research Project, the University of Utah (1960–1967), and subsequently, a total of 67 group methods were developed and extensively field-tested. A recent compilation (Otto, 1970) of these methods revealed the following breakdown: core group methods (12 methods), other group methods (22), experiences for two persons, three persons and families (13), sensory and nonverbal experiences (8), and fantasy methods (12). Two methods have been selected for inclusion in this collection.

The peak-joy method is for use within a dyad or triad structure and seems to work best in a group of three, with one of the participants of the opposite sex than the other two, if possible. The two-person and three-person experiences are sometimes called "programmed experiences," for they take place within a specific sequential step-by-step framework of instructions. It is essential to recognize that these experiences, despite their structure, are self-directed in the sense that *much more goes on between participants than is indicated in the directions,* the nature and quality of the interaction being determined by the dyad or triad.

These self-directed programmed experiences also provide a welcome relief from the prolonged concentration on shifting interaction and the involvement with many people that are ever-present in a group session. It has been my observation that participants in a programmed self-directed experience return to the total group with more vitality to tackle group and individual problems and goals.

In contrast, the death-in-life experience is for use with a larger group. I have used the method effectively with as many as 40 persons. A limitation on use of this method is the size of the meeting room, because each participant must have sufficient space to lie down at full length comfortably. The death-in-life experience especially seems to set in motion processes involving self-confrontation and the working through of feelings. I have had a considerable number of reports that indicate that over a period of three weeks and longer following this experience there are growth experiences, insights, and change traceable to the use of the method.

The Peak-Joy Method

For use by two or three persons, this method leaves participants with upbeat or positive feelings. There is, however, one caution for use of this method. In 1968, while conducting a leadership training course for group facilitators on the East Coast, I was persuaded to use the peak-joy method with a group composed of clerics and nuns. It became clear that the method produced a different reaction when used with a group where most members were deeply steeped in the puritan heritage or where theologic or religious backgrounds delimited joyous experiencing. In this group there was considerable expression of hostility about the use of the method. Most participants thought use of the method was "irrelevant," "not very meaningful," or a "waste of time." Deeper probing and working with the anger resulted in a highly growthful confrontation around the question, "What is the meaning of pleasure and joy in my life?"

Use of the method begins with the group facilitator pairing off participants or forming triads. These should be stranger groups and couples; friends or relatives should not be paired. I usually ask dyads or triads to begin getting to know each other better and more deeply immediately after pairing has been completed. (This means that while I am still pairing, the group interaction is already under way.)

Once pairing is finished, I hand out one set of mimeographed instructions per dyad or triad and make the following announcement: "You have about one and one-half or two hours, and there are six parts to the use of the method. Someone in your group can take responsibility to see that you don't get stuck on one of the parts because you enjoy it so much. Retain some notion of time so that you can complete all parts."

The following material, which is used as mimeographed instructions, can also be read to the group, who can take notes, and a blackboard can be used to summarize instructions.

Introduction

Almost everyone has had great moments of joy in his life. These have been moments of exhilaration, of intense living laced with vivid pleasure. By and large, these are among our happiest moments. Peak moments of joy do not occur often enough in our lives. Perhaps this is due to the attitude we hold that these moments happen to us—and that *we do not make them happen*. We believe that our moments of peak joy are the *result* of happenstance and luck—Lady Fortune has smiled upon us.

The question must be raised: "Are we really helpless and incapable of arranging our lives so that moments of peak joy can be with us more often?" or: "Can we plannedly point our lives and experiences in a direction where this spontaneous illumination of joy becomes a certainty?" To deprive ourselves of moments of great joy speaks to the advanced stage of our self-deprivation.

Most of us will agree that there is insufficient joy in our lives. It is only by facing this fact and by planning positive change that a healthier balance can be established in our pleasure economy. It is also clear that if we experience more joy ourselves, we can give more joy to others. This is closely related to the concept that only by loving ourselves can we truly love our neighbor. All of us need repeated moments of great joy and gladness, for it is in these moments that we live most vitally and fully. We tend to describe these moments as "unforgettable" and then range them in the storehouse of our memories. It is as if peak moments of joy are so precious that we have a tendency not to recall them too often because memory of their passage kindles the pain of how much we miss them. Perhaps *the natural state of the human organism is one of joyful communion with others, with itself, and with the universe.*

Moments of joy give us new energy and vitality—the energy and vitality needed to actualize our possibilities. It is crystal-clear that our greatest moments of joy bring us a heightened sense of well-being, the feeling that we are glad to be alive and that we would like to share this abundance with our fellow man. It is in this spirit that the attainment of joy helps us to unfold our potential.

USE OF THE METHOD

The method is based on Abraham Maslow's concept of *peak experience,* which he defines as follows: "The word peak experience is a generalization for the happiest moments of life, for experiences of ecstasy, rapture, bliss or the greatest joy."[1]

This method is designed to help you to point to your course through life in the direction of more joy, to help you have more moments of peak joy as a means of actualizing your potential. The method is based on the premise that direction and intention determine outcome and that if we are willing to invest of ourselves to achieve a desired end, we are most likely to achieve it. It is possible to plan our lives and experi-

---

[1] Maslow, A. H. Fusion of Facts and Values. *Amer. J. Psychoanal.,* **23:**117–31, 1963.

ences so that the peak moments of joy can spontaneously illuminate our being.

The method is designed for use by three people. It is best if one of the three is of the opposite sex from the other two. The method takes from two to three hours, and, if possible, the triad should deliberately seek beautiful surroundings (nature, park, attractive room with fireplace) because they facilitate the process. The triad should follow the step-by-step procedures, which are explained in detail.

Figure 6-1. Getting to know each other. (Photo by Zev Guber.)

Step 1. Spend at least 30 to 40 minutes getting to know each other. If you already know one another, get to know each other more deeply. *Ask questions you would not usually ask.* If you are complete strangers, each member of the triad should spend six minutes sharing the most significant experiences in his life that he believes had something to do with the person he is today. If the person does not use his full six minutes, the other two members should ask deeply personal, searching questions, in an effort to know him better. Another 20 minutes or longer should then be spent in dialogue until you feel that you really know each other.

Step 2. The triad should take at least five minutes for silent time. Silently review your past and recall as many peak joy experiences as you can. Peak joy experiences are defined as *moments of great gladness and pleasure, of exultant affirmation that fills us with delight.* Abraham Maslow described these as "the best moments of the human being, the happiest moments of life, experiences of ecstasy, rapture, bliss, of the greatest joy." Take notes in key-word fashion and write down as many peak-joy moments as you can. A sample list of peak-joy experiences made by one participant read as follows:

1. The sea of cherry blossoms in the full moon.
2. In love with B.
3. On ship setting out for the first ocean trip—a great joy.
4. First sex with N.
5. On the seashore with R., New Year's Day.
6. Florida Keys, coral reefs, sun.
7. George Lewis jam session—his solo, New Orleans.

Step 3. Following the silent period, the triad should share what they wish from their lists. Open yourself and be as free as possible with your sharing. *Share the peak-joy experiences that gave you the most delight.*

Step 4. Following the sharing of peak-joy experiences, the partnership team should have another silent period of five minutes or longer (you may wish to take notes). Look over your lists. *Are there any patterns here?* For example, did many of your peak joy moments occur in nature?

Now briefly review your present existence and life style—in what ways can you *plannedly introduce change so that more moments of peak joy can come into your life?* What can you do so that you can have more moments of peak joy? Plan a course of action and outline, or write out the highlights of this plan. About 15 or 20 minutes should be set aside for step 4.

Figure 6-2. Sharing the peak-joy experience that gave you the most delight. (Photo by Gary Madderom.)

Step 5. The triad now shares their action plans designed to bring more joy into their being. Listen carefully to what your partners propose. Use your sensitivity and perceptivity—use your sensitive perceptions, feelings, intuitions, hunches. Do not hold back your perceptions and hunches. Share these freely—you can always preface your remark with "I have a feeling that . . ." In this process, interpersonal honesty is very important—"level with each other." Are the plans your partners are making sound? *Are there ANY OTHER WAYS in which they might bring more joy into their lives?*

Step 6. Help your partners select one plan that should have priority and that will help them embark on *a course of action* leading to more joy in their lives. Following use of the method, the triad should plan subsequent meetings for feedback and to help each other realize more joy. Remember:

Place Joy and Pleasure
in the Service of
Unfolding Your Potential

THE DEATH-IN-LIFE EXPERIENCE

The denial of his own mortality is one of contemporary man's most fundamental and destructive self-delusions. Most of us live as if life were to last forever. We go through life as if we had an infinity of days stretching into the future. Death is for the other person, never for us. It is simply too far away to really bother about. And yet, when we do encounter death in our experience, we turn away with aversion, fear, anxiety, a sense of shock.

These reactions deny the reality that death is continually with us throughout life. Many more times than we realize we have close brushes with death in urban traffic. In addition, when the nation is involved in an international power struggle or crisis, all of us face immediate and violent death through nuclear holocaust or biologic warfare. (See the Robert Kennedy memoirs, published in October, 1968, concerning the Cuban crisis.) It is one of the hard facts of our time that, to a greater degree than ever before in history, the lives of all citizens of this country have been placed in the hands of the President of the United States and the elected leaders. It is clear that our psyche (regardless of whether or not we are consciously aware of it) is burdened by the added dimension of a death threat, which peaks with each international crisis.

Not only is our psyche burdened with recurrent *death threats* (which have to be repressed) coming from the outside, such as violence on the streets and international crises, but we also carry the huge load of continuously repressing or "attempting to forget" the possibility of our own death. Every time we pass a funeral home, read an account of a death that "strikes home," or see a relevant death on television, the dynamism of denial, repression, and forgetting is activated. A great deal of psychic energy is used up in the process, in turn affecting the individual's vital and creative functioning. Yet, it has been recognized since early in man's history by many cultures *that the recognition of death in life* (the emotionally grounded gut-level acceptance of our mortality) *can be a tremendous factor in adding vitality and a heightened sense of being to our lives.*

The more we can accept the constant presence of death on an emotional level—death as a necessary antipodal element in life—the greater our capacity for living fully in the here and now, for enjoying and savoring life. It is only by fully accepting death that we are able to live fully. Deeply acknowledging death is tremendously life-affirmative. Acceptance and gut-level recognition of death as a force in life can mean more passionate involvement with life—and more passionate living. Full acceptance of death can make life an ecstatic communion, with the recognition that the cessation of life merely changes the quality of the communion.

As important, if not more important, by accepting death fully, we more readily accept the many little deaths that occur daily in our existence. We accept the death of our attachment to a thing, the death of a relationship, of a moment, or of a flower more easily. The acceptance of death as a never-ending process in our life allows us to enter fully into the dance of life, the *joi de vivre,* the childlike astonishment of discovery, of adventure, of pleasure, and of continuous joyful unfoldment.

It is the purpose of the death-in-life experience to bring participants into closer touch with death as a denied aspect of themselves, and to help them face mortality as a means to fuller self-realization and self-actualization. The experience also offers an opportunity for coming to grips with the fear of death. A final aim of the method is to present the participant with an opportunity for an integrative experience, leading to a clarification of life goals and life philosophy.

BEGINNING THE METHOD

The method should not be used until a climate of closeness, trust, understanding, and free-flowing communication has been established in the group. It is necessary for the room in which this experience is to take place to be carpeted, and the furniture should be placed against the wall to provide free space. Everyone should be able to lie down comfortably.

If desired, the following preliminary experience can be used to deepen the total experience. After everyone has found a place to lie down comfortably and without touching another person, the group facilitator can make the following announcement: "Please relax and close your eyes. Now for about five minutes (I will call time) *on a feeling level recall the death of someone close to you.* If possible, let this be an occasion where you have been a witness of death. Let yourself experience feelings. Another possibility is to dwell on the death of an animal, an experience that touched you on the feeling level."

Depending on the leadership philosophy of the person in charge or the group's level of previous group experience and sophistication, the rationale for use of the method contained in the preceding pages can be presented. An alternative way is to involve the group directly in experiencing by making the following or similar remarks:

We are about to have an integrative experience, called the death-in-life experience. Participation is voluntary and no one will be forced to take part.

There are three parts to this experience. *First,* go through your own death. Pick how you think you will die. Then let yourself feel your death agonies and go through the process of dying. This is the only part of the experience where you can make sounds as you are dying. The rest of the experience is in silence with your eyes closed. For the *second* part you then in fantasy experience your own funeral. *Third,* and finally, you may want to imagine what afterdeath is like or feels like. You can, of course, stop the experience at any time by sitting up and opening your eyes. After everyone is sitting up, we will have some voluntary sharing as to what happened.

This is a nonverbal experience and is done with eyes closed. Do not talk, but you can make whatever noise you want to.

To put yourself in the right frame of mind, we will have a few minutes of silence while you think about your death and dying. (About two minutes of silence.)

Now choose your own death, *the way you feel it might happen.* If it is an accident, let yourself feel the shock of the impact. If you are killed by someone sticking a knife into you, let yourself feel the impact of the knife. (The group facilitator demonstrates by closing his eyes and thrusting his closed fist against his chest, as if holding a knife.) If you die in bed, lie down to your death bed and go through the experience. Make any noise you want to while going through your death experience. Afterward, for your funeral and what happens beyond that, it will be a silent experience with eyes closed.

I will not participate but will be there to help you if necessary. When we are ready for the experience, we will all stand up and each one of you will then die in his own way and lie down.

Take your own time going through the experience of dying, and, if you want to, attending your funeral. Finally, you may want to imagine what afterdeath feels like and is like. Slowly open your eyes and remain resting when you come out of it. Sit up but do not move about. *Please do not talk;* give others a chance to finish their experience. When everyone is sitting up, we will have group sharing about what has happened and what is happening to us.

I will now slowly repeat the instructions, and we will begin with the experience. While I am repeating the instructions, those who do not wish to participate can leave the room or sit on the chairs we moved against the wall. (Those observing the experience often become deeply involved.)

It usually takes 20 to 30 minutes or longer for the total group to experience this process. Often the whole group will be sitting up quietly within that time but one or two persons will be lying on their backs still engaged in the experience. I have found it is helpful to stand quietly beside this person watching him. This will be sensed and seems to help bring closure to the experience. There is often deep sobbing, crying, or groaning by several participants throughout this experience. Touching persons while they are crying or going through a painful segment of the experience is not indicated. Most people feel death and

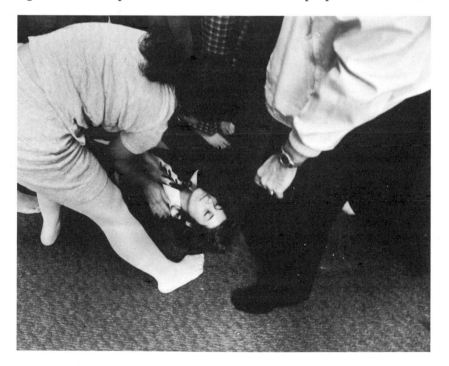

Figure 6-3. Death-in-life. (Photo by Zev Guber.)

dying is uniquely personal and private and do not wish to be comforted.

After everyone is sitting up, the group facilitator can initiate the sharing process by quietly asking the following question: "Who would like to begin sharing his experience and what has happened to him as a result of this experience?" I have found that many participants have such a deep experience that they want time to digest it first and do not wish to discuss what has happened. As a result, some group members will refrain from sharing their experience. For this reason, it is best to schedule a follow-up meeting to discuss what happened to participants in the interim between group meetings, attributable to the death-in-life experience.

Because of the depth and impact of the experience, it is best to schedule the use of this method at the end of an evening if used during a week-end marathon. An alternative is to schedule a lunch break, plus free time following the experience to give the participants a chance to integrate and synthesize what has taken place.

The following represent group members' verbatim reactions to the experience:

K. M.: As a result of my experience, I have more of a feeling of continuity—of totality.

R. B.: Until you come to terms with your own death, you tend to hang on to things. Things end. Anything you experience ends. When you experience death, you go on to other things in life.

L. J.: I was planted in the earth as a seed. I came up as a green shoot and went through the cycle many times. I know the seasons very well . . .

J. V.: I got the feeling it was going to be a release. My body released itself. My last moment was a moment of great love.

T. R.: (a businessman) I saw my children standing around my coffin and crying. I realized that I had spent too much time working, getting my organization going, and not enough time with my family. I am walking out of here a changed man.

W. L.: When I died, I began skipping through the flowers, through the trees, skipping through the brooks, and I was free, free, free—going away into the stars. I could see the earth receding behind me. It was a beautiful experience. I didn't want to go back. My feeling toward death has changed.

R. S.: The moment of death was very painful for me. I died and found peace. I feel very peaceful now. This makes my death more real to me.

F. I.: I have been thinking about suicide for the last eight months.

The storm is over now. I know I'll never do it. (Begins to sob very hard.)

H. P.: I died in bed and it occurred to me that I've kicked this whole life away. I haven't been actualizing enough.

K. D.: How bright and beautiful the world on opening my eyes. For the first time since I was a kid I thought what it was like after death. As a kid I thought it would be heaven and I would have an electric train. I am going to do some reading in the Eastern and Western religions.

R. L.: I became very aware of my love for my family—then decided "You did a very good job as a mother." It made me feel so good!

T. J.: At the burial I realized that I didn't love enough—that love is the force that matters. (Cries.)

Other than beginning to come to grips with the fear of death, some participants appear to begin a re-examination of their belief structure about death. Also repeatedly referred to is a feeling of "having a second chance at life," which was capsulated by the remark, "I will live life more fully now."

Because of the considerable impact and working through of feelings in depth that can be initiated by use of this method, it is suggested that only *skilled professionals* utilize this experience. This is particularly important if, by chance, one or more people who are undergoing psychotherapy or who are at a crisis in their lives are members of the group using this method.

BIBLIOGRAPHY

Kinter, R., and Otto, H. A. Human Potentialities Research: Application to Geriatric Programs. *J. Amer. Geriat. Soc.*, **12**:677–86, 1964.

Maslow, A. H. Fusion of Facts and Values. *Amer. J. Psychoanal.*, **23**:117–31, 1963.

Otto, H. A. The Personal and Family Strength Research Projects—Some Implications for the Therapist. *Ment. Hyg.*, **48**:439–50, 1964.

———. Personal and Family Strength Research and Spontaneity Training. *Group Psychother. J.*, **17**:143–49, 1964.

——— (ed.). *Explorations in Human Potentialities.* Springfield, Ill.: Charles C Thomas, 1966.

———. Actualizing. In S. Jourard (ed.), *The Self: To Be or Not to Be.* Gainesville, Florida: University of Florida Press, 1967.

———. Depth Unfoldment Experience—A Method for Creating Interpersonal Closeness. *Adult Educ.*, **17**:78–84, 1967.

————. The Minerva Experience: Initial Report. In J. T. Bugental (ed.), *Challenges of Humanistic Psychology*. New York: McGraw-Hill, 1967, pp. 119–24.

————. Toward a Holistic Treatment Program—Some Concepts and Methods. In H. Greenwald (ed.), *The Active Psychotherapies*. New York: The Atherton Press, 1967.

———— (ed.). *Human Potentialities: The Challenge and the Promise*. St. Louis: Warren H. Green, Inc., 1968.

————. Motivation and Human Potentialities. *Humanitas*, **3**:293–307, 1968.

————. *More Joy in Your Marriage*. New York: Hawthorn Books, Inc., 1969.

————. *Group Methods to Actualize Human Potential: A Handbook*. Beverly Hills, Calif.: Holistic Press, 1970.

————, and Hansen, K. W. The Multiple Strength Perception Method: A Four Year Evaluation. *Proc. Utah Acad. Sciences, Arts, & Letters*, **43**:138–42, 1966.

———— and Mann, John (eds.). *Ways of Growth*. New York: Grossman Publishers, Inc., 1968.

———— and Nelson, N. E. The Minister and Human Potentialities. *J. Religion & Health*, **7**:182–90, 1968.

Michael P. Andronico

7 Marathon Techniques in an Outpatient Clinic: The Minithon*

COMMENTARY

Michael Andronico, one of the innovators of the filial psychothera-peutic technique, describes the *minithon*—an extended group en-counter but an abbreviated version of the marathon. The author dis-cusses the advantages of the minithon for facilitating ongoing psycho-therapy, for use with collaterals of patients (e.g., spouses, parents, and children), and for brief limited therapeutic or personal growth goals.

BIOGRAPHY

Michael Andronico, chief psychologist at the Hunterdon Medical Center, is also a research associate at Rutgers University. His undergraduate degree was from Brown University in 1958 and he received his M.S. in 1960 and Ph.D. in 1963, both from Rutgers University. He has been a consultant to various school systems and a social work agency.

Dr. Andronico has been interested in intensive work with groups since

* The author wishes to thank Dr. Charlotte Weiss for suggesting the word "mini-thon."

1966 and has been a group leader in the Rutgers Summer Seminar in Inter-actional Processes, as well as director of professional and personal growth workshops for Princeton Associates for Human Resources.

In addition to his work with intensive groups, he has been active in the development and research of filial therapy, a method of teaching parents, in groups, to have play therapy sessions at home with their children.

Within the past few years there has been a sudden explosion of activity in the area of intensive group therapy and group interactions. Perhaps the most exciting of these methods has been the marathon (Bach, 1967) or "accelerated interaction" groups (Stoller, 1966). The mara-thon is usually conceived of as a week-end group starting early on one afternoon and either continuing nonstop through until late the follow-ing afternoon or stopping only for a few hours during the evening and resuming until late the following afternoon. The particular appeal of the marathon is that it permits an intense experience, a high degree of involvement that is achieved quickly, and that it offers an opportunity to cut through usual defenses, all in one session, albeit a prolonged session.

Myerhoff, Jacobs, and Stoller (1970) experimentally demonstrated that emotional involvement becomes heightened under marathon con-ditions, in comparison to shorter group sessions. Utilizing 18 hours as the common length of treatment, these authors studied two therapy groups. The experimental group received its 18 therapy hours in three six-hour sessions, whereas the control group received its 18 therapy hours in nine two-hour group therapy sessions. The basic dif-ference between these two groups was the "generally higher rate of oc-currence and variability in the expression of negative feelings," which the authors interpreted as reflecting the breakdown of the ego defense system, allowing for the expression of more intense and prolonged effect in the former group.

Most of the work in group therapy has been primarily done by private practitioners (Mintz, 1967). Navidzadeh (1968) has reported using this method in an outpatient clinic setting. He points out that limita-tions of funds, physical facilities, leadership, and manpower make it difficult to apply the marathon to an ongoing clinic setting.

In most outpatient mental health clinics, for practical staff and time reasons, patients are seen once a week rather than many times per week as is done in private practice, particularly in analytic practice. The goals of therapy are therefore usually more limited and short-range in these mental health clinics rather than the deeper and more compre-hensive goal of major personality change. The application of marathon principles could also be utilized in a shorter period of time, with less extensive, but still significant, goals. Greater numbers of people could also be reached in this way.

A shorter marathon, or minithon, has been employed at the Outpatient Psychiatric Department at the Hunterdon Medical Center during the past three years, by the present author. This minithon, an uninterrupted six-to-seven-hour session, has been used six times to date. It has been primarily used with ongoing groups, with certain modifications. Two of the minithons were held with only the members of their group present. The others were conducted with the ongoing group members as the majority and nucleus of the minithon, with the addition of some of their spouses and one or two other additional patients who were not related to any of the other group members. The minithon groups ranged in number of members from 8 to 12. The minithons were comprised of two ministers' groups, one mixed adult group, and an all-women's group. One of the ministers' groups had two minithons, one year apart. The first of these was comprised entirely of the ministers' group members, and the second was comprised of the male ministers plus most of their wives, with the addition of a female minister. The second ministers' group minithon was composed of the ministers plus some of their spouses. The mixed adult group also had two minithons, one year apart, with only the group members present. The women's group minithon included some spouses and patients from individual therapy.

FACILITATION OF INSIGHT

One of the advantages of the application of minithon techniques to ongoing groups is that they stimulate unconscious material to quickly come into consciousness and thus provide the groups with material that they can discuss in future ongoing sessions. This is done in several ways, one being that the greater length of time allows for more intensive experience. Members can spend a greater amount of time both experiencing and talking about the experiences they have had among themselves during the minithon. The greater length of time allows defense mechanisms to drop more readily because it is more difficult to maintain defenses over a six-to-seven-hour session than a one-and-one-half-hour session. In addition to the time element, the application of marathon techniques to the minithon changes the focus of the group from verbal exploration and discussion of feelings to action on these feelings in a therapeutic manner, enabling group members to add another dimension to their understanding of their own and others' emotional functioning. This is facilitated by the group members' being confronted directly with their own behavior as well as their verbal descriptions of their behavior. For example, one woman complained that she felt imposed upon by people and angry and resentful at people for preventing her from directly expressing these feelings. When it was suggested that now, during the minithon, she could be nasty either to certain individuals in the group who she felt were particularly hostile to her or to the entire group, this woman refused to do so. This then prompted a discussion as to why she could not, as well as to the insight that she herself was choosing not to express these feelings, rather than seeing the group as imposing upon her and preventing her from expressing herself. This experience and its accompanying insight enabled the patient to work more directly on this problem in future group sessions, and she has since made major positive changes in her ability to assert herself.

Inclusion of Spouses

Despite the obvious desirability of having mixed adult groups, it is frequently difficult for men to come to group meetings during the working day. Even with evening hours, the percentage of adult female patients heavily outweighs the adult male patient population in most outpatient psychiatric clinics. Thus, despite the desirability of having mixed adult groups, it frequently becomes a practical necessity when forming groups to have some groups comprised of all women. Another type of group that usually is a single-sex group is a ministers' group. One of the advantages of having a minithon with such a group is that it enables the group members of a one-sex group to experience interactions with members of the opposite sex in a therapeutic milieu. This provides future ongoing weekly group sessions with additional data and perspective for discussion. In single-sex groups, the sessions immediately preceding the minithon often reflect the anxiety of some group members in anticipation of having the other group members see them interacting with members of the opposite sex. This is particularly true of patients who have defensively portrayed an unrealistic picture of their interactions with the opposite sex to their group. It can also precipitate the unrealistic fear of competition in the rare instance of a female minister or female religious aid whose ego is enhanced by being the only female in her group.

Because some of the men who attended the minithon were husbands of members of a women's group, and some of the women were wives of men in the all-male ministers' group, additional opportunities for direct marital interactions were available, which also provided important data for future group sessions. For example, one woman in an all-women's adult group occasionally, in weekly sessions, discussed her dislike of her husband in strong terms and her dislike of men in general in mild terms. In the opening few minutes of the minithon this particular woman reacted in strongly negative ways to one of the men in the minithon group who was not her husband. This enabled her to see more clearly just how strong her feelings were against men in general.

Spouses of patients who are in psychotherapy and who themselves have had little or no experience with psychotherapy are often baffled, confused, and frequently opposed to the effects that psychotherapy is having on their spouses. The minithon experience helps these persons to better understand what their spouses are undergoing and also to better appreciate the implications of becoming more feeling-oriented. It also allows them to cope more directly with their own feelings concerning their attitudes toward their spouses in treatment, and to realize that the feelings that many of their spouses are beginning to express are a result of their past lives rather than something their therapy group "produced." For example, in a minithon that included the husbands of some women of an all-women's group, one husband said, "So you are the women my wife talks to on Tuesdays before she comes home all upset and makes my life miserable every Tuesday night," in an obviously hostile manner. Despite his initial anger at the group and his resistive approach to group therapy, before the end of the session he became more empathic with the group and his wife and her interactions with the group. He, himself, later entered therapy.

By having the spouse of a patient in the minithon, the therapist is able to view the interaction between husband and wife as well as having the other patients in the group see this from a better perspective. This different perspective can lead to new insight into the dynamics of the interaction as opposed to the one-sided presentation given by the patient in the weekly group sessions. A common expectation of patients' spouses is that members and the group therapist will side with the patient. Often when the therapist gives appropriate support to the spouse of a patient, this unexpected support results in increased willingness of the spouse to listen to the patient's problems because the spouse then becomes less defensive. For example, one husband of a woman in the all-women's group was resistive to a feeling orientation in the morning part of the minithon. He expressed his entire focus of concern on direct problem-solving in an intellectual, reasoning fashion. Later in the afternoon, after having received support from the therapist, this man became more understanding of his wife as well as of the other women. By the end of the minithon he overtly had given emotional support to one of the women in the group and he verbally recognized the efficacy and importance of emotions. Several months following this minithon, this man joined his wife in a brief series of successful marital counseling sessions.

The minithon also tends to increase group cohesion. The addition of non-group-members to the minithon frequently leads members of the existing core group to form together into a closer unit, especially in response to attack from a non-group-member against a group member. In future, ongoing group sessions, this "defense against a common enemy" feeling dissipates, but the closeness tends to continue. For example, two group members who had been very hostile toward each other during the regular weekly group sessions, especially in the weeks preceding the minithon, reached out to each other in positive and empathic ways for the first time when each of them was attacked by a non-group-member. In the following group sessions, these women continued to discuss their anger at the men who verbally attacked them and their appreciation of each coming to the other's defense. Although they still had negative feelings toward each other, they were able to better relate to each other. This set the stage for both of them to realize and experience that it was possible for them to relate amicably with people, even if they had once been overtly angry.

The mixed group enabled many types of interactions to occur. In the groups in which spouses were included, there were husband-wife, wife-with-another-man, and husband-with-another-woman interactions. Those people who did not have their spouses with them were often freer to interact with others, and there was a tendency for arguments to occur without couples themselves being enmeshed. In this way couples were able to view nonmarried couples in arguments and could indirectly address themselves to their own arguments. Many were reassured to realize that other people, as well as other couples, could argue as vociferously or as subtly, or could be as uncommunicative as they themselves were. Often, the interactions between a husband, or wife, and another group member provided an insight for that person's spouse. For example, the wife of one of the ministers observed her husband's difficulty in relating to other women within the group. She exclaimed that she had previously viewed his interactions with women in his role as a minister and had seen him as being confident and competent in that role. She had therefore assumed that his difficulty in relating effectually was with reference to trying to relate to other women on a deeper rather than a superficial level, away from his ministerial role. It was pointed out to her that her husband did, indeed, have difficulty relating to women.

This opportunity to incorporate important people in a patient's everyday life, such as a spouse or a close friend, into a therapy setting such as a minithon simultaneously provides an advantage while reducing or eliminating a disadvantage of incorporating spouses or friends in ongoing group sessions. The advantage of having such people in the minithon is that it provides those people as well as the patients of the ongoing groups with an opportunity to interact in a different manner, in a relatively safe setting, especially because the participants view the minithon as a once-only occurrence. Many people who are resistive to ongoing therapy will agree to one minithon session, and their participation often substantially contributes to the ongoing treatment of their spouses or friends. The disadvantage of members of the ongoing group becoming overly defensive about certain issues that they would not want discussed in front of their spouses or friends can be minimized in the minithon. Patients can, if they desire, avoid this type of defensiveness during the minithon, but then resume it during the following ongoing group therapy sessions.

EXTENDED TIME: AN IMPORTANT FACTOR

The extended time afforded by the minithon permits a group to work through many different stages of feelings within one session. In the morning, anger, suspicion, and hostility are usually prevalent, and during the afternoon, affection, warmth, and concern become more evident, with separation anxiety occurring near the end. Although each minithon does not inevitably follow this course, this does appear to be a common pattern. This pattern also occurs frequently during the course of individual and group therapies. Stated in another way, people initially tend to respond defensively during the early stages of the minithon. This defensiveness often takes the form of suspicion, anger, and hostility. Once people become less defensive and more comfortable, they relax their defenses. They share more of their deeper feelings and become happy, relieved, and reassured by the support they usually receive from the group, instead of the anticipated and feared rejection. This sets the stage for the warm, affectionate feelings during the latter stages of the minithon and the fears of losing these feelings once the minithon is over.

One advantage of the extended period of time is that many people can experience this progression of feelings in one day and in one place. This enables the patients to get a broader view of their own therapy, and it is particularly important for "nonpatients" (spouses of patients) to be able to get into and work through certain types of feelings without being placed in the uncomfortable position of having opened up certain feelings and let down defenses without having had an opportunity to work them through. Of course, all feelings are not worked through entirely, but compared with a single session, the longer length of the minithon allows for more feelings to be dealt with in greater depth and detail. It is not unusual for spouses of patients who come for an individual or joint session to leave the hospital or clinic feeling frustrated, resistive, and therefore less likely to return for more sessions.

In addition, it is easier for resistive spouses to attend a minithon when they are told that "other husbands" or "other wives" will also be participating. This reassures them that they will not be the only nonpatients there. It also helps them to feel that there will be a buffer between themselves, their spouses, and the therapist. This fear of being "ganged up on" is a common resistance among nonpatient spouses when they contemplate a joint session with their spouses and their spouses' therapist. The presence of other nonpatient spouses also reduces some of the patients' unconscious resistances to including their spouses, with the group members subtly applying pressure to each other to bring their spouses to the minithon.

As mentioned above, homogeneous groups such as an all-minister's group and an all-women's group are very atypical of society in general. The minithon, with the inclusion of spouses and other people, enables the homogeneous group to more closely approximate the real world in terms of heterogeneity. Another advantage of the minithon is that it can provide a testing ground for termination. Although this can, and is, done during regular weekly group sessions, the minithon, with its extended time, allows the patient who is ready to stop therapy to test out his ability to cope with his feelings, in intensified form, and to see how he adjusts to an almost new situation. The adding of some people who are not regular group members also allows the terminating patient to try out his abilities to adapt to new people and cope with new challenges.

POTENTIAL AID IN CRISIS INTERVENTION

Although it has only been used once by the present author, the minithon can be utilized as a helpful adjunct in crisis intervention with a person of sufficient ego strength. It has not been tried with psychotic or borderline patients by this writer. For example, one man who was being seen in individual sessions had reached a crisis in his marriage in that his wife had become very upset and insisted on a divorce. This man had interpreted his wife's desire for a divorce as total rejection and a distinct representation of all the rejection he had experienced by females in his life and a confirmation of his own, deeply rooted feelings of being inadequate as a man. The evening before the minithon, the patient had seen his therapist on an emergency basis, arriving for his appointment with a bottle of whiskey and a rifle. After the patient was helped to regain some confidence and composure, it was suggested that he participate in a minithon, which happened to be scheduled for the next day. The patient agreed, and during the minithon, he related very well to some of the women in the group. These women, in turn, responded positively and affirmatively to him, which reduced his strong feelings of impotence and rejection by women. He was also able to develop a close relationship with some of the men, thereby elevating his low feelings of self-esteem. He was not schizophrenic and did not appear to be on the verge of a psychotic break. His inclusion in the minithon was viewed as a positive opportunity for him to regain quickly some of the feelings of self-esteem that he had lost in the marital crisis. It was also viewed as an opportunity to lift some of the patient's intense depressed feelings and enable him to return to a point where he could continue to profit from his weekly individual sessions.

PROBLEMS CONCERNING THE MINITHON

As in most other situations, the advantages of a new method also pose problems that must be coped with. The increased intensity of the minithon approach often leads some people to become initially more defensive and resistive. One group member who was usually on the periphery of the group during weekly sessions withdrew even more during the first part of a minithon. Another member who assumed an active role in the weekly group sessions employed a joking defense by stating that he was conserving his energies until a specified time, more than halfway through the session. In this way he was able to prevent himself from relating to the group on a close basis until well into the second half of the minithon. Some people react in the opposite way and become more open and emote in a very rapid manner. The therapist should be aware of these two extremes and be prepared to deal with them.

The experiencing of such a high degree of emotional intensity provides much material for future ongoing weekly group meetings. One group member who had been very verbal during the weekly group meetings became unusually quiet during the minithon. When asked about his silence, he said that for the first time, he was beginning to realize that other people also had very strong feelings and that he was surprised to see this. He said that he wanted to hear from the others, rather than simply waiting until they were finished in order for himself to resume talking, and that he was taking this extended time to listen to others. In future weekly group meetings he continued to listen to others as well as to discuss his prior inability to stop talking.

This experiencing of a high degree of emotional intensity also can be utilized as an avenue of resistance for some patients in ongoing weekly group meetings. Some patients, when faced with material that was brought up during the minithon, expressed a desire to postpone discussing this material "until the next minithon." Some claimed that there now was not sufficient time during the weekly group sessions to discuss a particular issue. Still another patient, one in the all-women's group, said that she could discuss her feelings much better if there were men in the group. Again, as in other situations concerning resistance, the therapist should be aware of this type of resistance and be prepared to deal with it as such.

The inclusion of spouses, despite the many positive aspects mentioned above, also can lead to frustration on the part of patients in the ongoing groups. Patient's expectations and distortions as well as transferential responses enter here. Most of the patients in ongoing groups who were at the minithon with their nonpatient spouses gave lip service to their desires to increase communication and understanding in their marriage. Unconsciously, however, some patients regarded the minithon as therapy for themselves and viewed the participation of their spouses as an adjunct to their own therapy. Those patients who unconsciously perceived the minithon in these terms unconsciously expected that the therapist would also do so. When the therapist failed to comply with these unconscious expectations, the tranferential relationship was affected. One minister, for example, after having been relatively withdrawn during most of the minithon, complained of feeling empty and somehow dissatisfied with the minithon. He apologetically looked to the therapist for an explanation of his feelings. It was this minister's wife who had previously enacted a highly emotional scene, role-playing both sides of a conversation with her mother. After an interpretation, this minister was able to express his feelings of rivalry toward and jealousy of his wife for having gone through an experience he himself had wanted. It further generalized to his competitive feelings toward his wife in other areas of their lives.

SCREENING

The screening of patients for any intensive group experience is important. The utilization of a minithon with ongoing therapy groups largely reduces, if not entirely eliminates, this problem. The group therapist has already screened his patients for inclusion into the ongoing groups. All members of the groups reported on here were included in the minithon. Among them were two patients who had previously been diagnosed as schizophrenic but were considered to be in remission and sufficiently intact to participate in the minithon, with no obvious adverse affects. With ongoing patients, the therapist has the opportunity to function more efficiently because he knows his patients and is better prepared to step in sooner with the more vulnerable patient.

A brief screening session is usually sufficient for spouses of patients, some of whom were seen during the initial diagnostic intake procedure on the patient.

Patients who are seen in individual therapy can be included without screening, especially if these patients are patients of the minithon therapist. For those patients in individual therapy who are ambivalent about joining a therapy group, inclusion in a minithon can motivate the patient to enter group therapy. This is more likely to occur if this patient participates in a minithon with the members of an ongoing group that the therapist would like the patient to join.

Patients who are very fragile and those who are likely to have a psychotic episode under a high degree of emotional intensity, such as borderline schizophrenics with a tenuous grasp on reality, should not be included in a minithon.

This chapter has concentrated primarily on the application of the minithon to ongoing therapy groups, with some supplemental members. There are, of course, other applications to an outpatient setting, such as the use of a minithon or two as the primary or only form of "brief" therapy for patients whose goals are specific, limited, and short-range. The minithon could also be used as a six-month follow-up to short-term therapy.

In summary, the application of an abbreviated form of marathon, a six-to-eight-hour "minithon," has shown many indications of becoming a positive psychotherapeutic method in an outpatient psychiatric setting, especially as a supplementary method with varied, ongoing weekly adult groups.

Bibliography

Bach, George R. Marathon Group Dynamics: II Dimensions of Helpfulness: Therapeutic Aggression. *Psychol. Rep.*, **20**:1147–58, 1967.

Bach, George R. Marathon Group Dynamics: III Disjunctive Contacts. *Psychol. Rep.*, **20**:1163–72, 1967.

Mintz, Elizabeth. Time-extended Marathon Groups. *Psychother.: Theory, Research, & Practice*, 4:65–70, 1967.

Myerhoff, H., Jacobs, A., and Stoller, F. Emotionality in Marathon and Traditional Psychotherapy Groups. *Psychother.: Theory, Research, & Practice*, 7:33–36, 1970.

Navidzadeh, Buick. Clinical Application of Marathon Group Therapy. Presented to the 1968 Annual Convention of the American Group Psychotherapy Association.

Stoller, F. H., Robinson, Margot, and Meyerhoff, H. L. Effects of Video-Tape Feedback on Student Participants in a Two Day Marathon Group. Unpublished manuscript, 1966.

John B. Enright

⫸8⫷ On the Playing Fields of Synanon

COMMENTARY

The kafkaesque techniques of the Synanon game (i.e., you are guilty of self-deceit until you either prove yourself innocent or confess) hold out a promise for growth that has as its basis the obliteration of resistance. The Synanon game players have no patience with resistance. With drug addicts, the character itself (the psychic soil in which habit flourishes) is assumed to be defective as regards solving problems of daily living. Therefore, people come to Synanon for a surgical psyching that has gotten results in ways that other therapies, more tolerant of resistance, have not.

BIOGRAPHY

John Enright describes himself as follows:

"I was born in Yakima, Washington, and grew up there a totally conforming good boy and model student. On scholarship to Yale, where I was a thorough misfit, I left my earlier interest in history to major in psychology, after identifying strongly with a psychotherapist I saw there. The field of psychology turned out to be irrelevant, if not actively antagonistic to achieving the life-style and quality of experiencing I was seeking, but I persisted in getting a Ph.D. at the University of California at Berkeley and fitting myself into the image for a few years. For most of my life, personal and professional activities have been quite separate. Now I seem to be achieving a kind of integration in which what I do seems to be different manifestations of one process. Thus, personally I am developing my will and spontaneity, conceptually I am integrating the very diverse methods of growth and change I have been involved in, and practically I am making a living by teaching change methods, and by consulting on the design of change programs (educational, therapeutic, or growth)."

Recent publications include two chapters in *Gestalt Therapy Now*, edited by Fagan and Sheperd (published in 1970 by Science and Behavior Books), and a chapter entitled "Synanon; a Challenge of Middle Class Views of Mental Health" in *Community Psychology Perspectives on Community Mental Health*, edited by Adelson and Kalis (published in 1970 by Chandler Publications, San Francisco).

I had walked from the mental hospital where I worked, through Golden Gate Park, on a quiet April evening, just at dinnertime when humans were scarce, and rabbits and quail were out. I had reached a mansion on Pacific Heights just at 7:30, and now 14 of us, a few seeming "at home," but many obviously total strangers, sat staring at each other from the comfortable overstuffed chairs. I knew only one person in the room even slightly, and our relationship was hardly a promising one; on the previous Friday, howling with protest, he had been discharged from the hospital. I had done the exit interview, telling him firmly and frequently that in no sense of the word was he "sick," much as he wanted to be, and that his only salvation would be to begin to take some responsibility, however small, for his own life, instead of clinging to his favorite image of himself as a helpless football of fate. At that time, I had had no concrete recommendation as to where or how he could achieve that, and I certainly had never expected to see him again.

G., who introduced himself as a lawyer, ex-drunk, and Synanon member, had talked for a few minutes about the Synanon philosophy and the two rules of the club; nonviolence, and abstinence from illegal mind-altering chemicals (and legal ones also, on the day of playing the game). The "game" (which at that time seemed to me a silly and provocative thing to call group therapy) was about to begin.

The next few hours presented a bewildering kaleidoscope of interaction, incomprehensible to me at the time. Looking back on the vivid memory of that evening years and many games later, however, I can see most of the basic patterns of the game. Most immediately impressive was the quality of attack and challenge, focused on *actual behavior* and *values as expressed in behavior,* with an almost total disregard of feelings as initially presented and values as verbally expressed. Attention was first directed at Jim, who introduced himself as a "group counselor" at juvenile hall, and whose life goals were to help troubled adolescents. The game participants quickly amended this to "guard at a kids' jail," and went on to make a very convincing case that he worked there only because it was the most convenient and undemanding job he could find. There were also dark hints that he was a latent sadist, who had not yet acted out these tendencies grossly only because he was better supervised than most guards. I remember the peculiar feeling I had when the game had finished with him that both his and the game's views of "reality," however wildly incompatible they seemed, were completely plausible and, in some sense, "true."

During the attack on Jim it had emerged that another man in the game was a friend and coworker of his, though he had volunteered nothing about Jim. The attack on this friend opened with something like this: "You call yourself a friend? Sitting there hiding the truth about Jim, letting him go on hanging himself with his dumb behavior? All he needs to really be in trouble is a few more 'friends' like you, supporting his craziness. Typical street ethics. Now, what's he hiding about you in return? Save us a lot of time if you tell us."

The friend was quickly dismissed as a hopeless liar, with all the dishonesty but none of the courage of Jim, and the game went flying on. (Suddenly, Jim, who a few minutes ago was apparently viewed by all in the room as an untouchable moral leper, was being called "courageous" for having been as open about himself as he had, and again I felt the power of this ability to shift frames of reference fully and quickly, to see life and behavior almost simultaneously from many vantage points. Jim also obviously brightened at this comment and began participating more in the game.)

I thought I had learned one practical lesson from this attack on Jim's friend; so when the game's attention was directed on my ex-patient I had something to say. This turned out to be no help at all in diverting attention from me, in fact, seemed to draw it, and shortly I felt all eyes on me while G. was saying sarcastically, "You call yourself a teacher and a therapist; why are you the most scared and hostile person in the room, *Doctor?*" I remember little specifically of what followed for the next 45 minutes; most of it was to be repeated in game after game from then on and had to do with my ineffectiveness, dishonesty, cowardice, and aloofness. (This memory blank too seemed to point up a game pattern; at least early in their Synanon careers, people tend *not* to do their best learning while the attack is directed at them, but rather at other times, through identification and action.) As sud-

Figure 8-1. You call yourself a teacher and a therapist? (Photo by Zev Guber.)

denly as the game had turned onto me, it flipped away. Perhaps someone had thrown a remark at me that attracted attention to him; perhaps someone had used a moment's pause to turn attention to whoever was next on his personal agenda. I was not aware enough to notice at the time.

Two other interactions from that game remain very vivid. At one point during the attack on a suburban housewife who had been a drunk for some years and now had been sober a precarious six months, the tone of the game suddenly changed. G. sat back and began talking about his own days as a drunk, particularly the first few months of sobriety. His account was alternately serious and hilarious, but always vivid and personal. I remember particularly the description of his "automatic arm," which at parties would suddenly have a drink in its hand, with no conscious awareness up to that point. These vignettes were not exactly advice, and not even particularly directed at the housewife, but there was obviously something for her in it, and she was listening very intently. Later, in games, when G. or someone would "run his story" to me at some point of identification, I often experienced a peculiar kind of warmth and comfort in knowing that someone else had been at this point and gotten past it apparently quite successfully.

The other most salient interaction came near the end of the game

when G. turned to the fiery little brunette woman I had tagged to myself as "assistant leader" and asked a very casual question about a
phone call she had neglected to return. She tossed off some reason and
seemed to dismiss the matter, but G. hung in, rejecting her excuse and
pressing the question. For several minutes, which seemed a total waste
of time to me, G. pursued this, with the woman becoming increasingly
evasive and uncomfortable. Finally, weeping, she admitted the call was
from someone connected with the call-girl past she was trying desperately to forget as the date of her respectable marriage approached.
G. pointed out very gently what seemed obvious to all of us—that going
into her marriage with such a load of unresolved guilt could only lead
to trouble—and gave her a *motion* to bring the subject up herself
in every game she played for the next few weeks.

Three facets of this exchange impressed me. I noted again the power
of paying persistent attention to simple *behavior* and how close attention to this could lead to strong and important feelings more directly
and effectively than attending to the processed and familiar "feelings"
with which a person was immediately prepared, even eager, to deal.
Second, I noticed that the game was powerful almost in proportion to
the degree that the participants knew each other and had outside
contact. This last episode involved three people who clearly knew each
other well. The simple behavioral facts that were so powerful tended to
be *life* facts, known from other sources, rather than facts that developed from the here-and-now of the game (though these were also used).
Finally, I was impressed that this most powerful and sustained episode
of the game had been directed at an apparent "leader." It seemed no
one was immune (though it was to be some months before I was to see
G. really cornered effectively in a game). There had, in fact, been a
continuum of leadership in the game; some "leading" much of the
time, some sporadically, and some of us not at all. But "leadership" did
seem to be up for grabs. And I was tremendously impressed with
quality of leadership, most evident in the obviously experienced and
skilled leaders, but present in germ in several others; there were a
vigor, directness, and, above all, trust and confidence in their own
perceptions that I had rarely seen in my life. Later, reading Emerson
("A man should learn to detect and watch that gleam of light that
flashes across his mind from within"; "and abide by our spontaneous
impression with good-humored inflexibility, then most when the whole
cry of voices is on the other side"), I had some notion of the quality
of life action he was referring to.

My first contact with Synanon had been three years before this game
when its major facility was an old armory in Santa Monica. At the time
of that visit I knew about as much as any well-informed citizen; that
Synanon had been founded in the late fifties by an ex-drunk, Chuck

Dederich; that in some strange way it seemed to "work" in getting addicts to clean up, where no other approach had; and that it always seemed to be in trouble with some branch of the Establishment. I was fascinated at my first visit, particularly by the honesty, the sense of purpose, and, above all, the feeling of mutual *caring* that permeated the atmosphere. I remember coming away from the visit almost wishing I had been a dope fiend,[1] so that I could join and share that atmosphere. Looking back, I see that the qualities that impressed me were precisely those most lacking in my own life at that time.

The personal and professional dissatisfactions that had been operating mostly out of awareness in 1963 had clearly surfaced in the next couple years. My marriage seemed empty and unsatisfying and I had no close friends. My whole line of interest and research up to that point—computerizing the interpretation of psychologic tests—seemed shallow and pointless, but I could find nothing else that seemed worthwhile. Seven years past my Ph.D., it was getting very difficult to maintain my favorite image as the bright young man with lots of promise. I felt increasing pressure to produce, but despaired of finding anything in myself worth producing. In 1965, I began group therapy with an eminent Bay Area psychiatrist, but was finding that frustrating and unhelpful.

During 1964 and 1965 Synanon had been struggling to get established in San Francisco, making many friends and supporters and then losing most of them in a battle to keep a racially integrated house for its ex-dope-fiend members in wealthy, exclusive Pacific Heights. For a year or so in 1965 Chuck Dederich had played a Sunday night Synanon game with some "square" (nonaddict) sponsors and supporters, including G. After Chuck left San Francisco, the members of this group began playing the game with their friends and associates who had become interested. Word spread rapidly, and on Easter Sunday of 1966, 90 people appeared at the old warehouse that was then Synanon's San Francisco headquarters and formed a "game club"—"whatever *that* is," as G. said at the time. Quite by chance, I heard about it the next day and the following day played the game already described.

In the 1970's, the notion of people meeting in groups to discuss themselves very personally, without those groups being called "therapy," is so familiar that it is hard to remember how recent and revolutionary that idea is. The very term "encounter group" was hardly known at the time Synanon was offering the game and membership in a thriving social movement to the public for dues of $10.00 per month. For many people, Synanon was the first chance to satisfy the

---

[1] *Dope fiend* is the Synanon term for drug addict. The majority of Synanon residents are ex-dope fiends.

hunger for community and interaction that seems to underlie the growth of the encounter movement. Certainly it was among the first to emphasize that such groups could be an end in themselves, could be enjoyed for their own sake, and need not be totally for the purpose of "cure" or "growth" or "therapy" or some such serious goal.

However, I cannot emphasize enough that Synanon is far from being an encounter group. Its basic goal is to produce strong, honest, self-reliant people who can manage their own affairs and have some fun doing it, yet who also have some energy left over for the increasingly grim struggle to save our world from destruction by our species—and even have some fun doing *that*. Most encounter groups, as I understand them and conduct them, are on a very different trip. However, almost as a side effect of working toward its goal, Synanon seems to have some success achieving some of the goals by encounter groups and has certainly taught me a great deal about how people can be together in groups more enjoyably and productively. In this chapter I will describe the social movement and learning community called Synanon in some detail. My starting point is the personal experience of one overintellectual, aloof psychologist of 38 years who plunged very deeply into the experience and gained a great deal from it. My bias is therefore positive, though I hope to balance my account with a statement of some of the ways Synanon falls short of its potential for many people.

Synanon is an inclusive community that is devoted simultaneously to social action and the personal development of its members. Its achievements in getting a large number of ex-dope fiends to stop using dope on a shoestring budget with no government or professional "help" are well known. Its contributions to race relations and innovations in education are significant, though less well known as yet. At the same time, the individual development of each of its members is of the highest priority. Emerson says, in his essay on "History," "The world exists for the education of each man." Synanon exists so that its members can learn and teach each other a coherent philosophy of life, and have some fun in the process. This learning is not only an intellectual process. It takes place through *demonstration* and *example* in a close face-to-face community and works through intellect, emotion, and action concurrently.

These two functions of Synanon—social action and personal growth —are not separate. In fact, it seems likely that part of the reason Synanon "works" while some of its copies do not is precisely because personal growth *is* a part of and partly a side effect of *involvement* in processes outside the self, in wider social issues. And, in Synanon's view, the developed man uses his new competence and fuller self to work even more effectively on the social problems. Dederich would complete Emerson's quote above by saying, "—and the educated man works to raise the level of existence of the world." Without this final step of effective action in the world, it is questionable that much "growth" has occurred.

A few background facts are necessary to understand the detailed description of Synanon that follows. One is that the Synanon Foundation is first and foremost a residential situation, with well over one thousand full-time residents, who live and work in Synanon and for whom it is a whole way of life. Many of these, especially the long-time members, the crucial role-models and pacesetters, were long-time dope fiends, made clever and tough by the harsh, live-by-your-wits-or-die life of the streets. Though previous to their Synanon experience they were skilled liars and con men, and quite socially irresponsible, they generally are not crippled in their ability to express aggression and hostility and directly and forcefully and, in fact, rather enjoy a good contest. When finally "turned around" by long participation in the Synanon dynamic, many have become quite powerful and effective people, committed to Synanon and involved deeply in it. Most of the residents, of course, have not been in for a long time, but are in the process of becoming more involved in the organization. The presence of this core of full-time, committed members makes most of what happens in Synanon possible. They carry the major load of work and most activities are designed for them. It is very doubtful that an organization with the coherence and intensity of Synanon could exist with only partly involved nonresident members. The other side of this coin is that in any conflict between the needs of residents and the interests of nonresidents, the former come first, and I will give some specific instances of this later.

A nonresident member of Synanon lives in the community, has no history of narcotic use, and is usually working and leading a normal life. He may or may not have "problems" or "symptoms"; these are irrelevant to his interest in Synanon. Such an individual will join the *game club*, usually beginning by playing the Synanon game one night a week. Some people stay at this level of involvement. Many leave after a brief exposure. A few become increasingly involved and take on more responsibility, in ways that will be described later. There is no limit on the degree to which a nonresident can get involved if he wants to; indeed, a category of "resident nonresidents" is developing to accommodate those who wish more involvement. A full understanding of Synanon requires knowledge of its history and the structure of the resident situation. Though many of the descriptive comments in this paper could also be applied to the resident situation, some, particularly the conclusions, do not apply. For descriptions of the resident situation, or the Synanon foundation as a whole, the reader is referred to Endore (1968), Enright (1970), and Yablonsky (1965).

It is easy for a visitor or newcomer to Synanon to miss the fact that the character and quality of Synanon are deeply dependent on the personality of its founder, Chuck Dederich. To a large extent, Synanon is the "lengthened shadow" of Chuck. Its strengths are his, its weakness and lacks are his. For many years (and possibly still), Synanon has been an inverted pyramid resting on him, with only his charisma, creativity, and egotism keeping it moving. Most of the long-time residents of Synanon quite simply and undramatically feel, and will say, that Chuck saved their lives. It is little wonder they admire and copy him. Synanon can be described as a chain of role-models; in that image, he is the final link. To have one man so central and important seems to make many of us Americans, with our lip service to democracy, uneasy. I fought the recognition of Chuck's importance for some time; now I simply accept it and am glad the depth of his morality matches his strength.

The structural details and techniques of Synanon as described in this chapter will probably not correspond to the Synanon of the early 1970's. It is based on Synanon as it functioned from 1966 until late 1968, when I chose to become less intensely involved. Yet, I hope the reader could walk into a Synanon house in 1971 or 1972, look at the apparently very different forms and titles in use then, and still recognize the essence. Looking backward at the accomplishments of this nonviolent, drug-free society during its brief existence, it is tempting, and easy, to see all its direction of growth as the result of farsighted, rational planning. To those of us participating at some of the choice points, it is also easy to see many of the major decisions and directions as products of the wildest accidents and whims. For example, in 1969, the Bay Area house was located on the edge of the ghetto in Oakland, and Synanon was achieving some results in race relations that no government agency with ten times its meager budget of small donations could even dream of doing. Yet, a few months earlier, Synanon was a personality quirk away from making its Bay Area headquarters in a stuffy, lily-white suburb many miles away, where it would have ended up involved in some other crucial social issue. In both its internal structure and external impact, Synanon changes with astonishing rapidity. Not bound to be consistent with its own past, or to fit anyone else's image, its energy flows quickly and efficiently in whatever direction its philosophy seems best able to be actualized.

There is one final comment necessary before plunging into the description of the Synanon philosophy and technique. Most of it— "growth," philosophy, saving dope fiends—sounds like a very serious business, an impression probably reinforced by my style. Whatever else Synanon is, it is also a game. Some of the most hilarious moments of my life have been in games; I have come out weak with laughter. Many very official titles in Synanon are spoofs such as "primate," "game warden," "grand poobah," and the "king-freak chair." Chuck has commented more than once on the eve of some crucial decision that seemed inevitably ruinous to the more cautious among us, "Oh well, all I have invested in it is $33.00" (referring to one of the legends of Synanon's founding). Whenever I start to take Synanon too seriously, I think of an episode in a game, in which a man, staring at the floor, was talking himself more and more deeply into self-pity. Usually, such activity gets short shrift in a game, but this time G. waved us into silence, while he inserted a cigarette in each nostril. About the time the rest of us had copied him, the man, no doubt getting suspicious at the unusually patient reception of his woe, looked up at a whole circle of lugubrious walruses staring solemnly at him. Any human event can be seen as a tragedy, comedy, subject for careful analysis, and from any number of other points of view. At its best, Synanon seldom loses sight for long of the comic view.

The major source of the Synanon philosophy is the work of Ralph Waldo Emerson, particularly the essays "Self-reliance," "Power," and "Compensation." Dederich has often said that he read "Self-reliance" as "a personal letter to me," and the essay indeed can be read practically as a handbook of the game. Emerson's view is that man has an inner direction, strength, and certainty that are unbelievably powerful, if he will only listen to and act decisively on his inner voice, whatever the apparent consequence. Conformity, consistency, concern for reputation and looking good in others' eyes, and fear of failure are some of the enemies of awareness and free expression of this voice. There are three qualities (practices?) (virtues?) (habits?) that will maintain or regain this in-touchness with the inner voice and the ability to express it. These are honesty, courage, and total acceptance of responsibility for what one does and what happens to one.

Honesty—veracity—the representation of things as they are rather than as we wish them to be, or wish others to think them—sounds too simple to be the bedrock of a philosophy. Yet nothing seems harder to attain than that transparent, effortless, paradisic state in which anything I do or think can be known to anyone without harm to me. The moments I have been in anything approaching this state seem unbelievably precious and worth any effort to prolong and reattain. The effort to maintain my phony image, and to hide that which is shameful, illegal, embarrassing, or in some way thought to be damaging, absorbs a significant amount of energy—at least, great amounts of energy seem to be released when this effort is temporarily reduced. And one lie seems to be sufficient; it becomes the nucleus around which others quickly gather. One friend, a long-time Synanon member, compared that one lie to yoghurt. For seven years he never fully confessed to his misdeeds in Synanon, but always hung on to one. Just as one spoonful of yoghurt can convert a gallon of warm milk to a gallon of yoghurt, one lie was enough to keep him "dirty," dishonest, guilty, and ready to lie more. Freud is said to have rejected as a patient an official in the Austrian government who insisted he would have to conceal certain state secrets—nothing personal, mind you. These "state secrets" would have provided the necessary nucleus.

By now, I imagine that many of you have dissociated yourselves from this discussion, saying something like, "This doesn't apply to me, though it certainly does to all those others." Not so. To get in touch with your own lying, start by looking at your arguments that you don't lie. Or look for our particular synonyms for lying. "I don't want to hurt her." "This fact is not relevant here." "It's not important." "I forgot." "My account was true in essence, if not in detail." "Uncle Sam will never miss it." "Everyone does." These are some common ones. Or look at some fragment of your life story that you have re-counted many times and examine it very carefully for literal accuracy. I discovered in Synanon that my life story as I told it to myself and others was a pack of lies and cover-ups, designed to make me look good, and to conceal facts and feelings I was ashamed of. I am pushing this point of view because I think most of us have no idea to what extent lying, and the misdirection of energy to maintain it, cripple us for effec-tive action in the world. How can I stand up to my boss on a matter of principle when I have been sneaking away from work an hour early the last month? How can I take a position with my wife on how to bring up our children if I am having or contemplating an affair? How can I consider running for public office if I have been hiding some fragment of a shady past? And so on. The web of distortions necessary to conceal our derelictions blocks intimacy and leaves us unable to act firmly and rightly when necessary. If a man could live totally honestly, he could shake his universe, instead of tiptoeing guiltily through it.

It may be that total honesty alone is enough to lead to my doing what is right for me; if I see myself and the world clearly, right action may not be difficult or require any courage; it may simply seem in-evitable. But something like *courage*—the willingness not to draw back from what I know to be right, even if I fear or don't "feel" like doing it—seems to be a necessary quality while learning to know myself and the world. F. S. Perls, the founder of Gestalt therapy, has often said that every neurosis is based on a phobia, on avoidance of the difficult. This is a useful way of looking at much human unhappiness and neurotic symptoms. Underlying them is often a feeling that could be expressed in some phrase such as this: "Surely I can get what I want without doing this difficult, fearsome thing." Or, as Emerson put it, "We are parlor soldiers; the rugged battle of fate, where strength is born, we shun." Much of what happens in Synanon can be seen as creating opportunities (and providing pressure) to take action that will risk stepping into the unknown or require the courage to leap directly into the feared situation.

Responsibility is the recognition that I, not society, circumstances, mother, my subconscious, boss, children, or wife, have taken the steps to bring me where I am now and generated the emotional atmosphere I live in. The liberating effect of gut-level acceptance of this point of view would have been unbelievable to me before I accepted it to the degree I have so far. When I truly see that I did it, I also see I can do otherwise; I am no longer impotent and subject to the will or whims of others. And, as an important side effect, resentment—the emotion of impotence—evaporates, and the energy that fueled it is freed for positive, self-directed action.

These are the core concepts of the Synanon philosophy. Many of the ways Synanon has developed for presenting and teaching these concepts look superficially like "techniques" that can be described separately, and presumably transplanted to other settings. This is a misleading impression. The "techniques"—the game, stew , trip, cerebration, reach—work only in the over-all context of the Synanon *community*. And much of the behavior influencing in Synanon happens not through any identifiable "technique," but simply through members interacting, demonstrating the philosophy in action, and role-modeling for each other. It seems less misleading to me to first describe this richly textured community and some of what happens in it, before focusing on the more clearly identifiable "techniques" mentioned above.

As the San Francisco Bay area "game club" began to approach a thousand in number, Synanon discovered that there is a distant limit to the number of people who can form a close, mutually knowing, face-to-face group. It also became clear that the success of Synanon methods required a group with such qualities. The optimum size for such a group, which we decided to call a *tribe*, seems to be between 40 and 100, depending on the amount of contact members have with each other. With more contact, the larger size is possible. This optimum size, interestingly, seems to be the same as for groups of baboons, the most important primate other than man that committed itself to coming down from the safety of the trees. The tribe of which I was leader for about nine months consisted of about 35 people—the lower limit in size. For most of its members, during their first months of membership, the tribe was the primary contact with Synanon. Members played the game almost exclusively with each other and socialized and attended seminars and worked with other tribe members. With longer membership, individuals would be involved with more games and activities outside the tribe, in the larger Synanon community. Each tribe deliberately was as varied as possible in age, race, socioeconomic status, and so one. The more diversity, the more tension and energy in games, and the more the increasing social and racial polarization of our time could be reduced. (A beautiful example of this occurred the night before a large Berkeley protest march, when a marcher and a member of the National Guard, destined to confront each other the next day across a barricade, had a chance to shout it out in a game.)

The great *variety* of modes of interaction is an important feature of the Synanon community. The game provided a place for honesty and confrontation almost unknown in our society. In addition, tribe members often worked together. For example, the tribe would go out together on a Saturday afternoon selling tickets for a benefit drawing, perhaps ending up with a party. There was always some construction going on at the Synanon house, where people could volunteer to work together. The yearly Synanon fair required months of preparation, and the fair itself was an orgy of exhausting but enjoyable work. There were numerous parties, both tribal and Synanon-wide, each requiring a committee to prepare and organize, and each committee meeting, with its tensions and disagreements, provided more fuel and material for the game. For a while it was a strange feeling to have ordinary, everyday interactions with people who knew my worst secrets, and whose secrets I knew. Gradually this became second nature, and much easier to do outside of Synanon as well. Gradually, those of us who stayed in long enough to feel the liberating effects of such open living began to bring more friends and coworkers in. At one time or another, I was involved in Synanon with my doctor, dentist, and mechanic and with various colleagues, students, and numerous current ex-patients. I did not always enjoy having some mistake at work or some bit of arrogance with a student brought up in games, but each time it became easier, and I learned more from it. And, of course, there was some recompense in being able, for example, to lay into my dentist for his inefficient secretary. The quality of relationship in the tribe could almost be described as familial—closer and more interwoven than most of the friendships formed in the wider society.

The possibility of knowing others as whole people instead of through the partial relationships that characterize our society makes learning by *role-modeling* a central fact in Synanon. A newcomer to the tribe would usually spontaneously pick two or three people he admired and to some extent would copy them. The tribe leader or tribal elders were most frequently selected, but by no means necessarily; a patient of mine in her mid-sixties very much admired and copied a girl in her late twenties. This process is explicitly encouraged; frequently role-models would be suggested to someone who seemed stuck at some point in his Synanon growth. Just as *selecting* a role-model is encouraged for the newcomer, so is *being* a role-model encouraged for the older member. He is constantly reminded that his actions are a demonstration of a way of life, an experiment in applying a philosophy, and that others are looking to him as an example. This at times was helpful to me when I felt about ready to quit trying for a while. My awareness that my life truly *was* an example to some others in my tribe helped keep me doing what was right for me.

The Synanon philosophy is communicated implicitly and constantly in simple community living. It is taught and demonstrated explicitly in some of the specialized procedures or techniques Synanon has developed. It is part of the philosophy that an effective philosophy of life is more than an intellectual position; it must be *felt* and *lived* as well and, therefore, must be taught at all levels of being. For convenience, the techniques can be classified roughly as aimed at *intellectual* learning, *emotional* or "gut-level" learning, or directly at changing behavior through *action*.

Two major tools of intellectual learning at present are the *cerebration* and the reach. In both of these, great emphasis is placed on eliciting through discussion what the participants already know, rather than attempting to instill or "teach" anything. In the former, two or three concepts are written on a blackboard, (e.g., "time" and "responsibility"). Participants will discuss these for several hours, weaving in personal experience as well as abstract intellect. In a long cerebration, the concepts will be considered in different combinations to give even greater depth to the discussion. The leader's role is to keep the discussion alive and involved and relevant to the Synanon philosophy, but otherwise not guide or direct it. In the *reach,* simple physical relations (e.g., why does chalk stick to blackboards?) are used instead of abstract concepts, and 24-hour unbroken meetings are used, to give fatigue a chance to weaken habitual rigid thinking patterns. The thrust of these approaches is to *bring out* rather than to put in and to *stimulate to learn* rather than teach. Learning will be rapid when a person knows what it is that he wants to know, and he can be trusted to find it himself. The emphasis is also that intellectual knowledge and skill be *integrated* with emotion and the whole self. Abstract, intellectually elegant notes are discouraged, if they result in keeping intellectual grasp and understanding unavailable to immediate use under challenging circumstances. It is also not expected that intellectual grasp of a subject or point is adequate in itself, until it has been thoroughly wedded to emotion and action. The goal of all the intellectual techniques, as well as reading, is simply to have the intellectual concepts readily available, to tie to emotion and action whenever possible. A member might mouth some slogans about responsibility or truth 20 times in a game, before one day he will suddenly be hit in the face with the real relevance of this concept for him in his life. Then, it begins to be truly his. It becomes still more part of him every time he applies it to himself or teaches it to someone else.

The great tool for gut-level learning in Synanon is the *game*. It is the heart of Synanon, the earliest technique developed, and the most central. (And, like a heart, it cannot survive or function outside the total organism.) Its importance is suggested by the fact that I have had to refer to it 20 times already in this chapter, even before describing it. For most nonresidents, it is the first introduction to Synanon, and their primary activity for some time. (Though if they keep it their only activity too long, they will find little benefit in it.)

In the game, 10 to 15 Synanon members meet, anywhere from 2 to 24 hours, usually about three. The rules are the same as anywhere else in Synanon: no violence, and no consciousness-altering chemicals. The composition of no two games is quite the same. The individual will play mostly with fellow tribe members, plus a few drop-ins from other tribes. Spouses sometimes are together in a game, sometimes separate. The tribal leader is responsible for insuring a balance of skilled and new game players and making sure the game is seeded with conflict and the possibility of action. A member can arrange to be in a game with someone he has something to say to. (I used to tell my tribe there were two ways to insure being in a game with someone: to ask to be, and to ask not to be.)

Within this setting, the whole range of human experience is possible. Players try among other things to tell the truth about themselves and others as best they can. An attempt is made to strip away every mask that is put on, every hat that is donned, and to drive a person out of every position he takes. An attempt is made to create crises and emergencies, to drive people to the end of what they know, and hopefully beyond that point, to force action where no action seems possible. A man is basically always alone in a game; all friendships are left at the door, as well as all status and titles. Alliances are fleeting and *ad hoc*, and when the purpose of one alliance is finished, that very alliance may be examined, to see if the allies are concealing anything about each other. In a good game there is an abundance of comedy. The epic may be reduced to a gag, and a momentary lapse of awareness may be magnified into a crime against humanity. In the game, people work through their disagreements, carry out their quarrels and dominance struggles, express their points of human identification with others, and make the first tentative exploration of new parts of themselves, discovering these parts primarily through action, rather than through talking. There can be no guarantee of confidentiality of this situation, of course, but members are asked not to carry any information out of the game, and certainly not out of Synanon. Gossiping outside of Synanon, when it is discovered, is attacked very strongly in games, and a person who persisted might be suspended for a while.

A game typically opens with an *indictment* of a piece of misbehavior, large or small. Perhaps the indictee left a dirty coffee cup after the last game, perhaps his wife is annoyed that he was two hours late last night without an explanation, or perhaps a friend of his secretary has discovered he is embezzling funds at his office. Whatever the face-value importance of the indictment, the game is off and running with it. Other players bring in confirmations or supporting evidence and begin to weave a web around the indictee. His explanations are examined very critically, and usually dismissed. On the rare occasion he defends successfully, he may open himself to a new indictment. I remember vividly successfully defending myself against the charge that I was brusque and pushy at committee meetings—that I "played the game outside the game." Carried away by the success of my defense, I commented that, indeed, I was perhaps not pushy enough, perhaps even mousy at the meetings. Immediately, I was faced with defending my mousiness and ineffectiveness. In the hands of a master, the indictment can be a work of verbal art. I once watched Dederich take a leisurely three hours to parlay the poor location of the toilet paper holder in the men's room into a detailed analysis of exactly what was wrong with everyone involved in the management of that particular Synanon house. With increasing skill and experience in the game, the indictment can reach breath-taking levels of subtlety. A skilled player may talk for five minutes about some dereliction before anyone in the room is sure who he is talking to. If the indictment is worded generally enough, everyone in the room is anxiously searching his memory to see if he is the lucky one. Or, if I know that someone on a committee has been performing poorly, I will indict the *chairman* of the committee for his sloppy management, insuring, among other things, that later in the game the chairman will heatedly take care of his delinquent member. Or, if I know X knows something about Y and hasn't brought it up, I may indict him for not indicting Y—"You must really hate Y, to encourage his continuing in his dumb behavior."

A new player will frequently try to defend with a counterindictment. This is rarely successful. Someone else's misbehavior is no excuse for mine. It may later come under close scrutiny on its own merits, but not as a defense. I have often been amused watching a husband and wife new to the club learn this fact about the game. Wife would indict husband (unfortunately for our culture, that is usually the way it would start) and then with almost incredulous delight watch the game develop her complaint into a massive criticism of the husband's whole life-style. Everything wrong with the marriage—and faults would be found she had never dreamed of—would be clearly seen as springing from his

inadequacies. Suddenly there would be a reversal; the same incidents would be gone over in detail again, and an ironclad case be made
for the wife being totally to blame. Both, in other words, would be
seen as 100 per cent to blame for their joint misery. The game's attention to them might end with a joint indictment for their wasting our
time with their trivial complaints that would be easily settled if they
would just read the Synanon philosophy and act on it.

In nonresident games with many new players who may as yet have
had little contact with each other outside of the game, indictments are
less available, and the game must start elsewhere. Often, simply a person's appearance or detail of dress, with its implications for his self-
image, might be a starting point. In the hands of a skilled player, this
can be beautiful. I once watched an overweight psychiatrist in a game
reduced to tears when a skilled resident player took a ten-minute verbal
trip, describing in exquisite detail exactly what the psychiatrist would
be doing and saying and how he would be living ten years in the future.
Somehow, this New York Irish street kid—a heroin addict at age 12—
knew what the life of the son of a Jewish small businessman from
Brooklyn was like, and what it would become if he didn't pay some
close attention to his choices in the next few years. In the hands of a
less skilled player, this attention to superficial details remains superficial, and the game comes across then as inept bludgeoning.

A game might also start with casual questioning of someone until an
inconsistency or probable lie appears; this is seized on and developed.
For a while, I opened games by asking someone to state his deepest,
most central life value and then demonstrating out of his own mouth
how he did not live up to it. Games emphatically do *not* start, though
newcomers keep trying, by taking complaints and "symptoms" seriously. With boring regularity, people new to games try to start with
some variant of the cliché, "I'm frustrated, alienated, and I can't communicate." (This has become such a cliché that in California there is a
sweatshirt commercially available with that message stenciled on it.)
The typical response would be: "Listen, you sloppy, overage adolescent; the only trouble with you is you're fat, pimply, and have nothing
to say; there's nothing wrong with you that Clearasil, a diet, and a few
good books wouldn't cure. If you can't communicate, you're probably
lying about something; what is it?" The tired mutations of self-pity that
most people dignify with the name "feelings" are unacceptable to a
game. Equally common, and equally unacceptable, are genetic accounts
that purport to "explain" my current existential despair and ineffectiveness. I remember one solemn youth who tried, with a tear forming
in each eye, to sell the game the notion that he was unemployed, unhappy, and unattached because his mother had once left him in a toy
store for a few hours when he was three. With gales of laughter, we

spun this story out by speculating that perhaps some customer, mistaking him for a new model doll (it wets, it cries, it even talks!), had wrapped him up and taken him home.

The position of the game seems to be that anything a person already knows about himself is probably false and irrelevant and is certainly misused to maintain his narrow, unchallenging, and less than completely satisfying life. (And his life is assumed to be all of those things, whatever he says.) Any valid self-knowledge will survive the acid bath of doubt the game will put him through. We want to shake his assumptions about life and himself, to test and question, not justify and excuse. The usual manipulations just won't work. The suicide threatener will receive an offer to drive him to the bridge on my way home. (Though in fact, along with everyone else, he will be invited to stay for coffee after the game, not as a reward for his manipulation, but simply because he is a potentially interesting and creative human being.) The uptight lady who is shocked at the dirty words will be called "superstitious," because she is afraid to make a particular noise. "How come you can say 'cuff'—that's the same sound backward?" A skilled game player can usually sense the difference between feeling-crying and self-pity, manipulative crying, and he is quite short with the latter: "When the flood is over, maybe you can tell us something real instead of all this crap."

We want people in the game to examine what they actually *do* in their lives, not what they think they do, and examine the *values they actually live by,* not the ones they mouth. Rationalizations, cover-ups, "I forgot" are spotted as lies by the world's greatest experts in lying and are probed and examined until the person is forced to see what he is really doing. If it is not grossly illegal or destructive, we usually don't even care if he then changes or not—newcomers often misunderstand that—we just want him to see it clearly. In a poor game, a lot of time is often wasted trying to get people to admit something about themselves that the game has been pushing. Good players never bother; they shoot their shot and move on. If it is true, it will connect; if not, belaboring won't help. As part of this effort, it is necessary to get people to stop defending others. Every supporting argument by someone else, no matter how valid it may be, weakens a person and reduces the likelihood that he will see himself clearly. Considerable effort in newcomers' games has to be devoted to silencing the "Jewish mamas" and getting them to examine what their phony "helpfulness" does for them.

It is part of the game that a person is never right in anything he does. Fairly early in my Synanon career, I was one of five put in charge of discussion groups. One of the other five was attacked in a steering committee game for scheduling a game with his group instead of a discussion—something I had also done. That next week, I furtively de-scheduled my game, giving my group members some phony excuse. The next game, I was attacked for *not* having a game with my group. There was, of course, no policy on the matter; each person was expected to do what he thought best—*and* be able to defend it. It was hard for me to believe that it was truly up to me; I kept looking for the "right" thing to do.

As people are discovering in the game what they actually do in their life, we simultaneously encourage them to use the game as a place to try out new ways of being and acting. The mouse is encouraged to roar, the loudmouth told to shut up and listen for a few hours. The polite and deferent husband is maneuvered into a position of arrogance vis-à-vis his wife, and the bully is subdued and shouted down until he exhibits some uncharacteristic politeness. Newcomers will be given a simple task to "open their mouth" at every person in the game, describing them, expressing their feelings toward them, and so on. Simple practice in influencing others and acting rather than reacting is much of the game. At about my sixth month in Synanon, I spent most of each game for several weeks simply practicing the art of directing the movement of the game attention from one person to another, learning the timing and technique of transition until I could make the game shift almost any time I wanted. The ability to function coolly under stress, holding one's position and continuing to influence others effectively under fire, is a skill many people in our society have not learned; in a game, there is ample opportunity to make up for lost time. Going into a game is a little like being parachuted into a jungle, with a guarantee of being air-lifted out three hours later. The task for those three hours is to survive, and maybe even enjoy the trip. Part of me knows all the time that the tigers are paper, but my gut is not entirely sure, and I learn a lot about survival in that time. To enhance the usefulness of the game as a practice field, there is a convention that no final decisions are made in a game. A man might quit his job or a husband might announce his irrevocable intention to leave home, but it is understood that such statements have to be confirmed outside the game before leading to action.

From this point of view, the game is to emotional life what exercise is to physical life; a place to challenge and push myself beyond the relatively low demands of life. Because I jog or play tennis regularly I feel better in normal daily physical activity and have an extra reserve of stamina available for emergencies such as running for a bus. If I play the game weekly, hold my own against its spirited and exaggerated attack, and give as good as I get, I am readier for the emotional emergencies of life, and the usual emotional demands are child's play.

Much human energy seems to go into justifying, defending, and hiding one's thoughts and actions, and part of what happens in a game is designed to make this waste of energy obsolete and unnecessary. Explanations and defenses are never accepted; in addition, we go zealously after the (usually trivial) secrets a person is keeping about himself. Early in his game career, a player will be asked, "What's the worst thing you've ever done?" The first few answers, of course, are not accepted. When something of some apparent importance is finally revealed, its real triviality usually becomes immediately apparent, even to the hitherto guilty one. One man, in a paroxysm of tears, confessed to masturbating with a bottle stuck in his rectum. When his tears died down, and he looked guiltily around, someone asked him, "What kind of bottle?" He had to join in the ensuing gale of laughter.

When the superficial defenses against an indictment are flattened, and the person begins to consider some flaw in his life seriously; when a few layers of his self-pity have been swept away by the humor and ridicule of the game; when he has faced some of his shame about his past choices, real sadness and despair begin to emerge. At this point, in a good game, the tone changes dramatically. The experienced players then will open up about times in their own lives that in some way are similar to what the individual is struggling with, offering these fragments of themselves not particularly as advice, but primarily as evidence that others have been there, and gotten past that point somehow. Some of these moments in a game have been very intimate and precious for me, whether I was primarily on the giving or receiving end. As long as a person presents his past as a record of bad things that happened to him, which therefore excuse his current misbehavior, he is attacked mercilessly. At the moment he faces with regret and contrition some of his own destructive *choices* in life, he is met with empathy and support. The attitude toward his own past that is modeled by the good game player is one of total responsible acceptance, without the twin dangers of regret or boasting. To the extent he can do that, his past is then available as a source of knowledge about himself and others that he can use in a game and his whole life. The use of *identification* is the most powerful tool of the game; for me, all the preliminary attacking is largely to let off steam and get the individual to the point where he can hear such identification. Of course, the person who profits most from this identification is the one who tells his story, not the one who hears it. The teller has a priceless opportunity to review some fragment of his life, peeling off one or two more distortions as he does so, seeing it more and more clearly each time, and each time tying himself a little bit more closely to the human race, as well as to the individual he has told it to.

In Synanon's constant effort to combine intellectual and gut-level learning the *perpetual stew* was born. Twenty-four hours a day, seven days a week, 18 people meet in a large circle. Every two hours, two leave and two new ones take their place. Thus, at any point in time, most of the people in the room have been there for several hours and are thoroughly warmed up to the process, sweeping the newcomers very quickly into their level of intensity. Some are in for 72 hours (with two six-hour sleep breaks), others for 24; still others have signed in for four-hour units. Much of this time, the group is playing the game, but at any time Chuck or one of the other directors of Synanon may wander in and talk from ten minutes to ten hours. At various times, talks will be given by someone in the stew on his profession or on some field of special interest, or tapes of talks or famous games in Synanon will be played. Once, a graduate student from Harvard, who knew math but not people, and Chuck, who knew both, jointly taught a two-hour lesson in plane geometry. Chuck had the members of the stew (including some almost illiterate ex-dope fiends) asking questions they didn't know they knew, and understanding the answers. With the sense of endless leisure the stew provides, the game takes on a different dimension; at one point, the attention of the stew was devoted to me for as long as an average game takes—two and one-half hours. The added time was necessary; it took the game that long to force me to see my responsibility for some things I had been blaming on others. My defenses against accepting this responsibility could never have been dented in the brief period of a game.

At another point in the stew (in my memory, everything of significance in the stew seems to have taken place about three o'clock some morning), G. spent an hour demonstrating to everyone's satisfaction that my life work as a group therapist was not only dishonest but impossible, quoting up-to-date data from Farson on the efficacy of leaderless groups. His conclusion was that the only honest thing for me to do was become a hod-carrier.

At one point, the stew at the Tomales Bay facility was being broadcast to the entire facility. At any time, anyone on the Synanon property could tune in and hear whoever was then dragging his most intimate secrets into view. I know this sounds reprehensible to most Americans, with the exaggerated sense of secrecy we have developed. Having lived a few years with this point of view that no constraints on the truth are necessary or desirable, it seems quite acceptable to me.

The *trip* is a highly structured, 48-hour event that most people will take once, if at all, in their Synanon life, and then only after several months' experience in the club. Through psychodrama, intense group pressure, intellectual challenge, music, fatigue, and a variety of different intense emotional stimuli, the attempt is made to push people through whatever point they are stuck, to some glimpse of the freedom that is possible in life. "Push" is too mild a word; the most brutal attacks on dishonesty and the most intense pressure toward truth occur in trip and pretrip games. A person *must* pass through some of the horror of his life and experience his responsibility for that horror in his whole being before the freedom becomes real. Once he does accept that responsibility, the experience of love, joy, and oneness with the other trippers—and often, for a while, with all of humanity—can be extremely intense. Many come off the trip describing the experience in terms reminiscent of religious experiences, often with feelings of being reborn. For me, the effect seemed to be to push the knowledge of what I had to do with people from intellectual level to gut level. On the trip, I experienced responsibility for my closed-up, withholding, deceitful relations with others and could see that this way of life was killing me emotionally. For the next few days, I literally could not hold back or lie to others about my feelings; my stomach would tighten with anxiety at even the tiniest white lie. The name "trip" was deliberately chosen to imply some goals in common with the psychedelic trip. We feel in Synanon that much of the subjective experience and the possible permanent value of the drug trip can be achieved, and possibly even more solidly achieved, without drugs.

The descriptions of the techniques of teaching the Synanon philosophy through intellect and emotion cannot be complete without considering how these techniques interact with the community and, above all, with the methods of learning through *action*. Ultimately, all learning is through action; words are never considered adequate evidence of learning. For a time, for example, individuals leaving the stew were asked to make some commitment for specific future action relevant to whatever had come out of their stew experience. I ran into this emphasis on action in my first game, when G. gave the brunette a motion to bring up her call-girl past in each game. In the same game, my ex-patient was given a motion to wear clothes that would make him look like something other than a "senile fag." These *motions*, as they are called in Synanon, come in all shapes and sizes, from simple here-and-now suggestions to rather important life steps. I was given a motion once to open every game by indicting the strongest woman in the room. Later, as tribal leader I put myself through a motion to stop hiding from people behind my paper work after games and sit for a minimum of one-half hour at the table in the coffee shop where I knew the fewest people. A dull and dumpy woman who sounded like a therapy addict was trying to tell the game for the nth time how bad she felt about being fat, and what a rotten marriage she had, when the fact leaked out that she was an amateur potter. Immediately, we took up a collection in the game for money to buy clay, and told her to take it to the resident in charge of the activity program for 800 ghetto kids and offer her services to him. We promised that if, at the end of one month of helping him, she still felt just as rotten, we would listen to her tale of woe.

At the other extreme of seriousness, a resident who split (left) and wanted to return might be asked to sit in his hotel room for a month, writing a letter each day, giving a different reason for wanting to return. At their worst, motions might often be flippant and hostile, often amounting to no more than bad advice. At their best, some were the most elegant behavior therapy prescriptions I have ever heard. One purpose of the motion is to position the person to feel what it is like to act in certain ways he has not tried before. If he continues, frequently certain feelings and impulses, hitherto unexperienced, might arise. The other effect is to elicit different feedback from the world, which again allows him to change his mode of experiencing. For both these purposes, it is not necessary that he understand why he is carrying out the motion, or even like to do it; it is often sufficient simply to do it—to "go through the motions." This emphasis on *action* as a primary way to learn appears throughout Synanon, in matters large and small. Games, for instance, start on time, and anyone late does not play that night. The reason is simply that people value that which they arrive on time for, and devalue that which they arrive late for, so if we do not permit them to arrive late, they will value the game more, and hopefully play it better. *Act as if*—practice the form until you achieve the essence—is constant advice in Synanon.

As an example of learning through action on a large scale, my own first experience with this method is still the most vivid. I had been playing the game about four months when I received a summons to a special meeting. (Synanon always acts as if its activities and needs take precedence over everything else.) Here it was announced that some fight promoters had offered to put on a heavyweight prize-fight benefit for Synanon, and we game club members were invited to sell tickets for it. I was further invited to become a ticket captain, supervising and encouraging ten others. I had managed to go through most of my life not only not selling, but practically not speaking to anyone, except as a student, teacher, or professional, and I certainly had no intentions of *selling* any tickets to a *prize fight*. However, I didn't have the courage to say that directly in a game, taking what I thought was the safer position that I would like to, but . . . The "but" was followed over the next six weeks with a remarkable series of rationalizations, each of which was cheerfully demolished in game after game. The last "reason" was my objection to the occasional brain damage suffered by fighters. This reason disintegrated when someone innocently asked if I would object to a wrestling match. When I shouted, "Yes," they had me; wrestling is not a dangerous sport, and it was obvious even to me that I was refusing out of cowardice and snobbery. For the next month I carried tickets around, but was unable to sell even one. I have never in my life experienced such self-defeating behavior so vividly; as I walked up to a prospect I could *feel* myself marshaling his arguments against me, and by the time I opened my mouth it was two against one, he and I against me. And, of course, every week the game would deride and make fun of me for my failure. I was very close to leaving the club, in spite of my strong attraction to it, when finally someone in a game indicted me with, "Well, John, let's examine why you are such a total failure in a simple thing like this. First of all, you're *going* to the fight yourself, I presume?" "Of course not," I answered. "You've been to one before, I trust?" "No." "What! You call yourself a psychologist, a student of human behavior, and you've never been to a *prize fight?* I suppose, you phony ————, you've even had the gall to lecture on displaced aggression, when you've never even been to see it yourself, never heard the crowd roar at a punch and felt the identification with the desire to hurt? My God, I can't believe it." He went on at some length, but his point was made; I meekly said I guessed I would go. Somehow, that broke the impasse for me, and I started selling as well as teaching and role-modeling for my ten supervisees. After that, it was never difficult for me to sell, to talk to city councils and store owners to get permission for Synanon to solicit funds, and so on. Some kind of barrier of aloofness and fear was broken, not only in Synanon, but in the rest of my life as well. The game had operated here not to help me get any "insight" or understanding, but simply as a pressuring and motivation device to push me into some *action*, actions I had never done before, and could barely imagine doing, but, when done, left me freer, stronger, and more able than I could have imagined. It is also so typical of Synanon that shortly after all this, a resident who had been in the forefront of those pushing me commented in a game: "Well, John, it looked for a while as though you might have enough guts after all to stand up against the pressure we gave you, but you didn't. Too bad; you were looking pretty good for a while." There is little time wasted in Synanon praising someone for doing something that is in his own best interest; he might make the mistake next time of doing it for praise instead of for himself.

There were endless other opportunities to get involved in learning through action—"to seek and assume responsibility," in the Synanon phrase. The other major one for me was *tribal leader*. I was among the first group appointed when the tribal system evolved, and for a month or so I basked in the status and planned all the glorious things I was going to do in this position. Then, all of us were summarily fired and replaced by residents. When I was reappointed after a few months, I had learned my lesson, and I got to work. As tribal leader, I learned a tremendous amount, at a very practical level, that I had missed while growing up in my isolated boyhood, and certainly had not learned in academic psychology: how to motivate and inspire people, stand up to criticism, and take and delegate responsibility.

Desmond Morris says that most hobbies, cults, sports, and so on exist primarily for the purpose of providing opportunities for status. "In each case, the overt nature of the activity is comparatively unimportant. What is really important is that the pursuit provides a new social hierarchy where one did not exist before. Inside it a whole range of rules and procedures is rapidly developed, committees are formed, and—most important of all—leaders emerge. A champion canary-breeder or body-builder would, in all probability, have no chance whatsoever of enjoying the heady fruits of dominance, were it not for his involvement in his specialized sub-group."[1] In Synanon, rather than this being an unacknowledged, inefficient by-product of some other activity, it is a recognized part of the process. Learning to assume wider and wider responsibility, with its associated status and leadership skill, is part of the reason for being there. And, being done consciously, it tends to be done well. People are moved from position to position not only for the sake of the job, but very much to further their own personal development. (And, incidentally, jobs are rarely filled twice; there is usually a change in job description or at least name every time a person is moved; so no one ever follows exactly in another's footsteps, but has the joy and challenge of creating his own job.)

Some of the interrelations of all these techniques with each other and the community have been described, but two additional points are important. The game exists as a place for people to shout, scream, and cathart partly *so that* they will behave themselves elsewhere in the world or the Synanon environment. Taking motions and acting-as-if is hard work. The housewife who has stopped drinking, the husband who has stopped philandering, the service station attendant who has stopped rifling the till have a lot of tension built up and feelings to express. These tensions are great fuel for the game. Before every major committee meeting, the members involved play a game, to get all the interpersonal rivalry and petty infighting expressed and out in the open, so that the battles are not fought over business issues. Thus the game and acting-as-if reinforce each other; each becomes easier and makes more sense in context with the other.

Another way of looking at the interrelation of all these Synanon procedures is as a series of concentric circles of action and influence. First is the game. In an atmosphere of no violence, no reprisals, and no consequences in the real world, a person can begin to learn to take

[1] Morris, Desmond. *The Human Zoo*. New York: McGraw-Hill, 1969, p. 57.

positions, expand himself, try out his strength, and in short, learn to be a *cause* instead of an *effect*. When a person has begun to master the game environment, he is ready for the next circle, of committee work in the tribe, perhaps a tribal leadership, and then responsibility in the Synanon Foundation. Hopefully, he also begins to seek and assume more responsibility and exert more influence in his family, in his job situation, and wherever else he wants to. The battle of Waterloo, it is said, was won on the playing fields of Eton. On the playing fields of Synanon, the individual can prepare for his crucial life battles. He can learn the ways and pleasures of personal power and genuine responsibility and become that rarity of modern life, an adult, who can manage his own affairs, take care of others, give back to the world instead of take, and maintain and extend human culture and civilization.

So far I have presented Synanon at its best, in order to make its goals, principles, and techniques as clear as possible. But its faults and failures grow out of these principles and methods just as much as its successes, and it is necessary to study how it falls short of its best, as it too often has. There are few experiences in life more hilarious and exciting than a good game, but there are few drearier than a bad one. A bad game is full of ineffective and unpleasant badgering, fruitless and unending dominance struggles, boring emphasis on profanity and negative feelings, baiting and bullying. In a poor game, acting-as-if comes across as deceitful posturing. The necessary rejection of self-pity is extended to the blocking of expression of genuine emotions. "Motions" frequently amount only to thoughtless and hostile bad advice. For perhaps a majority of the thousands of people who sampled Synanon briefly and chose not to continue, such games were probably their dominant experience—pure attack without flair or care.

There are two immediate reasons for a bad game: lack of enough experienced players, and lack of outside contact among the players—contact that provides indictments, knowledge of each other, and some reasons to care. For far too much of the game club's history, too many games occurred with neither the experienced players nor the supportive web of outside friendships. These games happened whenever too many people were taken into the club without a large enough cadre of experienced players to ensure good games and to attend to the Synanon growth of the individual newcomers. At least once, when the San Francisco club was almost doubled in size overnight, and almost destroyed as a result, the immediate motive seemed simply to increase the flow of dues to help the foundation through one of its numerous financial crises. The development of the close human contact among club members was made particularly difficult by such floods of new people. In addition, Synanon's absurd and paranoid position that activities should be held only on Synanon property inhibited many kinds of contact—e.g., informal socializing, picnics, pack trips, activities involving children—that would be natural for nonresidents. Tribal leaders and game club managers were frequently appointed because of their wealth or influence, or to give them leadership experience. Badly out of touch with the needs of the average nonresident, such leaders, copying Chuck's flair for drama without his wisdom, often made decisions that were quite destructive. In one instance, all the tribes were dissolved and reformed, wiping out in one day networks of human relations that had taken months to develop. Underlying these immediate reasons is the basic fact that the Synanon foundation does not exist primarily for casually involved nonresidents. The nonresident club was created by Synanon as a source of donations and recruits for the inner circle of deeply involved members, and as a training ground in leadership for members of that inner circle. It is frequently a step-child, not provided much wise or positive leadership by Synanon, but on the other hand not allowed to move too far in directions that might be appropriate and natural for it, if these moves seemed to require even the slightest adaptation by Synanon. For example, at one point the game club began to develop an exchange program with the Esalen Institute, and one of Esalen's leaders did several hours of sensory awareness work with game club members. This work was very well received by the game club members, but apparently some of the residents in positions of authority in the club were threatened by it, and the exchange program gradually died out. Later, a Synanon copy did develop such an exchange program that was very satisfactory to it and Esalen. From one point of view, these criticisms are pointless; Synanon created the game club for the purposes mentioned above and owes it nothing. At the same time, it is possible to regret that Synanon did not give the club more autonomy and let it develop in directions natural for it—"start it and then get out of its way," to use a favorite Synanon phrase. It is quite possible that in the long run, such a policy would also have served the Synanon Foundation better, as well as creating a better game club. From a more self-reliant point of view, it is also a pity that some of us in the club did not seize such autonomy and create a club closer to our hearts' desire, even in the face of opposition from the foundation.

In addition to the above problems that follow from some of Synanon's policies, there are aspects of the life-style that many nonresidents find unpleasant. Most of these qualitative features spring from the fact that almost all Synanon members during its first few years were antisocial, character-disordered people, with histories of drug and alcohol abuse. Many of the life-style features developed appropriately for that group have persisted, often unnecessarily. The atmosphere is often frantic and pressured, with little time left for the individual to engage in solitary or artistic pursuits. This pressure and excessive group orientation are probably necessary for the recently addicted person, but are unpleasant impositions on the nonresident. There is often a crass and unbeautiful quality to Synanon life and a wholesale acceptance of some of the very values of the wider society (size for the sake of size, unrestrained pragmatism and materialism) that many nonresidents are trying to get away from. There is a distinct lack of attention to sensory awareness and physical grace and development. While it is true that the recently admitted ex-dope-fiend member probably could not handle strong sensuous feelings well, or be able to control symbolic physical aggression, it is a pity that some of the powerful techniques of physical contact therefore have been forbidden for the nonresidents.

In spite of all the creativity and intensity of Synanon, and regardless of the success it enjoys in its own unique development, it has not proved, and is not likely to prove, acceptable to large numbers of people who are looking for the kind of contact, community, and growth that seem to be promised by encounter groups. However, partly because Synanon *is* marching to a different drummer, it has developed, or stumbled on, some very valuable lessons for encounter groups. My goal in this chapter has been to present a description of Synanon sufficiently complete to allow the reader to see these contributions himself. I also want to spell out what I have learned from Synanon about three of the commonly stated goals of encounter groups—*insight, intimacy,* and *authenticity*—and about the frequent tendency in such groups to concentrate attention on *here-and-now feelings.*

Insight, or awareness, can lead to spontaneous behavior change in some people under some conditions. Since this method of change seems superficially so undemanding and certainly easier than the hard work of acting-as-if, many people are tempted to sit back and wait for the insight, avoiding action and involvement, and putting their energy into understanding why they cannot change instead of changing. Such insight addicts are legion. In Synanon's view, it is sounder to take the position that "the gods help those who help themselves"; it is safer to look on insight as an occasional gift that comes while I am doing my conscious best. In a game, "going for the insight" is viewed as a "cop-out," or avoidance of action.

Intimacy, love, and caring are precious states of being and feeling, as welcomed by Synanon people as any others. It seems, however, that real intimacy is not found by seeking and grasping directly; it seems too elusive for that. I view it almost as a by-product of the search for honesty. When I no longer feel I must hide parts of me—my guilty secrets—I seem to be able to look more directly at my fellows. When, in addition, I have expressed fully my anger and hatred. I seem freer to find and express love. Two men in Synanon whom I ended up liking very much I began by hating with a passion—and expressing my hate. I could always tell when a game had been particularly rough-and-tumble by the tendency of the participants in that game to stay together for coffee, and by the excited buzz over their table. Finally, there is something about the satisfaction of shared hard work that facilitates intimacy. One moment of close friendship for me was just before dawn, when a friend and I were frantically putting up the last booths for the Synanon fair. Synanon, then, provides the possibility for achieving some of the prerequisites of intimacy—honesty, a place to clear negative feelings out of the way, and something worth doing together.

Too frequently, when a person says he wants to be "authentic," he means he wants the freedom to retain his narrow, automatic way of doing things; he means "familiar." Synanon certainly discourages automatic, familiar, accustomed behavior, and many encounter group habitués who wandered into a game have complained bitterly that their authenticity was being blocked. (In that sense, the overprotective Jewish mamas are being authentic too.) Synanon feels that until a person truly has a choice, he cannot be authentic. A person meek out of cowardice is not "authentically meek": he is just a coward. When he *can* roar effectively, and *chooses* to be meek, that is another matter. I now authentically dislike prize fighting and selling tickets to prize fights; before, I could not. Synanon provides an opportunity to achieve the breadth, capacity, and flexibility that make authentic behavior possible, but on the way toward this state, much apparently "unauthentic" behavior is necessary.

The emphasis on *here-and-now feelings* is a frequent convention of encounter groups and, for some people at certain stages, a welcome relief from contrived politeness, dry intellectualizing, and boring tales of what happened when. The group that practices this way of being can be an exciting and rewarding place. However, I have come to see in Synanon how each of these emphases—here, now, and feelings—can become a way of avoiding dealing with difficult and important matters.

The preoccupation with *here* frequently leaves out other important people in my life, who know me far better than my group and with whom my relations are far more important. With practice, it becomes relatively easy to express feelings toward unimportant strangers with whom I have no ties and no commitment and, above all, who do not know how I behave the other 166 hours of the week. Many people learn the encounter role quite efficiently, trot it out for weekly use, and go right on acting (and acting out) the same way elsewhere. Synanon counters this tendency in several ways: by encouraging outside contact among members, by facilitating games between spouses and friends and coworkers, and by structuring the game to encourage bringing in relevant outside behavior. In Synanon my presentation of myself "here" is constantly checked against how I have acted elsewhere, and any discrepancies are seized upon with delight. I cannot act a role indefinitely, and so the game in time will see me as I am. Eventually, in spite of my best efforts, I might even see myself as I am.

The other danger of limiting myself to the here too long is the loss of wider goals and ends. My group may be a very exciting and accepting place, but if it becomes an end in itself for too long, I may end up devoting time and energy to it that I might wish in the long run had gone into something bigger than myself that I could be proudly part of. A person must stretch beyond himself and feel the wind in his face at some time in his life in order to be fully human; it would be sad if the delights and stimulation of the group replaced this stretching out and doing something in the world.

Now is from one point of view the only reality, and if I express the now fully it will contain all the relevant past. In practice, the emphasis on now lets me think I can avoid dealing with some uncomfortable and guilt-provoking matters in the past. I have seen husbands and wives particularly in therapy and encounter groups delude themselves that they could achieve a here-and-now honest relationship without revealing some old secrets.

A good game, when it is moving rapidly, is very much a here-and-now activity; anyone too concerned about past or future could not think/act nimbly enough to remain with the action. But it is taking place in a *context* that ensures spatial and temporal continuity of the game with the rest of life.

The expression of *feelings* is a frequent preoccupation of encounter groups. Many people seem almost not to know what they are feeling most of the time and have difficulty expressing even what they know, and so a place to practice and learn to experience/express their feelings is very valuable. In some sophisticated groups, however, the expression of feelings becomes almost the only focus of attention. When someone in such a group emits a particularly choice feeling, the effect is much like that of an operatic aria; all action stops while the feeling runs its course. Frequently it is followed by an admiring or critical discussion while the group is waiting for the next event.

The problem with this is that feelings, pleasant and unpleasant, exist primarily as the organism's ongoing evaluation of actions and events, not as ends in themselves. "Good" feelings occur with actions that are right for me; it is good for me to do this thing, be in this place, and so on. "Bad" feelings mean stop, leave this vicinity, and so forth. Feelings carried too far out of context are meaningless and distorted, produced for manipulation or as ends in themselves, for "kicks."

Synanon guards against the misuse and distortion of feelings in a group by providing *contexts*—social, behavioral, and moral. Because a person's fellow game players usually know him well in other settings, with any luck, someone in the game may have been present at the event about which he wants to discuss his feelings. If not, good game players will not let him talk very long about feelings without insisting on knowing factual details about the event. I remember one boy of 30 who went on at some length about how much he loved his girl, even though he felt she was doing him wrong. Almost accidentally (he was a smooth talker) it emerged that he rarely let a week go by without beating her up. He was told, of course, to cease at once or be expelled from the club. If a person is engaged in destructive behavior, who cares how he feels about it? The question worth discussing is how he justifies it morally. If it is seriously hurtful, we are not interested even in justifications, only in his stopping it. If he stops beating his girl, many interesting feelings will no doubt rise to fill the vacuum.

As mentioned, the game may err in the direction of oversuspicion of feelings. However, when strong here-and-now feelings come up that do not seem manipulative, the game is quite respectful.

I have discussed some of the lessons I have learned from Synanon that are directly relevant to encounter groups. More broadly, I have seen and felt the value for growth and living of a coherent philosophic basis for talk and action, and of *involvement* in a caring community, and in goals larger than the self. There is much about Synanon I have found personally unpleasant, and reject, but there is far more that is of enduring value. I hope I have, in a phrase commonly used in Synanon, "clapped both hands" and expressed both sides fully.

Bibliography

Austin, B. L. *Sad Nun at Synanon*. New York: Holt, Rinehart and Winston, 1970.

Casriel, D. *So Fair a House*. Englewood Cliffs, N.J.: Prentice-Hall, 1963.

Endore, G. *Synanon*. New York: Doubleday, 1968.

Enright, J. Synanon: A Challenge to Middle-Class Views of Mental Health. In D. Adelson and B. Kalis (eds.), *Community Psychology and Mental Health*. Scranton, Pa.: Chandler, 1970.

Morris, Desmond. *The Human Zoo*. New York: McGraw-Hill, 1969.

Synanon Pamphlets: #1 *The Human Sport* by G. Endore. #2 *Outrageous Impudence* by G. Endore. #3 *The Perpetual Stew* by G. Endore. #4 *The Trip* by B. Harrison. #5 *Synanon: The Learning Environment* by G. Endore. Available from Synanon Foundation.

Yablonsky, L. *The Tunnel Back: Synanon*. New York: Macmillan, 1965.

Daniel H. Casriel

9 The Daytop Story and the Casriel Method*

COMMENTARY

In the previous chapter, we have been introduced to the Synanon encounter groups. In this chapter, Dan Casriel discusses how he has built upon these groups and developed techniques and rationales for an intense experiential group confrontation and therapeutic consequences.

BIOGRAPHY

Daniel Harold Casriel was born in New York on March 1, 1924, and has been a psychiatrist engaged in private practice in this city since 1953. He is the founder (in 1964) and psychiatric-medical superintendent of Daytop Village, a residential drug treatment center described in the text. Among his other accomplishments are the following: since 1964, consulting psychiatrist to the Probation Department of the Second Judicial District of the New York State Supreme Court; since 1966, clinical associate professor at Temple University Medical School; since 1969, director of the Department of Psychiatry of GROW; he is a past president

* Printed by permission of the author.

of the American Society of Psychoanalytic Physicians; and the founder and psychiatric director of Areba (1970). He is the author of *So Fair a House*, published in 1963, as well as of numerous journal articles.

I want to talk about two things. One is the Synanon-Daytop concept of the "therapeutic community." The other is a new group process that has been evolving for the past five and one-half years and that successfully treats not only the problems of the drug addict but the total spectrum of neurotic and personality disorders.

Therapeutic communities are groups of people living together helping each other get well. Synanon, the first of these communities, is now about ten years old. Daytop, the program with which I am now affiliated, has been in existence for five years. Approximately seven and one-half years ago, I first visited Synanon during a tour I made to evaluate drug addiction throughout the country. At the time, I was on a research grant sponsored by the National Institute of Mental Health, and Synanon was the only group that I felt was doing anything significant about the problem of drug addiction. It was this feeling that impelled me to write a book— *So Fair a House: The Story of Synanon* —and to become an active supporter of Synanon, helping the organization to get established on the East Coast in Westport, Connecticut. But after two and one-half years, I broke off this relationship for several reasons and helped to found Daytop Lodge and Village on Staten Island in New York City.

The basic philosophic differences between Daytop and Synanon are, I believe, very significant. First, the problem of drug addiction is so huge that government funds are essential to cope with it. Public financing accounts for about 80 per cent of all the treatment, educational, and research programs going on throughout the country. Private foundations account for an additional 10 per cent, and individual contributions—the dimes, the dollars, the ten dollars—account for the remaining 10 per cent. Synanon, at the time when I left, refused to take government support because they felt this would lead to intolerable interference. I, however, felt that a lot of valuable time was being wasted in fund-raising rather than in dealing with more crucial issues. A second important factor was that Synanon became in time a "closed culture" where people could get rehabilitated, become free of drugs, and then stay to work in a community called Synanon City. Although this might be fine, it wasn't my prime interest. I felt that I wanted to rehabilitate the drug addict in order to get him back into the community.

These were two basic differences. The third difference lay in the fact that Synanon didn't pay its staff members, who, therefore, were beholden to the whims and wills of the administration, which, in those days, was Chuck Dederich. I felt that staff members never could really be mature and free under these conditions. At Daytop, the concept was that anyone who worked at a job would be paid. Both staffs, at Daytop and Synanon, had their hearts and souls invested in something that had given them new life and to which they were committed. With these points in mind, Daytop was born.

Daytop Lodge was the initial research program established by the New York State Supreme Court a little over five years ago. During that first year, we had our share of troubles. It was one thing to write about the theory and structure of a therapeutic community, and another to implement it on an hour-by-hour, day-by-day, week-by-week basis. Daytop Lodge amalgamated into Daytop Village, and the Village grew and thrived for about three and one-half years, but one and one-half years ago it stopped growing and thriving. During the first three and one-half years the population expanded to about two hundred, but in the past year and a half, it increased in size by only about 40. In the end there was a confrontation between myself and the board on the one side and the executive director, an ex-addict, on the other. He left, taking all his top-level staff and many of the younger people, but amazingly enough 40 of the people who were the second- and third-level echelon staff, who had been in Daytop from 18 months to four years, sided with the board and me. They remained. On December 2, 1968, we went back into Daytop, 41 of us. Five weeks later, I was happy to report we now had a population of 120. Fifteen weeks later, we were close to three hundred. We are able to absorb new people at the rate of about 15 to 20 a week, which is something we were never able to do previously. We have a better philosophy and a more dynamic program than ever, and I hope to see Daytop Villages spread over the country by the score during the next few years. What's happening? The residents are becoming aware of the therapeutic power of love. There is no longer purely a hostile encounter, but also sympathy and concern. The hostile confrontation, when a newcomer starts to act out negatively, isn't used anymore. The older residents and staff tell the new arrival, in effect, that they are in charge and they will teach him how to do things the right way. And if he does something the wrong way, he will get called down for it. But basically the message is: "We are concerned about you. Somebody saved our lives and we want to save yours. If you don't want to save your life, that is your problem, but give us a chance. We want to help; it makes us feel better."

As a result, very few are leaving. We used to expect about 40 or 50 per cent departures, with 25 per cent of them leaving in the first day, 25 per cent the first week, 25 per cent the first month, and 25 per cent later on but before they were completely cured. We now have a "split" rate of less than 50 per cent of what it was, and of those who leave more than half return. We expect a holding power of over 80 per cent. Of the 99 residents who graduated, 92 are known to be functioning productively without crime or drugs, two have lost contact, and five have relapsed into addiction.

The original Daytop Lodge was funded by the National Institute of Mental Health and controlled by the New York State Supreme Court, Department of Probation, Second Judicial District. The Daytop project was a five-year study in which the Supreme Court would select 125 felons from among the cases pending before it and put them at random into five different types of groups, including one control group. The plan was to count, after five years, the number of drug-free days that each group of people had during that period. Urine tests would be administered both to the Daytop group and to a second group of 25, who were put on probation and followed by a specially trained probation officer. Their urine would be tested to see if the knowledge of such testing would be a deterrent to taking heroin. A third group of 25 was to be assigned to another probation officer without urine-testing. A fourth group was to be placed with a probation officer who, at that time, had about two hundred probationers on his list. These 25 would be just thrown in with the other people and would be given urine tests. The fifth group, the control group, would consist of 25 people placed in the average case load of two hundred given to a probation officer. That five-year program was finished November 1, 1968.

The residents of Daytop are almost all previous hard-core heroin addicts. Daytop is supported by the state. It is free to residents of New York State. About 75 per cent of the Daytop population are what I call "primary" addicts. These are addicts who have grown up in the lower social and economic areas of the city, and who have never developed a meaningful life-style or a significant human relationship. The other 25 per cent I call "secondary" addicts. They usually develop drug addiction a little later in life. They have finished more schooling and have had more of a normal, middle-class life pattern. They might have been married and have developed some significant relationships that they were unable to maintain. They generally have had some sort of job or vocation, sometimes highly skilled. *Hard core* refers to addicts whose life pattern has been for at least one year exclusively centered around heroin. *Soft core* refers to people addicted to heroin for only one or two years, who have not in that time given up all other vestiges of normal living.

About five years ago, when I started my first therapeutic groups in private practice, they were based on a Synanon type of provocative encounter. These groups have since evolved into what I believe to be a totally new process that I call a "third generation" of group process.

The first generation of therapeutic groups arose as an extension of individual psychotherapy during World War II, simply because the overworked psychiatrist didn't have enough time to meet the tremendous demands of the neuropsychiatric casualties that were flooding the hospitals at the time. Because of these demands, psychiatrists extended the principles of individual psychotherapy into a group process. To a great extent this is the process still applied, with modification, by most of the professionals using "group therapy" today.

About a dozen years later, after the initial experiences of group therapy had been absorbed, a new generation of groups evolved called the encounter behavioral groups, which are the ones Synanon typifies. An encounter group is a provocative verbal confrontation by each member of the group with any other member of the group. When I first was exposed to this type of group, I was so stimulated by its apparent effectiveness that, after experiencing and taking part in the process for about a year, I established encounter groups for my patients in psychoanalysis and psychotherapy. The results from those groups were quite startling. People progressed more quickly in a few sessions than they had in weeks and months of analysis. I began to see a different perspective. My groups, however, didn't stay like the Synanon type of group. I'm not an ex-addict and my patients were not ex-addicts. I had been a middle-class neurotic and my patients were middle-class neurotics. I, therefore, amalgamated the behavioral confrontation of Synanon with the psychoanalytic introspection that I had learned and that my patients were experiencing. A totally new qualitative difference gradually started to emerge in the groups about two years ago, which resulted in a flood of new insights, for both myself and my patients.

About four years ago, I noticed that group sessions never seemed to last long enough. There was just never enough time to get some people to respond. Daytop lent itself to experimentation, and so we established longer and longer periods there. Groups started to go from an hour and a half, to two hours, to five hours, to ten hours, and one day, lo and behold, the director came and said, "You know, we had a group that lasted into the morning. And something very dramatic happened around dawn. It was like a new birth or a new day; it was just sort of very beautiful!" I requested this extended group session for the entire Daytop Community, and my version of a marathon group was born. I found that after 15 or 18 hours a very close, warm feeling settled into the group. The new element, which was not labeled, has become recognized basically as love and concern. The marathons have now been going on for over three years, and they have become more and more efficient and more and more effective. What people felt in the marathons they carried back into my group process, and today, my two-hour groups are like a marathon—very emotionally intense.

Thus, I was forced, gradually, to re-evaluate classical theory and adaptational psychodynamics in order to understand what was happening. People such as addicts, homosexuals, and others with severe character disorders who, on a theoretical level, weren't supposed to be getting well were getting well. And they were responding in months. Professional literature had suggested that if they could get well, it would take many years. I had to start to develop a new theory to account for the success of my clinical process. As a starting point, I used Adaptational Psychodynamics, which is the name of the major modification of freudian psychodynamics taught at Columbia University's Psychoanalytic Clinic for Training and Research, to try to understand what was happening. I then proceeded to modify that theory until a new theory as well as a new process evolved.

First, in my present theory, I accept the fact that all motivation is based on the pursuit of pleasure or the avoidance of pain. People react to pain, the classical therapists say, in one of two ways: by flight or fight, fear or anger. I hypothesized a third way of reacting to pain: isolation by withdrawal. Individuals who react to pain or danger with the defense mechanism called isolation are those people whom psychiatrists consider "character disorders." A neurotic attempts to cope with pain or danger primarily by either running in fear or fighting in anger. To control the excessive fear and/or anger, the neurotic personality will develop certain symptoms that are ego alien, something the person doesn't like, such as dissociative, obsessive-compulsive, and conversion reactions, phobias, hysteria, depressions and other character disorders. The character disorder then in turn reinforces the initial isolation through some encapsulating device or "shell," which creates further isolation. This encapsulating "shell" may be heroin, alcohol, barbiturates, amphetamines, or any other mind-affecting chemicals, or it can be the shell of homosexuality, of criminality, or of nonfunctioning. It also may be the shell of overwork—or anything else that keeps a person away from close human interaction. Now, by this new simple theory, the treatment of the drug addict at Daytop and the character-disordered person anywhere becomes quite simple and understandable.

At Daytop, there are two cardinal rules—no physical violence and no chemicals of any kind—and, by inference, no other shells under which to hide (there are no locked doors, you can't isolate yourself, you can't remove yourself from human confrontation). By those two basic rules, we effectively eliminate two of the three ways that all human beings react to stress or danger. They can't fight in anger and they can't withdraw into isolation. There is only one thing they can do, and that is to react with fear. Fear can cause people to react in two ways. They can run out the door, or they can stay to confront their fear. Those who stay do so for two reasons. First, what's waiting for them on the outside is jail, starvation, death, or disease. The second reason they stay is because of overwhelming identification. They see around them only people with whom they shot dope. They sort of trust another individual member, thinking, "He is one of those dope fiends just as I am, and he is not going to give me away." So initially they stay because they feel an identification. When addicts enter Daytop they are given two proscriptions, as I have said, things they cannot do. If they stay they are given two prescriptions, things they have to accept. These are: "Go through the motions" and "Act as if." To "go through the motions and to act as if" means that you do as you are told, and if you don't know how to do it, act as if you *do* know how, and we will tell you when you are wrong. This is basically a type of retraining developed by the "behavioral" school of psychology. The behaviorists use this type of retraining to combat negative behavior and to accentuate positive behavior. If you act a certain way, you will start to think a certain way, and finally you will start to feel a certain way. But it isn't quite that simple. You also have to be confronted simultaneously on your behavior, your attitudes, and your emotions.

Analysts have developed a technique of confrontation—the treatment process of psychoanalysis and modifications of psychoanalysis. Behaviorists range all the way from very simplistic systematic, almost mechanical techniques to complex living experiences such as those at Daytop. If you ask an analyst about the behaviorists, he will say they are very superficial, but if you ask a behaviorist about analysts, he says they analyze their belly buttons for seven years while the patient and his world are coming apart. It is not an effective or efficient process. If you ask the existentialist about either one, he will say they are both wrong. He maintains that human beings are different from animals; they have a language and can think and articulate. Therefore, you can confront a human being with his thoughts, his logic, and his rational understanding, which will in turn change his behavior and his feelings. The truth is that all three schools are right (and wrong). Nobody gets well unless he changes all three areas: his attitudes, his acts, and his feelings. He has to change his ABC's: affects, behavior, and cognition.

In psychiatry, there are three general types of people whom psychiatrists deal with: the psychotics, the neurotics, and those with character disorders. To me, if somebody is psychotic it means he has a metabolic or biochemical imbalance; he is a schizophrenic or a manic-depressive and he needs some sort of medication. The neurotic, as I have mentioned, uses flight and/or fight as his major mechanisms of defense. The person with a character disorder uses isolation.

The difference clinically between a neurotic and a person with a character disorder is that one is in emotional pain and the other is not. It's the difference between a person with an acute toothache and a person with rotten teeth. The person with an acute toothache feels hurt; that tooth pain won't let him alone. He has to see his dentist because he is hurting. The person with rotten teeth, on the other hand, although his teeth are decaying in his mouth and he might lose all of them, does not feel pain. As long as it doesn't hurt, he says, "Well, I know my teeth are bad (my personality is decaying) and they're ceasing to function, but it doesn't hurt, and if I try to do something about it, they'll hurt me; so I'll keep away." Every once in a while, you get a person with a character disorder who gets an "acute toothache." He comes running and screaming and says, "Doctor, do something. Save my life: I'm dying." The drug addict who gets caught, like the homosexual who breaks up with his boyfriend, is very depressed, very upset, and very anxious and comes in imploring, "Do something. I'm in terrible pain." But as soon as the immediate situation clears up or passes, he drops out of treatment.

In addition to the three major classes of personality I further divide people into four levels of personality integration: adult, adolescent, child, and infant. Now, what's the difference between an adult neurotic, for instance, and an infantile neurotic? An adult neurotic will come in to me as a psychiatrist and say, "Doctor, I don't know what's wrong. I've got a job, I'm married, everything seems to be going all right, but I'm depressed. I don't really enjoy life anymore. I have a slight feeling of tension. I don't sleep well. I just don't feel happy. Can you help me help myself? Will you try to help me understand myself so that by my understanding I can try to do something to help myself?" An infantile neurotic usually comes in or is brought in by a husband or parent or friend and finally says, "Oh Doctor, I think you are God. You are wonderful. Here I am. Cure me." The implication is, "I'll be your slave; I'll pray to you; I'll worship you; you do it for me. I am helpless; I am incapable of helping myself." The one between, the adolescent, comes in and says, "I don't know what the hell I am doing here. I think you are full of crap. But they told me to come, and I've got pains in my belly; so here I am, but I defy you to help me."

The same is true of persons with character disorders. The typical adult type of character disorder affects the successful businessman who doesn't seem to have any problems. He is very successful. He comes home at night, kisses his wife, pats his kid on the head, turns on the television, eats, and goes to bed. Twice a week, like clockwork, he has intercourse with his wife, and he is happy. It's his wife who comes in very depressed and says, "Doctor, I don't know what's the matter. My husband is a very successful businessman. He is nice to me. He doesn't drink, gamble, or run around with other women. But I just don't enjoy life. I'm very depressed. I can't seem to communicate with him. He doesn't seem to have any feelings. And I keep asking him, 'Why don't you communicate with me? Why don't you talk to me?' and he answers,

'What have I got to talk to you about? You're nice, I enjoyed the meal. Now, let's watch television.' And when I complain to my girlfriend, she thinks I'm crazy. Bill is a wonderful guy, and I just don't know what it is, but I'm terribly unhappy."

I used to put the wife in analysis. After six months or a year, or a year and a half, I found out that she really didn't have any human, emotional communication with her husband. It was like living with a roommate whom she went to bed with twice a week. When she became aware that this was what was happening, she started to make forceful demands on her husband. She openly expressed angry feelings toward him, and pretty soon Bill would come in and say, "Doctor, what the hell did you do to my wife? It's true she is no longer depressed, but now she is impossible to live with. She is a raving maniac, and all she tells me is to see Dr. Casriel and go into treatment and get into analysis, because we have no communication and no relationship. I don't know what the hell she is talking about." And I would say, "Well, she is talking about the lack of communication." He might respond, "What the hell do you mean? I do talk to her."

He comes back a second time, perhaps, and announces, "The only way she will let me alone is if I go into treatment." Well, in those days I would never treat a husband and wife together. So, either I would send him to a colleague or I would discharge his wife, put him into treatment, and get him on the couch three or four times a week. By the third visit, he would say, "Boy, Doctor, this is great. My wife is off my back. Things are wonderful at home. This is wonderful!" After about three months he would inquire, "Doctor, are you getting anything out of this?" I would say, "No." He would say, "Well, I'm sure not, and the purpose for which I came in is accomplished. She is happy and I'm happy; so let's call it finished." And I would reluctantly agree, saying, "I think you are right," but knowing nothing was really resolved. About three months later his wife would come back again, depressed. She would tell me, "He is just as bad as he was before." I would say, "Madam, he can't be treated, and you've got one of three choices: You can live with it; you can get a divorce; or you can go your own way and do what you want." The truth of the matter is that analysis is really effective only for the adult neurotic and sometimes for the adolescent type of neurotic. But anybody with lower personality integration than this or any character disorder is very hard to help by the classical methods of analysis.

I found in the marathons that no matter what symptoms a person came in with, whether they were drug addiction, homosexuality, anxiety, marital problems, work problems, social problems, phobias, or depression, the basic problem that everyone has is the common denominator of the inability to accept love. The second most difficult problem is the inability to express anger and to feel one's pain. The third most difficult problem is the inability to accept anger without fear or pain. The least difficult problem is the inability to give love. Anger, fear, love, and pain are the emotions that cause all the trouble. I have theorized a structure about this that to me makes a great deal of sense, and from which I can start to treat a person whose history I don't even know, whose name I don't even know. First I focus on the basic pain-pleasure balance, which is related to the early significant human relationship: the relationship of the small child to the significant adult, whether that significant adult is mother, father, aunt, or maid. The significant factor is the child's relationship to the person (or persons) who meets his needs.

If, in his state of dependent helpless reality, the pain outweighs the pleasure that the child experiences, or if he must go through too much pain to get his pleasure, the child sooner or later rejects that human relationship. He says, "It isn't worth it; I'll do it myself; I'll do it as quickly as I can by myself." He isolates himself from this significant human relationship. I call these people the rejectors, because they basically reject this relationship that has been too painful. The amount of love they have gotten wasn't worth the pain and frustration to be able to get food, or to get their diapers changed. They just had to cry too loud or long; they were too uncomfortable; their mother was too irritable, and they basically felt, "The hell with it; it isn't worthwhile." They learned very early in life to isolate themselves and to feel that a human relationship is more painful than pleasurable.

There are others who feel that no matter how painful a relationship is, the pleasure is just a little more. Or perhaps the person feels too helpless in isolation. But whatever the factors (and I am sure there may be myriads of them, genetic and others), the person accepts that human relationship, no matter how painful it is, because he cannot escape his dependent needs, and he feels the relationship is the best way or only way to have these needs taken care of (pleasure). I call these people the acceptors.

We now have, on what I call a basic identity level, a person who is either an acceptor, who needs and accepts and maintains a human relationship no matter what the price, or a rejector, who withdraws and keeps himself out of a significant human relationship, no matter what the price. The rejectors can, for instance, have affairs and even get married. A rejector who gets married can't really accept a human relationship or love. If he doesn't accept love in a marriage, or the significance of somebody loving him, he starts to feel trapped in that marriage. He feels he is giving and not getting anything in return. The reason he is not getting anything is that he won't let anything come in. He becomes irritable and annoyed about marriage and further isolates himself and withdraws. The acceptor, on the other hand, maintains that relationship no matter, for example, how much she gets beaten, or, if the acceptor is a male, no matter how much his wife cheats on him or lies to him.

Surrounding the identity level is what I call the dynamic level. On this level I have found there are four basic feelings that one deals with: love, pain, fear, and anger. There are two basic emotional vectors that we may use to confront our feelings. One is love and the other is anger. What was so therapeutic about the Synanon type of attack therapy was that it confronted human beings with anger. It broke through their shells. But that isn't enough; it's only half the story, because there is nothing therapeutic about anger except its capacity to open a person up so that he can change. Only love is curative. To be really able to grow and mature one needs to have love.

In my groups we have practiced exercising, enforcing, and expressing these four feelings. I found, as we progressed, that feelings can have different levels of intensity. Let me give you an example: anger. I have found that there are four levels of anger. When I first got into the Synanon groups, I used to hear the participants really scream in murderous rage, and I thought, "My God, they must really be emotionally well." Coming from a middle-class neurotic background, I could never get this type of anger out; so I assumed they were well, because here I was anxious, while they could get that anxiety out and become angry. But I noticed that after a year or two years, they were still screaming angrily and I was still anxious; so I decided they weren't any better off than I was.

More recently I have noticed in the marathons that something was happening to rage. A deeper level of anger set in. I was now able to classify the levels of anger into four levels. It is only the fourth level that is therapeutic. The first level is "intellectual" anger quietly thought and expressed. When the second level of anger comes out in a loud scream, you can hear it in a person's throat, sort of mixed with anxiety. I call it riddance anger, because it always comes out, "Get away; I've got to get away from it," or "They have got to get away from me. *Get away from me!*" The third level is even deeper, and it comes out in your chest; I call it murderous rage because it is the type of anger that wants to kill: "*Let me at him, I hate him!*"

Individuals have to feel that third level before they can get to the fourth level. They have to feel secure enough for that third type of anger in order to feel the fourth level, which I call "identity anger." People feel it in their belly, and it comes out as a feeling that "I'm angry because I've been hurt; it wasn't fair what happened to me, God-dammit, and I'm angry. I'm angry and nobody is going to do that to me again; no more. I'm not going to let *anybody* do that to me. *No more;*

no more!" You feel it in your total body, and you feel aware of a total you, a total whole identity. You can then become aware that you are entitled to be loved without pain. You really are entitled to be loved without paying a huge price. It comes out, "I am really lovable. I am lovable because I am me. I am just lovable. I was lovable from the moment I was born, and if somebody doesn't love me I can find someone else who will. Also, I am *entitled* to be loved *without* getting A's. I am entitled to be loved without climbing ropes or doing tricks. I'm entitled to be loved without having to pay in blood, or pain, or sweat. I'm just entitled to be loved."

In addition to the levels of emotions, there are various areas that these emotions are expressed in, anxiety for instance. If somebody attempts to express anxiety or pain in my group, it depends on what level he is at, and I can pick it up very quickly. If a person says, "Oh, poor me. You know Johnny left me," or "Betty left me," or "I just lost my job, poor me," people who know him tell him, "Knock it off; stop feeling sorry for yourself; stop babying yourself." They tell him to "knock off" that type of anxiety, a symptomatic anxiety expressing itself at a symptom level. We do not deal with symptoms. Knock off the symptom —whether it is drugs, alcohol, or anxiety—and get down to the problem. But if an individual simply says, "I've been hurt," he is not asking for sympathy or support. He is just asking for empathy as a human being. "I've been hurt; let me share my pain with you. You are not responsible for my pain. You don't have to do anything for my pain. Just let me share my pain with you, and I'll let you share your pain with me." As human beings we can share our pain and not really be irresponsible because we all are inevitably responsible to do things for ourselves. But it feels good; it's nice to know that there is someone there who understands and who is concerned. We become aware that we have value and can be loved for ourselves.

We help people exercise feeling on the "dynamic" level whether it is fear, anger, pain, or need for love. And on this level, we can help them really to scream out as loud and as strong and as full as they can. And suddenly, or gradually, you find a person getting into what I call his identity level.

Now the interesting thing about the rejector is that he has learned to program anxiety internally. He knows how to "take it by himself," to run his own life, to cope with tension, and to work on his own. He establishes his own pleasure, by himself, and he really never trusts or enjoys the love of another human being. He just enjoys his own accomplishments. If somebody pays him a compliment, he says, "That's nice," but it sort of rolls off his shoulders. He doesn't really absorb another person's love or concern for him. When the rejector becomes aware of the total isolation he has lived in all his life, and that he really has been devoid of love, he feels a tremendous amount of pain. The last time he felt that pain was long, long, ago. But he has to feel that pain now in order to experience the love of other human beings.

On the other hand, the person who is an acceptor, who can't conceive of living a life apart from another significant human being, has learned to accept and handle pain. She is always in pain. She is suffering, and when she isn't suffering she will seek ways to suffer. She would rather experience a tremendous amount of pain than the defensive anticipation of pain, anxiety, or fear that she feels in isolation. Fear and anxiety truly panic her. She has never learned to handle or resolve these feelings. When she finally starts to realize that anxiety won't help her, that she can really live in this world as a separate self-respecting human being with her own identity, she feels a tremendous amount of freedom, and she says, "My God, I don't have to accept pain anymore to live," or "I am, I exist, fear won't kill me, and the assertion of my own individual identity will not make other significant human beings disappear or be angry and reject me."

What is a healthy person? He is one who can expect love without the fear or anticipation of pain or danger, just as he can cross a street without the expectation of getting hit by a car. A person who crosses a street knows there is danger in crossing a street. Similarly, a healthy individual, in getting involved in a significant human relationship, knows that there is some potential danger in that relationship. When a man who crosses the street finds midway that there is too much traffic and danger, he runs back to the safety of the sidewalk. In the same manner, a healthy person who starts to establish a human relationship and finds it getting too painful or dangerous gives it up and starts again at a better time.

One interesting thing about my treatment process is that we never discuss symptoms. Let me give you an example. In previous years if a homosexual would have come to me, I would have accepted from my training the idea that he is very rarely curable or treatable. If he were treatable if might require six, seven, eight, or nine years of analysis to cure him. I usually would get a homosexual who came to me because Peter just left him. His beautiful relationship with the man of his dreams just broke up and he was terribly unhappy. He used to come to me and say, "Oh Doctor, I feel so miserable; this boy I am madly in love with just left me." And I would say, "Poor Johnny, tell me all about it." And Johnny would tell me all about Peter and the relationship with Peter and draw out the details of his homosexual relationship. I would half listen and half not want to listen. And then I would say, "Well, tell me how this all started." Then he would tell me that he had a tyrannical mother and an absent father, or a tyrannical father and an overprotective mother. After about six months of this and one hundred hours on the couch, he would come in all "bright-eyed and bushy-tailed," and he would say, "Oh, Doctor, you have helped me so much; I feel so good, I found a new Peter and I am going away to California with him and he is wonderful."

Now it is different. Now I get the same type of fellow coming in for the same reason, but I say, "I am not interested in your Peter, and in your depression," and he is very upset. He says, "Aren't you a psychiatrist?" And I reply, "Yes, but I am not interested in your symptoms." He inquires, "What do you mean, 'my symptoms'?" I ask, "Do you want to get well?" He replies, "What do you mean, 'Do I want to get well?'" I respond, "Would you like to be heterosexual in terms of your thinking, your behavior, and your feelings?" And he answers, "Well, that can't be done." Or, "No, I like homosexuality. What's wrong with it? Why, are you prejudiced against homosexuals?" I tell him, "I don't care if you sleep with a sheep. If you are happy, fine. But if you want to come in, I can't get you well from nine to five and have you act out sick from five to nine. I can get you well if you want to." He asks, "What does that mean?" I explain, "That means you can be heterosexual in terms of your feelings, your thinking, your attitude, your dreams, and your performance, which will change to become much more productive."

About 90 per cent are curious enough to inquire, "What do I have to do?" And I tell them, "There is an old song you have to remember: 'You've Got to Accentuate the Positive, Eliminate the Negative, Latch on to the Affirmative and Don't Mess with Mister in Between,'" and I stress that this is important. I say, "Don't tell me in three months you just got a new job as a towel boy in the men's room. I don't want to hear that." So he asks, "What do I have to do?" I tell him, "You've got to stop acting homosexually and you've got to start acting heterosexually. Then come into our groups and tell us what you think and feel about it."

If he is basically adolescent, he will think, "This Goddam Casriel! I don't know what the hell he is trying to make me do. I don't believe him anyway." If he is sort of a child, he will feel, "Oh poor me. He is making me give up the only little joy I've got and now I have nothing." And it is usually one of those. What happens? He goes into the group and the first people he meets are ex-homosexuals. They will say, "We know how it is with Peter. We went through it." And he will inquire, "Are you really heterosexual?" They answer, "Yup." He asks, "Well, how do you do it?" They explain, "Just do what we are told to do; start dating a girl." He remarks, "Yes, but I don't enjoy girls." He is told, "Well, date them anyway, and go to bed with them, and come in and talk about the way you feel after you go to bed with them."

He comes in a few days, maybe a week or so later, and states, "Well,

I went to bed, but I didn't feel anything; nothing happened." And so they point out, "You know, if somebody had a gun at your head would anything happen? What would you do if somebody said, 'Get an erection or we will pull the trigger?' You'd say, 'Pull the trigger.' " He also starts to evaluate his distortions of what a man is. He becomes aware that his concept of a man isn't a man at all. Some of the misconceptions homosexuals can reveal "in their belly," not in their head, when they get confronted with them are that a man can have instant erection, his penis is about three feet long, he can put a woman into bed and give her thirty-seven thousand orgasms, and he leaves her in a pool of sweat unable to move a finger. He can get up and his chest size is about 97, and he will scream and run like Tarzan, and that is a man. At that point, the group breaks down, and some member says, "My God. I've been going to bed with my wife for 16 years. Don't tell her this; she is lucky if I do it once a week." Maybe it is a little more subtle than that, but the homosexual does start to abandon some of his distorted fantasies.

I have used homosexuality as an example because it is dramatic. It really doesn't make any difference whether the problem is just a mild depression or anxiety or what most people come in with—the inability to develop a significant, close human relationship. If a person does not feel lovable, he cannot accept love, and he cannot believe that anybody could love him. The feeling is, "If he loves me, he must be an idiot. How can I love him?" Or, "He doesn't really love me. He wants me for my body." A man feels, "She wants my money. She just wants to get married." Or, "They really don't know me very well. I had better run before they get to know me." You see the same patterns over and over and over again.

What does all this mean? I would like to see this group encounter process offered in schools from first grade to college. If we were to have this process in every school we would reduce emotional sickness dramatically. Young people would really be in touch with their feelings and know who they are and what they are, and what they have to do for themselves, and what they are entitled to do for themselves. I feel that this could be genuinely feasible because it is relatively easy. The entire process takes about six months to a year for rehabilitation and about another 90 hours to learn enough so one can teach it—it is really quite simple.

Part C

Innovations

Harold S. Streitfeld

10 The Aureon Encounter: An Organic Process

COMMENTARY

Introducing the section on innovations is Hal Streitfeld's chapter on the Aureon encounter. This encounter emphasizes the role of the body and incorporates principles from Gestalt therapy, Eastern philosophy, and meditation exercises. Presented with various rationales, the reader is provided with vibrant examples of how such techniques occasion dramatic group interaction.

BIOGRAPHY

Harold S. Streitfeld is founder and director of Aureon Institute in New York City, a growth center in the Human Potential Movement, the first in the East. He received his Ph.D. in clinical psychology from the University of Chicago in 1952. The giving and receiving of psychotherapy —psychoanalysis circa 1946, Gestalt therapy circa 1954, bioenergetic analysis circa 1961—have been his dominant occupation and preoccupation. Now he is mainly interested in bringing his 25 years of learning and experience in this field to bear on normal neurotics in encounter groups, to the masses in microlabs and on television, to his fellow professionals through demonstration and writing. Besides this article—his first attempt to set forth a theory about what he is doing—he is coauthor of a book entitled *Growth Games* published by Harcourt, Brace, and Jovanovich in 1971.

Inspired by Esalen, I founded Aureon Institute in the spring of 1967. Its stated purpose was to make available on an experiential basis to both the general public and the professional community the techniques, findings, and philosophies of leaders in the humanities, the arts, and the sciences. My personal aim at that time was to integrate the various approaches to the body that I had been separately exploring for 20 years.

To that end, Betty Keene (a foremost disciple of Charlotte Selver) and I offered a combined workshop on sensory awareness and bioenergetic analysis in April, 1968. In subsequent workshops, I introduced other body approaches and, to enlarge the framework, invited "body people" such as Ann Halprin, Albert Pesso, Mary Whitehouse, Ida Rolf, and Irmgard Bartenieff to Aureon. My role at these workshops varied from leader, to coleader, to participant.

I soon began to experiment on my own with combining body approaches and encounter techniques. From these experiments emerged the Aureon encounter, which, beginning in September, 1968, was offered on a monthly basis. Like a pupil who studies history in one class and philosophy in another before he can integrate his knowledge into a world view, my first efforts were compartmentalized. Although it was initially necessary to isolate the various approaches and work with them one at a time, my ultimate goal during those 18 months of exploration and experimentation was to achieve a true synthesis of these various methods.

By the fall of 1969, I was able to formulate the following description:

> The Aureon encounter draws upon diverse approaches to therapy and encounter, fusing them into a unique and truly organic process that is characterized by structure and flexibility. Each step in the growth of the individual and the group follows a natural sequence, which begins with a series of warm-up games or exercises designed to open up feelings. Attention is then focused on an individual who wishes to work on a feeling, or who appears to be "sitting on" one. By methods that arise naturally from the circumstances, the participant's feeling is brought to the surface, expressed as fully as possible, and resolved to his satisfaction. The resolution of anger, fear, love, sorrow, or more subtle emotions may be accomplished by manual work on body blocks, fantasy trips, communication games, encounter, ritual drama, or any one

of a number of techniques, including those created on the spot by the group.

When the feeling has been satisfactorily resolved, the group offers feedback—a process that at once rounds out the experience for the volunteer and also reveals a new feeling in someone else that has arisen from the emotional intensity of the preceding situation. This feeling, in turn, is worked on and brought to a natural conclusion. The cycle of feeling/resolution/feedback/feeling repeats itself in an ever widening network that ultimately embraces each participant, transforming a cluster of separate individuals into a cohesive entity capable of spontaneously coordinated actions and responses, yet free enough to permit individual autonomy.

Description of an Actual Aureon Encounter

To put some flesh on the "bones" of the preceding description, I will recapitulate an actual encounter that took place in October, 1969. Although it is not completely representative, this encounter has the virtue of having been taped and photographed. Present as participant-observers were a writer and a photographer from a national magazine who were assigned to cover the encounter. (The article never appeared in print.)

There is a group screening procedure for participation in Aureon workshops. However, the participants in this instance were notified of the unusual circumstances. Those attending agreed to sign releases. Besides the two magazine people, the group contained ten other participants: two married couples, one married woman, three single men, and two single women. Their ages ranged from the twenties to the late forties. Six participants had never been in an encounter group; three had participated in previous Aureon workshops. With a professor of English literature, a college English teacher, and two professional writers, the group had an unusually literary dimension. Finally, my co-leader was Martha Orrick, an encounter group leader in church work who has a special interest in Tai Chi and meditation.

The workshop took place in a lounge on the thirty-third floor of a Manhattan office building. Like all previous Aureon encounters, it started at 10:00 Saturday morning and concluded early Sunday evening. Our meals were taken together in nearby restaurants. There was a break from 11:30 Saturday evening until 10:00 Sunday morning.

Martha and I did some planning before the workshop. She agreed to begin the workshop with a demonstration of Tai Chi, a Chinese gymnastic form of movement and meditation. After the demonstration, the group was asked to pair off so that we could experience some of the Tai Chi techniques under Martha's guidance.

When the group was warmed up, we sat on the floor in a circle and each person gave his first name and offered one statement about himself. I asked the group if they had any feelings about where we were holding the encounter or about being photographed or written up by the magazine. When these feelings had been expressed and worked through, each person was asked in turn what he or she hoped to get out of the week end.

Because space does not permit a detailed examination of the entire workshop as it unfolded, I will summarize the sequence of events during the first day and then closely describe a crucial experience that took place just before dinner.

It is my practice to follow up on feelings as they arise in the group. I worked first with Andrew, who, in introducing himself, had said that he wanted to "get his batteries recharged." In contrast to his statement, he appeared as charged up as a race horse at the starting gate. It seemed to me that he needed to *discharge* some of this energy. I encouraged him to move, and he elected to run around the group, hopping

Figure 10-1. Mobilizing feelings of sadness. (Photo by Zev Guber.)

over our legs. Next, I turned my attention to Harriet, who had many feelings of dissatisfaction. In an encounter with Jim, she was able to mobilize her sadness. I also worked with Bill, who was shy and quiet, helping him to make contact with the other participants. Finally, I brought Phillip, whose wisecracks were continually cutting off the sad feelings of others, onto center stage. I touched upon his underlying despair and his suicidal fantasies, which his recent divorce had intensified. Though he got into the feeling, he continually choked off the sobs that arose in him. The room was quiet.

Figure 10-2. At the height of her mystical experience. (Photo by Gary Madderom.)

Diane, who was lying on the floor, was the first to speak. She said she felt detached. I felt an image rise up in me of her being levitated, and I suggested that she be rocked. The entire group lifted her up and rocked her. Diane, who for the past three years had been practicing yoga, was able to let go and take the experience all in. When the group began to feel the strain of holding her, I got on my hands and knees beneath her to support her weight while the group continued to rock her. Unlike many people, Diane permitted herself to breathe very deeply and fully as she was being rocked. I, too, was breathing quite deeply, and I could feel energy currents passing through me.

After a while, I slid flat on the ground, face down, and the group lowered Diane onto my back. When, finally, we both sat up, something very unusual occurred: Diane began to undulate her back in wavelike motions. She talked about kundalini yoga, telling us she could feel the energy moving up her back. We could almost see it shooting out of her eyes, which were bright and sparkling. When she was speaking, I kept looking deeply into her eyes and breathing along with her. Then we locked eyes, and I remember a strong upsurge of energy into my head. The group was spellbound as we silently sat there for several minutes. Then, spontaneously, Diane began to chant, "Ommmmmmmmmmmmmmm," in a deep, vibrant voice. (Tom, who had heard many such chants, later told me he had never before heard Om intoned like that.) We all picked up the sound, chanting with her.

Figure 10-3. Funeral pyre. (Photo by Gary Madderom.)

Just as her Om had arisen spontaneously, so it gradually faded away. When it was gone, I brought Diane back into contact by asking her to look into all our eyes. After she came out of her trancelike state, she suddenly remarked, with sudden insight, "All of this mystical crap— it's really just energy moving through your body."

According to Houston, Hatha Yoga "incorporates the practices of posture regulation, breathing exercises and meditation. . . . Its ultimate aim is to arouse what is called *kundalini,* a universal vital energy which [starts] at the base of the spine. . . . It is claimed that if this energy can be directed to the head center, a mystical state is attained and the yogi becomes aware of a mystical unitive consciousness."[1] As a result of her psychedelic research, Houston makes a distinction between mystical and religious experiences, the former having to do with the dissolution of personal depths into the transpersonal (becoming one with the Other), while the latter one has a confrontation with the Other (variously described as God or Fundamental Reality). According to this distinction, it would seem that Diane had a mystical experience.

Although everyone had been caught up in Diane's experience while it was happening, a number of people could not make sense out of what they had seen once the tension decreased. In the ensuing discussion, the group split over whether or not they thought Diane had had a mystical experience. Andrew accused me of trying to put something over the group until, in reviewing the sequence of events, he became aware that I hadn't deliberately set up the experience. Although Andrew could deal rationally with Diane's behavior and his reaction to it, Mary, on on the other hand, reacted like a child whose entire conception of the world had been shaken. Of all the group, she, in fact, was the most threatened by Diane's experience.

Martha, my coleader, took Mary and two other people who were also skeptical of Diane's experience into the middle of the circle, where they discussed the event among themselves. At one point Mary remarked that she didn't care what happened to other people. Later, Tom said to Mary, "You said, 'I don't care.' I don't think that's true. I think you do care." I interjected, "I think it *is* true. I've got an idea. Mary, pick out the people you most trust and bring them into the center with you."

When she had done this, I encouraged her to act out her sadistic fantasies by forming a "conspiracy" with her trusted friends. Together, I suggested, they could decide what they wanted to do with the rest of us. After a secret palaver in the center, they grabbed each of us in turn by our hands and feet and stacked us up in the center like logs

---

[1] Masters, R. E. L., and Houston, Jean. *The Varieties of Psychedelic Experience.* New York: Holt, Rinehart and Winston, 1966, p. 249.

Figure 10-4. Guided daydream on the growth of a tree. (Photo by Gary Madderom.)

of firewood. When the "pyre" was complete, they broke into an Indian war dance to celebrate their victory. This symbolic burning at the stake resolved the divisive feelings that had split the group, which then reunited with great hilarity and warmth.

After the laughter subsided, I brought the group back to the circle to discuss their reaction to Mary's bonfire ritual. Phillip happened to mention how much he identified with such tragic heroines as Emma Bovary and Anna Karenina. Myths and images being one of my particular interests, it seemed natural to suggest that each person confide the mythic hero he or she most identified with. This exercise proved extremely revealing and fruitful. By making conscious nebulous feelings, such an image clarifies a person to himself. At the same time, it clarifies him to others because the chosen image tends to capture the essence of the person. Jim, a group worker at a narcotics addiction center, for example, identified with Don Quixote; Mary chose George

Sand, the nineteenth-century French authoress who wrote under a man's name, wore men's clothes, and smoked cigars. Diane identified with Queen Victoria, and Harriet with Jackie Kennedy. On this reflective note, we broke until Sunday morning.

Sunday began as Martha and I had planned; with silence, Tai Chi, and then a blind walk on Sixth Avenue (in a blind walk, the group pairs off; one partner leads, the other agrees to keep his eyes closed throughout the walk). Upon everyone's return, we again formed our circle and shared our various reactions to the experience. Then Martha took us on a guided daydream, in which we were asked to identify with the growth of a tree, starting from the seed. During the ensuing discussion, Jim appeared sad. We brought him onto center stage, where his work culminated in a declaration of love feelings between him and Phillip.

Noticing that Harriet was crying, I asked her to share her feelings with us. At the beginning of the week end, Harriet had abrasively complained of a number of dissatisfactions. My first impression was that she was a "troublemaker" who had an underlying need for a real tantrum. This impression proved erroneous, for as she became more and more involved, it became apparent that she was a person of considerable competence and ability who had a real but frustrated sense of longing in her. Her father had been weak, and Harriet grew up feeling she had to be strong enough to make things work out well for everyone. The group soon became aware that Harriet had both a desire to let go and a fear of entrusting herself to anyone. On Saturday, several interactions and confrontations opened up these feelings.

When I asked Harriet to share her feelings with us at the end of Jim's encounter with Phillip, she replied, "I just can't say 'I love you' to anyone and I don't believe anybody is going to say it to me . . . I feel like I'm acting all the time. I can't get down to me."

As she continued to speak, I felt a scream rise up in my throat. Suspecting I was feeling Harriet's need to scream, I pressed her to do so. She began to object, but I persisted. "Keep going. Come on. Scream."

HARRIET: It doesn't come. I always feel like I'm acting.
  HAL: Then act.
HARRIET: (sobs)
  HAL: Now—that's not crying. Scream!
HARRIET: (attempts to scream, sighs, lets out another small scream that ends in a sob) I really don't feel like it.
  HAL: Keep going.
HARRIET: (more sobbing, then screams a little louder)
  (Similar dialogue continues. Harriet, with encouragement, continues to let out small screams, followed by sobbing.)

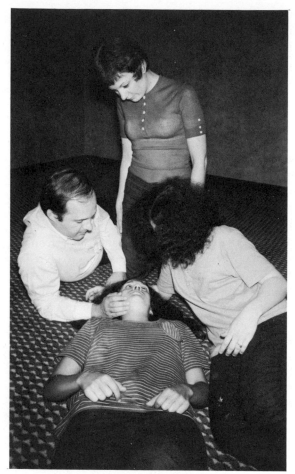

Figure 10-5. Your smile is preventing you from screaming. (Photo by Gary Madderom.)

HARRIET: (bigger scream) I didn't even scream when I gave birth. I heard the women around me screaming, and I . . .
(I have her lie on her back. As I continue to encourage her, Harriet's screams gradually become louder and deeper.)
HARRIET: It's like getting into yourself.
HAL: That's right! (laughter from the group)
HARRIET: (more sobbing)
HAL: We're going to act as your control. Do you think you can give up your control, Harriet?
ANDREW: The control's in your face, around your mouth. Your smile is preventing you from screaming. (Andrew begins kneading her face and keeps this up throughout the rest of this long session. The group draws their circle close around

Harriet, holding her hands, massaging her feet, making contact.)

HARRIET: (fighting against losing control, sobbing, emitting little screams) Save me, save me! I want to get away from me. I want to let go. I want to get away from it all.

(I keep encouraging her to breathe and scream. Then I ask her to look around at us.)

HARRIET: Who'll take care of me?

HAL: You don't let anyone in.

HARRIET: (long sigh, then silence)

(Leonore, reminded of Harriet's description of her father, suggests she repeat the syllable "da da da")

HARRIET: (repeats syllable, which becomes unsteady with emotion) My father was so weak. I had to be strong for my father. You make me think of my father. My mother and father . . . I have to be strong for them.

HAL: Let your father go.

(A long dialogue about letting go of her family and finding her own identity takes place between Harriet and the group.)

HAL: Open your eyes and look around.

ALL: Harriet, Harriet, look at us.

HAL: Harriet, look at us, look at us here, now.

HARRIET: There are currents going through my whole body.

HAL: That's right.

SOMEONE: They're in your feet, too.

HARRIET: It's like . . . groovy.

HAL: That's it, let it go through you.

HARRIET: Oh (rhythmic sobs), it's a real . . .

HAL: It is, it's just the release of all the energy you had bound up in you. Open your eyes now, Harriet.

HARRIET: Oh . . . oh . . . (long sigh)

HAL: Open your eyes and look around. Look at Martha's eyes.

HARRIET: (still in rhythmic release) I was so beautiful. I love. I think everyone is so beautiful. Oh . . . oh . . .

HAL: That's right, just stay with it. Stay with it.

HARRIET: Oh, you're working so hard. I always had to work so hard to please.

HAL: Now you don't have to do anything. All you have to do is receive.

HARRIET: I can't do that.

(A kind of duet follows in which Harriet keeps jumping into the past or the future, and the group keeps pulling her back into the here and now.)

HAL: There's no other moment.

HARRIET: How come you're not telling it like it is?

HAL: We're running this show. We're in control, and we're not going to let you tell the way it is.

HARRIET: But that's . . .

MARTHA: We're running it. Don't take it away from us.

HARRIET: He hates me.

ALL: No. No. We're running it. Take it in.

HARRIET: (interrupts again)

HAL: Harriet, look at us. That word, "us." Are you here? Take it in. How about Andrew's fingers. What do you feel from Andrew? What do you feel from us? Feel Andrew's hand.

HARRIET: Oh, my fingers. Oh! Oh!

HAL: That's alright. It's just a release of energy. You're not used to this.

HARRIET: I've never made love for real.

HAL: You make love for real now.

MARTHA: Take in our love. Feel it. Make love to us. (As she continues, Harriet relaxes.)

HARRIET: (in weak, uncontrolled voice) Everybody looks real. (group laughter) What will happen to my mother and father? (laughter)

HAL: They'll have to take care of themselves. (laughter)

HARRIET: (alternating between loud laughter and rhythmic crying. Then, suddenly terrified, she thinks of her children, whom she had forgotten for several minutes.) Oh my beautiful children. Why didn't I think of them? My beautiful children. (Realizing that her children are alright without her, Harriet's terror vanishes and she is able to accept their autonomy.)

After a break for lunch, we reformed our circle. Mary, I noticed, looked woebegone. My mention of this eventually led into a long conversation between Mary and Phillip, in which she admitted her mistrust of people, her dogmatic attitudes, her fear and antagonism toward men, and her use of silence as a weapon. Throughout this diaolgue, I urged Mary to verbalize her feelings, instead of allowing them to remain on the nonverbal level (as in the ritual burning). I also requested that she inhibit her tendency to cry and that she instead express her anger more openly and directly. To overcome her verbal blocking and subsequent withdrawal into silence, I suggested she repeat a sound, word, or phrase until the block in her throat loosened. The word "shit," which she first tried, did not mean much to her. When Leonore came up with the word "bitch," Mary looked very pained and murmured, "Oh, my God."

Then I found the right phrase: I asked her to say, "I'm a cold bitch." Mary began to scream, "I don't want to say that. I don't want to say that. It's not really me." Crying and moaning, she continued to protest. Then I asked her to say, "I don't give a shit about anybody." "Do I have to say that?" she wailed. "Yes," I said, "and breathe more from your belly." She screamed loudly, then weakly repeated, "I'm a cold bitch," through her convulsive sobbing.

Then I said, "You know what I'd like you to say now? 'I'm a hot bitch.' Would you like to say 'hot bitch' instead of 'cold bitch'?" With a great sigh, she replied, "That would be fine."

Then everyone offered suggestions about how Mary could be a "hot bitch"—how to move, how to breathe. The group laughed and applauded, clapping in rhythm as she warmed up to being a "hot bitch." Phillip said, "I like you better as a bitch in heat than as a cold bitch."

With more encouragement to keep breathing deeply into her belly, Mary began to undulate with real pleasure. "It's every woman's natural calling, and it gets lost somewhere along the line," was Phillip's final comment.

As our feelings subsided, there was a long pause until Paul spoke up: "I have something I'd like us all to do, which is pretty good for loosening up." He had us lie in a circle with our heads on each other's

Figure 10-6. Chuckle-belly. (Photo by Gary Madderom.)

bellies for a game that has been called chuckle-belly. The game begins with one person saying, "Ha." The next person in the circle says, "Ha-ha," and the next, "Ha-ha-ha," and so on. In a few minutes, we were all laughing uproariously. Our laughter mounted higher and higher. Then I realized that David, the photographer, had joined the group. When I asked him to take a picture of us, he replied that he did not want to leave the circle. Reluctantly, he got up and then—quite spontaneously—began to act the part of a flamboyant Italian movie director (accent and all), which brought us to ever-greater peaks of shrieking laughter. My own deep laugh added to the general paroxysms. We went on this way for 25 minutes. At the end, I said, "What an orgy. That was more fun than any real orgy."

By this time, David, who had gotten very much into the spirit of things, had come out from behind his camera. He wanted to go further and do something with all the women. He asked all four to lie in a row on the floor. At that point, he appeared stymied, so I suggested he roll over them. He followed my suggestion with great glee, enjoying himself immensely. Someone remarked that David was "doing what every man fantasied."

Leonore finally sat up and reported mild anxiety feelings about David and the rolling incident. Ordinarily, I would have responded to her remark and brought her onto center stage, but the hour was late, and I decided not to start something that we might not be able to finish.

I gathered the group into a final circle and asked for reflections on the week end so that we could verbally conceptualize and reinforce some of our experiences. Then, Phillip began the goodbye with me, "What a crazy bunch." We hugged, shook hands, talked, and parted.

EVALUATION AND FOLLOW-UP OF THE ENCOUNTER

Was this a typical Aureon encounter? Two features were atypical at the outset: the presence of the magazine participant-observers and the degree of preplanning that Martha and I did with the Tai Chi, the blind walk, and the meditation. Ordinarily I plan only the opening procedures. The presence of the participant-observers did not seem to influence the workshop after the beginning, when we all brought out our feelings about them. However, they may have influenced the make-up of the group, for some people chose not to attend because of them.

As the actual encounter unfolded, several other atypical features emerged. Most striking was the relative lack of work on anger and hostility. Then, too, though men outnumbered women in the group, the women were worked on much more (my three detailed examples are all women). Several people remained in the background and did not ask to be worked with. Because the group was small to begin with, a couple of people were able to have two rather lengthy turns and therefore go deeper into themselves. No one in the group triggered off any excessive emotion in me. Therefore, I did not engage in any encounters, nor did I go on center stage. Both positions I have taken and am willing to take, if need be, and I make this clear to the group in the beginning. Finally, this particular Aureon encounter was unusual in the amount of good feelings—hilarity, humor, and joy—generated. I cannot account for this unless it was because so much sad feeling had been worked through.

Although a systematic follow-up on these people was not attempted, I did have informal contacts with several. I met Diane in another workshop several months later, where she told me that she had lost 20 pounds since the October encounter. In a telephone conversation, Andrew volunteered that he had become more accepting of feelings and more open to the responses of his students, in contrast to his previous more dogmatic approach. He said that his wife Mary was still rather shy, but had become involved with the woman's liberation movement and had also successfully "done battle" with a learning theorist in the school where she was studying for a degree in guidance.

Leonore, a teacher, had begun to introduce a more open, circular form into her classes. Neither Bill nor Elaine had returned on Sunday. I learned subsequently that both had left because they felt they had not been getting anything out of the experience. However, Elaine joined an ongoing weekly group soon after, and Bill, after one more attempt, gave up groups altogether in favor of individual bioenergetic work and zazen meditation. Harriet reported she had more energy and was doing things she had once hesitated to try.

THE ROLE OF THE THERAPIST IN THE AUREON ENCOUNTER

Like Stewart Shapiro (Shapiro, 1967), who considers himself "a group of instruments: a recorder, a collater, and a transmitter" who has learned "to respect his inner messages . . . and to express them because they can be helpful in varied therapeutic situations," I, too, regard myself as an instrument in the group.

Diane described my role in the October encounter as follows: "It seems to me the most important thing I got out of the week end was the understanding that if you pay attention to someone, you really hear what they're saying, not just what you *think* they're saying. I watched you. You paid attention to what people were saying. You didn't drop it for a minute. That's why you could pick up intuitively what they were up to and what they needed—because you weren't listening just to their words, you were listening to their whole vibrations."

The word "vibrations" is not just a figure of speech. Pierrakos writes: "Living organisms are resonating systems that respond to each other's vibrations. Some people believe that they can pick up waves that others emit: others refer to this sense of rapport and communication as 'being on the same wave length.' People are sensitive to other people's states of excitation in a physical way."[2]

I think it possible to explain the origin of some of my unusual intuitions and interventions in the October encounter as arising from my body-self. Twenty years of work on my body-self—a journey that has taken me from Gestalt therapy, to reichian orgonomy, to bioenergetic analysis and many other approaches to body awareness—has softened it, has increased its elasticity and vibratory frequency, and has made it an instrument receptive to feelings in myself and in others. These years of stretching, breathing, massage, encounter, and life experiences have literally opened me up. Consequently, when I work with someone in a group, I can become so involved that I identify with his state of being. That is, I am instantly aware when feelings arise in someone because they have started up in me as well.

Instances of these "sympathetic vibrations" occurred in the October encounter on several occasions: when I sensed Phillip's underlying despair by the pain in my own body; when I picked up Andrew's need to move strongly by a kinesthetic image of this kind that came to me; when I sensed Harriet's scream in my throat; and when I felt Diane's need to rise by the image of levitation that sprang up in me. In other encounter groups, I have been able to "catch" someone's sexual feelings by the sudden sensation of those feelings in my own body—even though the person may have converted his sexual feelings into anger. By this kind of kinesthetic identification, I have also been able to tune in on the positive, joyful feelings beginning to spread in someone, but which that person is unwilling to risk asserting. My body-self is particularly helpful in situations such as Mary's, whose so-called "bullshit tears" were covering up her fear of showing anger. Because I sense the underlying hostility, I do not get taken in by the superficial feeling being expressed.

One can legitimately ask how I know whether I am feeling someone else's vibrations—feeling their feelings—or simply experiencing my own reaction to them. Though both situations occur, I have trained myself to discriminate between the two. If I am confused or doubtful, I verify. I may, for example, say, "I'm feeling anxious and I don't

---

[2] Pierrakos, John C. Rhythm and Pulsation. In *The Rhythm of Life*. New York: Institute of Bioenergetic Analysis, 1966.

know whether the feeling's originating in me or in you." There are also times when my "instrument" picks up a feeling, but I do not know who it is coming from. In such cases, I may make a remark such as, "I'm feeling some heaviness in the room," and open this comment up for clarification. I do not mean to imply that the body-self is infallible, or that I always "read" it accurately. My interpretation was incorrect, for example, when I thought Harriet needed to release a temper tantrum.

TOWARD A THEORY OF ENCOUNTER

In referring to this kind of group work as "encounter," I am not suggesting that it is separate from therapy, although I believe there are differences between encounter and therapy. One of the main distinctions, it seems to me, is that encounter deals with the present: with here-and-now feelings, with discovering an expanded self, with expressing one's true feelings openly, with confronting other people, and with receiving feedback from them. Psychotherapy, on the other hand, is concerned with freeing individuals from their past by releasing and intensifying repressed emotions so that they can be drained off from past figures.

Obviously, the distinction between encounter and therapy is not always clear-cut. Within the group situation, the two often merge imperceptibly. Furthermore, in any small group the need for both therapy and encounter arises. In the October experience, for instance, Phillip needed to probe his past in order to touch upon the despair and suicidal fantasies that had sprung up subsequent to his divorce. Harriet, on the other hand, was deliberately kept in the here-and-now by me and the group, who sensed her underlying need to forget others. The Aureon encounter typically oscillates between encounter and therapy according to the needs of the individual participants and the group as a whole.

The group process is more complicated, however, than the preceding distinction. In order to understand the qualities of sunlight or the nature of the sun, its rays have to be separated into the spectrum. Similarly, to comprehend the complex but unified phenomenon of the encounter group, we must break it down into its component parts, yet keep in mind that all the parts are interrelated. In writing this paper, I have developed four principles that I regard as convenient toeholds on a theory of encounter and that I will describe with illustrations from the October group: the mandala, the Gestalt, the energy, and the connection principles.

The Mandala Principle

The mandala motif is helpful in understanding the group process. The lost inner balance and one-sidedness we all suffer from can be worked on in the group perhaps even more effectively than by meditating on a mandala. The presence of our opposites in living flesh rather than as colored diagrams can facilitate an expansion of the self; can call into awareness our disowned parts; and can lead to a union of opposites: anger as opposed to sympathy, control versus letting go (Harriet), trust versus the opposite of mistrust, mysticism versus rationality (Diane), masculinity as opposed to femininity, or child versus adult (Mary). David, who had such a one-sided development as an observer behind his camera, was given the opportunity to experience his performer half —a side he usually kept under wraps. Such a successful experience can bring an individual one step closer to unifying his opposites.

However, the mandala concept does not apply to the group situation with total smoothness. At this time, I can offer only the glimmerings of the relationship, for the encounter group—unlike mandalas of other times and places—is a living, moving, dynamic mandala. More precisely, perhaps, a group *must become* a mandala, must evolve into a harmonious and integrated whole. The mandala must be formed without its parts' (the participants) being forced into place. Like a true mandala, the group must retain its differentiated wholeness.

How does the mandala concept function in actual practice? First, from beginning to end, the Aureon encounter takes place in a circle. I insist on this. Immediately upon entering, all the participants remove their shoes and sit on the floor in a recognizable circle (even though the absence of a backrest can be uncomfortable). A circle, of course, has not only a circumference, but also a center. In the group, whatever arises on the circumference that requires prolonged attention is brought to the center. The center may contain a single individual, two people encountering each other, or several people who share something in common (like the group who were skeptical of Diane's mystical experience). Though the circle may disintegrate during interludes of work or fun, the group always returns to "our circle." Throughout the encounter, the circle provides the dependable structure in which everything takes place.

The Gestalt Principle

Each moment in any encounter group contains infinite possibilities. On what basis, then, does a group move from point A to point B? Is the order just a matter of chance or of paying attention to the "wheel that squeaks the loudest?"

Some groups—apparently those that originate from a psychotherapeutic framework—are characterized by a fairly rigid structure; Ellis's rational emotive encounter (Ellis, 1969), Perls's Gestalt groups (Perls, 1969), and Lowen's bioenergetic groups (Lowen, 1958), for example. Many encounter groups, on the other hand, have no structure and flow with no particular direction. In the Aureon encounter, I try to maintain a balance between structure and movement. Under the mandala principle, I considered the structural aspects. The Gestalt principle explains, in my opinion, how a group can and should move.

The organic process mentioned in the title of this article refers to the Gestalt principle. The Aureon brochure describes a process in which a "figure"—namely, a feeling—emerges from a background, becomes a task for the group and its leader to work on, is hopefully resolved, and then recedes into the background as someone else's need or feeling comes to the foreground. In the October encounter, examples of this figure-ground relationship occurred when Jim's sadness emerged after Martha took us on a guided daydream; when Harriet spontaneously cried after the encounter between Phillip and Jim; when Mary appeared sad after the lunch break; and when Leonore admitted her anxiety after David had rolled over her and the other women in the group. In each case but the last, these feelings emerged spontaneously from the ground, were resolved to some degree, and receded naturally into the background from where they had sprung.

The figure-ground principle explains the way the focus in an Aureon encounter shifts from the group, to the individual, and back to the group. Part of my role as leader is to consider the needs of the group as a whole. To meet these needs I may, for example, suggest a group game that provides some kind of release. Just as often, a participant may lead the way—as Paul did when he suggested the chuckle-belly game that proved such a fine vehicle for group merriment. By contrast, I find that relentless work on a succession of individuals is a rigid and forced way of proceeding.

Laura Perls (Perls, 1968), in writing about the utility of the contact/support concept in working with individuals in Gestalt therapy, affirms that it does not "reintroduce a dichotomy into the holistic concept of the functioning of the organism, but is a differentiation according to the figure-ground principle."

This contact/support idea applies to the encounter situation when the group, by its support, helps intensify and clarify the contact an individual is making. Just as I have increasing confidence that my body will support me in moments of crisis, so does my confidence grow that the group will come through at such times. Every week-end encounter has its impasse. Experience has taught me to withstand the anxiety of these blank pauses when nothing comes forth. From such voids, I have learned, spring the most creative moments. Both the ritual fire burning and the chuckle-belly incidents, new experiences for me, emerged spontaneously and unexpectedly from what has been called "the creative void."

THE ENERGY PRINCIPLE

Wilhelm Reich's theory of character rests on his discovery of the way in which energy moves and blocks in the human body. In the 40 years since the publication of his epochal *Function of the Orgasm,* intensive clinical work on energy movement has been undertaken in terms of individual treatment. Little, however, has been written or researched on energy movement as a group phenomenon. Baker, a reichian therapist, writes: "The principle of therapy is quite simple: merely to remove the chronic contractions which interfere with the free flow of energy throughout the organism and thus restore natural functioning. There are three avenues of approach. . . . They are (1) increasing the inner push of the organism by building up its energy; (2) directly attacking the spastic muscles to free the contraction; and (3) bringing into the open and overcoming his resistance to the therapy and the therapist."[3] Let me deal with these approaches in inverse order, as they apply to the group situation.

Regarding Baker's last point, I would like to offer a word of warning: On the whole, resistances are more easily overcome in a group than in a one-to-one relationship because a participant has many more "therapists" to deal with at one time. This advantage is, ironically, the danger. I have seen groups cajole and browbeat a person so that he is dragged along against his will by strong group pressures. An individual in such circumstances may very well achieve some sort of breakthrough. In the long run, however, this work may come to naught because he has not deliberately decided to cooperate and can too easily disclaim responsibility for what took place. I now put a stop to such pressures and pointedly ask the individual a question such as, "Do you wish to work on this?" Only if he responds with a clear "Yes," do I or the group continue.

Baker's second avenue of approach—that of directly attacking the spastic muscles and freeing the contractions—is extremely important, in my opinion. The musculature in the human body has many qualities, but an essential one is its elasticity. Muscles expand and contract,

[3] Baker, Elsworth F. *Man in the Trap.* New York: Macmillan, 1967.

vibrate and pulsate. Those that are free of chronic tensions vibrate smoothly, whereas chronically contracted muscles or groups of muscles vibrate little or not at all when the body is placed in positions of stress. Lowen (Lowen, 1958) uses the analogy of an automobile to describe this phenomenon. When the motor in a finely tuned Rolls Royce is running, its vibrations will be smooth and even. By contrast, a flivver will vibrate jerkily and unevenly.

In the human body, vibrations are not in themselves feelings, but are rather pathways through which feelings flow into all parts of the body. The goal in all work on the body is to free the contracted areas so that they can again vibrate, allowing the individual to pick up feelings and let them flow freely through him.

Work on spastic muscles can, to a certain extent, be undertaken in an encounter group. Andrew intuitively did this when he kneaded Harriet's face as she was letting go. In the group situation, chronic muscular tensions may be temporarily freed in a number of ways: through a strong emotional experience, by having the individual deliberately tighten the tense area or assume appropriate positions of stress, or by direct manipulation of the contracted area.

Why, one might well ask, is it necessary to deliberately intensify someone's emotion? Another concept from Gestalt therapy is relevant in answering this question. Perls writes that "the formation of comprehensive *Gestalten* is the condition of mental health and growth. Only the completed Gestalt can be organized as an automatically functioning unit (reflex) in the total organism. Any incomplete Gestalt represents an unfinished situation that clamors for attention and interferes with the formation of any novel, vital Gestalt."[4]

It is the emotions that finish off situations: anger in frustration, grief in mourning. The emotions are prevented from doing their job by the tension barriers erected against them. If the individual is to live in the present, he must complete these past situations once and for all—get out the tears, exhaust the rage. Psychoanalysis failed to do this job because it lacked the necessary tools. Together, Gestalt and reichian therapy may produce a more effective approach.

My work in the area of intensification is an attempt to integrate Gestalt and reichian approaches into the group process. Emotions directed toward past figures must be intensified in order for them to break through the blocks that have been constructed over the years to hold the emotion in check. Water held behind a dam can be released either by opening the dam or by raising the water level until it overflows the dam. The most direct way of raising the individual's level of

[4] Perls, Laura. Two Instances of Gestalt Therapy. In Paul David Pursglove (ed.). *Recognition in Gestalt Therapy.* New York: Funk and Wagnalls, 1968.

feeling is through the spontaneous or deliberate intensification of his breathing.

Kelley (Kelley, 1965) has suggested two methods of intensifying breathing, which can be employed independently or sequentially. I used both techniques in the October encounter. First, I had Harriet and Phillip in turn get down on their hands and knees, pant from the belly, and then take several deep belly breaths. Then, they were instructed to flip over on their backs, open their eyes wide as in fright, and let out a sharp, abrupt "Oh" on the outgoing breath (this procedure is called "startle breathing"). Although one of these breathing methods often suffices to release the topmost feeling in an organism, neither Phillip nor Harriet immediately responded. In Phillip's case, it was first necessary to find a key phase ("I wish I were dead," and later, "There's no way out"). Though these phrases released some choked-off sobs, I was not successful in getting Phillip to cry uninhibitedly. Harriet, on the other hand, did reach an involuntary level of emotion when she temporarily relinquished her self-control.

Hyperventilation, it must be mentioned, does not always produce an emotion. A pure energy release may occur, as in Diane's case. Because yoga had prepared her body for the experience, she was able to enjoy and go along with the feelings it engendered. A person less accustomed to a sudden energy release may be alarmed by the tingling, numbness, and buzzing that these currents produce. Such a person needs both reassurance and an explanation of what is happening. As the body accustoms itself to an increased energy flow, these sensations will diminish and finally disappear.

I might add that although some of these group experiences are intrinsically more potent than others, even the most powerful can fall flat.

THE CONNECTION PRINCIPLE

Previously I set forth unification of the individual as a goal. Such a goal is hardly unique with me; in fact it is a goal everyone is striving for. But rarely are the steps necessary to reach this goal spelled out. In my opinion, probably the most effective work being done in this area is coming out of the Synanon approach. Here in New York, some very important amplifications and alterations of Synanon have developed in the work of Daniel Casriel and some of his followers. As yet there are no reports on this approach in the literature, and it is not included among the techniques being presented at Esalen. This manner of working with emotions has not been covered by the previous three principles.

More than most other approaches, this one takes cognizance of the fact that certain emotions can be used as defenses against other emotions. For example, anger can be used defensively to keep away from painful, vulnerable feelings and crying can be used as a defensive cover-up for anger. It is necessary to place some demands on the individual to consciously inhibit the superficial emotion and to work at getting into the deeper emotion. For this work of getting into these emotions, certain emotionally expressive devices are used. A typical one used for getting to anger is this: The person stands in the middle of the group, bends his knees, clenches his fists, and breathes deeply from the diaphragm, building up a density in his body. He starts by saying, "I am angry," "Damn," or whatever word seems most appropriate. He focuses on the object of his anger. Gradually his voice gets louder and deeper. He is strongly encouraged by the group to stay with the feeling and not just to have an uncontrolled discharge or to settle for a partial build-up. (Most often a person does go through a series of "partial build-ups" often over a period of weeks before he can achieve a fully connected feeling.) Casriel suggests that there are four levels of anger, and the intensity and depth of the anger are in terms of the level of depth in the body from which the anger comes. As you go deeper from the head downward, the feelings get stronger and there is a different quality in the vibrations that we all can sense. When the anger finally reaches into the depth of the belly—gut anger—this frees the pleasure feelings in the genitals and allows them to stream out. These good feelings often require a great deal of encouragement to blossom forth because their exposure is risky in our culture.

Mary is an example of someone working through her feelings of pain, deepening them, and finally reaching pleasure feelings at the point when I asked her to say, "I'm a hot bitch." This verbalization climaxed a great deal of previous work that had begun the preceding night when Mary acted out her feelings largely on the nonverbal level. When she finally got to the phrase, "I'm a hot bitch," she became unified and connected. She asserted her womanhood—an assertion to which she and everyone in the group responded with pleasure.

New Directions

In this paper, I have tried to formulate a tentative theory of encounter as it has thus far emerged from the Aureon experience. But the Aureon encounter is a dynamic rather than a static process, one which is continually changing and developing. Even as this article is being written, I am moving in new directions. In future encounters I would like, for example, to explore the swirl and movement of energy streams that flow in, through, and around a group of people. Although I am currently aware of these energy currents and actually work with them, I do not yet know how to write about them.

To expand the scope of body work that can be undertaken within the framework of the encounter group, I am planning to invite the participation of a licensed masseur, who could demonstrate how the group, as a whole or in pairs, can work on each other's chronic contractions. I would also like to probe the function of imagery as an organizing principle that relates to the life of the individual participant and to the group as a whole. The relationship between imagery, both visual and kinesthetic, and the body is another area yet to be explored in the Aureon encounter.

Although it is a simple matter to introduce new modalities into the encounter group, the challenge is to find a way to integrate such devices into the total framework. Integration, not compartmentalization, and flexibility, not rigidity, are my primary concerns. In the light of such concerns I was particularly pleased to hear Andrew say it was the *variety* of experiences in that October week end that impressed him the most.

In my work, I try never to lose sight of the end goal of all therapy and encounter: what the participant, as a result of his experience, can carry over into his everyday life. In the final hours of the October week end, I asked the group what had happened to them during the encounter that could facilitate this carry-over. Andrew's articulate response, springing from immediate experience, captures the essence of the principles formulated in this paper:

"The crucial thing about an encounter group is that it's a safe world. You know that within this safe world, people won't fall apart if you let off steam. What happens when we go outside is that we put on some armor. But once you learn what it's like to be in a safe room without the armor, you can become aware when you put it on. It's damn important to realize that the armor is on and to know that it can come off again.

"The safe group teaches you about how you can trust people. It does this by showing you what fantastic intuition such a group has. Hal Streitfeld's intuition is special, but everyone in this group has that. The group itself develops a kind of extraordinary wisdom that is dependent on the quality of trust and safeness. In an environment in which it is safe for people to be themselves, beautiful things happen." And beautiful things did happen that week end in October.

Bibliography

Baker, Elsworth F. *Man in the Trap*. New York: Macmillan, 1967.

Bradford, Leland, Benne, Kenneth, and Gibb, Jack. *T Group Theory and Laboratory Method*. New York: Wiley, 1964.

Casriel, Daniel. *So Fair a House*. Englewood Cliffs, N.J.: Prentice-Hall, 1963.

Christiansen, Bjorn. *Studies in Respiration and Personality*. Oslo, Norway: Institute for Social Research, 1965.

Ellis, Albert. A Weekend of Rational Encounter. In Arthur Burton (ed.). *Encounter*. San Francisco; Jossey-Bass, 1969.

Govinda, Lama Anagarika. *Foundations of Tibetan Mysticism*. London: Rider. 1959.

Jaffe, Aiela. Symbolism in the Visual Arts. In Carl Jung (ed.). *Man and His Symbols*. London: Aldus, 1964.

Kelley, Charles E. Orgonomy Since the Death of Reich. In Charles E. Kelley (ed.). *The Creative Process*, **5**:1–82, 1965, pp. 1–82.

Lowen, Alexander. *Physical Dynamics of Character Structure*. New York: Grune and Stratton, 1958.

Maslow, Abraham. *Toward a Psychology of Being*. Princeton, N.J.: Van Nostrand, 1962.

Masters, R. E. L., and Houston, Jean. *The Varieties of Psychedelic Experience*. New York: Holt, Rinehart and Winston, 1966.

Moses, Paul J. *The Voice of Neurosis*. New York: Grune and Stratton, 1954.

Murphy, Michael. The Reformation of Experience. In Herbert A. Otto (ed.). *Human Potentialities*. St. Louis: Warren H. Green, 1968.

Perls, Frederick S. *Gestalt Therapy Verbatim*. Lafayette, Calif.: Real People Press, 1969.

Perls, Frederick S., Hefferline, Ralph E., and Goodman, Paul. *Gestalt Therapy*. New York: Julian Press, 1952.

Perls, Laura. Two Instances of Gestalt Therapy. In Paul David Pursglove (ed.). *Recognitions in Gestalt Therapy*. New York: Funk and Wagnalls, 1968.

Pierrakos, John C. Rhythm and Pulsation. In *The Rhythm of Life*. New York: Institute of Bioenergetic Analysis, 1966.

Rogers, Carl. The Process of the Basic Encounter Group. In James F. T. Gugental (ed.). *Challenges of Humanistic Psychology*. New York: McGraw-Hill, 1967.

Shapiro, Stuart. Myself as an Instrument. In James F. T. Bugental (ed.). *Challenges of Humanistic Psychology*. New York: McGraw-Hill, 1967.

Thomas, Hobart F. Encounter—The Game of No Game. In Arthur Burton (ed.). *Encounter*. San Francisco: Jossey-Bass, 1969.

James Elliott

 The Nude Marathon—
A Conversation with
Paul Bindrim*

COMMENTARY

Nude marathons examine nakedness in terms of the hang-ups of people about their bodies. Body image problems are seldom directly dealt with in ordinary therapies. When dealt with at all, they are put in terms of fantasies concerning the body. But to explore nakedness— to discuss fantasies and feelings about one's body, the bodies of others, testing fantasies against realities! Paul Bindrim has had the courage to experiment in this direction, not for sensationalism, but for purposes of analyzing and undoing self and body image difficulties in people.

ABOUT PAUL BINDRIM

Paul Bindrim is a licensed clinical psychologist who has been in private practice in Hollywood, California, for over 20 years. He received his degrees from Columbia and Duke Universities and has taught at Finch and

* Reprinted, in part, from *The Group Leader's Workshop*, Portfolio IV (P.O. Box 1254, Berkeley, Calif., 94701).

El Camino Colleges. He originated and led the first nude marathon in 1967. Since then, he has conducted over 75 nude sessions throughout the United States. This work has been reported in *Time* (1968) and *Life* (1968). Paul has made presentations at major universities and professional conventions, including those of the American Psychological Association and the American Psychiatric Association.

His publications include articles in *Psychotherapy* (1968), *Psychology Today* (1969), and a chapter on cultivating peak experiences in *Ways of Growth* (Otto, 1968). Chapters for the following books are in preparation: *The Encounter Group: Issues and Applications* (Solomon and Berzon, 1970) and *The Human Potentials Movement* (Aaronson, 1970). The Canadian Broadcasting Corporation has produced a documentary on his work. His forthcoming book on nude marathons is being published by Macmillan and a sound-slide seminar on the subject will be released by McGraw-Hill.

Paul Bindrim's address is 2000 Cantata Drive, Los Angeles, California 90028.

Nude encounter groups were first suggested in print by Abraham Maslow, who wondered in his book *Eupsychian Management* what would happen if groups took off their clothes. "People would go away . . . ," he speculated, "an awful lot freer, a lot more spontaneous, less guarded, less defensive, not only about the shape of their behinds or whether their bellies were hanging or not, but freer and more innocent about their minds as well. If I can learn not to be conscious about the fact that my ass is hanging, or that my belly sticks out too much, if I can throw off this fear, this defense, maybe this act of freedom will enable me thereby to throw off a lot of other defenses. . . ."[1]

The marathon itself was pioneered by George Bach and Fred Stoller in the early 1960's and, essentially, is a very long, almost always overnight group running as short as 12 to 15 hours or as long as 48 to 72 hours, but most commonly lasting 24 hours, the length of time together with the lack of sleep accounting for the more intensive work that goes on.

Put the two together and you have the *nude marathon*—a variety of group that has come to be associated with its originator, Paul Bindrim.

While conducting ordinary clothed marathons some years back, Paul Bindrim noticed a tendency on the part of the group members to disrobe as they got emotionally closer. In "A Report on a Nude Marathon," he writes: "On a few occasions, when a pool or hot baths were

---

[1] Maslow, A. H. *Eupsychian Management: A Journal.* Homewood, Ill.: Irwin-Dorsey, 1965, p. 160.

Figure 11-1. (Photo by Dan Miller.)

available, the participants spontaneously engaged in nude swimming after the marathon had ended. These spontaneous excursions into nudity seemed to increase interpersonal transparency, remove inhibitions in the area of physical contact, decrease the sense of personal isolation and estrangement, and culminate in a feeling of freedom and belongingness. It seemed quite possible that the inviolable sense of privacy that man maintains by wrapping himself in a tower of clothes, or retreating to the castle of his home, might not only serve to safeguard his individuality, but also, perhaps, in effect, be a self-imposed padded cell through which he can limit his contact when he basically distrusts and fears interaction with other persons. It seemed that disrobing might constitute a symbolic attempt to open this cell of isolated psychological privacy to healthy group interaction and intimacy. It seemed possible that if a participant disrobed physically he might, by this gesture, gain the freedom to also disrobe emotionally. If this were true, it might be desirable to first disrobe and then interact, thus shortening the process and intensifying the beneficial results."[2]

---

[2] Bindrim, P. A Report on a Nude Marathon: The Effect of Physical Nudity upon the Practice of Interaction in the Marathon Group. *Psychotherapy: Theory, Research and Practice*, 5:180–88. 1968.

GROUP FORMAT

The groups are usually conducted at a motel or private home with a heated pool. "You need a place where you can make all the noise in the world," Paul told us. "Think of people screaming at the top of their lungs like they're fighting for their lives: this is what you have to be able to have. You need a place that's screened so you can be nude, too—and it has to be in a state where it's legal to be nude in private groups."

People are screened by telephone, unless they've been referred by a therapist. Each registrant is sent two printed sheets—a "Nude Encounter Workshop Agreement" containing the ground rules and a sheet instructing them to bring certain "peak stimuli" to the group. Each person brings a sleeping bag.

The group ranges in number from 14 to 18, balanced so as to be approximately half men and half women. Minors are excluded. The session lasts from 7 P.M. the first day to 4 P.M. the following day and is divided into four parts: (1) Seven to nine hours of verbal and non-verbal encountering; (2) four hours of sleep, meditation, or silence; (3) about seven or eight hours of nonverbal work; and (4) two or three hours of verbal integrative work.

"The objective of the first part," Paul explained, "is to get a good, functioning encounter group going." Part 1, which lasts from 7 P.M. until some time between 2 and 4 A.M., begins with a discussion of the ground rules led by Paul. "For instance, I tell them that we permit physical encounters, which means that people can hurt each other, but they may not injure each other. A slap in the face may be worth 10,000 words, but if it knocks a few teeth out, it's against the rules. Of course, anybody who doesn't want a physical encounter doesn't have to have it; it's up to him."

After everybody understands and signs a copy of the ground rules, Paul gives a very brief intellectual introduction, after which group members introduce themselves and talk about what they do or why they came and ask each other questions. "I begin on the head level," Paul said, "but we hold an egg timer on them: they get three minutes to lay their egg before they go on. It's not worth any more than that. And yet if you don't do that, they won't feel that they know each other well enough to go much further.

"Then we do what I call 'getting acquainted the way animals do.' I tell them that if they put a strange cat in the room with their present cat, the first thing that would happen is that the two would eyeball—look directly into each other's eyes. And then the next thing is that they'd interact physically. And so I want each of them to do this with every other person in the room—to eyeball until they have an urge to do something to the other person and then go ahead and do it. And after they're in a physical interaction for awhile, then to start talking. But they're not to touch until they've eyeballed and gotten an urge of some kind. Otherwise, touch becomes very stereotyped. You can hug everybody instead of shaking everybody's hand, and one is as ridiculous as the other. I pair them up to eyeball, and as soon as they've finished eyeballing that person, they're to find somebody they haven't eyeballed yet, until they've eyeballed everyone in the group. And during that process, all kinds of things happen. Fights start. People hug each other. People dance with each other or slap each other or wrestle with each other. And then they talk. I ask them not to talk too long, because there's a lot more to do.

"And when that's finished, we talk about anxieties regarding nudity, fantasies they've had, like, 'What's the worst thing that can happen to you as soon as you go nude?" You know, a woman who's had a mastectomy can get undressed a lot easier after she's told the group she has only one breast and that she feels that they'll react with shock and reject her. Or a woman may be worried that her breasts are too small, and I'll ask her, 'What fellows here would you be most upset to have see your breasts, and what would their reactions be?' 'Oh,' she might say, 'they'd be disgusted with me. They'd look at other women; they wouldn't notice me.' 'All right, please look each of those men in the eye and say, "When I get undressed, you'll see that my breasts are too small and then you won't be interested in me. You won't notice me." Now say it to each person.' Then they go down the line looking in the eyes of each man, saying it to them, and by the time they've said it to five or six people, they begin to laugh. The anxiety has been discharged.

"Or some man may say he's afraid he'll get an erection. And then some other fellow will pop up and say, 'My biggest worry is that I *won't* get an erection.'

"Then we generally go to the men's and women's dressing rooms to undress. I don't like the lingerie display. It's not a natural thing. After people have experienced nudity, lingerie and underwear mean nothing, but prior to it they fit in with a burlesque show. There's no reason to go through that. So after they undress, they meet in the room, which by now is darkened.

"I've walled off a little area that is a kind of pen, and they step into that little area, and they're asked to mill around with their hands at their sides and experience physical contact—but neither trying for it nor avoiding it. Usually I have a record playing, *Music for Meditation*, and afterward, while I'm milling with them, I'll sound an 'om' (making a humming sound) and they'll begin to join in this. As they mill around with body contact, they get into a kind of psychedelic state; that's usually the first turn-on that happens. Then after the milling, I'll have a projector come on with colored slides, and there'll be some fast-tempo dance music, and there'll usually be mirrors there. And perhaps I'll turn on a strobe light.

"What this means is that they're not standing around gaping at each other; we go right from clothing to the intimacy of touch. We bypass the visual voyeuristic-exhibitionistic phase, which is what they're all afraid of anyway. So by the time we come back to looking, they're already so intimate that it's not that bad; the hang-ups don't happen that would happen if you didn't get right into the touch area. And in a sense, we've already gotten into the touch area with clothing on by the physical interaction that follows the eyeballing.

"Then following that, we will do many different things in the group, depending on what the group needs. If I feel that people are not able to express themselves because they're angry and they can't trust the group, they have a period of time that is a kind of telling-off session, where each person puts somebody in the hot seat and tells him to his face why he dislikes him, and other people in the group may tell him too, but the one who's in the hot seat can't say anything. This is just one approach. I work in whatever way I feel that that particular group needs.

"Another exercise is what I call 'crotch eyeballing.' We put them on their backs in a circle on cushions with their feet in the middle, and behind them there's another person who grabs their ankles and brings their ankles back up over their heads so everything hangs out. And you're looking at everybody else with it all hanging out, and when it all hangs out at one time, it's not an issue, whereas you might be quite embarrassed to be in that position if you're the only one. Then I ask them to talk about their sex practices, the things they feel guilty about, and so forth, the things they don't want anybody to know about. We all have a head end and a tail end, but we rarely look at our tail ends together; we sit around in a group looking at our head ends. Well, let's look at our tail ends for a change and see what the other end of the animal looks like. Then, after we work on the animal level, we're able to talk about it. The verbal exposure follows the physical exposure.

"There's another exercise I used for a couples group once. I found that the husbands and wives were hanging on to each other, and we had no group spirit; so I made an inner circle of women and an outer circle of men, and each man was facing a woman, and every four minutes the outer circle rotated one place, and as they faced the next woman, they eyeballed. I'd say 'Eyes for 30 seconds,' then 'Hands— continue eyeballing and holding hands for 30 seconds,' then 'Necks—

eyeball and hold necks for the next 30 seconds,' and 'Now close your eyes and react spontaneously.' Then after it was over, I said, 'All right, men, now sit down but not next to your mate, and let's talk about what we experienced.' And by this time we got a nice mixed salad going; we'd gotten over that hurdle of the insular nature of the paired couple —the allies.''

At some time during the evening, Paul asks each person to choose a partner to help with the peak stimuli he has brought. Peak stimuli are "the things that you most enjoy smelling, tasting, touching, looking at, and listening to," and each person tells his partner where his peak stimuli are located so they can be brought when needed. "When they *are* needed," Paul explained, "the individual will not be in any condition to get them; he'll be deep in an emotional experience." Partners are chosen after group members have gotten to know each other well enough to know who they like and who likes them.

"We wind up the first part of the marathon some time between 2 and 4 A.M.," Paul told us, "and I tell them that from now on, until I give the word, there is to be silence. They can make any sounds they like except words. If they *absolutely* need to say something, like where's the toilet, they can write it down. But no lip movements, no reading, no playing chess. I don't want them to use their heads in any way. If someone feels he's *got* to talk about something going on inside him, you can be damn sure that if he doesn't talk, he's going to get further than if he does. I stipulate that if I feel that talking is necessary, I will be the one to talk, and I will whisper what I want to say into the person's ear so as not to disrupt the group. I tell them about my hand signals, too, when I want them to rock somebody, or give him skin contact, or when I want the group to form a conveyer belt.

"Then the period of silence begins, and we go into meditation around a single candle. At the Topanga Center, we have an underground cave. We walk down a 200-foot tunnel that's dug into the dirt, and it's pitch black in there. We feel our way into that tunnel, nude, holding each other's hands as we go, and we can smell the earth. Halfway through the tunnel there's a little chamber where we sit in a circle, and I light one candle in the middle of the circle, and there are glasses and a bottle of wine. Then I turn on the Alan Watts record *Om,* and it begins by saying, 'You know who you are. Stop kidding yourself. You've always been around. You'll always *be* around.' He goes into this thing on a verbal level very skillfully, which gives people a further turn-on, particularly if they're head-oriented people; it helps them get out of their heads. And then the record switches over to the "om"—sounded by oriental instruments.

"While that's going on, I pour the wine and give a glass to each person, and then we all bring our glasses together over the candle, and the candlelight shines through the wine, and then we sit there and watch the candle, and as each person wants to leave and go to sleep, there's a little candle they light from the main candle to give them light to find their way back through the tunnel to where they will sleep, and that's the way we begin the silence.

"They have four hours' time during which they can rest or meditate or wrestle with the things that have been stirred up in them in the earlier part of the evening, and during that period of time, I just go to sleep.

"The next morning, somewhere between 6 and 8 A.M., I play a Brandenburg concerto to wake them up, and they have a light breakfast: orange juice, hot rolls, and coffee. When I'm using the Topanga Center, I take them through the tunnel again, and, instead of stopping at the center chamber, I go right on through to the other end of the tunnel, where there's a staircase, which they climb for about two stories—in absolute dark—and then when they come out through a door, there they are on a beautiful hill, with trees, and the sun shining and the wind blowing on their skin. This often results in some of them having a peak experience there.

"Then they go into the pool, and the regressive procedures begin. They form two lines facing each other like a conveyer belt, and the person at the head of the line lies down and is rocked and passed down the line, so that everybody sees all these human bodies passing in front of them, and as you are rocked and slowly passed along, by the time you get to the end of the line, somebody has to help you get back on your feet.

"The whole group gets turned on by that; I try to do it with everyone before I work with any one person if I can. But sometimes somebody's in something so deeply that I wind up working with first one person, then another, and there's only time for a few people to go on the conveyer belt."

Paul works on a nonverbal level with whatever happens during this period, using a variety of techniques. "If someone starts to cry," he said, "I might float him on his back, and people would group around and begin to rock him and hold him while his partner lets him experience his peak stimuli and another person feeds him with a baby bottle.

"Or I might massage them, opening up their body armor. The thing I do is open up the head area first so the expressions can come out. If people are repressing anger, they become very angry when I massage their muscles. They've already been told that this is the most beautiful opportunity they'll ever have in their lives, probably, to be totally free to express rage. They're encouraged to try to hurt us in any way they wish; they can be totally irresponsible. We will restrain them enough so that they will not damage themselves or us. So we're holding their arms and legs, and they start to rage, and they beat with their arms and legs, and they roar. Sometimes we have two people face each other, too, and growl.

"This period usually goes on from 8 A.M. until 2 P.M. But I'm trying to start earlier—work from six in the morning until 12—and then leave myself four hours to do the integrative work."

The last period starts sometime after lunch and is a time for words. "We talk and try to tie things together intellectually," Paul explained. "Each person tells what happened to him, and what he got out of it, and then the group tells him or what they see in him, and how they feel about him, and sometimes I'll use psychodrama or some other technique to work with what they're talking about." The final part of the marathon ends at 4 P.M.

"I ask them to write me a letter a week later," Paul added, "specifically stating what happened to them, what changes they've experienced, and what insights they've had. I tell them to concretize it as much as possible without overconcretizing it. I think there are evolving organic experiences that, if the person tries to nail down too firmly at this stage, will be walled off. So I don't ask them to be *too* specific."

A month after the marathon, Paul schedules a follow-up session, running from 8:00 P.M. until 11 or 11:30 P.M. If they need help before then, they can call for an appointment.

"I make tape recordings of everything that goes on in the marathon itself and in the follow-up session," Paul told us, "first, for possible research value; second, to draw from in writing a book; and third, to protect myself in the event that anybody wanted to claim that something had happened in a session that didn't happen."

Paul also conducts midweek nude sensitivity training groups that meet once a week from 7 to 11 P.M. in a private home with a pool. The purpose of the midweek group is "to integrate this new awareness into the ongoing life of the everyday." Nude meetings led by Paul alternate with clothed leaderless sessions.

RESULTS

Generally speaking, participants' immediate reactions to nudity fall into seven categories:

1. A sense of pleasure derived from the freedom to look at other persons' bodies and to be looked at.
2. A personal sense of comfort, exhilaration, and freedom.
3. The desire to touch and experience skin contact and a sense of being inhibited in this respect.

4. Pleasure arising from the sense of group closeness and the relaxed expressions on the faces of the other participants.
5. A sense of the naturalness of the nude condition, and a feeling of relief at not having reacted inappropriately.
6. The experience of being high or unable to sleep for most of the remainder of the night.
7. A sense of concern about one's physical body when comparing it with other members of the group.

Do people report any carry-over to their life outside the group? "Yes," Paul told us. "Following up one month afterward, my impression is that 50 percent of the people experience major changes in their lives. We haven't done any studies yet, but people do report things like a decrease in alienation, greater warmth, greater openness, a greater degree of relatedness to other people, and a greater feeling of aliveness. Also, greater acceptance of their body, increased comfort with their body, no longer feeling that it's ugly or dirty or misshapen or in some way undesirable. Greater capacity to express love via physical contact—this is especially reported by men, who often learn to express love by physical contact with their male children.

"About half report improvement in their sex life, some in terms of frequency, some in terms of enjoyment. Really, of course, it's understandable, because in the course of the 24 hours, 'Daddy, has been saying it's okay to be sensual, it's okay to be nude; where you approve of this, you release sex guilts and permit greater expression in this area.

"Many people have reported that others say they look better. This I think is because they allowed themselves to be warm, loving, and sensual, and this in turn means better-looking. A few people have focused more on physical fitness than before. Another thing they report is desensitization to skin color.

"Oh, by the way, aging is also a problem of body image. It's very important. Many active, really warm, alive human beings assign themselves to isolation because they feel they are getting too old. So they are going to be rejected. They very often are more turned on than the younger ones. And besides that, when they are nude they are more beautiful. You know the ugliest part of the human body as people age is their faces. You know why? Because the face shows the continuous kind of strain we are under. More than any other part of our body. And so most people when they get undressed look younger and look better. In fact I know of only one person in the 43 sessions that I have run that I think should stay dressed. All the others have looked better with their clothing off.

"Still another thing they report is a drop in their sex stereotypes. In other words, the fellow who only likes blondes finds he likes brunettes too after a nude marathon. It's a kind of freeing process, also a freeing in terms of age. Many men find they are more free and open with older women, who normally would have disgusted them. So the age barrier seems to some extent to be transcended.

"Married couples seem to get a greater degree of freedom and also a greater sense of security. That is, they are not as jealous as they were before. Attractions now take place openly rather than covertly; so they realize it's not something to be concerned about. A woman might be concerned about her husband looking at the ankles of girls passing by, but after she goes to a nude marathon and he's hugged a few of them and even had an erection, and he still loves her and isn't interested in replacing her with another woman who, after all, only turned him on sexually, and at that, momentarily—she feels a greater sense of security.

"Other areas reported are those concerned with sex problems, particularly impotence, which has been resolved in a matter of a marathon or two in many instances. Exhibitionistic symptoms have been dropped —gone for four months, the last I heard. Nude marathons have been used along with behavioral therapy for homosexuals, lesbians, and the sexually inhibited. We've had many instances of men who, following a few of these sessions, are dating and going to bed and living a more normal life, and some of them are 45 or 50 years old. We've had good results with women who are the old-maid type, too."

Have there been any negative results? "Not that I know of," Paul told us. "There could be. It's possible. Not everybody comes to the follow-up session, and sometimes you don't know why they don't come. My feeling is that as long as you're running a group where the door is open and people are free to leave whenever they want to—a group where people know what they're getting into ahead of time—I don't think you're too likely to have serious negative results. In addition, I don't pressure people. A lot of techniques sound something like the third degree without the lights; there, I think, you get into problems. But not if a person can leave if he wants to. People who might be too badly upset by the process probably don't even come."

Has anybody ever left? "Oh sure. Particularly since we've begun working on the stomach and opening up body armor. This thing gets pretty wild—people screaming. It looks worse when you're looking at it than it feels when you go through it. Once in a while we'll have someone who isn't ready for it. There's no way of describing it to them beforehand, but the door is open, and I've had some people walk out. I've had some people talk to me first and then leave. Other people I've been able to reassure that they won't have to go through this thing if they don't want to. It's strictly optional. Actually, we don't have time enough to put everyone through it anyway. I structure it that way; so we have a number of places for people who just watch this process.

"I imagine you can't do this work with 500 to 1,000 people and not have somebody who has a negative reaction to some degree. I can't conceive of that. Also, I would have to say that sometimes, when progress is being made, the halfway point is negative. A person can be so dumb in a depressed state that he doesn't even know he's depressed. As you get him to express his anger, his depression becomes an active depression, and he feels worse than he did before. Whereas before he was lying in bed all day and sleeping, now he's getting up, and the world looks miserable, and he's moving around looking for a job, and he can't find one. So he's depressed, but it's an improvement. Now he knows he's depressed, where before he was asleep. So you can have interim states where a person is improving, but it doesn't look that way.

"The remarkable thing about this is that there is so little negative comment. In other words, what has kept us going is that practically everybody who's been involved has either come out of it neutral or is a very enthusiastic supporter. You get negative reactions from people who haven't been to a nude marathon. And you get plenty of them.

"I think nude marathons will be very valuable in working with people who have physical deformities. In rehabilitation, for instance. Very often, the psychologic handicap is greater than the deformity itself. Women with mastectomies often no longer have any sex lives. It's amazing how a man can overlook a missing breast in a woman in a matter of a few hours and not even know it. I wouldn't believe it possible if I hadn't gone through it myself. Then there are all the imagined defects for which people want plastic surgery that they don't even need. Nude marathons also help suicidal persons. We have rapidly eliminated that symptom in a number of them. When they see the magnificence of human life, they are not as prone to take their own lives. A feeling of aloneness is a very strong suicide indicator, and suicide-prevention groups try to help the suicidal person know how much other people need them. It gives them a sense of relatedness. I wouldn't be surprised if nude marathons could do this in quite an overwhelming way. I wish they'd send me some of the suicidal cases they're afraid they can't get anywhere with."

THEORY

"If a child falls down and scrapes his knee," Paul explained to his audience at the 1969 Annual Meeting of the American Association for Humanistic Psychology, "he holds his pain in and doesn't cry, and he runs to his mother, and when she puts her arms around the child, he begins to cry. Now the analogy is that human beings have hurts within themselves that they need to express, that they're holding in because the daily environment is not one in which they can trust the group of people they are with. So what I do is to set up a highly supportive situation in which these emotional needs that are being held back can spontaneously break out. When they spontaneously break out, I feel they are most ready to be worked with, and then I work with them. But I don't probe for them. I may spend five or six hours setting up an environment that is highly supportive and in which there isn't, in my opinion, any major therapeutic change taking place in the participants, but in the next two hours, the whole group goes off like a string of firecrackers, and instead of spending an hour with each individual dragging all this stuff out, it comes out spontaneously and can be handled in a matter of minutes. It's a supersupportive approach. It's the end product of what Rogers began a long time ago, when he tried to support people by his verbal responses to their emotional state. I'm using an environment that permits and makes regression safe. What it does is to recapitulate the environment of childhood, of babyhood.

"The silent period is as important to regression as nudity is, because babies don't talk, and if you want somebody to regress to prelanguage levels, and you talk to them, they're not going to do it.

"What I'm doing is working on the animal disclosure level first and letting the cortical level come second.

"When we wake you up at eight in the morning, give you some breakfast, and take you into that warm-water pool, what we have added to nudity, which is one factor of babyhood, is skin contact, which is another, and nonverbal communication through sighs, gestures, and touch, which is still another factor of babyhood. Then we have womb temperature water and the lightness of floating, which are other factors of babyhood, and the feeling of being rocked the way your mother rocked you and being held in people's arms and given thorough skin contact all over your body with their faces and hands, which is another factor, and finally, we give you a bottle of warm milk with a nipple. In this secure state, you will spontaneously begin to cry or show rage, and then we will add still another factor of babyhood: the right to be irresponsible. You can flail, kick, cry, do anything you want—it's the responsibility of the group to watch out for you and take care of you. And we have four heavy men, one on each arm and leg, and you're in the pool. What can you possibly do to hurt yourself or anybody else?

"Then we add another dimension of babyhood, which is the right to let emotions go into screams and immediate vocal expression instead of the inhibition we learn as adults, and these people scream fiercely.

"Then I do one more thing. I alternate this highly supportive love-giving state with working on the body armor, massaging the tensions in the muscles that are used to hold back negative emotions. I find that by massaging the muscles in the head, neck, and jaw, expression is freed. For example, if you want to hit and you don't want to hit, the end result is a cramp in your arm. The way to relieve the cramp is to massage it. Massaging a cramp is more painful than the cramp. Tension is like a chronic cramp—one that you've gotten so used to living with that you don't even know you have it. At this point, with everybody hanging onto your arms and legs, I have one person begin to work on the stomach area. First, there's physical pain. Then, emotional pain. While someone's working on your stomach, I'm working on your head. And as I relieve the tension in the jaws and face, the pain in the stomach is translated into a scream. And the people who are holding you scream, too, as the emotion becomes transmitted in the state of nonverbal, nude, womb-water unity.

"What happens, apparently, is that recall from early babyhood is far more *somatic* than it is visual or auditory, and so the somatic element of recall happens first. Sometimes you don't get beyond the somatic. But frequently you will get visual and auditory flashbacks to the exact event. Or if you provide the environment for regression to babyhood, and the traumatic event that is blocking the person is one that happened later in life, you will get that incident instead. For example, if, when we float a woman on her back, she holds her legs tightly together, we will put two men on her legs and pull them apart, and she will go right through the ceiling. The woman has been raped or has had an unwanted pregnancy, and she's keeping her vagina protected. Now as soon as we know that, we alternately spread her legs, and when we feel the time is right, we put her legs back together again, and we hold her and rock her and give her a bottle, and then we spread her legs again and out comes more terror, but there's nothing happening to reinforce the terror. From a behavioral therapy viewpoint, we're simply deconditioning her. And then I'll hold the pelvis, and I'll start making her make sexual motions, and again she'll go through the ceiling. Or maybe I'll get between her legs with my shoulders and apply the kind of pressure characteristic of a man who was trying to rape her. And again she'll go through the ceiling. And alternately, we rock, support, hold. And then repeat, until finally there's no longer any reaction.

"When you're doing this, she will have recalls—perhaps of being raped, or of a husband who is giving her children she doesn't want in a marriage she doesn't want to be in, or perhaps an uncle molesting her when she was six years old. These will be flashbacks, but we don't talk about them at that point, because if we did, we would block the process. When we end the silent period at two o'clock, we turn the cortex on and talk. Until then, the whole object is to get at what's there precortically.

"In the integrative session, we say, 'Now, what did you experience and what meaning does it have for you?' And then we work with the individuals until they understand. Perhaps a woman says, 'Oh, now I know why I can't really let myself go with my husband! I was really more emotionally involved with my father. I wanted *him* to make love to me, not my husband, and that wasn't possible, so *nothing* was possible sexually, and now I feel relieved.' And she comes back a month later and says, 'My God, I'm having orgasms; it's tremendous!' That's one example."

One theory has it that Paul's conveyer belt is like a birth canal and thus recapitulates the birth experience. "I'd like to record the intra-uterine sounds of a woman," Paul said, "and play them back through an underwater loudspeaker for the participants while they float in the warm water.

"We know that emotional problems are also helped. People are afraid to be close to people. From a behavioral standpoint (the behavior therapy point of view), most of our problems are phobias. And if you come close enough to what you are afraid of, and nothing happens, it's not reinforced. If a horse kicks you, from that point on you're afraid of horses, but if you progressively come closer and closer to horses and they don't kick you again, gradually the fear lessens. And before long you can ride the horse once more. Now I suppose you could sit on a couch and talk about horses but there's nothing like getting near the real one. Can you imagine if you were a therapist and a patient came to you and said, 'A horse threw me, Doctor. Can I lie on your couch and get over my fear?' Then you sit there and have that person ramble on day after day about how he fears horses, on that couch? Or are you gradually going to take him toward a horse back at the stable? Then you say, 'Oh Mr. Bindrim, you're oversimplifying the complexities of the psyche,' as some people have said to me—which is a way of calling me a dirty name. But you know, there are horses in our past, there are experiences we have had and we can approach them through our fantasies. And if they actually are fears you can get rid of, so much the better. If a man is afraid of women, and he comes close to a woman, he is going to have fantasies. It's going to activate the whole thing and make it easier to work with. For example, it's no surprise that one fellow who had sexual relationships and even an ongoing relationship with one woman for as long as three years never married. He raises horses and he disliked females so much he would not even have a mare in the stable. Following a nude marathon, he felt he got the full impact of what he was missing by not relating emotionally, and within two months following the session he was married. So it becomes a powerful instrument in these areas. I think that at the present time we need to evaluate some of these results really carefully and statistically. Some are very clear. Others will call for more extensive research procedures.

"This procedure can result in dramatic regression—a regression to preverbal levels, even to birth levels. Sometimes adults virtually turn into babies in the swimming pool. I had a fantasy the other day that if some people felt they had to conduct these sessions with clothes on, we could hand out diapers at the door. This might be the standard clothed setting and it would be alright. I think the extent of the regressions that occur are the most interesting because, if we want to use a freudian term, 'regression in the service of the ego' is very important. To begin with, we can get back to the way we felt as babies and thereby not only become aware of whatever repressed feelings we have, but also deal with these feelings. It's not enough just to know. If you feel an insatiable hunger and a lack of trust in human beings, you may discover that at the root of this is neglect you suffered before you could talk. And how can we 'talk you' to that point? In fact the very act of talking will block the regression. And yet we can reach that point, and if you can feel that agony, and if you can claw and be a baby, and if at that point you can be given a bottle of warm milk, or better still if I only had a lactating cotherapist (that will come too, some day, you know), this can reach that hunger as nothing else can. And when you come back, for some strange reason you don't feel this emptiness and aloneness anymore. And you feel a sense of easiness around people, a new kind of aggressive creativeness in the way you conduct your life. Some things that happened to us before we could speak have devastated our guts to the point where we are unable to cope with the normal things that happen in life.

"Why should this be such a good method of producing aggression? In the first place, we begin at seven o'clock at night. We go on with a basically ordinary encounter session, except that we are also getting used to getting nude and physical contact. By the time we reach four in the morning we usually have a group that's a real group relating and communicating well, that's really close and intimate with each other, where people don't jump if someone puts his arm around somebody. We're used to erections by then, all this kind of nonsense that people are afraid about. That's all gone, that's over. At four o'clock we begin a silent period. And you can have some rest if you want and meditate. We give you about four hours to stew, about everything that has been shaken up. There's nothing like stewing, nothing like being silent with yourself. Most people talk to escape themselves. Then by eight in the morning, after having breakfast, with the silence still continuing, we go into the warm-water pool. So to begin with, we've taken away language. In other words we've gotten back to where the only modes of communication are those that you knew before you could speak, when speech meant nothing to you. As we enter the pool, human beings begin to communicate with each other through grunts, through groans, through sighs, through screams, through looks in the eyes, through tears. And that communication is very powerful, far more powerful than language. In fact, if you're crying that you hurt, other people in that group see it and begin to cry with you. That means a thousand times more than anybody saying, 'Oh, I'm so sorry you feel that way.' In fact, those words are an insult. They are a substitute for the real.

"Without language, the way a baby is in the womb, with full skin contact, huddling, and closeness, we place you in the water of the pool where people can hold you in their arms even if you weigh 200 pounds, and where a group of people can cover your body as completely as a mother once did when you were small. In this environment you can be like a baby, being rocked the way a baby is rocked, or perhaps held so that you can rage with full rage the way a baby does, with arms and legs and everything going, and screaming like hell at the same time, and doing damage to no one and feeling the same helplessness you felt when you were a baby. There are people holding your arms and holding your legs, and they massage your body and begin to touch some of those tender places in your stomach that are like buttons. When these 'buttons' are massaged and pushed they first create a feeling of pain, and then release the emotion that the tension in those muscles is holding back, so that you begin to re-experience some of the fears, the dreads, the hurts, and the deep agonies that you knew as a child, and that you have literally been carrying around with you all your life instead of unloading them. The idea is to experience and thereby to unload. To use an analogy, if you have a rotting fish in your house, you might sweep it under the carpet so that you won't have to look at it, but the smell won't get any better. When you carry it out by the tail, it will stink worse than ever. But once it's disposed of, it's gone. And the same applies to these gnawing feelings of anxiety and hurt that we live with; they are like the rotting fish that needs to be experienced fully before it can be gotten rid of. This is one procedure for doing it, in this warm water, with the skin contact, with the rocking, with this concern of people, with the absence of language, and finally with a bottle.

"It is surprising how people reject the bottle. Those who reject love from adults also reject the bottle on this primitive level. And after they spew the milk out five or six times, the right muscular tensions have been released, and they are free and they cry and they scream. Suddenly some little Mr. Milktoast or a woman who is terribly repressed in terms of her rage suddenly lets go with full force and violence and nothing happens. It's all right. It's O.K. to feel that way; it's O.K. to express it. And then they are held and rocked with skin contact and warm water of the pool, and wow!"

"After LSD expert Stan Grof attended a nude marathon, he reported that many of the processes were like what happened in LSD sessions. Describing a woman in the marathon who felt her body was ugly, Stan said: 'She could spend years in analysis talking about her body, and I don't think she would get anywhere. In the LSD sessions, this would be changed, but she still would be left with the trial and error of real-life situations. But this was fantastic for her. There was a 9:6 male: female ratio; so she was held by someone most of the time. I don't think even with repeated LSD sessions this kind of problem could be tackled as successfully.'

Some people who are afraid of the emotional level prefer to remain on a touch level. They are trying to get from touch what the rest of the world gets from emotional relationships. We could call them the fiction set, the hypersexed, the sexual freedomites. If you have had anything to do with the orgy thing, or explored it at all, you know what an ice situation it is. In fact, you are told right off, 'If you want emotional relationships, please don't come down to our orgy. You'll ruin the club.' We've had Don Juans, one-night-standers, both men and women for a long while. Simply the fact that they get together and have an easier route together than the local neighborhood bar is just an improvement in communication. But there's no greater warmth involved in it at this level. I think that extended families, where there are emotional relationships between the multiple pairs, are on a different level. But there aren't too many extended families. There are quite a few individuals who are afraid of emotional relatedness and therefore prefer to experience sensuality without emotions.

"There are people who have achieved the emotional level of intimacy, but who are afraid to move on to the spiritual level, which is the finer level. This is the peak experience level. This is the level of commitment to life, where you feel more than the paired relationship, which is so frequent on the emotional level. The emotional level reads like this: 'I have now found my one and only, and you and I are going to make it against the rest of the miserable lousy world out there.' On the Susskind program when I asked David what shoulder he cried on, he said that of his wife. And I said, 'What does that say about your attitude toward the rest of the world? Don't you trust anybody else?' And he had to admit it. This kind of symbiotic relationship on the emotional level can become very sick, can become very ingrown. We can demand too much of each other, literally eat our children.

"From there we move on to this broader spiritual level of the peak experience that Maslow describes in which we feel a part of life. We don't really have to know someone first to feel a part of him to begin with. I would liken this to being a piece of a jigsaw puzzle among all the other pieces, and the only thing that is your claim to individuality is that you are isolated, that you can draw lines around yourself. That makes you an isolated piece, a unit. Whereas the other extreme in the final intimate blending is that you've got all the pieces of the puzzle together, and you, the remaining pieces, are then put into that hole that's left. And as you drop into the puzzle, you disappear. You literally leak out into the rest of the puzzle. At first it's frightening, because you are losing your identity in terms of isolation. But suddenly your identity is one of meaningful relationships with your society. You are what you are doing and who you are intimate with in the context of your life. Without the other people you would not exist, in any meaningful sense. So we move from the isolation of identity to the meaningful relationship that establishes a new nonisolated kind of identity.

"It is the extent of the nude marathon to help the person, to accept him at whatever level he is on. What good does it do you to play a game with a sexual exhibitionist? Here the poor guy is waving his penis around because he is afraid to have contact with anyone. And so, you put him in jail. As soon as he gets out of jail, he says, 'So now I'll wave it without getting caught.' And you keep playing the game! What do we do with him? We let him wave it for 20 hours. Do you know what happens after 20 hours of waving it? It gets kind of tiresome. Other people are holding each other and experiencing love and closeness, and he says, 'Jesus what in the hell is going on there? There must be something to that.' If you can entice him into the experience and help him to feel it, the first thing you know he's not interested in waving it anymore."

RESPONSIBILITIES

"First, there's a responsibility on the part of people working in this field to define what we're doing and distinguish it from other things," Paul said. "If you're running a skinny-dipping group, call it that. If you're running a nudist camp, call it that. If you're running a permissive encounter group that allows people to take their clothes off if they wish to, call it that. If you're running a nude marathon with psychodrama, call it that. There's a hell of a difference between the regressive type of nude marathon that I'm running and an encounter group that provides baths for nude bathing after the group is over. But all these things tend to be put in one bag.

"Second, there will always be people who will learn how to do the mechanics of a nude marathon, such as the warm water and the rocking and so forth, and they're going to unlock some pretty potent stuff. If they are not sufficiently seasoned as therapists, they're going to be scared. I've had a lot of therapists working with me who get very frightened when things open up and start to fly. In fact, sometimes I've had to comfort them more than I did the person who was blowing. Not only will they have to go with what opens up, but they'll also have to do something about it. It's not enough to unlock these feelings; you have to work with them when they are opened up, and this calls for a person who is not frightened by violence or by powerful emotions. It's not so hard to unlock these reactions, but you have to be very sensitive and pretty committed and willing to take risks yourself in order to work with them. I don't think nude marathons are something for a new, naive, immature, inexperienced therapist to plunge into, let alone inexperienced persons who have been to two encounter groups and have decided they'd like to hold the next one nude.

"Another thing that can happen to a neophyte in this area is that he is likely to be seduced. Who is to see that *he* follows the ground rules? To say nothing of the individual who thinks it's a ball to run nude marathons because he thinks it's an easy way to find women. And just because a fellow has a Ph.D. doesn't necessarily qualify him. It calls for a good deal of mature judgment. I'm not a fuddy-duddy when it comes to sex. I'm certainly not opposed to sex. But I know that when you're going beyond the mores of the society, and you're doing it in a professional and not an underground way, you have to be very certain of yourself as well as the way in which you set things up for others.

"There are also legal factors. At the AAHP convention we had people bathing nude in the pool and calling it a nude marathon, which is ridiculous in the first place and second is a violation of Maryland law. This is irresponsibility, and we have to remember that we are responsible to our society. So if you're running a nude session, make sure the law allows people to be nude together. And don't do it in a yard where other people can see you, for that constitutes indecent exposure, and you're in trouble. And be careful of minors; don't have them in your group, or you may be accused of corrupting their morals.

"Also, you have to place responsibility for acting out sexually on the participant. You can't be everywhere present, and you're not a policeman. But it's your responsibility to structure the marathon so that people cannot wander off by themselves.

"I have a set of ground rules that participants receive *before* they come to the session. This is a legal contract they sign. It's your responsibility to let people know *before they arrive* what they will and will not be doing. At an American Psychological Association convention, participants in a division 29 workshop were asked to strip down to bras and panties and underwear, and no one who went to that workshop was told ahead of time that they were going to be asked to strip. That's unethical, as far as I'm concerned. A person should know ahead of time what he's going to be asked to do if it is contrary to commonly accepted mores.

"It's also important to let participants know that the medical model is not being followed. We are in fact dispensing with the medical model. We are saying that emotional reactions between participants and the leader are central to the encounter. We are not holding our distance. We are expecting no more of the participants than of ourselves. This has to be in print, because the person is anticipating that you will be in the role of doctor, with himself as privileged characters. You must clarify that you have equal rights in the session and equal limitations. This should be clear before they arrive.

"Another responsibility is to openly report what you do. Recognize that when you are in an area that's going contrary to the mores of society, it's your obligation to report your results to professional societies, so that nobody will think you're just playing hanky-panky for your own kicks. But the second aspect of that responsibility is the responsibility of the psychologic associations themselves to *permit* you to report. At present, many of these associations have failed to meet this responsibility because they are afraid it will damage their image. And in this respect, I consider their ethics to be questionable. The welfare of society is more important than their image when the two are in conflict.

"There is also a responsibility to do research. You are entering a new area that is threatening to your society, and it's your responsibility to carefully evaluate your results as soon as possible. This may mean beginning with the very loosest kind of questionnaires and winding up with the tightest possible types of research that can be done. But there is also a responsibility on the part of the institutions to make this research possible. I've spent four or five mornings with Ph.D. candidates so they can make sensible requests to do their dissertations on nude marathons, and one person after another has been cut down by his department. It is also the responsibility of psychology departments to permit research to be done in this area. And the same applies to the NIMH if they don't provide grants in this area because they think the area is not respectable. So the responsibility for research and reporting goes both ways.

"Then we have a responsibility to the press. Publicity in this area cannot be avoided; it can only be directed. You have a choice. If somebody from the press wants to interview you, you can say, 'No,' and you're very likely to get a loaded story about what must be going on behind those closed doors. The essential thing with the press is if you're not hiding anything, be open, but demand that the representative of the press thoroughly experience what you're doing, not just listen to a quickie tape or a lecture and then write an article. Make him come into the session. Make him participate. And if he isn't willing to do it, close the door and tell him it's his own responsibility because *he* won't take the personal risk involved. And they will understand. I've gotten good publicity throughout.

"The last responsibility is to establish a new kind of organization that will encourage research in formerly closed areas. It goes much further than nude marathons. Because we're now entering an era in which active exploration of new cultural models will be commonplace."

How does Paul feel about being identified with nude marathons? "I thoroughly accept it," he replied when we put that question to him. "I'm willing to let my future rise or fall with what happens to nude marathons, and I'm training people to run them as rapidly as I'm able to. I feel confident that there's a great deal in this area to be explored. I'm all for research in this area, and I don't think anything will happen other than confirmation of the validity of what I'm doing. Meanwhile, the main danger is that the public and the profession may not understand what we're doing, and that some persons may exploit the area."

BIBLIOGRAPHY

Bindrim, P. A Report on a Nude Marathon: The Effect of Physical Nudity upon the Practice of Interaction in the Marathon Group. *Psychother.: Theory, Research and Practice,* **5**:180–88, 1968.

Bindrim, P. Nudity—A Quick Grab for Intimacy in Group Therapy. *Psychol. Today.* **3**:24–28, 1969.

Maslow, A. H. *Eupsychian Management: A Journal.* Homewood, Ill.: Irwin-Dorsey, 1965.

Ruth C. Cohn

 Living-Learning Encounters:
The Theme-Centered
Interactional Method

COMMENTARY

Ruth Cohn suggests that what we learn and the way we learn it are too frequently irrelevant to actual human situations. What tends to happen in traditional learning situations is that material presented may remain emotionally unassimilated, i.e., not relevant in depth.

The theme-centered interactional method is defined and illustrated in an effort to demonstrate that learning, psychotherapy, and encounters all have in common an opportunity to provide a *live experience* for people. This opportunity can be realized when the leader respects and is responsible to the resources within the group so that confrontation techniques then become the vehicle rather than the limitation to personal growth.

BIOGRAPHY

Ruth C. Cohn's professional background is that of psychology, philosophy, and psychoanalysis. Her living space includes pre-Nazi Germany, Switzerland, and the United States. Her interest has grown to include a variety of therapeutic approaches with individuals and groups, which include experientialism and Gestalt therapy and the initiation of the theme-centered interactional method. This approach is geared to use knowledge of group therapy and group process for the improvement of group leading and group communication.

Ruth C. Cohn has been on the faculties of National Psychological Association of Psychoanalysis (N.P.A.P.) and the Group Therapy Department of the Post Graduate Center for Mental Health. She is the founder/director of the Workshop Institute for Living-Learning. Publications include a variety of papers on countertransference training of therapists and supervisors and on training intuition and various articles on the theme-centered interactional method.

SCOPE

When lively people communicate with each other about a thing, a task, or a theme they are in a living-learning situation. When people strive for awareness of each other beyond their functional roles (such as being the bus driver or the salesman), they are in a living-learning encounter. Living-learning encounters are our daily privilege of being alive and in touch with each other.

Living-learning is the celebration of being a human being who can take in and change around and create something new. Living-learning means enjoying pictures, perceptions, new feelings, new relationships, thoughts, motions, and skills—and never having to be bored. Living-learning is the joy of freedom and mastery and leisure and adventure alone or with another—the surprise of the unexpected, and the curious expectation of what now and what next and never being still for long.

The term "living-learning" was coined by Norman Liberman on the occasion of our founding the Workshop Institute for Living-Learning in 1966. We searched for a term that would express the process of learning as exciting, alive, and with-it. This concept implies the contrast to dead-learning that most people endure in their acceptance of splitting life into hours of learning (or having a job) and hours of being free and living. Students are asked to "learn" so they can "live and make a living later on in life." This separation of living *and* learning is a sad cultural fact and not a biologic necessity. The baby reaches out for his toes, watches a colorful windblown pinwheel, gurgles sounds toward articulated words, kicks and wiggles and coos—or, if he fails, may rage and cry. His learning is his living. Our culture pushes children and adults to learn and work faster and encourages competitive rather than cooperative games and schooling. What could be a living-learning growing process becomes a competitive rat race—planting ulterior motivation and ultimately defeating itself destructively.

The theme-centered interactional method[1] is a systematic attempt to bring living-learning encounters and their excitement into working groups—such as academic classrooms, staff meetings, conventions, research teams, and social action groups. The method is a derivative of group therapy, teaching, and communication approaches. Like group therapy, it offers respect for the individual's growth and promotes the group's awareness for each person's participation within the flow of the group members' concerns. Group therapy has, however, one theme and one theme only: "I want to feel and function better." The W.I.L.L. method shifts the emphasis from this one theme of developing an individual's growth potential to any and all tasks or themes that individuals can be concerned with—without losing the focus of each person's uniqueness. Themes may, for instance, refer to police trainees as "trouble shooting without a gun," to high school students as "turning on with mathematics," to staff relationships as "being myself—being black or being white," to therapeutic research groups as "using different methods in different therapeutic situations," and so on.

The number of possible themes in interactional groups is unlimited. The participants may be children, adolescents, or adults. The themes may be concerned with educational, scientific, artistic, and organizational themes and also family, commune, and community living. The optimal size of a group ranges from about 12 to 20 people. However, the principles of the method are also applicable for large meetings and are helpful in private life and smaller groups.

This chapter will give a survey of how the theme-centered interactional method is being used in working groups.

Historically, the theme-centered interactional approach evolved spontaneously in one of my psychoanalytic training groups in 1955. As I conceptualized the method, ideas and techniques from other sources were integrated. I learned most from the Atlanta Psychiatric Clinic (especially from Carl Whitaker and John Warkentin) and from Gestalt therapy (especially from Fritz Perls and James Simkin). Progress in techniques followed by using the theme-centered interactional method in the Workshop Institutes for Living-Learning—our staffs working in the community and training professional and paraprofessional group leaders. The method, despite its firm structure, can embrace an unlimited number of techniques or games. These may include those derived from psychodrama (Moreno) and behaviorism, or the video techniques of Ian Alger and Peter Hogan, or the personal and interactional games of Dan Malamud, or the encounter techniques of Elizabeth Mintz and Virginia Satir. (Hogan, Malamud, and Mintz are mem-

---

[1] Sometimes referred to as the W.I.L.L. method taught at the Workshop Institutes for Living-Learning in New York City and Atlanta, Ga.

bers of W.I.L.L.; they and other creative people have shared in improving the method with their ideas, work, and friendship.)

LIVING-LEARNING—A HOLISTIC APPROACH

I encounter you means I meet you; it means I want to know you. It means I open my senses, my feelings, and my mind to you. It also means I want you to know me and open myself up to be known. We encounter each other if you too want to encounter me and know me. I might want to know all of you that can be known or just a very little bit, and vice versa. The fuller the encounter, the richer we become.

To learn something from my encounter with you means to keep something of you in my existence. I can never take into me what is inside of you—because your perceptions, data, thoughts, and, of course, feelings are always yours. The message from you to me changes on its way from your sending to my receiving. If both of us were to watch a painter painting a picture, there would be at least three images of this picture in the room: the painter's, yours, and mine. (Yet there *is* a picture in the room. You—I—We center our learning in each other *and* the picture.)

I can accept the simple fact of our being psychobiologic islands as a beautiful adventure. I can playfully enjoy chance and choice of an infinite number of encounters and learning adventures. I can accept that we live in this world as separate and autonomous individuals, yet that bridges, ferryboats, jets, and rockets bring us into close proximity —and so can songs, words, smiles, and touch. Or I can fight our separateness and communion by trying to establish fantasy symbiosis or establish autistic isolation, thereby losing the perspective that all islands meet under the ocean and that galaxies are bonded in space.

Whenever a person tries to deny the island quality of human existence—the quality that keeps human beings separate and connected— his communication to the other becomes unrealistic and in a deeper sense comical. When I try to convince you of something that is self-evident to me (because of my particular background and characteristics), I act like a mother who tries to force-feed a child. The child swallowing the unwanted has his own self-propelled living force and may not digest the food—he may vomit, get ulcers, and hate his mother.

By the same token, if a teacher tries to "make" students learn data or opinions from him *his* way and expects students to learn what he knows, he does not take into account people's uniqueness of perceiving, feeling, and thinking and their framework of background and motivation; these differences change every fact, every concept, theory, and method into individual particles of personal systems. Force-feeding of food corresponds to force-feeding in teaching and communication. The food may disappear in the child's body as the teachers' words, data, and utterings may disappear in the student's learning apparatus, but such forced learning, lacking vital involvement, is dead-learning. It is likely to come out undigested or it may poison the student into lethargy or rage, or—most frequently—into lifeless conformity. The most important music, words, or formulas—Bach's, Shakespeare's or Einstein's —have no bearing on students whose receptive and integrative organs are preoccupied with other scholarly or mundane matters, or are pained or fatigued.

Writing down these thoughts, I feel foolish. The statements in this last paragraph seem self-evident to me. Yet the facts show that schools and schoolbooks, organizational meetings, and round-table discussions go on with dead-learning programs and methods as if people were data-processing machines with input, integration, and output mechanisms that can be fed and forced to function with a little bit of repair (reward and punishment) and refinement of procedures. The facts that what you say is not what I hear and what I know for sure is opposed by you —and may be opposed by myself tomorrow—are hard facts to learn; they may have to be stated and restated over and over again from generation to generation—like the commands of "Thou shalt not kill" and "Gnoti Sau Ton."

Living-learning is a concept within a holistic philosophy of man. It encompasses the wholeness of sensing, feeling, thinking, and believing in the wholeness of being a creature who integrates past and future in his present somatopsychic, mindful existence. And this philosophy encompasses man's bondage in causality as well as his freedom of choice and his being a separate individual and a participant in the social and material universe. The seeming paradox of being a separate biologic unit *and* being a social participant presents each individual with conflicts, unfulfilled wishes, and dynamic strivings to balance the never-balanced.

Living-learning encounters occur between two, three, or more people. Living-learning encounters can be spoken, danced, kissed, fought, or cried. They can even be—with more difficulty—written or read. I, writer, and you, reader, right now are in such a difficult encounter. The writer-reader unit is a nonfeedback encounter. I, writer, want to influence you, flow into you, make a difference to you, have an impact on you—with my written-down feelings, thoughts, experiences. Yet I must take the risk of not being heard. I must accept and confirm the existential writer's situation of loneliness-by-no-immediate-response; I must ride on the wings of a fantasy encounter—and you??? (Point 8 in this book's Editors' "Instructions to Contributors": "Above all—involve and interest the reader.") What methods are there to bridge the gap from my sending to your receiving?[2]

Living-learning can occur in solitude and in interchange with other people. Living-learning may be experienced in reading or in lonely ecstasy of seeing a sunset over the ocean, or understanding a mathematical formula. Yet even in solitude most people relate their feelings and fantasies to an absent person or group—the parent, the lover, the teacher, the class, the staff ("if only they were here, I could tell them"). And in absence of such fantasy there still is the participation with others by the mere fact of shared language, shared symbols, and a shared conceptual world. No one is ever alone inside himself—he contains his partnerships with the past, present, and future environment within himself. It is only in participant autonomy that we exist. This participant autonomous I-We relationship in living can be promoted constructively in humanistic communication groups and can be dehumanized in dictatorial and dead-learning settings.

Our schools and boards are as yet resistive or ignorant of the useful role of interactional groups. Classes and meetings are primarily theme-and-leader-directed. The experience of students and group members is therefore that their inner needs or wants, abilities and interpersonal interests, preoccupations and conflicts are ignored or negated. Living-learning energy is converted into dead-learning. Boredom, sleepiness, rebellion, and resignation ensue. *The international uprising of students* and workers, I believe, is not only a phenomenon of economic and racial origin or rejection of nuclear world destruction but *also an expression of a desire to be respectfully heard, to be counted as creative individuals, an antidote against anonymity within an overpopulated world.*

The W.I.L.L. method represents an approach to personalize the impersonalized world of mass education and mass communication. It encourages the individual's self-realization of his sensing *and* feeling *and* thinking potential and his relating intimately and usefully with people who can become important to him. The method is built on faith that a task can be accomplished both more meaningfully for each individual and more successfully in accomplishment if the physical, emotional, intellectual, and spiritual uniqueness of each person is respected and enhanced within the group's involvement with the theme. Therefore, the method promotes awareness of the I and of the You as individuals as well as the We of the group as a whole, cohesion results from the awareness of all I's of each other and the theme. *The theme-centered*

---

[2] The common writer's block can be better understood by realizing the inherent difficulty of communication by memory and fantasy.

interactional group strives for awareness and furthering of each I-potential and We-cohesion and the accomplishment of penetrating a theme or fulfilling a task. Thus, the I-We-It triangle is the structural image of the theme-centered interactional method: the connection of three points of equal importance—the individual, the group, and the theme.

GROUPS

The interactional group is a lively place in which learning takes place. I first became aware of its unique living-learning potential when I compared the deadness of most classrooms, staff meetings, and especially lecture halls with the passion and enthusiasm engendered in therapy groups; and the repeated statements of group therapy patients that the group has been their most important learning experience in life. The interaction in group therapy centers around the participants' personal difficulties and growth potential. The interaction in such groups is concerned with your and my problems and achievements and with living with each other in the space and time of the therapy sessions. However, you and I may add other themes to our interaction than those concerning our personal lives. A group is a group is a group (and not a cluster, crowd, or mass) if all persons within a given time and space share concern for themselves, for each other, and for a theme or task.

ILLUSTRATIONS

Father, mother, and child may be together in the kitchen. They are a family by definition; whether this family is a group depends on their concern with each other and their relatedness to a theme (task). Father may fix a gadget, mother cook dinner, child draw a picture. They may be isolated individuals or they may have concern for each other's feelings and activities. They may share implicitly or explicitly a theme such as "doing things for family living," "making our house nice," "getting things done together," or even "spiting each other." Such themes would be expressed in verbal and/or nonverbal communication.

The triple concern for each (I), for the group as a whole (We), and for the activity and/or theme (It) makes father-mother-child in the kitchen a group rather than a cluster of people. *The rationale of a group thus is the I-We-It triangle. This triangle symbolizes the importance of the respect for the individual with his psychosomatic and spiritual needs, wants, and beliefs, the group as a cohesive team, and the subject matter as the concern of all participants.* The degree of group cohesion depends on the dynamic balance of these I-We-It factors. If for any length of time one or two of these factors are neglected or dominant, group cohesion dissolves and the people in the room become a cluster or a mass.

Cocktail Party. People mill around the room. I meet another "I" and another one. Each "I" has his own pursuits: meeting friends from old times, meeting new people, showing off clothes, getting money for a cause, enjoying food or drinks or conversation, looking at pictures on the wall. There are meetings from "I" to "I" but no common theme. No "We" evolves (beyond possibly some fleeting subgroups with private themes). *This is a microlab of isolation within a mass.*

Lecture Hall. A professor or minister speaks about a theme to many people. If the speaker has good thoughts, lively manners, and clear and convincing ways of speaking, and if he is aware of or at least in tune with the interests of his audience, he creates a multiple theme-to-I relationship between himself and the audience. Many isolated I's thus relate to the speech and the speaker. A "We" is not created because there is little communication from the listener to the speaker and from the listener to his peer listeners. Many lines lead from the I's to the speaker and to the It: the We is represented only by nonverbal and unchecked "thin" lines drawn between peers. I call this the "star relationship" in which all lines go from participants to the speaker and the theme. Under the I-We-It perspective, the We falls short. No group ensues. (*This is a microlab of cultural indoctrination.*)

Academic Seminar. In an academic seminar teacher and students are concerned with themes. The overt theme may be Plato, trigonometry, forestry, or cubism. Covert themes are the teacher's status and the students' grades. Teacher and students may or may not be involved in the overt theme. Their passion may or may not be elsewhere. The "It" (the theme) is in the foreground; the I-involvement may include a thin intellectual layer and exclude all other living-learning energy; the We-cohesion may be spotty. No group has been created. (*This is a microlab of competitive civilization.*)

Family. A family trims a Christmas tree. Father puts up the tree and the lights. The big children put on decorations. Grandmother fixes broken hangers. Mother helps little children to cut out paper trimmings. If the activities are an expression of the family's feelings and the desire to do this together, a group has been formed. The parents, ideally, function as "coleaders" of this group and are concerned not only with trimming the tree but also with helping the family develop manual, esthetic, and interpersonal skills and with supporting the grandparents' emotional and useful position in the family. (*This can be a living-learning group.*)

Group Therapy Group. A group therapy group is involved in the theme "I want to feel and function better." The participants may be interested in one man's difficulties in getting along with his employer. The patient exposes his feelings toward his boss and toward the therapist. The group members relate their perceptions and interpretations to the copatient. They also talk about their own feelings toward this man as well as their involvements with authority figures. The group therapist relates in personal ways to the one patient, the group, and himself. The people in this session are a group concerned with the I-We-It. (*This too can be a living-learning group.*)

THE THEME-CENTERED INTERACTIONAL GROUP (THE I-WE-IT APPROACH)

In initiating and practicing the theme-centered interactional method I have endeavored systematically to create a group structure that promotes living-learning in classrooms, research groups, round-table conferences, and any place where people meet for educational, organizational, research, or other community purposes. Such models that occur spontaneously in families and in group therapy have rarely come forth in educational and organizational settings, which have been concerned with either theme-centered programs or personal care for growth and health.

PHILOSOPHY

The philosophic basis for the theme-centered interactional method is holistic.

The wholeness of man has a multitude of aspects: He is a psychobiologic entity who senses *and* feels, *and* thinks, *and* believes. He is a being, determined by and determining his past, present, and future. His vantage point is his here-and-now. His past, present, and future contain chance and choice. Man is a participant partner of the universe. His partnership is determined by all and determines all others.

From the basis of these axiomatic assumptions it follows that man, as a psychobiologic unit in time and space and as participant partner in the universe, is both autonomous and interdependent: An individual, an I, functions and lives well in the flowing process of his existence if he lives within the awareness and consideration of his self-reliance and partnership; he becomes a burden to himself (sick) and to mankind (asocial) if he distorts his autonomy into the practice of autism and his interdependence into the illusion of grandiose independence or helpless dependency.

Promoting the living-learning spirit of each person in an interactional group means to accept each individual's inalienable right and reality to be autonomous and interdependent.

Only the I, only the individual, is in the position of inward knowledge of his sensation, feelings, desires, and aspirations. No outside perception equals intrapsychic self-knowledge. The outsider, on the other hand, can perceive and intuit much about the other person if he functions with awareness of and sensitivity to reality rather than to his own projections. Such perceptions and intuitions can be helpful to the other's inward recognition and self-realization.

The existential condition of the self being in the center of his own world gives each person the responsibility for his own experience and activities. (Nobody can substitute for me as the core of my own existence.)

THE "GLOBE"

The theme-centered interactional method relies on awareness of what constitutes an interactional group and use of these constituents dynamically. The group is the meeting of people who are concerned with each other and a theme. The method encourages free-flowing awareness of all structural factors.

The I-We-It factors designate the group's balance at any given moment. A group, however, does not exist unto itself but is embedded in the larger circle of environmental circumstances. These circumstances include the givens of time, space, motivational, hierarchic, and functional auspices of the human environment in which the workshop takes place. These data include strict or flexible time schedules—such as hours per week, week ends, and evening or day series. The space may be set within classroom organizational quarters, a rented house, a retreat, offices, or any other (preferably secluded) space. Flexibility in the widest sense is possible—one can make group arrangements at street corners, conventions, bars, and so on (but these are rather minimal operational conditions for the method).

The globe includes the purpose of the workshop meeting. The purpose may be set by the group; a group may contract a leader; or people may respond to an advertisement. The purpose or goal may, however, also be set by people who have power over others—such as prison officials over prisoners, teachers over children, administrators and employers over employees.

The globe includes the constellation of the group membership. Are they all strangers at the beginning or do some people know each other? Are they hostile or friendly to new people? It is vital to know the constellation of group participants. Once I led a group of ministers for a week end, knowing that they came from different churches and places. I did not realize, however, that half of the group had met weekly for half a year but the others were strangers. There was an undercurrent of hostility between these subgroups of various kinds, which could be worked through only after the globe factors were known.

Sometimes a "captive" group receives the group leader as a spy and perceives the workshop as a planned brainwashing procedure that is to be resisted. Only when such globe factors are cleared up can living-learning encounters take place. Most difficulties in interactional workshops arise not from overt interactions, but from opaque interfering constellations, or from real or suspected manipulations by outside forces.

As soon as these are recognized, they become workable challenges for group interaction.

Examples.   I was asked to give a workshop on staff relationships in a western psychiatric clinic. The work seemed easy. People were eager and cooperative. Only after a relatively long time, did I become aware of the fact that those staff members who were unfriendly to the medical director (who had arranged for this workshop) had not come to participate! The two-party system showed up by nonparticipation.

I was invited to lead a workshop in a southern growth center. A few months later I received a letter from another not-too-distant organization stating that they had agreed to join this series. This was confirmed. A few days prior to the meeting I was informed by the representative of the first organization that there were more registrants than I had stated as my maximum. I said that this would be alright if I were allowed to bring a coleader. This was acceptable to the person I spoke to. On my arrival—a few hours prior to that of my coleader—the representative of the second organization greeted me in great anger. *He* had not agreed to accept a coleader and he would therefore advise his group to leave if they so chose. My young coleader (who just happened to be black—a fact not previously known to the organizational representatives) and I went through a miserable period of clearing the air before anything else could be accomplished. This was a typical "globe" error.

I had been invited to go to England after giving a speech at a convention in Vienna about the theme-centered interactional method. The invitation was for me to be the "consultant for the staff" of a group therapy association for a two-week training session for mental health workers and teachers. I assumed that I was consulted to introduce the W.I.L.L. method. It took the staff and me four days of agony until we recognized that they wanted me to help them improve their own method rather than acquaint them with mine. Because I was on theoretic and practical issues in opposition to their credo (group leaders as observers rather than as participants), we found ourselves in a difficult position. The misjudgment of the globe here put the staff and me in conflict.

The environmental globe in which each interactional triangle takes place does not exist unto itself but, like all stellar globes, is embedded in the universe and influenced and coguided by all other globes and the universal condition. Thus, *an interactional workshop takes on characteristics of its individual members as well as their connectedness to their societal relationships.*

In a theme-centered interactional workshop the group leader functions as the guardian of the method. He guards a multiplicity of factors: the "globe" triangle (space-time-environmental condition) and the interactional triangle of the multifaceted "I," the intricate "We," and the establishment and pursuit of the "It." The first and most important task is the setting of the scene in cooperation with the person(s) who shares in the responsibility of establishing the workshop series. Time, space, environment, and themes must be optimally geared to the purpose of the group meetings. Following are some examples of corelating the purpose of the program with an experiential theme-centered design.

Examples. (for experientially relating the theme to the globe).

Purpose. Training group therapists as group leaders and staff members of the Workshop Institute for Living-Learning.
Time. Fall, 1966. A week end.
Place. Renee Nell's country place (a halfway house in Connecticut). The halfway-house residents participated (as community representatives in the program), Renee Nell as guest member of the staff-in-training.
Theme. Multiple groups: Segregation-collision-coexistence-integration.

One of the *built-in theme experiences* of that training week end was the inclusion of various forms of segregational experiences. These were to be in four of eight complementary groups: *residents (of the country place) and professionals,* blacks and whites, men and women, Jews and Christians. Each participant belonged to one category of each of these pairs. Each section worked together in such a segregated state for one-half hour. *Each person* therefore *had four different experiences of being segregated with "his own kind."* Each subgroup had a group leader belonging to the category he led.

Schedule
Friday Evening

On arrival	Buffet supper (professionals and residents)
9:30–11:00 P.M.	Principles and techniques of the theme-centered interactional method, Ruth C. Cohn

Saturday

9:00– 9:30 A.M.	Breakfast
9:30–11:30 A.M.	Theme: segregation (rotating half-hour groups)

	Segregated groups	Group leaders
Living room	Residents only	Renee Nell
Library	Professionals only	Ruth C. Cohn
Living room	Blacks only	Win Adams
Library	Whites only	Norman Liberman
Living room	Men only	Stanley Hayden
Library	Women only	Vivian Guze
Living room	Jews only	Leonard Schwartz
Library	Christians only	Hans Priester

11:45– 1:15 P.M.	The theme-centered interactional method Theme: *multiple groups: segregation-collision-coexistence-integration* (professionals only), Ruth C. Cohn
1:15– 4:00 P.M.	Lunch and leisure (including indoor and outdoor sports)
4:00– 5:30 P.M.	Theme: *segregation and collision* Various group members and leaders Professionals and residents
5:30– 7:00 P.M.	Theme: *Coexistence and integration* Small heterogeneous groups Professionals and residents
7:30 P.M.	Dinner
Evening	"Happenings" led by Renee Nell and residents

Sunday

9:00– 9:30 A.M.	Breakfast
9:30–11:00 A.M.	Practicing theme-centered interactional workshop techniques with small heterogeneous groups on themes such as "freeing

Sunday

	creativity," "freedom and bondage," "non-verbal communication," selected by residents and professionals
11:15– 1:00 P.M.	Workshop on leadership of theme-centered interactional workshops and creating the workshop institute Professionals only
1:00 P.M.	Lunch; end of program

Notes Referring to One Experiential Part of Dealing with the "Segregation." At breakfast I assigned two rooms, library and living room, to the various paired groups, truly by size or at random. I stated the theme as, "How does it feel to be in this group, not permitted to go to the other room, to the other people?" (Each group had a trained theme-centered interactional workshop leader, except the black group whose leader happened to be ill.)

The *resident group* felt the segregation as a hostile act. Why were they "condemned" to the library while the "head-shrinkers had 'their' living room?" Hostility prevailed and cautiousness to strangers was recommended.

The complementary *group of professionals* felt relatively at home. No feelings of discriminating or feeling discriminated against were expressed. "It feels like always." "We know this situation so well." "I have never been in a room with three Negro colleagues." The group, whose theme was meant to lead to experiencing segregation as professionals, related instead questions of interracial segregation. The in-group experience of being together, blacks and whites, in one professional group, was emotionally prevalent. (Therefore, more than a half-hour's time would have been needed before the theme-imposed experience could have come into productive awareness.)

After half an hour the schedule called for separation of *blacks and whites*. The black therapist walked out of the living room to join the one black resident guest in the library. The three empty seats of our black colleagues were filled by white residents. This was painful to some of us. The room became overcrowded with the influx of about 18 residents added to the 12 white professionals. "This is not a group." "We are too many to communicate." The residents expressed their antagonism about our intrusion into *their* living room. We felt the same way about *their* coming in. We were emotionally divided into "us" as a familiar group of New York professionals and "them" as country place residents, and vice versa. After some expressions of hostility, our interest in meeting each other became predominant. Yet the immediate experience of the deserted and filled-up chairs remained a visceral undercurrent in some of us.

The black group felt their small size as disturbing. Having one black resident among three black professionals became the theme. The thinness of the report emphasized hesitancy to explore our prejudices. (This changed radically in the following theme-centered workshops.)

The clock sent the men into the library. The *women* stayed in the living room and were joined by the one female black therapist. We were comfortable in group size, giggly in spirit. Knitting needles tap-danced. Chatting was easy. "'Why don't we miss the men?'" "It is only a half-hour—it is so nice to feel like we are back in college—feet up and not care." The fact that a female black therapist was present mentioned by one white colleague. This statement hurt the group spirit. The lightness was lost. We worked on this.

The *men* reported an unhappy group spirit. They felt put upon. "Let me get out of here." "We are heading for a collision." There was great interest about what might go on in the women's group. Small subgroup discussions ensued. Breaking the closed door open was imminent when the clock struck for the last paired segregation group: Jews and Christians.

There were rampant hostility and fractionalism in the *Jewish* group. "I hate German Jews; they feel superior." "American Jews discriminate." "Every person I like is a Jew to me—I don't care whether he is or not." "I don't *feel* that I'm Jewish—I just *know* I am." "How can you say you are Jewish if you don't care that your child marries a *goy*?"—Again the intragroup split was dominant. Some comfort and discomfort about the absent Christians were expressed.

The *Christians* did not feel like a group. They felt discriminated against. "*They* must have a good time." "*They* are a closely knit real family; *they* always are." "We are not a group at all—we are a non-group of non-Jews."

The segregation experience stayed on. There was self-consciousness about who would sit with whom at the lunch tables. We talked about this too. *In most groups self-segregatory experiences had overshadowed those of being discriminated against.*

Another Example (for programming and building relevant experiences into the here-and-now of the theme to be explored).

THE GLOBE
    Advertised workshop; developing growth potential (general public) and group leadership training for W.I.L.L. staff (25 participants).

Time. Week end, 1967.

Place. A group leader's office apartment; use of two rooms.

Theme. "The Challenge of Change" (exploring participants' attitudes toward major and minor changes in living; changes that have to be accepted and changes that the person initiates; bringing up individual's general attitudes and imminent changes in their living, including marriage and divorce, job changes, family changes, aging, moving).

GROUP LEADERS

Ruth C. Cohn and Vivian S. Guze.

PROGRAM

Friday Evening. Total group meets for a few minutes, then divides into two rooms with one leader each.

Saturday Morning. First half: splitting up the groups of Friday night.

Second half: groups stay, leaders rotate to the other group.

Lunch together, informal.

Saturday Afternoon. First half: groups divided into married couples (who came together) and single participants; each group with one leader.

Second half: total group together with both leaders.

Saturday Evening. "Come-as-you-change" party.

Sunday Morning. First part: two W.I.L.L. staff leaders-in-training lead groups (the initial Friday evening group; leaders are now participants).

Sunday Afternoon. Training session with group leaders-in-training only; practice-centered discussion.

In the "challenge-of-change" workshop experiences of changes outside the group are explored within a setting that imposes changes in rapid order onto the group members. Surprisingly, in the various challenge-of-change workshops I have led, the swift change of group members and group leaders and rooms has not ever led to withdrawal and hesitation of the participants but rather to an acceleration of self- and-other involvement around the theme. The challenge of meeting new people and new situations and dealing with this theme has propelled the urgency of living-learning rather than delayed it.

Another Example. At the convention of the Art Directors of New York in 1967 Peter Hogan was to show his video tape of my workshop with eight art directors on the theme "The Art of Perceiving," and I was to discuss this video tape. Before the tape was shown, I asked the audience (approximately 200 people) to follow for a moment the (same) instructions I had given to the workshop group of art directors: to be silent for a few minutes and to be open to that which came easily into their awareness. After a few minutes I asked the reverse: to try to perceive something they had not and would not ordinarily perceive spontaneously—to perceive something in this room and situation that had escaped their attention before. Peter Hogan then showed the video tape. We both discussed in free interchange with the total audience whatever experiences or questions came up. The focal point of every single statement from the audience was their own experience rather than the observed video-taped workshop, which had dealt with the same phenomena. "How do I perceive? What do I perceive? What do I leave out? How do I deprive myself? How do my blind spots in perception handicap my work? How can I improve my visual, tactile, auditory, olfactory, kinesthetic senses?"

THEME-SETTING

As is apparent in the above three examples, theme-setting is an important facet of the theme-centered interactional workshop. The theme has to be in tune with the participants' interests and motivations. The wording of the theme is of great importance. The more stimulating, personalized, and positive the wording, the more likely cohesion around the theme can be achieved. Words have a hypnotic impact. "Toward a Team Approach in Our Agency" is a better title than "Faulty Communication with Our Staff"; "Being Myself and Being at Work" is more challenging than "The Impersonalized Job World," and so on. The ". . . ing" of the verb and the "noun "I" in the theme-setting are helpful aids.

Introduction to a Workshop.   The introduction to a workshop series serves to promote awareness of personal, interpersonal, and thematic connections. Whatever introduction the group leader chooses, his purpose is to promote I-We-It awareness, a constructive spirit, and each person's awareness of his autonomy and interdependence.

In the above example of introducing the art director's workshop on "The Art of Perceiving," both in the small group and at the convention my introduction was spoken slowly with words like these: "Please be silent for a little while; sink back into yourself and think about ways you usually perceive things in your daily living—in your work, at home, in the street—which senses are you aware of using most? How do you remember taking things into you—so you can feel them, use them, have them at your disposal?"

And after a few minutes of silence another suggestion: "Please remain silent but shift your attention from your thinking and your memories to where you are now. How does it feel to be in this special group here, perceiving whatever you perceive—of yourself, of your body, of others, of the environment? What are you aware of here and now, without pushing yourself to perceive anything special? Just let things come into you as they always do." After another few minutes: "Now try to switch again and try to perceive something you did not perceive before—something you usually don't perceive but can make yourself perceive right now."

Such suggestions bring to the fore thoughts about the given theme and previous experiences and concepts—connections of thoughts and memories with the here-and-now and with the immediate experience of the self, the group, and the environment. Personal experience is emphasized by the request for silence and awareness of feelings and perceptions in the here-and-now. The final suggestion puts a theme-centered task into the foreground.

The introduction of silence in the beginning is opportune in many, by no means all, circumstances. It promotes an atmosphere in which the "I" can communicate with himself, a situation that is frequently repeated during the workshop series. Alternating between being by myself and reaching out appears to be a fundamental living-learning rhythm often neglected in our living ways except for the grace of having to sleep!

Although initially silences are often rejected by group members as "religious stuff," as "Quaker meetings," or as anxiety-producing, silences are usually cherished later on. The ebb and tide of being within myself and being with others *and the permission to be really with myself while being with others become a new and beautiful experience.*

It is important to estimate the levels of anxiety and hostility in advance planning. The introductory procedure is gauged to reduce rather than increase anticipated negative feelings. In "captive groups" such as parolees or staff members of organizations and agencies, the main point of order in the introduction is the attempt to establish a working relationship with the group leader. This may be achieved by short lectures and explanations, by very cautious exposition of what the group leader intuits of the anxiety and anger in the group, or by inquiries concerning what the group would like to do with this time if they had free choice (other than leaving the room). The principle behind the variety of chosen techniques requires that the introduction promote awareness and communication between each I, the group interaction, and the theme.

As soon as possible, but only in response to the ongoing process, ground rules are stated.

Ground Rules for the Participants. *"Let each one of us try to give to this session and to get from it whatever each one of us wants to give to and to get from this situation, from this group and the theme."* This ground rule clearly states that each individual is responsible for himself. It cuts through the usual expectation of group members that the group leader carries sole responsibility for the well-being and achievements of the group. This group rule states that each person is responsible for getting and giving in the interaction with all others.

"Be your own chairman. Speak or be silent as you want to and be aware of your own agenda." People in traditional groups, be it in schools or committees, raise their hands and wait to be asked by the chairman or teacher. The pendulum of history now seems to swing to the extreme of the other side: each person must do what he feels like, that is, "do his own thing." The encouragement to "be your own chairman" does not promote dependency on the group leader nor does it give up responsibility toward the group and the task. "Doing what I feel like—my own thing" promotes self-expression of feelings, whenever, wherever—with little foresight or planning for myself and others. (I may feel like smashing my television set because I see a hated face on the screen with no consideration for my own future loss or consideration for the other television users.) *"To be my own chairman" means to include what I feel like doing into the givens of the reality situation:* other people, time-space factors, aids and obstacles, and my own contradictory needs, wishes, goals, and so on. A good chairman has the outline of an agenda—a flexible idea of purpose, and an awareness of the fact that *he functions with responsibility toward a task and toward people.*

The participant as "his own chairman" has a multiple job: he is primarily the "chairman of himself" (in fact, this was my initial formulation later replaced by the more popular guidewords of "be your own chairman"). He is the only person who can achieve awareness of "his *inside* committee members": his own desires, tensions, pains and pleasures, conflicts, and goals. His contribution to the workshop includes his offering of experiences, his self's awareness, his relationship to others, and his personal connections to the theme. He is truly "egocentric," i.e., each person's center is within himself. All other people are peripheral to this center, even though each person as partner of the universe transcends simultaneously his selfness. *Each person transcends his egocentricity in two ways: through his communications to others and through being part of this world.*

The "be your own chairman" formulation of the autonomy-interdependence principle has had a profound effect on people within the group process as well as thereafter. "I am a theme-centered interactional workshop," said a sophisticated colleague. "I regard all my needs clamoring for attention as my 'committee members' who have to tell important things, but I have the right and obligation as my own chairman to weigh their voices with regard to my own intent and agenda. What do I, as the total self, want to do—after listening to 'my own group inside': to stay in bed, to wash my hair, to read a book, to take care of many other chores, to be with my friends?" Or, another person's statement: "In any group I was inclined to be silent and to listen to others always waiting to be drawn out. When you said, "Be your own chairman," I was very angry at you and felt you just wanted to shirk your responsibility. Then I started to understand that nobody can ever substitute for myself. I have been more independent ever since." Another statement: "I did not want to go to my sister-in-law's party. I don't care for parties but my wife likes them. She also does not want to offend her sister by not going. So I thought: 'What have I learned in the living-learning workshop?' 'To be my own chairman.' She wants to go to the party; I want to paint the bookcase. I will try to convince her to go without me. It really worked after she understood. The whole family talks about 'being my own chairman.' Strange as it seems, we seem to enjoy ourselves much better since we know that each person is his own chairman—even our little ones. We as parents are also the cochairmen of the family group—as you are in the workshop."

Another ground rule in the workshop is: *"Disturbances take precedence.* State when you are bored, angry, preoccupied, in pain, excited about something else—state when you are out-of-it for whatever reasons and can't get back on your own steam."

Passionate involvements with issues not belonging to the theme, emotional preoccupation, outside problems, conflicts with other group members, physical discomfort, and so on may be "disturbances" that take precedence. The participants are advised to take the responsibility of telling the group when they do not concentrate. Stating discomforts or involvements is likely to help a member re-enter the group fully. This happens whether the disturbance or involvement has been fully explored or has just been stated and recognized.

The disturbance, however, is kept in the center of the group discussion only until the "missing group member" has been helped to come back to the group. This rule, like all others, has to be applied flexibly and handled delicately. In cases of deep-seated disturbances such as psychotic preoccupations or conflicts between married partners, or the grief of a mourning person, *tactful decisions are necessary between pursuing the person's disturbance or just sharing and recognizing it as existent and acceptable.*

It is a strange and beautiful fact that time spent on disturbances or passionate interferences invariably pays off. The rule is effective, human, and expedient. If, in a conference or classroom of 45 minutes' duration, 30 minutes or more is used to clear up interferences, the remainder of the time is open for important living-learning encounters. To learn this "economic" lesson over and over again is hard even for an experienced leader. (This rule is most clearly a derivative of psychoanalytic knowledge: In psychoanalysis, awareness is directed on defenses that work against the patient's goals. Work on resistance takes precedence over work on content.)

Examples. An academic seminar of economics was scheduled within the context of teaching the theme-centered interactional approach. The theme under discussion was "Stock Market and Money Market." The inspiring teacher gave a spontaneous lecture of about 15 minutes, exposing in simple and factual ways the difference between these two markets. The adult class of about 17 group leader students listened quietly and with interest. I functioned as a "participant supervisor." After 15 minutes I interrupted the teacher (as we had agreed). I said that two women seemed not to be with it. Several participants got angry; the lecture was interesting, and it would not be fair to stop the teacher because of a small minority. The teacher was frustrated but agreed with the experiment. The two women stated that they were not concentrating on the lecture. They never had been interested in economics, but did not mind sitting through this class. I suggested to them that they talk three minutes with each other about this lecture. Had they remembered anything—maybe one or two words? One of the two women, a Swiss citizen, explained that she had never seen any reason to be concerned with economic and political issues because in her country women had no right to vote; why aggravate herself over something she had no control over anyway? The other woman said she had heard the words "money market" and "stock market." For some reason the words "mountains of money" had occurred to her. These two different mountains had amused her, and she continued with a fantasy of one mountain of money and one mountain of ware. The two women's conversation was lively and impish, and the listeners as well as the speakers related to its humor. Within a few minutes the two outsiders felt included and the theme-centered discussion proceeded, with the "deviant members" genuinely expressing the wish to be able to widen their horizon in money matters.

In contrast to group therapy *the theme-centered interactional workshop does not venture to work through people's individual problems, desires, and preoccupations.* Sharing concern about them is meant to relieve the acute blocking and to enable the group to return to the theme as soon as possible. A psychotherapist group leader may use some short-therapeutic techniques such as role-playing, Gestalt interview, or encounter games. However, his emphasis remains on the process that centers around the given theme. In the above example, for instance, no attempt was made to go into any interpretation of the meaning of the money disturbances. Catharsis and group acceptance were sufficient to re-establish group cohesion.

Another ground rule is: "*Speak for yourself, state yourself, speak per I.*" This rule puts a damper on hiding one's own opinion behind other people's. Whatever I feel is my feeling, not yours. To state myself as "I" means to take responsibility and to risk personal commitment. In the extreme, a suggestive "we" spoken by a group leader or a strong group member may lead individuals to give up their responsible judgment. This "we" is a great danger, for it enables people to lose conscience and conscientiousness.

In this context I had an interesting experience on my first return to my birthland, Germany, after 36 years, on the occasion of the D.A.G.G. (Deutsche Association fuer Gruppentherapie and Gruppendynamik) convention in Bonn, 1969. I was the chairman of a panel, and included the several hundred people of the audience in the discussion. I gave some directions by explaining the theme-centered interactional method and giving some ground rules. At the end of the meeting, which succeeded in establishing a living-learning encounter between the audience and the panel, a participant approached me enthusiastically: "I know why you had us be silent and think and speak 'per I': this way you avoid mass suggestion and mass hysteria." This was a thought that struck me deeply coming from a German colleague—a thought that had not entered my mind in this negative perspective: "to avoid mass hysteria" rather than "to promote the individual's autonomy"!

Other ground rules concerning technique rather than principle are interjected whenever necessary.

Group Leadership

(Editors' instructions: "Above all—involve and interest the reader.") In writing the previous paragraphs I may have gotten too involved in my own thinking, having you, reader, only dimly in the back of my mind. I have, however, the hope that you have followed me with your own thoughts or—like listening to a story or folksong—without a direct bridge from the writer to the reader.

But now, writing about group leadership I feel like talking more directly to you. I want to interest you in group leading with this method by telling you about my own experiences. I want to use one of the ground rules of the method and speak to you "per I." Of course, you will understand that although principles and rules belong to the method, the style of each group leader is uniquely his own.

In my writing style I will speak to you about my leading style. You as the reading partner of this nonfeedback dyad will be stimulated (or not) to receive and to assimilate (or not) in your own way what I try to say to a distant (oh so distant!) living-learning partner.

I stated before that I believe that the most important single element of group leading is the discerning of the globe: the time-space-human-situational environment. In my 15 years of trial and error and of conceptualizing the method, I have learned that the prework—the preparation for a workshop series—determines to a large extent its success or failure. I spend several hours of preparation before every beginning workshop series. During the workshop things flow easily if I have been correct in my prework. My simile is that of giving a party. I am careful in choosing the guests. I arrange food, furniture, candles, and flowers carefully. Thereafter I feel as "irresponsible" as my guests. The theme is friendship, sharing, and fun. The external structure invites success. I am my own guest.

The *prework* consists of several facets: (1) I establish all pertinent data, such as who wants the workshop, and who does not; who pays for it, and what is the financial situation? What are the dynamic forces that make such a workshop desirable in the minds of those who want it and undesirable for others? Why should I or why should I not be the group leader if this workshop comes to pass? How many leaders would be adequate for the situation? What are the room conditions—can we have a circle and comfortable seating? How much time is necessary to accomplish what can optimally be done? What compromises may have to be made in time, money, and so on? (2) I use my fantasy (or meditating ability) to imagine what kind of situation I will encounter. (I always assume that the collected data will be partly correct, partly biased, and always incomplete.) With these fantasies in mind, I play around with themes and subthemes that may stimulate me and others to achieve what we are out to achieve. (3) I contemplate an introductory procedure that will fit the situation. All introductory procedures aim at setting a positive living-learning encounter atmosphere and awareness of the I-We-It factors. In prethinking the introductory procedure, the estimated level of anxiety, sophistication, anticipation from previous experiences, intensity of needs, and so on all play a role, as well as the question of whether I am to lead a group alone or with a coleader. (4) The prethinking also includes the question of how many groups and group leaders will be necessary if the project includes many people and subgroups (schools, hospitals, business, and so on).

Match-or-miss fantasies in the prework highly help or hamper any interactional group work thereafter.

These and other preconsiderations occur either in lone meditation or as teamwork with coleaders in interactional workshop fashion. We do not plan the theme-setting beyond a few sessions of any series but work out later grouping and theme-setting with the participants.

In the beginning of a workshop I try to promote an accepting, non-hostile climate. I believe that a negative atmosphere is not conducive to free communication and learning. The participants are not treated on the basis of "patienthood" or of "encountering brothers" but as people who come together for the penetration of a theme. Thus *the emphasis is not on curing pathology or meeting people or getting something done but on being myself with you while doing something together.*

My way of promoting a sensitive climate includes an accepting attitude to anything that is being said, especially in the beginning of the first session. I may reflect what is being said in a rogerian way, or recognize the value of the proposed statement. Or I may shift an inadequate remark slightly toward becoming useful or tell a suitable anecdote. In writing this down there seems to be more manipulation of content than actually occurs; *there is rarely any statement that does not contain a useful component, and it is this useful component that I seek to stress.*

Participant leadership starts at the very beginning. *As a group leader I am not only the chairman of the group but also the chairman of myself* with the same privileges and responsibilities as all other group members. In the introductory period, until a free and workable atmosphere has been established, I accept and even promote the "star relationship" by responding to everything that is being said.

I respond with my own feelings and experiences, propelling the group's interaction as well as establishing myself as a member of the group. Usually after 10 or 20 minutes some genuinely constructive direct statement is made from one participant to another. From then on I promote interaction mainly by taking a less dominant role. The rules and norms of group interaction that support awareness of autonomy and interdependence replace active leadership. However, the need for "dynamic balancing" of the I-We-It approach emphasizes the importance of leadership function as important throughout. I alternate between being the conductor of an orchestra, being the leading violinist, and being just any player. Yet very early in my theme-centered workshop experiences I found that groups do not stay centered around a theme when no one takes personal responsibility for the dynamic balancing. In advanced groups leadership can be established in rotation. Yet, without an appointed or declared leader the simultaneous emphasis on all triangular points gets lost. Groups tend to become (I-We) therapy or sensitivity groups or (It) academic discussion seminars. The dynamic-balancing task between the three factors demands consciousness of function as well as special skills.

As chairman of the group I use the fantasy of riding a bicycle with three pedals, labeled "I," "We," and "It." If the group, for instance, stays excessively with one participant for longer than he needs, to return to the theme I may step on the We or on the It pedal. I may do this by a direct request, such as taking a "snapshot" (concerning the We): "In a snapshot way would you please hold on to whatever you experienced at the moment when I stopped you. Make the rounds and say very briefly where you were at when I took the snapshot." This leads to knowing where each person's attention was. Such interruption leads to the "We." Everybody knows where everybody else is, and the group can decide whether to shift attention or to stay with the previous subtheme. *There are innumerable verbal and nonverbal techniques for shifting from one "pedal" to the other. More than anything else this shifting of pedals promotes the dynamic interaction and propelling force in W.I.L.L.'s living-learning encounters.*

As participant leader, I am chairman of the group—the chairman of myself—the person with inside awareness. *Being my own chairman as the group leader includes the awareness of myself as well as that of my job.* Thus I choose from all conscious images, thoughts, and feelings what I want to reveal as relevant for myself and for the process of the group. This conscious and careful choosing process I have called *"selective authenticity."* It means that *whatever I say shall be authentic, but not everything that is authentic will be said.* To be authentic does not mean to be indiscriminate. *It is ethical and functional to gear my overt expressions to the estimated receptivity and sensitivity of the people around me.* What psychoanalysis has labeled "timing" and "dosing" is valid for any group leader's interventions. It is sometimes difficult to decide whether I forestall communication because I am anxious or because I am authentically selective. I believe, however, that being aware of this question and trying to answer it in every situation is more helpful than indiscriminate withholding of the therapist's personal feelings as in orthodox psychoanalytic technique, or indiscriminate exposing as in radical experientialist encounter groups. I like my concept of "selective authenticity" as being helpful for both experiential psychotherapy and group leading. *The hippocratic oath of "nihil nocere"—never to harm—is applicable to group leaders' ethics as well as physicians' and therapists'.* Excluding rare cases of group leaders' sadism, the most frequent way participants are harmed is by indolence or ignorance. I consider it neglect if I do not put my attention on every workshop member individually. Although I ask each person to be his own chairman, I am aware of the fact that nobody is capable of using himself fully autonomously, and that the fact of interdependence demands me to (yes) "be my brother's keeper." To be my brother's keeper means a dual statement: to give him what he needs if I have it and not to interfere with his autonomy if he can make his own choices. *To give less than needed is theft; to give more is murder.*

I regard knowledge of *psychopathology* as a requisite for group leading in the community. I must have a feel for people's depressions, paranoid behavior, organic handicaps, and murderous tendencies. I do not try to "cure" people in theme-centered interaction workshops beyond aiding group members' participation. Yet rarely do I try to exclude a sick person from a workshop, partly because I feel that under good leadership such persons do not get harmed but may get help with regard to the thematic concerns and their relatedness to people; partly because most workshop groups are organizational or otherwise constituted through job or interest affiliations.

I may deal wtih deeper pathology by intentional and careful non-labeled recognition of the person's depression, anxiety, or confusion. I may take several minutes or longer to give full attention and recognition to that person's present experience. I may concentrate on bodily awareness, comforting empathic reactions, or promote a cathartic expression. Or I may turn the group's attention and my own away from the disturbed person for a while trying to give him privacy and comfort in that way. I try to use and train my intuition so that I feel whether turning toward or turning away is what the sick person needs in this situation. Comforting, not curing; understanding, not interpreting; turning toward reality, not fantasy—these are my most frequent attitudes. However, even here there are no absolutes. I remember a participant who was highly observant of his dreams, which he faithfully brought into every session. This participant was paranoid. I needed to help forestall psychosis and also to lead the group back to the established theme. I decided to let the person tell his dreams but to immediately relate the dream content to the theme and to occurrences in the group. This was helpful to the dreamer, who became more related to the group. Group members in turn related to each other and the purpose of the theme rather than to the individual dream interpretation.

I often spend some private minutes with persons in need in intermissions. Such personal attention tends to keep ill persons group-and-theme-related. I sometimes recommend outside help if this is possible and acceptable to the person.

Occasionally I use short therapeutic techniques such as role-playing, Gestalt encounters, catharsis, or psychoanalytic interpretations if this seems to be in the interest of the situation. However, in training group leaders, I discourage everyone from using techniques he is not fully acquainted with. Selective authenticity is also important in choosing according to skills and needs.

Toward the end of a workshop session as well as of a series I try to encourage the ventilation of feelings and thoughts that people may not want to take home. "What would you resent not having said or not having asked if we broke up now—30 minutes before we will separate? Imagine you were in the bus or car on your way home—what would you regret not having said or asked?"

This writing comes to an end. I know that I want to tell you much more. Yet there will be another workshop, another chapter, and some day a book—I do not have to continue now. I have said what I wanted to say here within this specific "globe": the purpose of this book, you, me, the editors, the space of this chapter.

(Point 8 of the editors' instructions "Above all: involve and interest the readers.") I would be delighted if I did. I would be more delighted if you would relieve the lonely writer-reader nonfeedback dyad and give me your reactions.

Stephen B. Lawrence

⫸13⫷ From Zazen to Videotape: Encounter Group Innovations

COMMENTARY

A tri-pronged innovative approach to encounter groups is found in this chapter. First, religio-philosophical thought and practice are tapped such as in zazen meditative exercises. Second, the technique of video-tape is used in novel and comprehensive fashion. Third, these approaches are explored with "new populations" such as institutionalized patients and geriatric groups. Stephen Lawrence describes his methodology in all these areas.

BIOGRAPHY

Stephen B. Lawrence is a clinical psychologist who received his bachelor's degree from the University of Wisconsin and his master's and doctoral degrees from Purdue University.

He has worked as a clinical psychologist for the Veterans Administration, the Indiana and California Department of Mental Hygiene, and the University of California and is presently chief psychologist at the San Bernardino County General Hospital and conducts a private practice in San Bernardino.

Dr. Lawrence is a member of the American, Midwestern, Western, and California Psychological Associations and is an officer and charter member of the Inland Southern California Society of Clinical Psychologists. In California, he is a licensed psychologist and marriage, family, and child counselor.

Stephen Lawrence is one of the pioneers in live telecasts of psychotherapy sessions and has been a prime innovator in the clinical uses of videotape, focused Zen group meditation for the mentally ill, and nude-group therapy. He has done extensive work with videotape marathon groups at psychologic growth centers throughout the country including Esalen Institute, Big Sur, California; Kairos Institute, San Diego; Topanga Center for Human Development, Los Angeles; Oasis Institute, Chicago; Aureon Institute, New York; Shalal Institute, Vancouver; and others.

For his professional work, Dr. Lawrence is listed in *"Who's Who in the West," "Personalities of the West and Midwest," "Who's Who in California," "International Biographies," "International Platform Committee,"* and *"200 Men of Achievement 1970."*

Much of my early work with videotape was done in a wide range of clinical settings. For some months, I was a consultant to the semi-underground Los Angeles Free Clinic, where most of the clients were "hippies" and adolescent runaways. The videotape "rap sessions" there always challenged and unglued our counselors' conventional thinking. Videotape feedback was also used at the U.C.L.A. Speech Clinic with groups of stutterers, with hospitalized and private patients, college students, children, and senior citizens, in Synanon-type games with delinquent adolescents, and with a host of other groups. With each of these populations, the video feedback appeared to be a significantly important therapeutic tool.

I am sure that each of the clinical innovations could have a story and a chapter in this history all to itself. In this section, however, I would like to share with the reader just some of the early encounter work with videotape and live television, some brief experiences with nude-group therapy, and a procedure that I more recently initiated: focused Zen group meditation.

WITNESSED PSYCHOTHERAPY

I will begin by first describing the organization, planning, and development of a novel treatment project, involving a variety of types of psychotherapy and encounter sessions that were telecast live on a closed-circuit television system in a California state mental hospital.

Figure 13-1. "Hippie clients" watch themselves on television during a "videotape rap" session.

This television project was developed by the hospital's Rehabilitation Department and functioned both as an effective part in the hospital's educational and recreational program and as a method of retraining patients in basic work skills. Except for one or two supervising employees, the entire television studio operations were staffed by mental patients. This included operating the television cameras, lighting, electronic control equipment, making background sets and scenery, writing scripts, directing programs, and other similar duties of a television broadcasting studio. The studio was considered to be a very successful rehabilitation project.

In the fall of 1966, I began a short-term project involving televising live psychotherapy sessions on this closed-circuit television system to the hospital. Because television receiving sets were available on each of the hospital wards, the potential audience for the sessions was the total hospital staff and patient population. The purpose of such a project was multiple. First there were the questions of technical feasibility, effectiveness of such telecasts, and the reception they would receive from the other patients and staff. It was also hoped to stimulate and increase interest in the small-group discussion program carried on by the psychiatric aides throughout the hospital. There were plans for some wards to hold their own small therapy groups immediately after

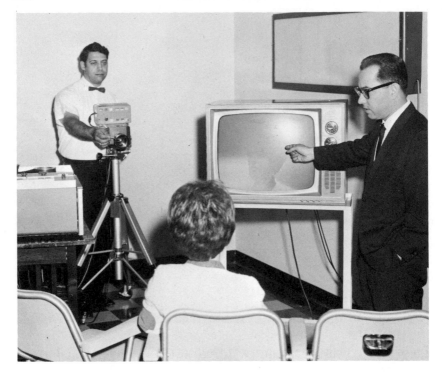

Figure 13-2. Dr. Lawrence (right) demonstrates use of videotape. Video technician points television camera at a woman whose photo appears in the TV receiver. (Photo by A. W. Sylvester.)

viewing a group session on the closed-circuit television. In this manner some practical demonstrations of group procedures and techniques could be provided for all those who conducted patient groups. This method would, of course, greatly conserve the limited time of the professional staff for teaching and training activities. Another major purpose of the project was an attempt to dispel and negate any existing unrealistic attitudes that have tended to characterize psychotherapy sessions in the past. It was hoped to open up therapy sessions for inspection and thereby reduce the frightening, threatening, or general discomforting aura that often seems to be associated with such activities. Also, if it could be adequately demonstrated that therapy could effectively be carried out under the conditions prevailing in a television studio, this could generate numerous research possibilities, especially with the use of videotape procedures for objectively evaluating psychotherapeutic encounters. Last, and possibly most important, there were hopes that the televised small-group therapy sessions could reach out therapeutically and beneficially affect the large number of patient viewers on the hospital wards. From a personal point of view, the concept seemed exciting, professionally challenging, and, frankly, a lot of fun.

The physical arrangements for the project included a 20-by-40-foot television studio attached to a small control room with a connecting glass window enabling the television director to watch the action in the studio. Patients were seated in a small circle of chairs with a coffee table in the center of the circle. The table held four microphones facing the group. Surrounding the circle of chairs was a battery of hot, bright television lights. Three large, mobile television cameras, operated by patient cameramen, moved continuously around the group. Chairs were provided around the edge of the room for observers. Therefore, during any particular televised therapy session, there were from 10 to 15 observers of the groups, including, usually, cameramen, patient studio workers, directors, ward personnel, visitors, professional staff observers and others.

PSYCHOTHERAPY GROUPS

The televised therapy groups were arbitrarily divided by myself into five categories. These groups, which were all voluntary, were each seen for one-hour periods on television, and at one time the project was telecasting up to six hours per week of therapy sessions over the hospital's closed-circuit system.

The first televised group was labeled "mixed-group psychotherapy." This was an ongoing group with relatively few replacements that met twice a week for one-hour televised sessions. The patients were male and female inpatients from an acute and intensive treatment ward. Generally, these were intellectually bright, alert, and relatively sophisticated individuals, i.e., those thought to be most suitable for verbal therapy. The second group was termed "family psychotherapy." This was conducted with consecutive patients who had left the hospital on leave, but would return once a week with their spouses and children for an hour of televised outpatient treatment. Care was taken to select families that were all relatively verbal and responsive. Some families consisted of husband and wife only, and others had several children participating jointly. "Revolving groups" was a name given to groups that each week would come from a different hospital ward for a one-hour televised session at the studio. This was an attempt to involve as many wards as possible in this project. It was assumed that those who had participated would probably be more likely to watch other patient groups on their ward television set. The patients for these groups were both male and female, primarily diagnosed as chronic schizophrenics.

Figure 13-3. Production team prepares to tape encounter group session to play back later on the TV receiver so that participants can learn what they look and sound like to other people.

A fourth group was a "sensitivity-training" session televised for one hour per week with the participants being a group of student nurses who were temporarily affiliated with the hospital. These young, enthusiastic, and highly verbal girls were accompanied in the televised sessions by their nursing supervisor. The fifth and last group was a "psychodrama" session conducted by another hospital psychologist who had considerable professional training in this area. These televised sessions were one hour per week with groups of patients individually selected from a variety of hospital wards. One or two other hospital employees served as assistants in these small psychodrama sessions.

It is seen, then, that a wide variety and type of participants were involved in the project, ranging from chronic schizophrenics to normal functioning staff members. All the group sessions were televised live, up to six hours each week over a period of several months.

An attempt was made to involve as many staff personnel as possible, rather than make the project a small isolated one. Therefore, the staff on each ward was requested to select the patients they felt might benefit the most from such an experience. The ward physician reviewed the selected patients and gave his written approval of the choice. It was also urged that the group be accompanied to the television studio by their own small-group leaders. This person was usually a social worker or psychiatric aide who knew the patients, had worked with them previously, or knew something of their clinical history.

The group leader would sit in on the televised sessions with me and functioned as a cotherapist. In this manner many wards were actively participating in the project and did urge other ward personnel and patients to become involved. As a further effort to encourage hospital-wide participation, the weekly television schedule was printed in the hospital's local newspaper, which is distributed to all staff and patients once a week. Also, five minutes before each televised therapy session an announcement was made over the hospital's public address system inviting interested staff or patients to view the program.

Before each session began, I would hold a warm-up period of approximately 15 minutes with each new group. The members were allowed to help set up the chairs, tables, and microphones and to look around the studio and generally become acquainted with the new surroundings. A brief orientation lecture was then given by the author, describing how the studio functioned, i.e., how the cameramen operated, the purpose of a director, the need for the hot lights, and so on. These procedures invariably caused the initial nervousness of the group to dissipate rather quickly. A further technique to reduce the group's tension was to allow the camera to circle around the group and let each member view himself on a television monitor before the broadcast time. The last five minutes of the warm-up session were devoted to allowing the group to verbally express their feelings about volunteering for the session, which also provided the therapist with an opportunity to observe the patients and form some initial clinical impressions about the members. The warm-up discussion usually flowed smoothly and quickly into therapeutic encounters as the program went on the air.

PATIENTS' REACTIONS

What kind of reaction did the participating patients have to being televised during psychotherapy sessions? First, it must be recalled that each group functioned under the following conditions: bright, hot lights shining on them; three large television cameras continuously circling around; cameramen talking to directors in stage whispers; other workers moving signs, cables, and the like; several observers in the room; and only 15 minutes' preparation for this experience.

In this author's experience, the groups consistently lost awareness of these numerous external factors within five minutes. The sessions were then, in my judgment, almost indistinguishable from therapy sessions in a private or secluded setting. Often when the televised hour was completed, the groups continued on for several minutes and had to be reminded the hour was over. The usual type of emotional responses seen in ordinary groups would frequently appear in the televised groups, i.e., anger, tears, emotional encounters, and the like. When the patients were later questioned, they uniformly agreed that after the first few minutes, the activity in the studio had very little or no effect on them. This confirms this author's personal experience of losing awareness of the external distracting elements in the studio once the session got underway.

Although there was never any overt difficulty with the patients in this situation, the technical equipment frequently malfunctioned, and human errors occurred in operating the machines with consistent regularity. Camera failure, microphones going dead, and electrical equipment burning out became a routine experience and promoted an atmosphere of continual excitement and mild apprehension for the studio workers and, at times, for the therapist.

PROJECT RESULTS

Toward the end of the project a more active and direct emphasis on teaching was made. During the last five to ten minutes of each televised group session, the patients would leave the camera area and the author would remain with the group's regular leader to discuss the just-completed session. This direct teaching situation, focusing on the "here-and-now" experiences of the group, appeared to be reasonably effective.

During the course of the project, approximately 200 patients participated in these live telecasts. The patients came from a variety of wards, ranged from small children to seniles and from normals to chronic schizophrenics—a generally adequate cross-section of a state psychiatric hospital population. The patients' reactions were uniformly enthusiastic. Not a single participant ever voiced any criticism of the televised sessions, and almost all patients were completely willing to come back again and repeat the experience. Of course, all the participants were volunteers for the group session, thereby possibly eliminating those who might raise objections to some of the procedures. Although no objective data were collected from the patients, the subjective responses were all exceptionally positive. When returning to the ward, the patients often were praised and encouraged for "doing so well" or "looking so good on television." Other times, their symptoms, such as depressed affect, overt hostility, or bizarre behavior, would be pointed out and emphasized to the participants by those who had watched the group on television. It was typical, then, that following the televised group experiences considerable feedback and further discussion arose over what had taken place.

Each of the group leaders who participated in the televised sessions were asked to complete an open-ended questionnaire on various aspects of the project. Again, there was uniformly high enthusiasm and praise for the experience with criticisms limited to minor technical problems, such as the discomfort of the hot television lights, the short length of the meetings, and problems in delivering the patients to the studio. The student nurses in the sensitivity-training group even wrote their supervisor urging that all future classes be included in the project.

As might be expected with a large and diverse staff, many of the professional employees had mixed feelings about the television project. Some had positive feelings, many had strong negative impressions, and most tended to be neutral. Certainly many of the concerns and issues raised warrant careful consideration and future exploration. Some of the problems involved legalities, such as release of information forms from relatives who might be discussed by patients, the question of complete loss of confidentiality, and concerns of who should be permitted to view these telecast groups. Several therapists noted they felt they would be unable to be spontaneous under such conditions. Subjective impressions from the therapists who did participate, however, seem to indicate that spontaneity was not a problem. Present, but rarely verbalized, was the concern that other professional workers might negatively evaluate the therapist's efforts as a group leader. Generally among the hospital staff, there was a moderate amount of interest and curiosity in the television project, but very little personal involvement.

In reviewing the project, this author feels a long-term teaching program would be needed to make these novel therapeutic procedures effective. Ward personnel would have to be personally involved, a difficult task with busy and overworked people. Further, considerable effort and hospital-wide coordination would be needed to motivate the staff and patient population to watch such televised sessions.

I personally feel the project was a success in many ways and that it did conclusively demonstrate the feasibility of carrying out such a program. Certainly, numerous possibilities for research in the area have been generated. For anyone who has the opportunity to participate in this type of professional endeavor, this author can readily attest to the very exciting and rewarding aspects of witnessed psychotherapy on closed-circuit television.

VIDEOTAPE ENCOUNTER GROUPS IN A
RETIREMENT COMMUNITY

From my experience videotape feedback has been a useful and significant tool in a wide variety of encounter group settings. But rather
than share with you, at this point, the multiple positive aspects of this
electronic aid, I would like to report on an unusual type of encounter
group in which videotape played a relatively minor role.

A review of the professional literature reveals that verbal encounter
groups have been conducted in a wide variety of settings with diverse
types and classes of individuals. As far as can be determined, however, none of these professional efforts have previously focused on
senior citizens in a retirement community. The reasons for excluding
this expanding and significant population are probably many, although
it is suspected that the prime reasons clinicians tend to ignore the
older citizen can be traced to the usual stereotypes and prejudices surrounding the elderly.

The senior citizen is, of course, a member of a social minority group
in our society and experiences a full range of discrimination in the
usual areas, such as employment, housing, and education. His status
is often characterized primarily by its categorical nature: he cannot
resign or escape by merit. Whatever his unique characteristics, he is
frequently treated simply as one unit of a group by those of dominant
status. Psychotherapists and encounter group leaders have not been
immune to the widely held prejudices against the senior citizen. They
also describe the elderly as rigidly defensive, emotionally repressive,
and manifesting increasing physical, mental, and intellectual deterioration. The elderly have consistently been dismissed as unsuitable candidates for psychotherapy or encounter groups.

Contrary to the above stereotypes, this author organized and carried
out a series of videotape verbal encounter groups in a retirement community. Before reporting on the actual sessions and their results, a
brief description of the retirement community will be presented.

THE COMMUNITY

This community of approximately 5,000 people is located 75 miles
from Los Angeles and is a self-contained city. There are several
churches, banks, restaurants, a 30-store shopping center, a comprehensive medical complex, an intracity bus system, and a recreation
center offering a wide variety of arts and crafts and similar facilities.
There are over 70 civic, social, and church organizations available to

the members. Residents may be either single or married, although one of the married partners must be over age 50. People under 18 cannot be permanent members. Children are welcome only as temporary guests. Many of the residents are employed in jobs, are professors, or are businessmen on a full- or part-time basis. In general, this specific retirement community is judged to be middle- to upper-middle class as measured by several factors, including the type of residents' homes. There are 24 different types of houses and apartments to choose from, ranging from $18,000 to $30,000. The community's brochure describes the surroundings as ". . . an environment wherein people may live in a country club atmosphere, among warm friends in comfortable homes, with almost all human activities at hand, and located in a warm, sunny climate."

THE CLASSES

The encounter groups were organized within the community's educational program, which includes the usual academic subjects, such as English, philosophy, and political science, and technical subjects, such as woodworking, typing, painting, and photo processing. Approximately 8 percent of the residents attend one or more of these classes, with the tendency for the same small group of residents to participate in many of the classes. A high percentage of regular class-goers are either women or have Jewish ethnic backgrounds.

More than 50 people originally signed up for the videotape encounter groups; 25 came to the first session, and over 25 other individuals "dropped in" once or twice during the semester. A hard core of 25 people remained active participants throughout the semester. The class schedule was published in the community's weekly newspaper, and through word of mouth others were encouraged to attend. The average age of the participants was approximately 65, with several members being over 75 years old. The class met one night a week for two hours with a ten-minute break in between. All agreed it was difficult to sit longer than one hour at a time, and sessions of more than two hours' duration, were felt by the members to be too fatiguing.

VIDEOTAPE FEEDBACK

The portable videotape equipment and video technician were introduced and explained to the group in the first session. Taping and playback to the group were begun right from the start. Although the members appeared to understand the overt purpose of the video feedback, it seemed to have no real impact on the group or individual participants. Despite questioning and encouragement, the videoplay feedbacks elicited little or no verbal reactions. The group appeared genuinely puzzled or simply tolerant of the video procedure and often viewed it as a kind of elaborate toy that did not have any relevancy to the immediate group verbal interaction. Even simple curiosity as to "How do I look" seemed missing in the responses of these people.

After several sessions, the video technician continued to silently tape the meetings without immediate playback to the group. These tapes were carefully reviewed by the author outside the class. Finally, the videotape was simply discontinued. None of the participants made any comments about these changes in procedure. This author has used videotape feedback in a variety of therapeutic settings with literally hundreds of individuals without ever previously getting this apparent blandness and seemingly total unconcern about the video feedback.

THE GROUP PROCESS

As the weekly encounter sessions occurred, this author was somewhat surprised to discover the group was not responding in any appreciably different manner from other similar encounter groups. Of course, the senior citizens had intrinsic problems peculiar to their age group and their similar community backgrounds, but this was to be expected. Concerns about rigidity, excessive defensiveness, reduced alertness, and other stereotypes of the elderly were unwarranted and did not develop. In fact, some of the most lively and sensitive members of the groups were over 75 years of age. Except for the group's inability to utilize the videotape, the process of the group was essentially indistinguishable from encounter groups with younger people.

In the first few meetings, the group responded with the confusion, lack of purpose, and "milling around" that are often typical of a nondirective, group-centered encounter situation. The members asked questions such as "What is the purpose of this group? "What is psychology? "Why do people act the way they do?" and other similarly vague and broad questions. Next there was the usual demand that the instructor give prepared lectures or at least firmly take the full responsibility for the direction of the class. After three sessions, however, the group began to speculate about the feasibility of making personal revelations and then gradually began to discuss the mutual problems in living for the retired senior citizen. Next, the group process flowed into more immediate, here-and-now personal encounters with the accompanying uneasiness concerning emotional transparency, but with the equally usual emotional supportiveness of encounter groups. Last, some techniques of physical contact and sensory awareness were introduced and seemingly accepted and experienced without any overt difficulties.

After only a very few sessions, then, the group took responsibility for the class, began to discuss meaningful personal material with considerable vigor, and, except for the apparent rejection of the videotape feedback, became significantly involved in the encounter process. This author also began to change his perceptions and stereotypes of the senior citizens (an awkward term; does that make others junior citizens?) and began experiencing the members more fully as complex, functioning individuals.

PROBLEMS IN LIVING OF THE RETIRED

Some of the rich clinical material of these sessions may interest clinicians and researchers in the area. Therefore, a brief review of the main problems in living of this particular encounter group will be listed. Many of the members indicated they had initially experienced anxiety and fearfulness when first contemplating retirement, especially the men. There were fears of inability to fill their days with meaningful activity and concerns about living on a significantly reduced income. Increased daily contact with the spouse generated feelings of possibly "being underfoot." Problems of losing ties with friends, relatives, and "the old life" were also voiced. Other group members noted little concern with this transitional period and, in fact, claimed to have been contentedly involved with the details of changing their style of living. One gentleman, over 70, noted he had made a list of things to do when he first moved to the retirement community a year ago, and the list is still on his dresser with nothing checked off. He has been too busy with his new community affairs to get around to his list.

Another major problem aired by the group was the experienced discomfort when old friends, and especially children and other relatives, failed to contact or communicate with the retired persons. Feelings of isolation, abandonment, and anger were experienced along with rationalizations for these significant others. One woman in the class mentioned that her reaction to this problem had been not to have meaningful contact with anyone in the retirement community for over two years. Her profound relief at knowing that other retired people had similar experiences was considerably moving.

Most of the group expressed negative feelings about the generally held stereotype of the aging individual as feeble, sick, inactive, and mentally dull, with a reduced personal worth. The group did not consider themselves as old, but rather agreed that the term "old" applies only to individuals 15 years older than yourself. In contrast to the problem of aging, many group members voiced strong condescending attitudes and criticism toward "young people" with their lack of experience and immature life style. On the other hand, considerable interest was generated concerning the "hippie movement," and there was a sincere desire to have encounter group experiences with this deviant group, which is at the other end of the age and social-scale continuum.

Other general topics included the inadvisability of living on past accomplishments and pleasures; parental duties and responsibilities toward grown children; social disengagement and the trauma of sudden drop in status, especially for men, on termination of employment; and the need for well-thought-out and practical plans for retirement.

More defensiveness and anxiety were noted on the topics of the possibility of physical deterioration and increasing dependency with aging. Some members refused to consider or discuss such a "morbid topic," although others approached it comfortably. Some were able to calmly consider and anticipate their own death and burial arrangements and the impact of their death on friends and relatives. Most participants, however, tended to say little on this emotionally charged subject, and the topic was covered in only one session. As can be seen from the above, a wide range of personal and emotional problems in living were closely examined in these encounter group sessions.

Extrapolating from this author's personal experience of encounters with groups with senior citizens, there appears to be no significant reason for the clinicians to exclude the elderly individual from such group participation. Observation of the group process revealed it to develop in a very typical manner, with the age factor playing a relatively minor role. This group does have its special problems in living, but so does almost any other special-interest group.

In terms of retirement community living, it is suggested that encounter groups might be a reasonably helpful method of easing the transition period for these elderly individuals who experience such difficulties. These groups are also judged feasible for dealing with a host of emotional and personal problems of this age group, such as feelings of isolation, abandonment, loneliness, physical decline, and death. Also, the group could be a vehicle for mutual sharing of the joys and pleasures of maturity.

From impressionistic data alone, it is suggested that adjustment to a retirement community follows a normal curve, as do most human characteristics. Some elderly persons seem to adjust quickly and without undue stress, others have painful transitional periods and later make inadequate and uncomfortable accommodations, often leaving the community, and the majority fall somewhere in between. If the critical factors for a successful adjustment could be identified, possibly psychologic screening for the retirement community could be a helpful service for both the individual and the community.

Last, this author wishes to note his gratitude to the retirement community for allowing this type of educational group to form and to the citizens of that community for all they have taught him.

VIDEOTAPE NUDE MARATHON GROUPS

Next, I would like to share my thinking about and experience with an innovation in the encounter group field that is probably the most controversial and emotionally charged technique of any procedure developed since freudian psychoanalysis: nude-group therapy.

Paul Bindrim, a psychologist who has practiced in Los Angeles for over 20 years, is credited with holding the first nude marathon groups during the spring of 1967. At the time, and again in the summer and fall of that year, Bindrim sent out over 4,000 individual flyers to most of the licensed people in the helping professions in California announcing his nude therapy groups. The response in terms of participants was extremely minimal; the response in terms of emotional controversy was sensationally maximal. I am sure almost every professional person contacted quickly developed strong emotional feelings about this taboo-shattering technique. However, no one apparently felt the need to get firsthand knowledge from Bindrim about his actual experiences with nude-group therapy.

My curiosity was too great to ignore the opportunity; so I visited Paul Bindrim in his Frank Lloyd Wright-type circular home in the Hollywood Hills to see what I could learn about this latest innovation. I found Paul to be a warm, outgoing, charismatic personality who was convinced of the potentiality of his newly developed therapeutic approach. At that first meeting, we talked for more than eight hours about his experiences with nude therapy, and I recall feeling that Paul had a great need at that time to share his feelings, hopes, and expectations with another professional colleague. He had been puzzled by the weeks of silence from other professionals since his announcements were first mailed.

During that fall meeting with Bindrim, I decided to take the professional risks he had already taken and hold a nude marathon group, but add the factor of videotape to such a session. Further, we agreed to submit a symposium proposal of our experiences to the convention of the California State Psychological Association to be held in January, 1968. Subsequently, I did conduct what was now the second nude marathon group and the first nude group with videotape feedback. The convention accepted our symposium proposal, and when Bindrim and I publicly presented our material to the convention, the mass media were quickly attracted to the concept of nude therapy. A steady series of articles, newspaper stories, and television appearances catapulted Bindrim and nude therapy into national prominence. Nude-group therapy was on the way to being incorporated and accepted as a specialized encounter group technique.

I felt more at ease a year later when *The American Psychologist,* a professional journal of the American Psychological Association, accepted my article on nude videotape marathon groups. Our professional establishment had acknowledged the existence of nude therapy and, therefore, indirectly, accepted the procedure as a legitimate area for exploration and experimentation. What follows are my thinking on and experiences with nude videotape marathon groups in the fall of 1967.

Nude-group therapy has come into being at this time partly because many of the old taboos are dying or dead. A more permissive society is already upon us. This is seen in the increasing nudity and frankness in today's films, in the blunt, often obscene, dialogue in American plays and novels, in the candid lyrics of popular songs, in the open discussion programs on television, in the political consciousness of the young, and in freer fashions and the often-discussed "sexual revolution." Behind this expanding permissiveness stands a society that has lost its consensus on such crucial issues as premarital sex, the purpose of education, race relations, drug usage, and the meaningful good life, a society that no longer agrees on the basic issues of what constitutes normal standards of conduct.

Although some perceive this new candor as a release from an American era of Victorian hypocrisy and repression, many are bewildered, concerned, and often angered at the swiftness with which all the old restraints are crumbling. These mores are changing so rapidly that many alarmed social thinkers fear a dangerous swing toward irresponsible hedonism and, ultimately, social decay. The analogy of the decline and fall of the Roman Empire has been applied to what is now perceived as developing in Western society.

Although most agree that this new freedom of expression is unlikely to reverse itself because the forces that have produced it are a permanent and irresistible part of modern life, many responsible individuals reject the notion that the new permissiveness is a sign of impending moral collapse. It is clear, however, that until recently agencies of moral order like the church, the government, the community, and the family have dictated what type of behavior will be allowed. Now these institutions have simply been overrun by individuals who are deciding for themselves which experiences they feel are rewarding and growth-producing.

With the typical cultural lag now receding behind us, many social scientists are beginning to see the tumbling of the old codes not as the beginning of a moral decline, but rather as the beginning of a search for new values. The breakdown of traditional values has broadened the options available to each individual as to how he will conduct his life and how he will deal with the new freedoms. Areas that were so heavily guarded or suppressed, such as nudism, are now open to this new moral atmosphere.

We are just beginning to discover what morality is all about. It is concerned with how we treat one another, not how much of our body we display. Nudity is just a part of a new way of being able to express feelings, and this area must be faced and accepted as a part of a general confrontation with life. And like the youth of today who demand the truth, psychology and social science must also "tell it straight; tell it the way it really is."

CHANGES IN PSYCHOLOGY

In the field of clinical psychology and especially psychotherapy, change is developing with a bewildering rapidity. The traditional one-to-one therapy situation, with its sharply defined roles and the therapist firmly secured behind his desk with the door closed and secrets flowing in one direction only, has almost become passé. From personal experience, I know both the exhilaration and the fear that have accompanied coming out from behind that desk: coming out to participate in psychotherapy on live television watched by hundreds of observers; to experience the aliveness of sensory awareness procedures and nonverbal techniques, often utilizing physical contact; to attempt to defend oneself in the Synanon games' "attack therapy"; to intimately share the tears and joy of 24-to-48-hour continuous marathon groups; and to accept the jolting experience of watching your own behavior on videotape playback and now nude marathon groups. Frankly, the intellectual and emotional nakedness in the above experiences was felt to be considerably more revealing than the experience of simple physical nudity.

For this author, the introspection, speculation, and preliminary planning for a nude marathon now, in retrospect, seem as valuable and enlightening as the actual group experience itself. The whole procedure, it was found, was steeped in caution and a strong concern of how my professional colleagues would judge such a venture. From previous personal experience, I have found that innovation in therapeutic approaches often leads to spirited opposition that at times has openly developed into hostile, defensive rejection by other social scientists and therapists of other schools. It has appeared to me that change, innovation, and pioneering in clinical psychology meet with the same forces of opposition and suppression that the Establishment everywhere instantly seems to be able to muster. This reactionary element in a science dedicated to change in a problem in psychology that warrants deep concern. So before a nude marathon was planned, this author carefully considered the contingencies of professional criticism and possible censure, of being labeled as unethical, cultist, unscientific, and by other similar tags usually given to those whose ideas and values differ from the majority. The fact that papers such as this one are now being presented at psychology conventions indicates that there definitely are strong elements of openness and permissiveness in psychology, and this is considerably reassuring.

PRELIMINARY EVENTS

In preparing for the nude marathon it was felt, for a variety of reasons, that an appropriate and natural setting for the group would be on the grounds of a nudist camp. Because social nudism is legal in only some counties in California, an appropriate and convenient camp was selected and arrangements for a marathon completed with the camp's director. The 24-hour session was held in one of the homes at the camp, so that the problems of food and other necessities were easily solved.

The participants, who were all over 21 years old, were volunteers solicited informally by word of mouth. Each gave his written agreement to follow the simple camp rules and also permission for video recordings to be taken with the knowledge that an abstract discussion of the group's experiences might be given for professional and educational purposes at a later date. The participants included two married couples and several single male and female individuals, most of whom had considerable background in psychotherapeutic experiences both as therapists and as clients. None were social nudists, although all had had some very minor experiences with nudity.

The videotape nude marathon lasted 24 continuous hours, during which the group remained intact with no subgrouping. Brief periods were spent in jointly exploring the campgrounds, in group sensory-awareness exercises, and in using the camp swimming pool. Videotape recordings and playback occurred during most of the session. Conveniently, the camp director sat in on parts of the marathon and was available for questions and feedback concerning his extensive experience with social nudism.

The group began fully clothed in the early evening with a discussion of anxious feelings the members might have about social nudism. There was also a brief discussion of each individual's previous experiences with nudity, most of which were solitary or in childhood. It was then jointly decided the group would walk to the swimming pool, disrobe, and swim briefly before continuing on with the session. At the time and later, all agreed this was a comfortable and smooth transition to group nudity.

As the group confronted its own nudity, there initially was much good-natured joking and laughter, with several members noting how pleasant and enjoyable the immediate experience had become. A number of topics related to the nudity were then discussed by the group, including present voyeuristic needs, the surprisingly easy control of sexual impulses, degrees of inhibition, physical imperfections, and the emotional adjustment to the new situation. In less than one hour, however, the group felt the topic of nudity and its peripheral areas had essentially been exhausted, and it was agreed to move on to other verbal encounters. At that point, the group felt that the nudity itself did not essentially contribute to a feeling of group solidarity. This was to gradually develop as the marathon continued.

VIDEOTAPE FEEDBACK

During the session each participant was given several opportunities to view his behavior and physical appearance through videotape playbacks. The first tape consisted of five-minute segments of each group member walking, standing, turning, sitting, and talking and included facial close-ups, shots from the waist up, and finally videotapes of full-body profiles. The participants viewed this five-minute taped segment twice: once in the group setting immediately after it was recorded, and again the next day alone, one at a time while the rest of the group ate lunch. The second tape was one hour long and consisted of candid views of the free group interaction, including group discussions and the participants moving about, changing seats, listening, and talking. This second hour tape was played back to the group approximately 12 hours later at the evening meal. During the playbacks the group members could comment and discuss what they perceived while watching their behavior and appearance on the videotape. Following the marathon, the author studied both tapes several times before they were erased. It might be noted that as in regular videotape marathon groups, the taping equipment and activities did not interfere with or inhibit the free-flowing group interaction.

The group's reaction to the videotape feedback appeared to be consistently, and often dramatically, effective. Without a doubt, it is a useful and meaningful tool in communicating another form or type of information in these group encounters. For example, most of the members had highly specific concepts and self-perceptions of their own physical appearance. These perceptions were not always shared by the rest of the group. Following the videotape feedback, however, these self-perceptions appeared to alter more in the direction of objective reality. Most of the group members' original self-body perceptions tended to focus on what they felt were negative characteristics, such as over- or underweight, poor body proportioning, unattractive changes due to aging, and other similar deviations from what is generally considered the ideal human physique. Despite repeated assurances that others did not perceive them in this manner, members continued to maintain these beliefs. Following the videotape playback of themselves, however, body self-perceptions were judged more congruent with the group perception.

One rather startling alteration in self body image occurred in a male individual who felt that all his life he had been physically unattractive, especially to women, and that now he had gradually become a "fat, little old man." Contrary opinions by the female participants were simply not accepted by him. Laughing and smiling while watching his video replay, he excitedly informed the group that "I'm not fat at all; I'm really rather husky and stocky and there is a nice masculine powerfulness about me. I like what I see."

In general, the women tended to be much more critical of their physical appearance, and video feedback often confirmed their original body perceptions, especially the usual shift in weight and proportion that occurs with aging. There did not, however, appear to be any critical evaluation of physiques by one member of another, but rather, as one participant aptly put it, "each body seems to fit nicely with each face."

The group voiced a consensus that none of us had previously taken a very careful look at ourselves in the nude. One couple noted that although they had been married many years, neither had a very accurate perception of how his mate appeared nude. All agreed the videotape had given them a dramatically more accurate image of their own body and judged this element of the nude marathon experience as very valuable.

OTHER ACTIVITIES

During a brief period in the marathon session, the group strolled around the campgrounds and jointly observed the other nudists. The most consistent impression was that now that we had been initiated, the nudists, and especially the nude families, seemed very natural and rather appropriate. Also noted was a feeling that other than the nudism, the camp activities seemed rather dull and lacking in the ability to sustain our interest for very long. Although our initial experience with nudism was uniformly judged as valuable, none of the group indicated any strong interest in the nudist style of life and, in fact, were rather critical of the typical nudist's rationale and the seemingly over-cautious and often incongruent rules and regulations of the camp.

Initially the participants exhibited some hesitancy and inhibition concerning physical contact, especially between men and women. This receded rather slowly until appropriate physical contact became comfortable and spontaneously natural. There were no observable sexual overtones to these contacts, and the group agreed that sexual arousal in this setting would be not only socially inappropriate, but a serious breach of our personal and group mores.

Throughout the marathon, physical contact was frequently initiated as a nonverbal therapeutic technique and spontaneously arose during shared episodes of intimate and warm personal feelings. Physical contact was also experienced during a series of sensory-awareness exercises conducted outside on the campgrounds. The members unanimously agreed that these experiences were significantly enhanced by being conducted nude. Several felt the procedures were joyfully enriching with an accompaniment of deep personal feelings of warmth and oneness with the group.

In conclusion, it is observed that the therapeutic encounter facilitated by nudity is not as radically a new concept as it may first appear. The approach has previously been used intermittently at some residential training centers, and mixed communal bathing and massage have been a standard adjunct for several years now at one of the leading California centers for exploration in the social sciences. Also, Abraham Maslow, Ph.D., 1967 president of the American Psychological Association, has been quoted as directly encouraging and sanctioning the concept of nude psychotherapy.

Like the new morality, this technique is already upon us whether we agree with it or not. Possibly it may be discarded tomorrow as other approaches are found to be more effective, but for now this author would appeal for a period of objective testing and evaluation of this new approach. Certainly much more objective data are needed, but even more vital is the necessity for a fair and adequate hearing for nude therapy.

This is not to say that nude therapy might be appropriate for all therapists with all clients in all situations; it obviously is not! But our very preliminary evidence suggests that nudity as a facilitator in the group process can be significantly effective with some therapists and some clients in some settings. In any case, videotape nude marathon groups with emphasis on sensory awareness and nonverbal physical techniques is "where it's at" today. The general thrust of all these new approaches developing so rapidly may leave most of us hesitant to deal with them, but in conclusion, let me quote Bob Dylan, the popular singer and one of the spokesmen for the new generation, who proclaims, "Something is happening and you don't know what it is, do you, Mr. Jones?" I suggest we find out what's happening in this area.

FOCUSED ZEN GROUP MEDITATION

A less controversial innovation than nude videotape marathon groups is a procedure that is certainly not new, but as far as can be determined has never previously been used with a psychiatric inpatient population. I am speaking about meditation, and in this case a specific type of meditative technique that I have developed and named "focused Zen group meditation."

Meditation has been used by man throughout the world for thousands of years in an attempt to find the elusive goals of heightened awareness, self-understanding, and spiritual peace. In the last decade, Americans have shown a growing interest in these ancient approaches to life, especially the Oriental and Zen styles of meditation.

Used in many settings, could meditation be an effective tool for encounter groups and with the mentally and emotionally disturbed? This was an intriguing thought that has been with me for a number of years, but until recently I never put the concept to any type of practical test. I first began studying Oriental meditation techniques in 1951 during and following a two-year stay of military service in the Far East.

When first learning of the existence of a Zen monastery in California, I felt that a visit there would be an excellent opportunity to explore the potentiality of meditation as a psychotherapeutic technique. Accordingly, after making the proper arrangements, I did visit and study at America's "only Zen monastery," the Zen Mountain Center at Tassajara, California.

I found that the students at the Zen monastery come from all over the United States, a few come from other countries, but most are from California. Their backgrounds have ranged from kindergarten teacher to psychologist and Peace Corps worker to hippie dropout. There have been a number of scientists, ministers, college students, housewives, poets, writers, and many others. Most are young, under 35, and generally they are the innovative, perceptive, unorthodox people who typically seek change and self-understanding.

Before a person can be accepted as a Zen student at the Mountain Center, he must satisfactorily complete the seven-day sesshin, or intensive practice period. Each of these days is divided into 50-minute periods of zazen, or silent group meditation, alternated with 10 minutes of kinhin, or silent walking meditation, from 4:00 A.M. to 10:00 P.M. Interposed during these 18 hours are three meals, a tea service, an hour work period, and a half-hour for bathing. These seven days, of course, are lived in complete silence.

When I talked to the students, they said the only preliminary instruction given for sesshin is "be prepared to sit." Most agreed they were tested to the utmost in this encounter with themselves, and many commented to me that it was the most strenuous mental and physical experience they had ever had. When the sesshin is completed, there is usually the mixed experience of accomplishment, joy, and acute alertness.

My superficial understanding of sesshin is that it is an opportunity to focus, with a minimum of distraction, on the essence of one's life or problems, more particularly, to let the happenings of one's mind and body come and go without interference, until one begins to really know his mind and body, until one experiences emptiness itself. This is traditionally called "to know your original face."

Meditation is also a time-space experience that like most life experiences has no real guidelines and that you must structure and solve yourself. The student decides for himself how long he will sit in one position, what thoughts he will focus upon, and with what dignity and composure he will meet and react to this challenge. Some students felt that the successful completion of a sesshin meditation period can be a peak experience in a person's life.

While at Tassajara, I personally participated in the daily routine with the Zen students while also discussing these experiences with them. The day begins at 4:00 A.M., with the sounds of a hand bell and then a wooden board being struck rhythmically by a wooden mallet, a Chinese monastery tradition over 1,000 years old. The daily schedule consists of meditation at 4:30 A.M. in the zendo, or traditional meditation hall. Then there is breakfast, a three-hour work period, midday meditation, lunch, a rest period, a study period, an afternoon work session, bath time, supper, a lecture, and then an evening period of meditation before bed at 9:45 P.M. Most of the activities are carried out in silence or with a very minimal amount of talking. I found that one quickly adjusts to this slow, formal, silent way of life, and the beauty and meaningfulness of the stylized simplicity of the Zen center gradually became apparent to me.

From these meaningful experiences and training at the Tassajara Zen monastery, I became convinced of the therapeutic potential of meditation with psychiatric patients. In the spring of 1968, I first began using meditation techniques with my private clients during week-end residential videotape marathon therapy workshops. In these experimental sessions I found the use of meditation often to be very dramatically effective. The meaningful memories, feelings, and emotional experiences generated by these clients in group meditation were

Figure 13-4. Psychiatric inpatients shown during focused Zen group meditation period. (Photo by A. W. Sylvester.)

highly stimulating to the group participants and convinced me that the technique was able to be used experimentally.

Utilizing psychiatric inpatients in a local hospital, group meditation sessions were begun for 30-minute periods, five days a week. The sessions have continued now for two years. For each session, 15 to 30 patients are taken as a group to a room in which the only furniture is straight-backed, armless chairs. The room is fairly soundproof, the lights are kept dim, and the air conditioning comfortably controls the temperature.

Because the traditional Oriental cross-legged position is too awkward and uncomfortable for westerners, straight-backed chairs are used. The patients are seated, facing the blank wall, in a single row of chairs next to each other around the room. The therapist sits alone near the center of the room so that he can see each patient as he gives instructions to the group.

Instructions are given slowly and with long pauses to induce a state of calm relaxation and to slowly lead the group into the meditation experience. A rigidly immobile posture is used, with both feet flat on the floor and hands held in the traditional Buddhist position of palms up, one hand on top of the other, and thumbs lightly touching together. Patients are instructed to tilt their heads slightly downward, to keep their eyes half closed, and to breathe slowly and quietly through their noses. Absolute silence continues throughout the session. Patients are also instructed to be aware of their thoughts as they begin to slow down and to be aware of all their bodily sensations as the group sits in silence without moving.

During some meditation sessions each patient is given a "meditation slip" to focus his thoughts upon. This is a slip of paper on which is written a single sentence, question, or brief phrase that is individually patterned each time for each patient. For example, a suicidal patient may be asked to think about "the effect of your death on those close to you." Other meditation slips may say, for example, "Think about the relationship with your spouse, or with your family." Sometimes very general topics are given to the patient, such as "love," "your future," or "your sadness." Each patient is instructed to focus his thoughts on these individual topics that are directly related to his psychiatric problem. During most sessions, however, patients are simply allowed to follow their own mental and physical processes without focusing on specific topics.

The rationale for the meditation slips is multiple. First, patients often feel that their therapist has superior knowledge or insight into their case, and therefore, these vague, general, projective statements are felt to have significant meaning and possibly to hold the key to their immediate difficulties. The slips tend to have the patients feel the therapist is personally aware and concerned about their particular situation. Such a positive attitude can be extremely helpful, especially in the typical overcrowded psychiatric unit. Also, the meditation slips are felt to be helpful in guiding those who have trouble handling a completely ambiguous, self-directed activity and focusing their experiences and thoughts on more definitive problems. As a tangible reminder of the experience, the slips are often saved by the patients and considered at a later time. If the open-ended, projective phrase or statement on the meditation slip is felt to be inappropriate or not personally applicable to them, patients tend to ignore the slips and follow other thoughts during the meditation period. Some patients have even taken the slips home and report they continued to meditate on these same topics on their own. Last, this procedure tends to encourage the therapist to participate more actively in the whole group experience.

Emotionally disturbed people are defensive people who have developed, usually over a lifetime, endless ways of avoiding, denying, and not dealing objectively with their problems. Patients develop complex verbal games to hide their basic feelings about problems from other people and even from their therapist. Considerable effort is often expended not to even think about critical life problems. Meditation, I feel, allows an individual a scheduled time and place to individually confront his own problem areas alone, without the necessity of defending his ego to others. It also aids a person to bring his own anxiety and body under more self-control, and with success here, the possibility is open for larger areas of behavior patterns to come back under voluntary control. Meditation may also allow an individual to become more aware of his own body and its relationship to the universe and hence tends to give more perspective to personal problems.

The preliminary impressionistic results of this experimental psychiatric technique are felt to be decidedly positive. In the first one or two sessions of group meditation, a new patient may move slightly, such as scratch his nose, shift body weight, or move a foot, but after that, all patients are able to sit immobile and silent up to 30 minutes. Very seldom does a person doze, and even grossly disturbed, very anxious patients are easily able to sit through the meditation sessions, with up to 30 patients participating in each of these daily periods.

Preliminary verbal reports from the patients themselves are also positive. The majority of them "work on their problem" during the sitting and generally report feelings of calm and being at peace. Thoughts tend to drift back to childhood memories and other emotionally significant events that shaped the patient's life. Many work on the reasons they became emotionally disturbed, and it is not unusual to see a patient sitting unmoving and silent with tears streaming down his cheeks.

Some patients report tension, but are instructed in the next session to try to analyze where the tension comes from. At times, very vivid daydreams occur that can be watched as if at a movie. Usually these experiences have direct or symbolic relevancy to the patient's immediate life problems.

A variety of physical reactions occur in the group meditation sessions, and these are probably due to confused nerve messages coming to the brain. The usual cues, such as vision, balancing, muscle tension, and movement, are greatly reduced in the meditation posture, and the brain may misinterpret the signals it receives.

Feelings of hands melting together, feet being glued to the floor, and body parts being lost are typical physical reactions. Often there is the feeling of the mind drifting away from the body and a temporary inability to move. Sensations of peaceful drifting, being asleep yet awake, and visual misinterpretations are frequently reported. These experiences generally seem to be pleasant and tend to enhance the meditation period.

Immediately following the group meditation period, a group discussion is held that quickly shades into a group encounter session. The wealth of significant clinical material that arises in the meditation periods is often utilized verbally in the encounter period.

Focused Zen group meditation has a number of advantages in terms of introducing this procedure into a clinic or hospital program with a minimum of difficulty. First, because it can be conducted by a single, trained staff member with large groups of patients, it is economic, efficient, and not disruptive to other programs. No equipment is needed other than chairs and a quiet, dimly lighted room.

It seems difficult to raise any objections to the procedure of just quietly sitting with a group of patients. There tends to be a feeling among more conservative or cautious personnel of "it certainly can't do any harm . . ." Also, the concept has an unorthodox, mystical flavor to it that helps hold patients' attention and interest, which is always a positive factor with a psychiatric population.

Focused Zen group meditation is certainly no panacea for the legion of the mentally ill, but our preliminary data seem to indicate that this experimental procedure has significant value for many individuals and, therefore, can prove useful when properly conducted in conjunction with other more conventional therapeutic tools. It also can be easily introduced and carried out in a variety of treatment settings, can be used with a wide range of emotional disorders, and is a treatment procedure that patients can feel comfortable with and easily learn. At this point in my experience, it appears as if this ancient art of Zen meditation can be developed into a modern therapeutic tool.

BIBLIOGRAPHY

Lawrence, Stephen B. Group and Family Psychotherapy Via Live Television. *State of California Psychological News Letter,* Vol. 10, Number 1, February 1967.

Lawrence, Stephen B. Videotape and Other Therapeutic Procedures with Nude Marathon Groups. *American Psychologist,* 24:476–79, 1969.

Part D

Populations

Frederick H. Stoller

 Marathon and Encounter
Approaches in Therapeutic
and Rehabilitative Programs

COMMENTARY

The marathon and encounter techniques applied to therapeutic and rehabilitative programs in institutions are explored and illustrated in this chapter. The point is made that a wide variety of populations in varying milieus can profit from encounter techniques.

BIOGRAPHY

The late Frederick H. Stoller was senior research associate at the Public Systems Research Institute, University of Southern California, where he was also associate professor in the School of Public Administration. A recent appointment had been as associate editor of *Comparative Group Studies*. Having received his Ph.D. in clinical psychology from U.C.L.A., he had been deeply involved in the group movement, having been a pioneer in the development of the marathon and in the introduction of videotape feedback into the group setting. Esalen, Kairos, and numerous growth centers had been the setting for his workshops. Prior to his death he had been attempting to develop a growth model to serve as a framework for future developments in the growth movement.

Dr. Stoller's unfortunate death occurred during the preparation of this volume.

If one were to base one's experience with clinical populations exclusively on the writings of the various psychotherapeutic schools, it would be easy to believe that society was made up almost exclusively of various clinical entities. Choose your literature and enter a world of hysterics, obsessive-compulsives, phobics, anxiety neurotics, or schizophrenogenic families. In this light, what is the world suggested by the encounter group? Largely middle-class, college-educated, and moderately successful in terms of material criteria, participants in encounter groups have frequently had previous therapeutic experience. Yet they come back for more.

Oddly enough, they do not appear to have more disturbing emotional problems than the remainder of the population. They may even have less (though they yell louder), but they do possess a consuming interest in increasing their self-knowledge and a sense of greater possibilities for one's life. The complaints they have mirror Wheelis' description (Wheelis, 1958) of the shift in problems being seen by psychotherapists in general: loneliness, insecurity, doubt, boredom, restlessness, and marital discord. The encounter approach appears at least to attempt to tackle many of these conditions if not "solve" them.

Within the circle that has embraced these new groups have been a very high proportion of workers in the helping professions. They share much with the population just described. In addition, they have a professional curiosity about new approaches to helping people. This interest, which has always been an appropriate characteristic of such professionals, now occurs during a period of broad upheaval: a broadening of the definition of those people for whom psychologic help might be feasible. More and more, attention is being given to those who are not "making it" within our society in as full a manner as is deemed appropriate (Rae-Grant, Gladwin, and Bowers, 1965). What has changed is not the existence of these groups but merely the realization that they are entitled to "equal time and effort," which has been heretofore denied them (Smith and Hobbs, 1966). At the same time there has been the growing awareness that the conventional psychotherapeutic approach is much too narrow and inappropriate for this population (Gould, 1967). Within this context the encounter group, with its emphasis on action, the development of joy and fulfillment, the appreciation of one's own capabilities, and the immediate exploration of new behaviors before the establishment of insight or understanding, has an attractiveness. In particular, the encounter group emphasizes styles of living and encourages people to explore new and alternative modes of life, not only for their possible utility but for the sheer fun of changing forms. Because so many of the "problems" and "difficulties" of the newer populations seem to involve less psychodynamics and more styles of life, the encounter group has an appeal for the freshness of its approach.

In similar fashion, the marathon group, with its emphasis on intensity and breakthroughs in behavior, seems appropriate for institutional programs. Unless the setting is being used explicitly for incarceration, the only excuse, in a rehabilitative sense, for institutionalization is in the learning opportunities that are inherent in people living and working together, such as has been exemplified in the Synanon approach and the Daytop program (Yablonsky, 1965; Shelly and Bassin, 1965). Characteristic of both these programs is the heavy emphasis on the residents carrying the bulk of the therapeutic work. As a consequence, the whole living experience is part and parcel of the rehabilitative possibilities. Such efficiency is far from the case when a therapeutic staff conducts a program for the residential population. Under such circumstances there is likely to be a considerable amount of "dead time"; institutionalization rather than rehabilitation will be taking place. It has been stated that considerably more mopping than psychotherapy takes place in a state mental hospital, and although this statement referred to the pretranquilizer days of almost utter neglect, the picture in "establishment institutions" of today is only relatively better rather than qualitatively different. The marathon group appears to be a natural solution to some of the problems inherent in the inefficient and ineffectual use of time and resources that is often endemic in such settings.

The major question to be addressed is not whether the encounter and marathon approaches should be used in therapeutic and rehabilitative programs but how and for what purposes. Unlimited enthusiasm for these approaches can only be entertained in lieu of an appreciation of their assumptions and goals. Before their appropriate use in therapeutic and rehabilitative programs can be dealt with, it is necessary to examine certain characteristics and assumptions of the encounter and marathon groups as well as to consider certain features of institutional programs and the populations involved.

THE MATRIX OF THE ENCOUNTER GROUP

Although much that goes on in encounter groups can be considered to be therapeutic and bears an undeniable relationship to psychotherapy, it is important to emphasize that entering an encounter group is not the equivalent of entering a psychotherapy program. If we trace the

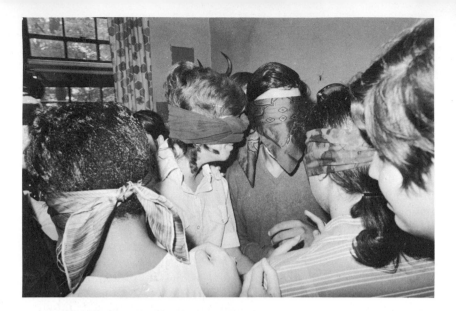

Figure 14-1. A "blind walk"—the encounter group's freshness of approach. (Photos by Zev Guber.)

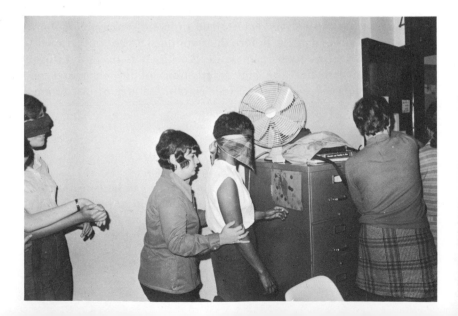

genesis of the encounter group, we can see that it emerges from a somewhat different tradition from psychotherapy. No matter what twists and turns it takes, the latter approach is clearly a direct descendant of Freud's discoveries and innovations; even the newer developments in the field are often reactions to and variations of his basic methodology. Psychotherapy operates within the medical model. It concentrates on people defined by themselves and others as having problems that, within the context of the treatment, are the most important thing about them. Built into psychotherapy is a basic assumption: that there is an optimal level of functioning, and those individuals who do not attain this optimal level will be helped by people in the role of expert and who invariably invoke a diagnostic model (whatever its terminology might be) in which the individual's status is compared with some over-all norm.

Much more in line with the encounter group's ancestry is the T group of the National Training Laboratories, an approach primarily interested in developing new avenues for learning with an emphasis on group process as a major focus of interest (Bradford, Gibb, and Benne, 1964). The clientele of such groups were primarily from a variety of institutions, and organizational change, through the use of group dynamics, was a primary goal of such programs (Schein and Bennis, 1965). As a consequence of developments on the West Coast, an emphasis on individual growth was introduced and the shift was made to sensitivity training, the so-called "therapy for the normal." Within this milieu a repertoire of techniques was developed designed to help participants explore their own functioning and expose themselves to areas previously avoided (Schutz, 1967). The development of growth centers such as Esalen has given a setting in which the encounter group is practiced along with a rich variety of approaches. The result has been a broadening and enrichment of the encounter group. Some example of the breadth of diverse interests involved, ranging from breathing to sensory awareness, from meditation to developing family strengths, can be gained through such a book as the one edited by Otto and Mann (Otto and Mann, 1968).

This heritage is of particular importance because in the relatively few years that such groups have been in existence, a number of assumptions have been developed. These assumptions have been dealt with in some detail elsewhere (Stoller, 1969), but unless one has some understanding of what they are, the mixture of interests and approaches inherent in the encounter group movement seems perplexing. In particular, these assumptions assume considerable importance in the application of the encounter group technique to programs that may require different assumptions.

If we return to the original point made in this section, it should be re-emphasized that the goal and contract with the participant of the encounter group differ from those of the therapy group. Rather than attempting to free the individual from disabling difficulties, the encounter approach tries to open up new areas of experience for the participants. Although these two goals would seem to be very close to one another, they are, in actuality, quite different operations.

For one thing, expansion into new areas may or may not help someone function more effectively in his life-space. Enrichment is, in itself, an adequate goal. It is assumed that each individual has within him areas and potentialities of which he has scarcely been aware, much less used. Although some of these oversights are due to neurotic blocks, some are merely due to a scarcity of experience or an investment of energy in one or more areas at the expense of others. Thus, the encounter group often finds itself dealing with styles of experiencing and the individual's freedom or reluctance to explore new modes of experiencing. It is for this reason that much of the work of the encounter group can look like play rather than always being deadly serious: its aims are often in the direction of enhancing "inner decoration" rather than establishing more effective functioning. The fact that the second goal is often attained through the former is really secondary; as soon as one purposefully attempts this, the operation becomes something quite different.

Figure 14-2. The work of the group can look like play. (Photo by Zev Guber.)

Such an unpragmatic goal can be puzzling to Americans. However, it must be understood that the encounter approach developed in a period of unprecedented affluence for large groups of people. It has been largely a middle-class phenomenon; basically its population is well functioning insofar as practical ability is concerned, and they are not plagued with concerns of survival. As if to follow Maslow's concept of being and deprivation motivation (Maslow, 1962), they find themselves interested in a new level of perception and experience. Hence the encounter group developed in the vacuum that their new value systems created; the fact that the encounter approach as it is now constituted is a rather crude instrument to achieve this new search should not deceive one any more than the first horseless carriages represented an imperfect vehicle. The encounter approach may be just as revolutionary.

Because of the population that has tended to be involved in the encounter programs, it has been assumed that the participant has the resources to move in any direction he wishes and is limited only by his own inhibitions and lack of imagination. As a consequence, there has been relatively little in the way of supportive services offered to the participant of the encounter group; he has been considered capable of pursuing his own course of growth and development once having been shown the path. Such lack of guidance may be overoptimistic, and future developments in the area of the encounter group may well be in the direction of supplying more depth and structure to an individual's movement. Nevertheless, the encounter group is not likely to alter the basic assumption about the individual's resources and will retain its avoidance of diagnostic categorizing and the development of case history material. Because of its heritage, the encounter group is a true departure from the medical model.[1]

Because the encounter is dealing with enrichment rather than amelioration, not all the behavior with which the encounter is concerned is rooted in long-standing conflicts. As has already been suggested, many blocks are the result of lack of experience. Consequently the encounter group has often moved very fast without the preparation one often finds in therapy. Group exercises and games are a frequent technique used to help participants sample new experiences. The emphasis on the nonverbal and the movement away from explanation and insight are very important aspects of this new thrust into enrichment and expansion. It is easy to make fun of "group grope" and

[1] To the degree that the important learnings come from others rather than from an expert it represents a further departure from the medical model. Groups in which the leader retains the central role and fosters most of the important learning represent a return to this model. The impact on the participant may be just as powerful as a diagnosis and prescription even if not couched in pathologic terms.

Figure 14-3. Group grope. (Photo by Zev Guber.)

decry the seeming anti-intellectualism of the encounter movement, but they represent very important antidotes for middle-class individuals who have spent most of their energies on goal-directed, rational behavior and who are hungry for a new dimension of experience. It is also implicitly understood by all the participants that these "sample experiences" are analogues for broader slices of life. Thus, touching does not represent a magic carpet to intimacy but a relative readiness and capacity for engaging in physical contact, a rich dimension of experience usually avoided. A good deal of the encounter technique is built on just such analogous operations, and unless the participant is in a position to understand this very readily, much of the encounter approach can have a forced and unreal quality.

Every human endeavor is goal-directed, and the encounter group is no exception. The goal, if it is possible to reduce it to simple terms, is to allow for a greater degree of flexibility in the individual. Thus he can allow himself to invest energy in a wide range of areas rather than remain within his customary inhibition and automatic tension. For the highly intellectualized, goal-oriented, striving, and gratification-delaying middle-class client this has often meant a very deliberate move away from self-analysis. The encounter group strives toward trust in self, a basic ingredient of spontaneity. In ways, this approach acts as a deliberate antidote to psychotherapeutic styles. It is likely that any style taken to its extreme represents a rigidity and fixation that are ultimately costly to the individual; therefore, the counter-movement to therapeutic self-analysis is not necessarily a complete negation of such efforts but rather a critique of the results of over-reliance.

THE MARATHON AS PROCEDURE

The marathon is less an approach than a technical variation, a re-altering of time and rhythm as it is customarily practiced in any given format. As such it does not represent a distinctly different line of development, as has been the case in the encounter group, but rather a technical innovation. Therefore, the marathon can be conducted in any of a variety of frames of reference from clear-cut psychotherapy to the encounter workshop. The marathon is, in and of itself, a complex technical problem requiring a high order of skill, as has been discussed elsewhere (Bach, 1966; Stoller, Marathon Group Therapy, 1968; Stoller, Accelerated Interaction: A Time-limited Approach Based on the Brief, Intensive Group, 1968). A number of features of this type of group are particularly relevant to treatment programs.

Marathons are often most effective when conducted as if they represented a unique opportunity for the participants. In this way the intensity and urgency of the experience, which are so important a part of the marathon, are maintained and enhanced rather than diluted (Stoller, Marathon Group Therapy, 1968; Stoller, Accelerated Interaction: A Time-Limited Approach Based on the Brief, Intensive Group, 1968). However, it was never intended that the marathon stand absolutely by itself as if it were the only growth experience that was necessary for any individual to undergo. Quite the contrary, the marathon was considered to be one of a series of growth experiences, whether it was part of an ongoing therapeutic program or merely one of a series of distinct experiences sought out by the individual on his own. Just as in the encounter approach, it has been assumed that the individual participant has the resources, both on his own and through his contacts, to continue the growth that might get precipitated within the marathon.

Another important quality of the marathon is that it does represent a break in the customary ordering of one's life. The pace and rhythm of participation in the world are forced to undergo a marked change, and some of the most important learnings emerge out of the fact that free and spontaneous participation turns out to be much less fatiguing and enervating than withholding, a profound analogue for one's conduct in the world outside the marathon. In any case, there is, as Maslow (Maslow, 1965) has pointed out, considerable merit to removing the individual from his customary behavioral structures in order to aid him to learn about himself. Everyone falls into patterns that become routinized in that they require little effort or a relatively minor mobilization of resources. This is just as true of therapeutic programs that last over a period of time; in one sense their routinization acts as a deterrent to the goals that are being sought. One important part of the marathon's effectiveness is that it is not a part of one's routine and is not meant to be.

Finally, the marathon shares with the encounter group the characteristic that it is much more profound in terms of its experiential qualities than in its didactic features. It depends, to a considerable extent, on the fact that participants learn to be together in a different manner than is customarily the fashion, that they learn to use alternative parts of their response hierarchies. The very manner in which participants pass through the microworld of the marathon, the texture of their experience under the variety of encountering or countering styles they employ (Stoller, 1969), is, in itself, an important outcome of the marathon. What is essential is that the marathon participants do experience one another differently as the group progresses; if they are hopelessly caught in labels for one another, such as diagnoses or vocational roles, this novel way of meeting both one another and themselves becomes very difficult.

PROGRAMMATIC TREATMENT AS A MODALITY

Programmed treatment attempts to go beyond the narrow confines of the client-practitioner situation; it is presented within the framework of a broader range of services and procedures designed to induce change. Whether offered in outpatient or residential settings they commonly feature the individual being processed through a series of prescribed activities once he is labeled or diagnosed as belonging to a particular category for which the program has been designed. Many of the psychosocial problems that confront the helping professions tend to be dealt with in this programmatic fashion.

A number of semantic problems arise when we deal with programmatic treatment. One of the most troublesome comes about when staff conceptualizes their concerns in psychotherapeutic formulations, ignoring the much more profound impact of the remainder of the program. The pioneering work of Stanton and Schwartz (Stanton and Schwartz, 1954) and the analysis of Goffman (Goffman, 1961), as well as the insights of many others, have indicated that the organizations have an effect that is rarely appreciated by those who are designing and administering the programs. At its most ludicrous it can involve elaborate discussions of psychodynamics at staff conferences while the patient is learning the role of the institutionalized inmate during the remainder of his time. The incidental learning of how to get along with the system's expectations can be far more important than the ostensible goals of the setting: the parallel with many of our schools is compelling.

If we examine the population and circumstances of such therapeutic and rehabilitative programs, we find that the people who become enmeshed in them are relatively impoverished in terms of resources.[2] It is almost by definition that these people lack many resources; it is just because of this that the extratherapeutic features of programs are developed. It is anticipated that through vocational training, education, and socialization they will have more resources available to them. It is clear that programmatic patients tend to be very much concerned with survival needs and operate in terms of Maslow's deprivation motivation. From this can be anticipated the fact that enrichment and inner decoration are of minor, if any, interest and that their tendency toward concreteness makes analogue bridging a difficult process.

In order to appreciate the actual position of the patients we are discussing, it is misleading to think in terms of diagnosis, case history considerations, and treatment prescriptions. Rather, one should conceptualize a distribution system through which people are moved from place to place until they achieve a particular identification: mentally ill, alcoholic, drug addict, delinquent, and so on. When this occurs, the distribution system deposits them in the appropriate collecting place. Consequently they find themselves in settings that define their role, in which everyone who is there has the same role designation. To the degree that they are supposed to learn new behavioral repertoires from each other, their homogeneity and rigid role definition create many indigenous problems. Should they break new ground for themselves, it is in spite of these characteristics of the setting rather than because of them.[3]

To the degree that programs tend to be complex, a variety of personnel will have contact with the patient. Generally there are a number of professionals who theoretically formulate the concepts that govern the program; they are in the minority and will have the least amount of

[2] Resources are the sum total of money, relatives, friends, talents, skills, capacity for attracting others, and other assets that enable the individual to move about as close to his own desires as possible.

[3] The only way to diminish the medical model in which people establish themselves as having a special requirement for guidance from an expert for a wide range of behaviors is when the "expert" is a peer who has managed to make many of the changes himself and functions as a real role-model in an intimate network.

contact with the patients. It is rare for an entire staff to be able to confront patients with a coordinated set of attitudes unless they have put considerable effort into working together, coming to terms in their philosophies, and confronting one another as to their actual behavior. What generally happens is that the housekeeping details of maintaining a complex organization involved in an intricate program take precedence over therapeutic goals, and much of the contact between staff and patients revolves around organizational maintenance problems. The thrust of such contacts is often of a very different order than the rehabilitative goals might dictate.[4]

Opening the discussion to the staff centers upon a very important dimension and provides a key to the introduction of the encounter technique and the marathon approach into such programs. It is important, however, to examine what happens to the people who are designated staff.

STAFF: THE NEGLECTED SIDE OF THE EQUATION

It is commonplace to state that therapeutic efforts are two-way affairs, that relationship is one of the most important ingredients in any rehabilitative effort. No matter what therapeutic system is employed, an enthusiastic and skilful staff is usually a minimum requirement. A frequent pattern in psychiatric history is the initial success of new approaches followed by a more moderate record; the enthusiasm of staff and its subsequent tapering off have generally been considered to be the key factors in this phenomenon. Therefore, what happens to staff is a vital aspect of such therapeutic programs but one that has received relatively little attention. Greenblatt and Levinson have pointed out that staff in a mental hospital can be under as much stress as the patients (Greenblatt and Levinson, 1965). Because patients are dependent on staff, the worker's welfare is of primary importance. Important as working conditions are, there are much more subtle factors involved.

Therapeutic staff do their work not because it is well paying but because of its personal rewards. They use themselves unstintingly to

---

[4] A major contradiction exists between efficient organization processes and an effective rehabilitative setting; the two may be incompatible. The well-run organization may represent a poor therapeutic milieu because of the priorities that are considered important. In an effective rehabilitative environment the important functions and decisions will be given over to the residents who have to struggle to attain the necessary level of responsibility and efficiency. When they do become effective, they are ready to leave the program. One should be wary of the well-run therapeutic organization; it will look good but its soul will be hollow.

the degree that they are reinforced. To expect them to behave differently is to expect them to function under a different set of behavioral rules from the rest of humanity. Over and above the money they receive, the reward system of staff operates on two levels: the regard and recognition they receive from their colleagues and the emotional response returned to them by their patients. In order for a coordinated program to function adequately, both are necessary. If only patient response is present without colleague recognition, the staff will tend to work in isolated pockets, in the same place but separately, much as private practitioners do who share the same professional building. Should response and satisfaction with clients be absent, staff will tend to play toward one another with elaborate staff meetings playing a major role in the setting; under such circumstances the patients can become a necessary but annoying interference with the important business at hand. Where both types of satisfaction are absent, the consequences are too awful to consider. It should be noted that staff satisfaction is not a static affair but one that changes over time much as spouse satisfaction erodes in many marriages unless something is done to alter the situation.

All too often, programmatic rehabilitative efforts actually represent organizations that process people. The analogy with an assembly line is an apt one, as Goffman has so sharply indicated (Goffman, 1961), except that the products are people. Assembly lines work best when the products being processed lie quietly and do not speak back to the processors, a difficult proposition when people are involved. In order to sustain this ideal situation, a variety of distancing and dehumanizing techniques are frequently applied to the patients. As Goffman indicates, patients frequently pass through such a process "marking time," barely being affected by the institution in any permanent way. However, the staff tends to remain, and it may be that being on the other end of such processing is ultimately more devastating for them. It can be speculated that staff, under the impact of remaining in such a system for too long a time, becomes exhausted, disillusioned, cynical about themselves and their organization, and contemptuous of the clients with whom they work. How long such a process takes for it to erode the original enthusiasm is impossible to say, but everyone has seen its effects at work. The only question is how ubiquitous and inevitable it is. If such a trend is to be subverted, processes for increased self-perception must be introduced.

Rewards are not always forthcoming from patients for a number of reasons. The population with which they are dealing often express their feelings in a somewhat different fashion than the staff person may be accustomed to experiencing. Positive results may be so long in forthcoming and so infrequent that the reward of success is too intermittent. In certain settings, such as prisons, staff is so prepared for recidivism that they cannot allow themselves to accept a success at the risk of looking naïve and of being disappointed later. In any case, the contingency schedules for staff should be regularly examined; the actual rewards for which people operate may reveal what is most important about the program.

The picture that has been painted should not be considered a condemnation of institutional staff. Rather, it is an attempt to appreciate their predicament in as realistic a manner as possible. Their circumstances are those of every human following his life pattern out and attempting to conduct his work in a self-sustaining fashion (Stoller, 1969). The work is of importance, over and above the human predicament, insofar as it affects the treatment of people within the therapeutic equation. Everyone is subject to an increasing blindness about his own behavior and his own effect on the environment unless there are steps taken to correct this process. When such a process affects how patients are perceived and treated, there is a particular therapeutic problem that can be ignored only at considerable expense. What will help staff enrich their own development is generally parallel to the therapeutic goals but not equivalent.

THE MODIFICATION OF THERAPEUTIC PROGRAMS

It should be obvious at this point that any attempt to replace a therapeutic program with the encounter group or the marathon would be completely out of place. The individuals involved require the development of resources, so that the marathon, by itself, would be inadequate. Populations of such programs have been so enveloped in deprivation motivation that many of the techniques and goals of the encounter group are irrelevant. And yet to eliminate them from consideration as part of the tools that are employed in programmatic rehabilitation would be to overlook their undeniable contribution as part of the modification of such programs, to enrich, to refresh, and to broaden what can be attempted.

One of the very important characteristics of the types of programs we are considering is that they are products of organizations. In general, the administrative forces of psychologic and psychiatric organizations are woefully naïve about the nature and problems of organizational structure. A body of sophisticated work has gone into the problems of organizational management, as the work of Argyris and Likert has indicated (Argyris, 1964; Likert, 1961). In particular, it has become fruitful to consider organizations as systems with sub-systems built into them to take care of various functions (Katz and Kahn, 1966).

Such a system would have an input and an output, specifically the input being people classified as having particular types of problems that are dysfunctional to both themselves and society and the output being people who are much less dysfunctional. A number of subsystems are necessary within the over-all system to carry out various functions, some of which are directly related to moving the process from input to output (throughput). Others are less directly related to production but are necessary for maintenance of the system. Systems analysis is less concerned with structure and hierarchic relationships and more with the cyclic flow of events. At key points various decisions are possible that will determine the future pathway that will be followed at any given part of the flow. For the moment, it is as if we are disregarding the people involved in such organizations and considering their acts as a series of decision points.

One of the important qualities that become apparent as one considers this model is that the system interfaces with its environment in a number of ways. One is that its goals are environmentally determined; that is, the kind of output with which it will be concerned is a function of environmental requirements. Should the gap between the system's output and the environmental requirements become too disparate, the flow of resources into the system will be altered. Such systems are considered to have a natural entropy; they will tend to run down unless new resources are fed into it.

One of the functions of an important subsystem is feedback, a means of allowing the system to have knowledge of the continual relevance of its output to its environment. One of the penalties of efficiency can be a built-in disregard of this important aspect so that changes in circumstances are not detected but the system continues to grind out its output regardless of subtle changes in the environment. Such changes are particularly difficult to ascertain in the therapeutic organization, and a constant re-examination of goals is of particular importance. In the circumstances of this type of organization, the influx of money, important as it is to the maintainence of the organization, is not the only type of resource counteracting entropy. It is equally essential that the system be open to new concepts, knowledge, and perceptions from outside or else it suffers from a very pervasive hardening of the arteries.

It is possible to build in operations that help the system look at its output, and most systems have some type of statistical information about their operations. However, it is really what is done with this and other less routine information that is important if the system is to grow realistically in terms of the staff's needs and the goals of the organization. Such growth is very different from the cancer-like growth of many settings. At this point it is necessary to shift from operations to the people involved; they are being asked to do one of the most difficult and important therapeutic tasks, a continued and open perception of one's own functioning. The encounter group, particularly as an organizationally oriented group, with external input is an excellent medium for continuing this ongoing searching look at themselves. Developing the capacity for continued honesty about one another and about the operation in which they are mutually engaged while continuing to undergo an interdependent undertaking is an extraordinarily difficult job. It is one that requires constant work so that regular encounter groups, within the staff, can have an important impact. It is highly recommended that such groups be conducted by a respected outsider who will help the staff members through the difficulties of mutual honesty.

Bringing in outsiders as important consultants to the functioning of the staff is one method of counteracting entropy. In the case of a therapeutic organization, entropy undermines the therapeutic and rehabilitative goals of the organization while the outer manifestations of the activity are maintained: people go through the motions without the substance. In a production system there will generally be mechanisms for detecting the growing inefficiency of equipment and the optimal time to replace them. In a therapeutic system, the important elements are people, and their slow erosion of effectiveness is generally less detectable. However, it can be assumed that, just as constant use wears out machinery, consistent routinized processes dull the edges of staff's effectiveness.

A major element in such erosion is the repetitive type of activity that may very well become inherent in an ongoing program. To the degree that this is the case, there is a necessity for refreshing changes of pace, both for the staff and for the clientele, as a way of renewing and recharging the processes of enthusiasm, energy, and fresh perception. Both the encounter group and the marathon arrangement represent ways in which variation can be introduced into the system without negating the throughput efforts. Because the encounter group has a somewhat different goal, that of growth and expansion into new areas, it tends to allow for a greater flexibility of activities. In particular, people can come together to enjoy contact with one another and to explore new possibilities in an enjoyable way. Because the encounter allows people to come together under a different set of strictures than is ordinarily the case, the possibility for refreshment in contrast to the usual goal-oriented activities is of a very high order. When staff and clients come together in the encounter group, the distancing inherent in the medical model is minimized. Staff-client participation in such groups can be used for this goal, in particular.[5]

The marathon group, on the other hand, can well be presented within the stricture of the therapeuptic goals of the program. Marathons can best be conducted when they are goal-oriented toward personal discovery and change. However, the pace at which they are conducted can be a very exciting one, allowing people to do things and to demand things of one another to which the usual time-restricted session does not lend itself. Here, it is the pace that can be attained through the momentum of the marathon that is, in itself, refreshing and renewing for all concerned. In one sense the marathon can be said to play the equivalent role for the client as the encounter group does for the staff member.

Kruschke and Stoller (Kruschke and Stoller, 1967), when experimenting with the marathon in a drug addict facility, found it extremely valuable in countering a set that had been inculcated in these particular inmates: an unvarying confrontation in which one member was elected "it" and the remainder of the group jumped on him. These particular men had become so automatic in doing this that it was apparent they were using the technique to escape confrontation themselves, merely taking turns being scapegoats. The marathon experience enabled them to learn to be more direct, honest, and mutual with one another and ultimately much more genuinely helpful. However, it was in motivating the men to make use of the rest of the rehabilitative program that the marathon was found to be most productive; in a sense, the men became "turned on" and invested their energies in truly embracing what was being offered them by the institution. They seemed much more likely to introject opportunities than go through the motions.

We finally come to the production subsystem, the central work of the therapeutic program. When we look at the system as a series of possible acts, it is obvious that the more possible types of alternatives there are available at the various choice points, the richer and more flexible program that is available. Thus, the encounter and marathon enable a treatment team to expand the tools available to them. It has already been suggested that the marathon has considerable facility in heightening clients' motivation for utilizing what is available to them. This leads to a primary principle that should govern applications of both these types of groups in institutional programs: *the introduction of the marathon and/or the encounter group into a therapeutic pro-*

---

[5] Within the context of the growth model inherent in the encounter group, the negative aspects of the medical format are most apparent when it is used to alter personal conduct and personality characteristics. Instead of a rational and helpful consultation with an expert, it becomes, for the client, a passive loss of self-definition as a person.

gram should always be with a particular subgoal in mind, which, in turn, is part of the major goal of the program.

Perhaps this over-all rule can best be illustrated by outlining a number of programs in which the marathon and encounter have been utilized as important parts of the process. Rather than an exhaustive catalogue of such efforts, which would not be possible at the moment, they represent an attempt to specify a variety of ways in which these approaches can be incorporated into therapeutic programs.

In the early days of the development of the marathon group, the author was involved in a program at Camarillo State Hospital. Its goal was to take institutionalized hospital patients, who were particularly low in resources, and provide them with some of the missing assets in a very concrete way. The marathon was utilized as a motivating and galvanizing force as well as to knit a group into a supportive unit. It was noted that a large group of mental hospital patients became involved in a vicious circle in which their lack of resources kept them in the institution, whereas the longer they remained, the more apparent was the gap between their capacities and what was required to function in the outside world. Rehabilitation money was made available to them so they could be supported for a period of two months while they sought work and attempted to get an established footing. It was planned that groups of eight would leave the hospital at a specific date, would have a place in the community wherein they could live together, and would receive counseling support. Given this departure date, groups of patients would be recruited about three months ahead and given this time to prepare for their departure. It was anticipated that patients would use one another for support, and in order to allow this to happen they would need a cohesive group. Marathon groups were conducted at the beginning of the three-month period and at the end, just before the patients were to leave the hospital. In the meantime the patients met regularly in groups and had their work assignments assessed in terms of implications for their functioning outside the hospital.

In this instance the marathon was employed to help motivation and to foster a tight-knit group, rather than to carry the entire burden of the program. It was also felt that the very specific goals, down to the date of departure, aided in the development of such assets as were available to the patients. In reflection, the primary shortcomings of the program were in not allowing sufficient time, three months not being enough, and in being too supportive within the hospital; having a greater choice of patients would probably have generated a more rigorous approach within the institution. However, the direction of the program was impelling and the use of the marathon proved to be an excellent device.

Following the marathon group conducted in a drug addict facility by Kruschke and Stoller (Kruschke and Stoller, 1967), a program was devised by Kruschke with the aim of developing a particular therapeutic atmosphere in the dormitory he supervised and enhancing the mutual helpfulness of the residents. He arranged to have residents admitted to his dormitory in groups rather than as individuals, and their first experience on admission was a marathon experience in which members who had gone through previous sessions helped out. Part of the plan was to have the group leave at the same time, the date of their departure to be determined by the group when all its members were deemed ready and to have worked on their departure plans. In this fashion it was anticipated that residents would be motivated to be more mutually helpful. The major difficulty that was encountered was pressure on the residents from men from other dormitories; any attempt to change part of the system without taking into account the rest of the system is going to develop difficulties. However, this was felt to be a highly productive use of the marathon in producing shared experiences and in developing a therapeutic style for the treatment setting that would ultimately be more helpful.

At the time of this writing, Bailey (Bailey, 1970) has planned a program at the same institution that puts heavy emphasis on the encounter group. The goal is to present the residents with a model of behavior other than the criminal-drug-addict role that so many correctional institutions reinforce rather than help modify. Part of this goal would be accomplished by the inmates going outside the institution and playing a helping role by doing such acts as giving talks on drug addiction to high-school students. Within the setting itself, the major activity will be a variety of group experiences, including marathons. Both staff and residents will be mutually involved in encounter groups as participants rather than the staff exclusively running the groups. It is hoped that this type of experience will open the residents to new role-models and break up the usually mutually exclusive groups. Putting staff and residents together in such groups is a very exciting possibility, which could well, within its own right, raise many new format possibilities for therapeutic programs.

Breeskin has made use of the marathon within a military clinic setting and found it very effective in helping couples work more effectively on their marriages. This effort has been paralleled in a number of informal attempts to bring family members to participate, in some fashion, in therapeutic programs. Because marathons demand a commitment of a week end, it is more realistic to bring in certain family members under this arrangement than under long-term participation. Breeskin found the inclusion of marathons in the ongoing program to be very effective.

In each of these programs the encounter and marathon groups were meant to enhance the possibilities inherent in the larger programs of the institution. One of the exciting prospects that the new types of groups present is the feasibility of new program designs. In order to be able to develop new programs, some idea about what needs to be accomplished is required, as well as some tools to achieve it. Although the encounter and marathon groups by no means supply all the answers, they nevertheless permit a greater degree of flexibility than the exclusive use of the conventional approaches. In particular, using staff personnel in new ways and allowing the clients to develop new roles for themselves have rich possibilities.

One final word. Programs have an unfortunate way of treating all clients in a similar fashion, devising a treatment approach into which all must fit. No matter what levels a group may bear, they are not all the same, and the smaller the range of approaches that can be offered them, the more the program is forced to disregard individual differences. Without necessarily developing an elaborate program, most organized programs could probably benefit from having a wider range of activities within their boundaries allowing people to be placed according to their characteristics. In this respect, the inclusion of encounter and marathon groups along with the more conventional approaches could offer a much more realistic program. A concept of multiple interlocking group therapy has been alluded to by Glaser (Glaser, 1969) in which a variety of groups with varying goals are designed to mesh in an over-all therapeutic milieu. The possibilities of encounter and marathon groups in such a design should be obvious at this point.

MARRIAGE OR COHABITATION

Many examples of possible uses of the new groups have represented a cautious introduction into the therapeutic setting. Such nervous cohabitation may be a consequence of the relative novelty of the encounter and marathon approaches and may be a realistic avoidance of a romantic overcommitment. Nevertheless, it is felt that there is room for bolder experimentation with the new modalities. Let us have a look at some attempts that are too informal to be more than suggestive.

In an alcoholic program, the staff grows weary of the customary verbose confessionals in which the clients love to engage (half-suspicious that the equivalent of an alcoholic buzz can be obtained through extensive descriptions of their former indiscretions). As much as to relieve themselves, some of the staff introduce a microlab with a broad base of nonverbal physical contact. The clients take to it enthusiastically, and a number of them report that, for the following week, their desire for alcohol diminishes. Although I am not attempting to tout the advent of *the* new successful treatment of alcoholism, it is possible that these procedures touch a dimension of affect hunger in such individuals that deserves further exploration. In this respect the encounter approach becomes direct treatment.

When encounter techniques are introduced into a program whose clients all emerge from a poverty culture, the technique of having the group rock an individual is introduced at key points. Invariably the individual experiences this as his having died, with the group carrying him to his grave. Allowing for a rebirth experience at this point can lead to an important and powerful experience. However, the interpretation of this event in so different a fashion by those from a less impoverished background leads to a whole range of different possibilities. Alternate techniques may be applicable to different groups, or the same techniques may have different applications. In any case, this represents a whole range of unknowns, deserving of exploration.

A final instance represents the inclusion of an individual in a marathon group who could be classified as having a substantial amount of disorganization, such as would ordinarily be found in a mental health setting. The experience of this individual when he is with people who do not all bear the same label is markedly different than would be expected in a more homogeneous group. The growth potential for him under this arrangement is infinitely more profound than would be the case in a treatment facility. It is very likely that, when people are treated directly in settings that do not fixate them in a particular role, the consequences will bear little relationship to prior experience.

Experience can be a powerful tool for the avoidance of certain errors. However, it can also place one in the position of the "old China hand" who knows the natives through his years of experience but can no longer see something that a fresh eye might see in a moment. Thus, the colonist may see what he wants to see. Much of this discussion has emerged out of experience and observation, and they are not completely worthless. However, the new groups represent an unknown quantity, and the groups of people we call clinical entities have more hidden about them than is known. What is known about them is known within a particular context. What is not known is how they behave under different contexts. In one sense, the marathon and encounter groups represent new contexts and may reveal surprising new aspects that are not anticipated. For those so inclined, the foregoing discussion should not be taken as a discouragement from experimentation with these new groups in "naïve" ways. When alternatives are available, all the present programs will be discarded. It can be anticipated that the present growth approaches represent a first step toward developing new alternatives. If the old and new eventually marry, there will be a very different household.

BIBLIOGRAPHY

Argyris, C. *Integrating the Individual and the Organization.* New York: Wiley, 1964.

Bach, G. R. The Marathon Group: Intensive Practice of Intimate Interaction. *Psychol. Rep.*, **18**:995–1002, 1966.

Bailey, R. Behavioral and Attitudinal Modification Project. Mimeographed paper. Los Angeles: Public Systems Research Institute, University of Southern California, 1970.

Bradford, L., Gibb, J., and Benne, K. (eds.). *T-Group Theory and Laboratory Method: Innovation in Re-education.* New York: Wiley, 1964.

Breeskin, J. The Marathon Group in the Military. Mimeographed. 48th TAC Hospital, APO New York 09179.

Glaser, F. B. Our Place: Design for a Day Program. *Amer. J. Orthopsychiat.*, **39**:827–41, 1969.

Goffman, E. *Asylums.* New York: Doubleday, 1961.

Gould, R. Dr. Strangeclass: Or, How I Stopped Worrying About the Theory and Began to Treat the Blue-Collar Worker. *Amer. J. Orthopsychiat.*, **37**:78–86, 1967.

Greenblatt, M., and Levinson, D. J. Mental Hospitals. In B. B. Wolman (ed.). *Handbook of Clinical Psychology.* New York: McGraw-Hill, 1965, pp. 1343–59.

Katz, D., and Kahn, R. L. *The Social Psychology of Organizations.* New York: Wiley, 1966.

Kruschke, D., and Stoller, F. H. Face to Face with the Drug Addict: An Account of an Intensive Group Experience. *Fed. Probation*, **31**:47–52, 1967.

Likert, R. *New Patterns of Management.* New York: McGraw-Hill, 1961.

Maslow, A. H. *Toward a Psychology of Being.* Princeton, N.J.: Van Nostrand, 1962.

Maslow, A. H. *Eupsychian Management.* Homewood, Ill.: Irwin-Dorsey Press, 1965.

Otto, H. A., and Mann, J. (eds.). *Ways of Growth.* New York: Grossman, 1968.

Rae-Grant, Q., Gladwin, T., and Bowers, E. Mental Health, Social Competence, and the War on Poverty. *Amer. J. Orthopsychiat.*, **35**:89–98, 1965.

Schein, E. H., and Bennis, W. G. *Personal and Organizational Change Through Group Methods.* New York: Wiley, 1965.

Schutz, W. C. *Joy—Expanding Human Awareness.* New York: Grove Press, 1967.

Shelly, J. A., and Bassin, A. Daytop Lodge—A New Treatment Approach for Drug Addicts. *Corrective Psychol. & J. Soc. Thought,* **11**:186–95, 1965.

Smith, M. B., and Hobbs, N. The Community and the Community Mental Health Center. *Amer. Psychol.,* **21**:499–509, 1966.

Stanton, A. H., and Schwartz, M. S. *The Mental Hospital.* New York: Basic Books, 1954.

Stoller, F. H. Accelerated Interaction: A Time-Limited Approach Based on the Brief, Intensive Group. *Internat. J. Group Psychother.,* **18**:220–35, 1968.

Stoller, F. H. Marathon Group Therapy. In G. M. Gazda (ed.). *Innovations to Group Psychotherapy.* Springfield, Ill.: Charles C Thomas, 1968, pp. 42–95.

Stoller, F. H. A Stage for Trust. In A. Burton (ed.). *Encounter: The Theory and Practice of Encounter Groups.* San Francisco: Jossey-Bass, 1969.

Wheelis, A. *The Quest for Identity.* New York: Norton, 1958.

Yablonsky, L. *The Tunnel Back.* New York: Macmillan, 1967.

Carmi Harari
Clara Harari

15 The Cotherapist Encounter— A Catalyst for Growth

COMMENTARY

Clara and Carmi Harari illustrate with dialogue and case example
their cotherapeutic approach to encounter groups and to couple's
groups in particular. They stress the significance of husband-wife
modeling provided the human features can transcend the therapists'
role.

BIOGRAPHIES

Clara Harari, M.S.W., a certified social worker and pyschoanalytic psychotherapist, was trained in New York City at the National Psychological
Association for Psychoanalysis. Wife, mother, and codirector of Community Consultation Services, she is consultant to the Association of Private
Hospitals and was formerly on the faculty of Lehman College. At present
she is taken with selective incorporation of experiential and Gestalt techniques. The marathon, a new form of work, is valued for its intensity and
catalytic and significant insights to participants. After continuous study and
mellowing with age, she finds that her alliance with youth and abhorrence
of professional language have caused her to consider writing more in an

era that wants to hear it as it is. She is coauthor of papers on "The Family Secret," "How to Fight in Marriage," and so on.

Carmi Harari, Ed.D., had V.A. training in clinical psychology following World War II. He has worked in hospitals, clinics, schools, courts, and social agencies. He has done delinquency research and is chief psychologist of the Domestic Relations Courts, New York City. He has had psychoanalytic training, as well as being involved in private practice and in individual, group, and family therapy and diagnosis. He cofounded Community Consultation Services in 1956 and recently helped develop it as a growth center affiliated with Esalen Network. He is on the faculty of Queens College and is president of the New York Society of Clinical Psychologists and chairman of the Association for Humanistic Psychology, Committee for International Organization. He has published articles on delinquency and group therapy and has also written for popular magazines. He is currently interested in "the humanistic model" in therapy. He is involved in education, community organization, and research and is interested in integrating "human potential" and "growth" techniques with more traditional approaches.

We have been asked to answer the questions "Why do we work together as a married pair of psychotherapists? Does the fact that we are a married pair make any difference in our work as compared, for example, to an unmarried pair of male and female cotherapists? What can the therapist pair contribute to their work that makes it superior to that of an individual group leader or therapist?" The answer to these questions rests in our own professional history and prior to that in our personal histories. We started working together professionally because of curiosity, opportunity, and necessity. As early starters in the field of couples and family therapy at a time when most psychoanalytic psychotherapists regarded such procedures as contaminatory of the transference and of the psychoanalytic process itself, we began to see from our own private practice couples or family groups on occasion in joint sessions as a variation on what was essentially individual psychoanalytic psychotherapy. At times, the need to have a male or female cotherapist deal collaterally with a family member or spouse and the convenience of our accessibility to each other led to cautious experimentation and trial, which with time became elaborated into both theory and technique. It must be stated also that the refreshing change of climate that brought family therapy to respectability and the innovative approaches in working with groups and individuals, including such concepts as conjoint therapy and multiple impact therapy

(Bell, Satir, Minuchin), encouraged us to further develop our methodology and theoretic speculation.

This chapter deals with our work as a married couple encountering each other over our lifetime together and using the learning and change from our own encounter in our direct work with individuals, families, and groups. As a pair of psychoanalytically trained psychotherapists we have learned to examine our own conflicts and interactions from the point of view of a continuing awareness of transferential reactions to each other related in a variety of ways to our professional work. We have discovered, for example, that a conflict arising between us seemingly out of nowhere may, with careful tracing, be found to originate in our own reactions to either part of a family whom we are treating conjointly and separately or to our work together in a group situation. The very examination of our own "underground" of conscious impulses and distortions very frequently leads to a refreshing awareness of hidden aspects within the treatment situation. In the process of continuous examination of our own conflicts and interactions, we have been able to become more open and direct and comfortable with each other. We view ourselves as a family that has fought together over many years and truly believe that a family that fights together has the greatest opportunity of working through the ordinary problems and conflicts of everyday life. We have experienced ourselves as fighting to maintain open lines of communication between each other as well as between ourselves and our children. The impact of a world full of war and aggression, stereotyped sexual role attitudes, and easy invitations to dependency on drugs or blaming the generation gap has made it essential for us to exert our own aggression in "fighting" for a kind of family authenticity based on integration and cohesiveness. It was very important to us to maintain open lines of communication, an acceptance of recognition of our individuality and difference, and a setting in which each family member could grow and blossom in his or her own way in contradiction to the negative impact of the outside world. We have always sought out the encounter between us and moved toward conflict rather than away from it and have found ourselves strengthened as a married pair and as a therapist couple.

Aspects of our own history were constantly replicated in our work with others and perhaps touch on the history of all families. Our encounter centered around the issue of expecting the woman to become predominantly mother and homemaker in contrast to her role as sexual partner, companion, and colleague to her husband. We believe that much of a woman's sexuality and energy is intuitively drawn toward the child-rearing role and therefore requires the counterbalancing pull of masculine need and energy to recreate a balance in the couple and in the family.

The difference between us emerged in our very encounter in writing this chapter with the opposite views and conflicts represented by two different approaches and opening statements. The male member of our team said, "Let's get started and then we'll know where we're going." Our female member said, "I need to know where I'm going before I start." We recognize that difference and conflict can be the basis for inhibition, inaction, and paralysis or can be employed as a constructive source of energy and forward movement. We found that when each of us said "where we were at" at a particular moment, it provided valuable feedback information that we could both use to go on and, as we will further illustrate, to "grow on." Our problem was how to take our opposite views and move together to produce a joint piece of work.

Seemingly, we approached each other from two opposite directions with our personalities and professional and individual differences emerging in a manner that could appear antithetic to the achievement of a joint product. We experienced our own anxiety, tension, and strain because we were uncertain about our own capacity to move from our own positions toward one of personal and professional comfort in talking together, relating around and determining the material for this chapter.

As we moved in our own interaction and permitted ourselves to move in the direction we were going without restraint (one might regard the analogy to physical laws dealing with inertia and the difficulty in achieving movement), the expression of positive and negative reactions to each other and to the common work at hand began to give way toward an evolution of more common ground and a conceptualization of the material for this undertaking. As we work together we often experience ourselves moving through difference, irritation, annoyance, and anger. We have frequently been concerned as to whether the strength of our own emotional responses would be separating and divisive or whether out of difference a sense of unity would be attained. With time we have come to trust our own responses and ourselves considerably more and have come to believe that the process in which we engage is essentially a sound one and that what emerges represents a true product of our interaction and carries its own authenticity. It makes us aware that in times of emotional storms, small or large, it is necessary to go on trust and memory of the "correct way" as a guide to the awareness of the present situation based on past experience. To stay with difference and conflicts is to provide the opportunity to go beyond them to resolution. In this very process we found ourselves feeding a line at a time or a paragraph to each other in what began to emerge as a harmony of sorts, discordant at times, harmonious at other times, but gradually coming together in what seemed to be becoming a workable blend. Even as this very blend was evolving, we became aware that our very way of working together was undergoing change from our last similar experience in writing together and was evolving into a new form of interaction that was in itself causing a certain amount of stress and strain. We paused to reflect that virtually each time we work together in one or another of the many joint activities we undertake there is a process of change and growth that appears to be qualitative in nature. It is as though there is a very definite metamorphosis of quantity into quality. Our working conception that I am I and you are you and we are a couple together was tested, retested, and experienced as a source of unity.

In our very use of a dictating machine, we found ourselves taking turns dictating with little concern about difference in style between one sentence and the next. We felt that if we dealt with the here and now as related to content as well as in the actual experience of writing together, this would be the best way of providing a suitable form for a joint effort. This, for us, represents an actual growth experience away from certain preconceived concepts that influenced our previous writing together.

We find that fuller acceptance of each other appears to emerge with a less threatened sense of our acceptance of ourselves. To the extent that we are able to accept ourselves, each other, and our differences and use this as a positive expression, we are able to help others to experience their own sense of self and difference.

In an experience with an ongoing psychotherapy group meeting in a three-hour session and co-led by both of us, the male coleader got up and left the room minutes after he was actively involved in an interaction with Betty—the 29-year-old pregnant group member—and came back with coffee and cookies for the group. Betty is a schoolteacher who was born in a rural area in the West and whose father was a country schoolteacher while mother ran a rather stern and orderly household. She has a brother a bit older than herself who is a teacher and a scholar. She came to New York at age 20 determined to make it on her own, supported herself, entered and completed college at a later age than most of her fellow students, and some four years ago married a man two years younger than herself who was having great difficulty in remaining in college and in completing any courses or program. Although she originally recognized a danger to herself and her family wishes, she sought therapeutic help initially for her husband and then came to recognize that she herself required help with understanding her own motivations and tendencies to subject herself to pain and disappointment through her combination of meticulousness, hard work, and naïveté. She had regarded her primary danger with her family as directed at her father and only in the course of treatment came to recognize the primary nature of her anger and competitiveness with her stern and disapproving mother. In terms of her interaction with the two therapists, her tendency with the male therapist was to engage in various forms of intellectually provocative play and to look for the sort of stimulation that she might have sought for and missed with her father; and in relation to the woman therapist, she regarded her as austere and distant and critical of her and tended to attribute to her a background very similar to her own with little basis in actual fact. With the male therapist out of the room, the female cotherapist carried on the interaction with Betty, which by that time had shifted to her naturally while other members of the group became involved in varying ways. It was at this point that two male members critically attacked the male leader for leaving at a "critical time" when "he was needed" by Betty and generally accused him of "copping out." When this interaction was processed, the group led off by Betty's declaration that she had greatly valued the attention of the woman leader and needed her at that point and had not really missed the male leader with whom she had been involved in the immediately preceding transaction. Checking back, the woman leader found that she had been conflicted because she was usually the one, although not always, who went for coffee and did the "mothering bit" and she felt the pull to Betty's evident need to which she was drawn at the moment. She reported that she experienced her coleader's leaving the room as resolving and relieving her conflicts and permitting her to stay with a situation she regarded as requiring her presence. The male leader responded that when he felt it was time for coffee and checked out his coleader's unavailability and determined that it was coffee time, it was up to him to do it if he wanted to. He emphasized the sense of acting for "I" for "myself" because of his need at a particular time to make his own decision as a paradigm for the entire group in self-affirmation and self-determination. As the attack on him was evaluated and examined by the group it became clear that they experienced themselves as being abandoned by "the father figure." This was too much for the male members of the group, who experienced themselves at this time as little boys called on to take care of their pregnant mother and the possible irrational emotional demands she might make on them. The ability of the group leaders to be individuals for themselves as well as for each other when needed to substitute or complement each other provided an example of flexibility and freedom and support for fixed role relationships or expectations. This fits in well with the concept of role-model that has been used so effectively in the treatment in recent times of drug addicts through encounter and confrontation techniques that partly owe their origin to Synanon and later Daytop Village and the work of David Deitch, Daniel Casriel, and many others and are carried forth in the effective work in the Addiction Services Agency

Figure 15-1. Her upset led to the group's "going around." (Photo by Nancy Polin.)

of New York City through its first commissioner, Efren Ramirez.

Betty had very much needed to resolve a problem with a woman stand-in for her mother at the point when the male leader left the room. What had triggered the whole episode had been the upset caused her by John when he arrived at the session and called out to her a cheery "Hello, pregnant lady." Her upset led to the group's going around and including the leaders who differed in their views of what had happened. The male leader regarded the greeting as "kind of warm, intimate, and positive," whereas the female leader said that she felt it as "impersonal and that it made Betty part of a category rather than a person." The woman coleader agreed with Betty's reaction and the male coleader differed. Anxious laughter greeted the revelation of difference between the leaders, and there appeared to be a quality of excitation and expectation of witnessing an escalating conflict between the two parent figures as though they were witnessing an old erotically tinged theme from long ago in which difference was equated with "right and wrong." We were struck by the importance of the living paradigm as more effective than verbal interpretation in such a situation in leading to insight and change. As we referred to our differences the air seemed to clear and the possibility emerged and was accepted that there could be difference without right or wrong. This contributed to a changed atmosphere within the session, and the possibility began to emerge that two different views could both be right and appropriate, even though perceived differently. A lively interaction ensued in relation to the different levels of communication and differences in reception of what is communicated depending on the individual needs of the persons involved.

For the group leaders, their evolving sense of freedom and personal growth led to their increased acceptance and toleration of each other's behavior without prejudgment or restriction. This recalled to them that in earlier periods of working together their later private review of the situation revealed anxiety not shared, at that time, with the group that the other coleader was doing something "wrong." The greater capacity to react immediately in the here-and-now provides both opportunity for correction of misperception and miscommunication as well as greater increases in the tolerance of difference and the unexpected.

The "family secret" (Family Secret paper, 1969, and Ackerman) had been used by the writers in the past to convey the quality of conscious and unconscious hidden agendas that occur in extended family groups with whom they work. This has provided a valuable means of leverage in entering into a group or family situation and discovering that there were more or less open "secrets" that represented at times a virtual conspiracy "not to see" or "not to know." An added dimension that emerged in our own growth and development was that beyond opening up the family secrets that interfered with communications and trust within families and by extension within groups, we began gradually to dispense with our own "secrets." Our secrets in relation to the groups with whom we work deal with the strategy or planning of how to deal with given situations or individuals within the group setting and sometimes encompass our interpersonal reactions, positive and negative, toward individuals and toward each other inside and outside the group situation. The extent to which we began to do our "stage setting" in working with groups and bringing our "secrets" into the group for open review and availability rendered us more human in our own eyes and served the group very greatly in providing them the opportunity to be immediate witnesses to a process of openness and reality that might reveal our own lack of perfection and superiority as well as doubts, uncertainties, perplexity, and disagreement. For example, in a marathon situation, one of us experienced that Herbert, who had sat quietly, depressed and within himself, really needed something from us in order to permit him to confront and deal with the source of his difficulty. At an earlier time we might have exchanged glances to signal our need to confer privately and away from the group. At the present time our approach is much more direct, so that one of us said to the other, "I feel that Herbert needs something from us at

Figure 15-2. Maybe we ought to ask the group. (Photo by Nancy Polin.)

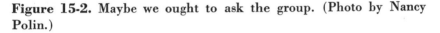

this moment but I don't know what to do." This permitted the coleader to respond, "I agree with you but I don't have any idea at the moment. Maybe we ought to ask the group." This reality transaction permitted the group to witness the need of an individual member of the marathon group, the group leaders' need and perplexity, and their own capacity to be called upon to help. And indeed they did by providing an activity that proved helpful and of a breakthrough nature for Herbert. Examination of encounter-transference phenomena suggests that when these are translated into the here-and-now reality of the group experience, they become richly motivating in terms of group and individual movement, change, and growth. We find that the expression of our own growth, change, and vulnerability is a potent force and provides a motivating example for group members to emulate the leaders.

As indicated above, the "role-model" behavior so significant in the encounter movement had roots in the treatment of drug addiction as well as in the National Training Laboratories model of the leader-facilitator from the field of group dynamics as originated in workshops in Bethel, Maine, and elsewhere. The pattern of providing a structure and a setting for activity or behavior, provision for feedback, incorporation of the feedback and an opportunity to replay, redo, or retry an experience and to observe the difference or gain as new feedback or new learning may fit in partially with reinforcement and learning theory in psychology and may reflect some aspects of Bandura's work (Bandura, 1961, 1962) as well as that of others who have called attention to the role of learning in therapeutic growth and change. The blend of ourselves as psychoanalysts, group psychotherapists, family therapists, leader facilitators, role-models, and even change-agents in the modern parlance all contributed to our thinking and behavior as we began to express and display ourselves more openly and less concealed within and behind our "professional selves." We regard our own growth process as having involved the merging of our own selves with our professional selves so that former distinctions have more and more been fading away. As our personal comfort with ourselves and each other has increased, our professional comfort with being "ourselves" has increased to the extent that we can risk more and reveal more without fear of harming the image we present for the effectiveness of our work with other individuals. In addition, we have grown in our interaction with our groups in our own personal and professional lives. Personal gains from our encounter experience have been noted in our greater readiness to stop, to back up, and to take a look at an ongoing situation between us with a full acceptance of the differences that may emerge. A personal illustration occurred around a project involving electric wiring, which after completion drew the male coauthor's acknowledgment that his wife's approach to the problem had been more direct and efficient than his own more laborious solution to the same problem. The capacity to accept difference as parallel rather than in a hierarchy of higher, lower, good, and bad is part of our own growing interaction and growth. The stereotypes of the "handy" mechanically capable man and the mechanically "inferior" woman as well as the subtle stereotypes of an intellectually and professionally more advanced male and the relatively junior or subordinate woman are among the stereotypes that first came to greater recognition within our experience in working with groups and were then followed into our personal lives.

We noted a tendency in jointly led groups over a period of time to regard the male therapist as the leader and the female therapist as a coleader. The distinction between a coleader and an equal leader is a subtle and important one reflecting the very heart of male-female relationships in a male-dominated culture. We regard it as having overtones with its subtle support of male superiority vis-à-vis females as does any other type of ethnic or racist superiority of one group in relation to another. The tendency to regard the female coleader as an assistant is seen as analogous to the situation in which, when a black-and-white pair of people are seen, the white man is often recognized as boss while the black man is regarded as his helper. This, by now, familiar experiment in social psychology to display stereotypes of racial attitudes also plays a strong role in ways of regarding relationships between men and women. In dealing with the problem of difference and superiority-inferiority we are also reminded of the earlier work of Delany, Mullan, and Harari who needed to deal with their own status and hierarchy differences to appoint a resolution both privately and with their social agency staff clients as an aspect of their "interactional consultation" work with groups of staff and administrators. They represented a black American Protestant, a white Catholic American of Irish ancestry, and a white American of Jewish background who were, respectively, a psychologist, psychiatrist, and psychologist sharing their specializations in psychoanalysis and group psychotherapy but under the leadership of the black psychologist who was the director of the consultation service of which they were a part.

The recognition of the male therapist that his own underlying sense of the situation was that he was "the real leader" despite his intellectual denial of this fact opened the possibility for the female coleader to confront him and the group with this distorted and prejudiced perception of the woman therapist. Under the cover of "democratic" and egalitarian expressions of the inner sense of difference and superiority-inferiority the tendency to deny becomes a genuine bar to communication, understanding, and growth, and in this the group leaders need first to examine their own condition. The more we were able to examine our own relationship and openly deal with it in group settings, the more group members were able to come along in their own recognition of themselves and their own masculine-female role stereotypes as well as other stereotypes that impeded growth and more effective communications and relationships.

The more we as a couple presented ourself with our own reality in honest encounter with each other, the more we became aware that we could deal with our very difference in the presence of others and offer to other couples a role-model in process of resolving conflict without "copping out" or "dirty fighting."[1] The positive value of fighting to a joint resolution of a problem without false acquiescence or overpowering of one partner by the other represents to us a "good" model of interaction. We, however, recognize that there are times when one partner may indeed win and be "allowed" to win in a situation in which there is real difference. Couples see us arguing and giving in to the pressures of time and the moment so that we are able to proceed, also resolving the disagreement where it is not as important to one person as to the other with but a shrug of the shoulder to show that one is willing to try the other's way, or where there is real recognition that

---

[1] Re our and others' use of this phrase, see Flora Davis, "Fight Training," citing us in *Glamour Magazine*, March, 1969, and *Reader's Digest*, June, 1969.

the other person's point of view is superior. The therapist pair is seen as a set of parents without secrets, dealing openly, handling problems of competition, rivalry, and jealousy, displaying difference, asking for help from each other (when needed), and displaying care and affection when appropriate. This becomes a different and significant experience for other couples.

The male leader is often regarded by our groups as a kind of "intellectual teaching parent" and the female is seen as "earth mother" (intuitive, warm, empathic, supportive but at the same time intellectually sharp). An illustration of this occurred around a woman's dream presented in a marathon situation in which there were only two fragments, which on the surface appeared quite distant and unrelated to each other. In this instance our male leader played the role of historical archeologist putting together the tiny fragments of an ancient vase representing the historical past as though one were to find shards of pottery, one representing a portion of the base and another a portion of the neck of a Grecian vase. The male leader began the patient job of reconstruction, of trying to fit, assemble, and establish the shape and contour of the missing pieces and of the total object or dream of which they were a part. The female leader reacted, chimed in with "trained intuition,"[2] risked several of her own associations to the two fragments: a mirror on the ground with a tiny edge around it with an apparent image and a fragment of a song from George Gershwin's *Porgy and Bess* called "I Love You, Porgy." Her intuitive association, "Mirror, mirror on the wall, who is the fairest of them all?" led to the trial interpretation that father never positively affirmed his daughter or saw her as she was, so that therefore she could not see herself. The further tracing of the dream to preadolescence led to revelation of her "unpretty" image of self and a virtual refusal "to be pretty or feminine" if not recognized by the most important person in her psychosexual life at that time—her father. Her mother had disapproved of her looking in the mirror at her own image and had covered a full-length mirror in her room with pictures from *Snow White and the Seven Dwarfs*.

With our own desires as a couple to find new and better ways through our areas of difference to mutual agreement that can free us to act and move together with greater spontaneity, creativity, and satisfaction, we find that our involvement with other individuals and couples is more intense and more satisfying to ourselves and brings a greater authenticity into our professional work and type of listening and reacting. Our own strong needs for individuality, mutuality, and "coupleness" come through very sharply to others and are very supportive because they

[2] Ruth Cohn has done much to develop this as a concept.

touch on basic problems of many couples. Our behavior as a couple becomes the backdrop to the professional situation to which we bring our professional selves. Our own openness and acceptance of where we are at, as a therapist couple, allow us to deal in front of groups or couples with our own imperfections and thus help those who consult us to allow themselves to be more human and deal more openly with and accept less painfully their own frailties. We thus use everything that occurs between us to help couples and individuals to understand themselves and what is going on between them more clearly.

The focus at all times is on individuals in dynamic group relationship structures and we serve as an added catalyst. We offer a positive self-image in some important areas of tension and conflict between people. In a recent couples marathon some milk was spilled by one of the wives while the male leader was nearby. He chose to deal with the situation and began to mop up the milk. The woman leader was genuinely appreciative of his doing this, although she could also have handled the situation; but the interesting occurrence was that a husband who backed away from demands made on him by his wife, resenting her pressure and fearing that he could not meet her demands, voluntarily joined in cleaning up the milk. The feedback to him and his wife was that despite his fear that he "could not be there" for his wife and her fear that he could not meet her needs, there he was doing what they both feared he could not do. His spontaneity when given a new role-model to emulate was most encouraging to the couple. The clarity with which we come through as male and female figures without rigidity as to male or female behavior stereotypes helps many couples to achieve softer, more flexible modes of behavior. They find that complementary behavior need not undermine their male or female identities. As we define for ourselves our areas of personal action and responsibility as different from our joint actions and responsibilities, we strengthen others and free ourselves to be ourselves and thus reinforce our own capacity to be more real and more helpful as a model. Our changes and growth are often noted as people "catch us" in a word or deed that feels different to them from how we were at another time. Their awareness of our growth and ongoing change without an obligation to remain the same increases their own tolerance of change and demonstrates that it need not represent inconsistency or weakness.

We have recently begun to see ourselves as two points with a taut string between us going through a kind of solar system. The symbolic and real pulling and tugging at each other, as we chart our course, has made for the best course that we as couple could follow, with the tension between us helping to define and redefine our course. Our recognition of our differences as personalities, as man and woman, husband and wife, son and daughter, and so on, has allowed us to help each other in complementary ways. In certain situations the woman needs to "pull" to win, in others to fight for the right to be separate and lag behind and sometimes to ask for support in order to catch up. The struggle for maximum communication in our personal and professional lives has had its ebb and flow as we have gone through the early couple period, the child-rearing stage, and the development of ourselves as separate and team professionals. The man's pull and strong desire that his wife meet him in the professional arena resulted in her needing to pull significantly in the direction of family and child-rearing responsibilities, which he ambivalently welcomed. Our couple balance depended on the pull both toward family needs and toward personal and professional needs. The degree to which our involvement in each area could vary was manifested in the division of responsibility between us for joint participation based on need and our real desire and conviction. Almost as in a dance we have moved back and forth between family and professional life. As a couple we have supported each other and made demands on each other and have done some very positive mothering and fathering of each other.

We have both always had a strong social and community sense as a backdrop setting for our specialized work; so although our training was different, we have enriched each other by taking from each other anything that was special and that we had learned or experienced. The cross-fertilization and interstimulation of our differences have never allowed for boredom, have increased communication, and have made for "constructive competition." Our male member contributed his training in clinical psychology with an emphasis on scientific method and clinical and psychologic diagnosis and his approaches to psychotherapy, and our female member contributed the art and sensitivity as well as rigor of another type from her training in psychiatric social work.

We believe that a therapist or a therapeutic couple, working within a framework of seeking greater intimacy, growth, and understanding, becomes a more potent therapeutic tool. We believe that the stance of each of us as persons, and as a couple, is a living demonstration of what others could want and get for themselves and helps unlock other individuals and families. Our dealing in the here-and-now with ourselves as well as with the group further demonstrates the experiential satisfaction of the moment that is possible in the very struggle for greater satisfaction and rejects the assumption that only in the future can there be happiness. We try to convey our belief that there is joy in the very struggle toward something more mutual, more creative, and more satisfying between us and demonstrate that that makes for the excitement of the moment and the anticipation and excitement of tomorrow. Our female coauthor expresses how she feels indebted to her

Figure 15-3. The therapeutic couple helps unlock others. (Photo by Nancy Polin.)

husband for the sense of joy of life that is so special to him. For herself, she regards her fight for equality as a woman and for an independent professional identity while assuming her responsibilities as a woman as part of a difficult struggle while learning how to be a complementary, supportive, and living partner in a couple relationship. In working with groups people are able to experience our female cotherapist as able to relate to men and women in the group in the presence of her husband, not as men and women in the stereotyped sense, but as human beings to whose needs, comforts, support, or clarification she can respond. As a female therapist concerned about the degree of alienation from which we all suffer, she senses how people need to be given permission to relate to people of the opposite sex in a wide variety of modes and levels and not only in a unidimensional manner that excludes all but sexual intercourse. Our capacity to relate to each person with whom we work as a human being and also, but not exclusively, as a sexual human being brings us and others closer together, renders us more open to each other, and increases the quality and quantity of human warmth, empathy, and understanding in our groups. This quality is often taken home and results in a more positive empathetic frame of reference in which problem-solving takes place outside of the group or individual situation in our office.

Our greater capacity to deal with the here-and-now has been most valuable in our professional and private lives, has allowed us to more fully enjoy where we are today and to anticipate where we might be tomorrow. We believe we are able to convey to other couples and individuals a sense of hope in the very difficult struggle between people to meet their own and each others' needs. The here-and-now encounter in experiential terms and deeper psychoanalytic work done with couples and individuals is borrowed from many sources, but placing ourselves into the situation represents our particular mode of joint and conjoint work.

Added skills and concepts have been taken from the areas of Gestalt therapy, sensory awareness, sensitivity training, T grouping, encounter, and psychodrama with a liberal admixture of an existentialist here-and-now approach to growth and change. From the relatively morally neutral psychoanalytic tradition in which we were raised we have found ourselves experiencing and living with newer humanistic psychologic emphases on values, goals, and human will.

Within our own life experience our view has changed substantially in relation to "success" and "failure," and we find ourselves less in tune with Western philosophies of conflict, opposition, and extremes and resonating more to the rhythms of Eastern philosophies, which emphasize the unity of opposites, the embracing of the negative, and the incorporation of conflict.

The cotherapist couple encounter each other as well as the individuals, pairs, and groups with whom they work and need to experience themselves and manifest themselves in the process of growth. Such growth, if it is to be a significant factor in change, must touch such fundamental areas of human life as sex, love, work productivity, and social values and goals. In our Western culture inhibition of these human expressions and needs are major manifestations of alienation and emotional disturbances.

We have come to accept our own irrationality as part of the continuum of our own humanity, and in this sense "nothing human is really alien to us."

In recognizing our own life journey in and out of emotional disturbance, neurosis, normalcy, and paranormalcy, we are recognizing that the arbitrary fences created by words, definitions, and diagnoses have very little to do with our own human condition. To the extent that we can accept our own psychotic potential and deal with it effectively, we can survive in a world that is often psychotic in its literal and implied threat to life and sanity in the form of violence, war, pollution, and corruption. We feel that the tighter the control and resistance to the acceptance of a view of a potential pathologic self, the greater the risk of a "break," "breakdown," or collapse of a rigid and tight defensive system; the softer our embrace around the totality of life including the negative and contradictory elements, the less the chance for a sharp break and the easier and more flexible can be transitions, changes, and available alternatives.

Countering force with force leads to impact, crash, impasse, and trauma at the junction, while a soft embrace of contradiction can lead to accommodation, warmth, and acceptance.

BIBLIOGRAPHY

Ackerman, N. *The Psychodynamics of Family Life*. New York: Basic Books, 1958.

Ackermann, N. *Treating the Troubled Family*. New York: Basic Books, 1966.

Bach, G. R., and Wyden, P. *The Intimate Enemy*. New York: William Morrow, 1969.

Bandura, A. Psychotherapy as a Learning Process. *Psychol. Bull.*, **58**:143–59, 1961.

Bandura, A. Social Learning Through Imitation. In M. R. Jones (ed.) *Nebraska Symposium on Motivation*, Lincoln, Nebraska. University of Nebraska Press, 1962, pp. 211–69.

Bell, J. E. Family Group Therapy. *Public Health Monographs*, No. 64, U.S. Dept. of Health, Education, and Welfare, 1961.

Davis, Flora, The right way to fight him. Interview with Clara and Carmi Harari. *Glamour Magazine*, March, 1969, pp. 178–201.

Davis, Flora. *Readers Digest*, condensed, June, 1969, pp. 91–100.

Delany, L., Mullan, H., and Harari, C. Mental Health Consultation: Similarity and Differences with Group Psychotherapy. Presented at American Group Psychotherapy Association, Annual Meeting, January, 1969.

Harari, C. How the New Consultant Establishes His Role. Presented, 85th Annual Forum, National Conference of Social Welfare, Chicago, May, 1958.

Minuchin, S., and Montalvo, B. Techniques for Working with Disorganized Low Socioeconomic Families. *Amer. J. of Orthopsychiatry*, **37**:880–87, 1967.

Mullan, H., Delany, L., and Harari, C. Mental Health Consultation in a Social Service Agency. Presented at International Congress of Psychotherapy, Barcelona, September, 1958.

Satir, Virginia, *Conjoint Family Therapy*. Palo Alto: Science and Behavior Books, 1964.

Donald H. Clark

16 Encounter in Education

COMMENTARY

Education has mostly focused on the accumulation of knowledge and skills with reference to their application to all forms of problem-solving. Yet the inner man has not been educated. And it is this isolated, split-off inner man who reaches out for contact. The teacher can reach the inner self of his pupils if he can be in depth relatedness to himself to begin with. Don Clark demonstrates the application of encounter methods to teacher training, bringing would-be teachers closer to themselves by exploring the inner meaning of learning.

BIOGRAPHY

Don Clark, Ph.D., is a writer, clinical psychologist, and educator in private practice in the San Francisco Bay area. For ten years he was a professor at City University of New York, and for five of those years he was Director of the Educational Clinic of Hunter College in the Bronx. His books include *Those Children* (Wadsworth, 1970), *The Psychology of Education* (Free Press, 1967), and *Emotional Disturbance and School Learning* (S.R.A., 1965). In 1969 he completed a nationwide study of the human growth potential movement made possible in part by funds granted by the Carnegie Corporation of New York. The statements made and views expressed are solely his responsibility and do not necessarily reflect the views of the Carnegie Corporation.

There are at least two possible ways to read the title of this chapter. First, there are the "encounter groups" or sensitivity-training experiences available in and out of schools around the country that are, by definition, educational encounters. But these encounter groups are only a part of a larger movement, sometimes called the "human growth potential movement," that is challenging our culture's definition of education. It is my guess that encounter groups will not often be mentioned 100 years from today when the history of this era is being discussed. Encounter groups will have evolved gracefully like the humans they serve who now realize that we lost our fur and tails at some point back there in history and hardly noticed the change. But the larger encounter in education, the implicit and explicit demands of the human growth potential movement, may well be viewed historically as a major turning point in education.

My interest in encounter groups grew out of personal and professional attachment to education and group therapy that goes back at least 15 years to the time when I was participating in a doctoral program in clinical psychology. Like others, I was never totally satisfied with either group psychotherapy or the classroom experience and intuitively experimented with bringing the two closer together to form a more satisfying hybrid. I developed my own style of encounter group of "sensitivity training in education," but was made restless by rumors of what other people were doing elsewhere in the country. In 1969 I took a sabbatical leave from the City University of New York and, armed with financial support from the Carnegie Corporation of New York, wandered about the country poking my nose in any door that looked as if it might lead to new understanding of the educational implications of the human growth potential movement. At first, I told myself that I was investigating "sensitivity training" in education but found this term maddeningly slippery in definition and representative of only a small part of the revolution quietly taking place.

In this chapter I shall talk less about the encounter group than about the family to which it belongs, the human growth potential movement, and its giant encounter with education.

WHAT IS THE HUMAN GROWTH POTENTIAL MOVEMENT?

The HGP movement is aimed at encouraging human growth that will unlock a greater share of human potential. The movement includes organizations, centers, schools, institutes, and publications, as well as unaffiliated workers. The most representative organization is the Association for Humanistic Psychology. A model center is the Center for Studies of the Person (best known for resident-fellow Carl Rogers but boasting an impressive collection of inventive individuals who are exploring humanness in family, school, industry, and community). Only a few new schools are totally involved in the movement (Johnston College at the University of Redlands is one). The single most powerful force in the movement is the Esalen Institute (best known for its director, Mike Murphy, and for Bill Schutz and his Joy workshops). The next most powerful force is the National Training Laboratories (where group dynamics took root more than 20 years ago and flowered into varieties of T groups, but where the accent is now on "organizational development" as opposed to "personal growth").

Representative publications for the movement include books like *Turning On* by Rasa Gustaitis (Gustaitis, 1969), magazines like *This Magazine Is About Schools*, journals like *The Journal of Transpersonal Psychology*, and informal communications like the *Sensitivity Training for Educational Personnel* (STEP) *Newsletter*.

The movement is most visible in its techniques. HGP workers are inventing new techniques at a rate that signals enthusiastic effort to satisfy long-denied human needs. Many of the techniques are invented by the participant, customer, client, or patient. Some of the techniques are adapted borrowings from the past. The use of the *small group*, itself, is a technique usually used in conjunction with other techniques. But not all GHP experiences take place in small groups. Some (like Jack Gibb's "intimacy in large groups" or Bernie Gunther's evenings of sensory awareness) take place with up to a couple of thousand people participating; some experiences (like Esalen's meditative massage) take place in pairs of people; other experiences (like other forms of meditation) are solo experiences.

The use of the small-group technique is no more and no less important a part of the HGP movement than other techniques, such as staring into the eyes of another person while saying, "This is an example of myself," rocking someone in a cradle of human arms, doing yoga, or trying to feel the way a small rock rests against your head. I emphasize this because if the use of the small-group technique is viewed out

of proportion, arguments spring up about whether "groups" are good
or bad, which is like arguing about whether talk is good or bad. The
answer obviously depends on how, where, and why the group or the
talk is used. The merits of the HGP movement can be argued, but there
is more to the movement than the use of the small-group technique.

HGP techniques are used in surprisingly different places. A church
congregation may be found lying on the floor, eyes closed, exploring
one another's faces with their fingers. Two industry executives may be
found arm-wrestling in the center of a concerned circle of peers. An
entire psychotherapy group may be seen forming into a wordless
organism that moves about the room with a style of locomotion and
a sound all its own. A college student and his instructor may be seen
in tearful embrace. A group of mental hospital patients and their
doctor may remove all their clothing while looking steadily at one
another. Or two friends, overly accustomed to one another's words,
may sit facing one another for 15 minutes with eyes closed, holding
hands.

Because (or in spite of) the techniques being used in such a variety
of places, there have been amazingly few trade union battles about
who owns the professional right to use these techniques. There have
been a few rumblings from social workers, psychiatrists, and psychologists reminiscent of the old fights about who could practice psychotherapy legally. But even these rumblings, restoking old fires, have not
come to much. It may be because the elders in each union are reluctant
to claim these controversial "unproved" techniques, whereas the
young practitioners are too busy and involved in their use of the
techniques to much care who else makes use of them.

It is possible to muster some agreement that "dangerous use" ought
to be curbed and that "adequate training" ought to be offered, but the
impetus for action fades as one zeroes in on definition. Experienced
HGP workers know that most of the danger stories are false or grossly
exaggerated. While most of the workers have some kind of professional
background (clergyman, teacher, psychologist, social worker, psychiatrist, or other kind of professional helper most often), they sometimes
come from dance, theater, or biochemistry. Those most experienced
know that we are nowhere near being able to spell out what goes into
"proper training." And HGP workers tend to have a sufficiently heavy
dose of truth serum flowing in their arteries to admit freely that the
helping professions make use of legal licensing and certification in a
manner that too often turns destructive incompetents loose on a trust-
ing public. Many of the HGP workers are anxious not to personally
participate in that kind of a pious travesty of "professional responsibility."

What holds the HGP movement together are the dedication to

exploration, dissatisfaction with pat answers, and a will to encourage any kind of human growth that may unlock a greater share of the human potential even if it flies squarely in the face of our culture's time-honored assumptions about what it means to be a "good" person. An HGP worker is more likely to be interested in learning about a group that is forming an intentional community where communal ownership of all property includes clothing and toothbrushes than in learning about new ways of encouraging potential dropouts to stay in school. Regardless of preconceived ideas of right and wrong, the communal experiment may provide some new understanding of what it means to be a human being, whereas the school experiment is designed to increase the efficiency of a cultural tradition that may have outlived its utility for human beings and almost certainly has been with us too long to unlock any new secrets about human nature.

THREE CATEGORIES FOR HGP EXPERIENCES

Even with the various backgrounds of the HGP workers and the diverse settings in which their techniques are being used, there persists a tendency for the focus of experience to fall into one of the three following categories:

1. Exploration
2. Instruction
3. Psychotherapy

An experience may contain ingredients of two or three of these categories, but it usually has a *primary* focus that fits only one category. (When it is an unfocused mixed bag, it is usually a pleasant or unpleasant waste of time for the participants.) But let me explain each of the three categories briefly.

Exploration is the focus when participants are offered the opportunity to find what lies beyond their self-imposed boundary walls of self-concept. Have you assumed that you are "introspective" and relatively incapable of spontaneous expression of feeling? You now have permission to try out some spontaneous expression and see where it takes you in your own feelings and how the other people (if it is a group) respond to this new kind of you. Are you well read and well informed about psychology? Try a 24-hour nonverbal experience in which you try to "listen to" your own emotions and the emotions of some other people, and you may find some emotions that have not made it into the books. Are you a well-adjusted and productive

Figure 16-1. Expressing spontaneously—making contact. (Photo by Gary Madderom.)

person? An adult play workshop may help you to explore ways that your life could be more full and satisfying. The examples are endless, but they all illustrate the reaching for the "new" and as-yet-unexplored.

Instruction is the focus when the leader of the experience has an idea as to the answers you should find or has a way of judging whether

you have "understood" or "profited" from the experience. By definition, you as participant are the sole judge of the success of your
explorations, but when you are being offered instruction that intends
to take you from "here" to "there," the instructor is in a position to
evaluate your performance. Most meditational experiences fall into
this category. Although the content or noncontent of the meditational
experiences is exploratory at times, you are being instructed in the
techniques of meditation. There are right ways and wrong ways, and
your instructor judges your stage of development or your achievement.
Some encounter groups fall just as easily into this category. If the
leader has some set ideas about what it means to be "emotionally
mature," "turned on," "well adjusted," or "mentally healthy" and is
working to help you move along a continuum toward that ultimate
objective, he is offering you an instructional experience even though
his vocabulary may sound more like psychotherapy or exploration. He
has the answers and you are looking for them. He may lead you

Figure 16-2. Releas-
ing tension. (Photo by
Zev Guber.)

through some "discovery" steps or may simply tell you the answers and try to help you accept them. In any event, it is instruction.

Psychotherapy aims to heal old wounds or correct emotional malformations. You say, "I hurt," and the leader of the experience says, "I will try to help you find ways to alleviate the hurt." In this category a group leader may have you use verbal and nonverbal means of expressing how you believe other people view you and then ask other members of the group to give corrective feedback when the truth is that they see you quite differently. Massage or sensory-awareness techniques may be used to help you release the tension that helps to bring on your chronic headaches. Psychedelic-like experiences with music and lights may be used to help you tune in on feelings that you have habitually kept out of awareness so that you can take the first steps in accepting parts of yourself that have caused unconscious discomfort. The intent is to help you fix something that hurts or to alter a style of living that injures yourself and others.

In all three categories it is not the technique used that identifies the focus of the experience but *how* and *why* the technique is used. It is very much a matter of intention. What are the intentions of the person offering to lead the experience and what are the intentions of the person wishing to participate in the experience? If we can begin to specify intention and determine whether the primary focus of an experience is exploration, instruction, or psychotherapy, we can decrease much of the confusion now surrounding HGP experiences.

ARE HGP EXPERIENCES A FORM OF EDUCATION?

The answer to whether or not HGP experiences are a form of education depends on how education is defined. The original meaning of the word "educate" is to lead, draw, or bring out what is in the person. It means drawing on the potential that an individual has, discovering it, and refining it. Using this kind of definition of education, HGP experiences are most educational when the primary focus of the experience is exploration. When the primary focus is instruction or psychotherapy, they are educational only in the sense that they will concentrate on facilitating individual growth.

In order to see clearly that HGP experiences are a form of education, one must rid oneself of the notion that what goes on in our schools today is a form of education. HGP experiences are very different from the traditional curriculum of a school. In our schools we have been accustomed to instructing, teaching, and training. The implication of instruction is that we put something into a student. We have information in the form of prepackaged questions and answers that we want to plant in the human who is our student. When we teach, we show or demonstrate something to the student. We are not drawing something out of him and refining it, we are trying to put something in. We want to show him how to perform a task or have him imitate a skill until he can do it with ease. The directive of our schools is to accept the wisdom of your elders, acquire the skills they already have, memorize the information they already have available and believe to be valuable, and accept established styles of truth-seeking. It is a kind of training that urges and rewards subtle conformity. Our schools pay lip service to education while performing training.

We can no longer afford our antique teaching or instruction of our young. We have used a variety of tricky and straightforward techniques to insist that our youngsters "discover" and accept the answers and skills we already possess. (A handful of individuals in each generation have taken unorthodox giant steps to find new answers and skills, and we praised them or persecuted them in accordance with how uncomfortable their deviations made us.) Our future concept of education must allow vast opportunity for new answers and new skills or we are as doomed as the dinosaur. The accelerating rate of change in the human world appears unalterable. We can try to harness it for our own use or be trampled by it.

Figure 16-3. Sensory education. (Photo by Zev Guber.)

We have heard a lot about "relevant" education in recent years. The cry was raised first from the ghetto where the training offered by the schools had little or nothing to do with the world in which the students lived out their days. It has been only a few steps from there to the realization that traditional schooling has not been relevant to anyone's real everyday life. Now everyone is clamoring for relevant education, but what is it? Boards of education are ready to seize the new "relevant education curriculum" and insist that it be followed step by step by every teacher in every school in their jurisdiction. They fail to understand that a relevant education cannot have a uniform curriculum because people really are individuals and a truly relevant education is an individual matter. There is no room for relevant education in a lesson plan.

The natives are growing restless, the customers are up in arms. Something is wanted and there is an increased willingness among a minority of teachers to try new ideas and techniques. HGP techniques are being used in nursery schools, elementary grades, secondary grades, undergraduate and graduate classes, in-service courses for teachers, and various other adult education courses sponsored by employers. In educational institutions the use of these techniques rarely carries official sanction though the principal or college president is aware that certain teachers are using them.

The HGP movement has hit schools just as it has hit other institutions and professions that profess to serve human growth needs. Why has this happened? Probably for the same complex reasons that actors and actresses are taking off their clothes and involving audiences; most of the nation under age 30 is giving marijuana a try; there are "blacks demanding" rather than "Negroes requesting"; young men are going to jail and to other nations rather than commit murder for the military; sex swingers are advertising their choices in underground newspapers rather than seeking cures; ex-drug addicts are setting up model communities where "squares" are permitted to come and learn; and growth centers modeled after the Esalen Institute are springing up around the country faster than one can count. It probably has something to do with the ever-present possibility of nuclear annihilation. There is no time for patience. One cannot reasonably be expected to wait for change. We want the fullness of the human experience and we want it now.

But while sporadic use of HGP techniques in schools continues and grows, there is little hope that it will dent the entrenched habits of our archaic institutions. The relevant education offered by the HGP movement is available outside of schools through the newly developing growth centers. Most of the experiences are available only to adults in these centers. If we want to make this kind of education available to our young through their years of schooling, we have some painful choices to make. It is not simply a matter of letting the youngsters meditate for a half-hour each day and then get on with geometry, social studies, and *The Rime of the Ancient Mariner.*

We know that skill acquisition and information accumulation can be handled with efficiency and pleasure if we pay a great deal of attention to the computer-assisted instruction techniques already available. We need better programs and more creative program authors, but they will appear if we offer cultural sanction and money. We know that most of the hours and years now spent in school can be devoted to individualistic human growth if we have the courage to face change squarely.

There is no doubt in my mind that the HGP movement offers education. I also have no doubt that we should seize the opportunity it offers to change our outmoded ideas about education and schooling. The doubt that looms large for me is whether we are ready to face the lies and half-lies that we have told ourselves for generations about what it means to be human. Are you ready to find out who you are? Am I ready? Frontiers are fascinating and frightening.

FINDING THE NATURAL VERSUS TRAINING THE NORMAL

Examples of the kind of "leading-out" education offered through the human growth potential movement but not available in the conformity training or "putting-in" experience offered by our schools tend to sound inappropriate or shocking because we have been trained not to think of "those things" as having to do with education. I have seen one such example clearly in the last year or so. It has to do with human sexuality. Sexuality is important to each of us. In the United States we seem to be obsessed with the topic and phobic about it all at the same time. It is a topic guaranteed to interest yet surrounded by both obvious and subtle taboos.

In encounter groups I was mildly surprised to see how often the topic of homosexuality surfaced. In all-male groups, it predictably came to the surface even faster and with greater force. I began to see how important and yet hidden a concern it is for almost all men. I saw men searching for more satisfying styles of expressing affection for other men. I saw anxiety about how to handle feelings that were sometimes undeniably homosexual. I saw men try to close off or exercise this "sick" part of themselves. I saw frightened men run to the protective category of "I am a heterosexual man," and I saw others unhappily resign themselves to the alternate category of "I am a homosexual man."

All the evidence we have about human sexuality suggests that a human is born sexual, not heterosexual or homosexual—just sexual. If his environment permits him the freedom, a human will happily express sexual needs with members of both sexes. Our culture officially frowns on homosexuality, and, because of this, psychiatrists and psychologists *assume* that homosexuality is wrong or "sick." This assumption has no supporting evidence but is one that is honored in our culture.

As one might expect, because the schools are our culture's training camps, we have tried in schools to train heterosexual citizens. We have taught people that homosexual impulses are "bad" and that they are to be denied and forgotten. If the individual finds it distasteful to repress or suppress the impulses, we suggest that he consider himself psychologically disturbed ("bad") and in need of treatment. Homosexuality can indeed be a symptom of emotional disturbance, but so can heterosexuality or any other natural human need that takes over a disproportionate share of one's life.

What has all of this to do with education? Everything. Here is a very important part of human life that has not simply been neglected but has been perverted by the training offered in schools. Your school experience did not offer you the opportunity to explore your sexual needs, to lead out of yourself whatever was your natural sexual potential, and did not offer you the opportunity to refine your own understanding of this potential and find the most satisfying ways to enjoy it in your life. If your education had been relevant to your unique self, this is how the topic of your sexuality would have been handled. You would have been encouraged to explore and evaluate and find your own answers.

Nor am I simply talking about the topic of sexuality that may have been covered in a "hygiene" (that word tells something about how we view sexuality) class or a sex education class. I am talking about the subtle reinforcements you got through all of your hours in school. Surely if you cannot remember examples in your own life, you have seen a little boy discouraged from kissing or fondling another little boy in a classroom or on a playground, and you have seen concerned teachers set to work to channel this feeling into sports or some other acceptable form of body contact. You know that almost any teacher is more upset about two boys getting into a hugging and kissing match than about two boys getting into a fist fight that ends in a bloody nose. Why? Wouldn't you think that a teacher would be more concerned about behavior that might cause bodily damage? The clear and sad reason is that our society sanctions war but does not sanction homosexuality. And our schools are geared to train citizens to adjust to society as it is now.

Our schools reflect our demand for "normal" citizens. That is a cruel but true joke. The joke is that there is no such thing as a normal person. "Normal" is a statistical concept at best, a synonym for conformity at worst. Try as he will to be the model "normal" citizen, any human individual will get into troubles because he is a unique individual who cannot possibly fit naturally into the pattern described by a statistical average of all individuals nor can he by nature be the perfectly conformed citizen. The more he tries to refashion what is natural in his individual make-up into the image of the normal man, the more misery he is going to have as a result of denying and hiding some true facets of self.

If the example of homosexuality is too heavy for you, try thinking about how natural it is for most young humans to keep their bodies in motion most of the time and to learn through happy individualistic investigation of whatever the physical world nearby has to offer. Then see us try to force them to be "normal" boys and girls who are not "hyperactive" (bad) but who sit quietly and concentrate on learning by doing "work" that is admittedly unpleasant but "necessary."

There is the choice. Do we view education as an opportunity for an individual to discover and refine his natural self or do we view education as an opportunity to train individuals to come close to being what we think they should be? In the past we have chosen schools to train conformity. But now are we restless, and more and more dissatisfied former students are being attracted to the human growth potential movement. Are we willing or ready yet to revise our notions of "good" and "bad"? If our television screens are true mirrors of our culture, we are not ready. It is still easy enough to see two men killing one another on television, but I have never seen two men make love on television. Youngsters are still expected to suffer through schoolwork. The message of our culture is still "conform if you wish to be accepted." But perhaps the growing attraction of the human growth potential movement signals the possibility of change. Perhaps our educational institutions will one day treasure the natural more than the normal.

Questions About the HGP Movement

A worried comment one often hears from professional teachers is, "All of this represents a kind of anti-intellectualism. People want to touch and taste and 'trip-out' but they don't want to understand by reading, discussing, and doing experimental research." The answer here, I believe, is that the intellectual approach as represented by the academic community has been offering its customers dry food for a long time.

The HGP movement, with its awareness of the body and nonverbal searching skills, is providing drink for some *very* thirsty people. My experience in the university setting with students is that once they taste the refreshing drink, many go on a binge and do indeed stop reading and listening to lectures. Eventually (usually a semester to a year and a half) the thirst is quenched and the student again becomes aware of his hunger. He then begins to look for readings, conversations, and lectures that interest him. He rarely gives up his right to satisfy his thirst but he combines it with attempts to satisfy his hunger. Intellect and emotion join forces in a whole person who demands reasonable satisfaction of all needs. This can be understandably unsettling to a university professor who has adjusted to a life in which he is the provider of dry food to unprotesting prisoners from whom he hides his own thirst. Is there reason to be worried about the anti-intellectualism of this movement? I think not. I see thirsty people drinking and I know that they will eat when they are hungry if the food is at all palatable.

A worried comment that one hears from all sorts of interested people is, "What are the dangers?" There are some dangers. A person can be hurt in an HGP experience just as he can be hurt in many other experiences in life. The assumption in the question, of course, is that he may be *more* vulnerable or more easily hurt in an HGP experience than in other experiences—a classroom experience for instance. I have not been able to find any foundation for this concern. People *are* hurt more often when they put themselves in the hands of a supposed expert and authority. We all know of someone who has had a hurtful experience with a physician, teacher, dentist, or lawyer. When an HGP worker presents himself as an authority-expert, the chance of hurting is increased. Fortunately there is a trend in the HGP movement away from expertise and authority so that an experienced leader is more likely to tell participants that he is there to explore along with them although he has a backlog of exploration techniques that he can make available to them. If he presents himself as a fellow-explorer, the chances of hurting anyone are minimized.

Stories of dangers usually stem from a writer's illustrative inventions or are the rumored magnifications and distortions of far-less-interesting true events. We have almost no reliable evidence or documentation of dangerous leaders pushing fragile but "adjusted" people into lifetimes of psychosis, ruining stable marriages, or provoking suicide. Most inept HGP leaders are more guilty of wasting someone's time than of harming him.

The third most common question asked by people interested in the educational implications of the HGP movement is, "But are these experiences of any lasting value? You get high on honesty and truth, get to touch some warm bodies, do some laughing and crying, and become sensitive to your own body and then you leave the group and go right back into the same hostile world. You can't sustain the high; so you end up right back where you started. What's the use?"

Here again we come to the outer edges of that persistent question of whether one defines education as a leading out or a putting in. If you are of the putting-in school, there is no way to defend the HGP experience.

A resident of the Esalen Institute parried the question by asking the value of seeing a sunset or of hearing a symphony. I think one could add a question as to the value of those school experiences not clearly geared to training some usable skill. One could also question the value of travel to distant parts of the world. You have probably had the experience of getting in touch with yourself, perhaps even changing in some subtle way, as a result of a sunset, a symphony, an off-moment in a classroom, or travel to some distant port. Something in you was led out. A new part of your human potential was exposed or an already-known part was viewed from a different angle. You were able to come to terms with yourself and the human experience in a new synthesis that made it easier to take some future steps in life.

We put an enormous amount of effort into the travel industry and demand no proof that a trip to the Greek Isles is of lasting value to the traveler. A summer trip to Italy may cause someone to re-examine his values because it helps bring dissatisfactions with life at home into focus. It could subsequently cause major behavioral changes, or it could yield only some precious memories to enrich later years. The trip could also turn out to be a tiring bore. The tourist may choose to return to Italy on another trip, see a new part of the world, or stay home and save his money. We congratulate travelers on a good trip and console them after a bad one but we do not demand research to demonstrate the worth of travel.

In schools we have deluded ourselves with supposed evidence of the value of the schooling. We have constructed tests to see if students can reproduce the information pumped into them and then congratulated ourselves on the worth of their educational experience when they are able to do nearly as well as a computer or a copying machine.

Growth potential experiences can be of lasting value to an individual, but it would be hard to promise that in advance. We can only wish the traveler a good trip and try to provide an interesting itinerary. A symphony, a sunset, or a course in nineteenth-century literature can be of little or great value to a questing, growing human. The HGP movement can only honestly claim to offer more sunsets and symphonies than most of us find in our day-to-day life.

TRAINING HGP EDUCATORS

If we are going to accept an HGP style of education, we need a new breed of educators. Teacher-training programs that now exist have little to offer him. He needs the widest possible exposure to the HGP techniques that exist, and he needs encouragement in an accepting setting so that he can begin to invent his own techniques and evolve a personal style (as an educator) that fits him.

Whether or not the HGP educator already has some background and experience as a psychologist, teacher, physician, priest, or other professional "helper," we can offer him an extended workshop in which he and other participants take turns as the educator, facilitator, or leader for the entire group and then gets full feedback from the other participants as to what was experienced as helpful and what was experienced as not helpful. We can also offer him the widest possible exposure to experienced HGP leaders who have had an opportunity to try out their techniques with many different people over a long period of time.

If he wishes to be an educator who works with children, we can offer him a wide variety of experiences in living with children. He need not be the observer or the professional. If he wants to be an educator in the ghetto, he can live in the ghetto with the children he wants to help. He can be encouraged to be open to the experiences available in the lives of these children so that he can be more adept at "feeling with" them. He can permit himself to be free to laugh, suffer, love, plan, play, and question with these youngsters as a fellow human being rather than as a condescending expert adult. He can participate in encounter groups with them and examine himself openly with them just as each of them examines himself openly.

It would undoubtedly be a mistake to set up a university program for training HGP educators. The university program would be set in the conformity-training atmosphere of a school. If we want a new kind of educator, he must himself have a new kind of educational experience.

We have repeatedly made the mistake of assuming competence when a person finishes a prescribed number of courses or passes an examination. The HGP educator is a facilitator who helps humans to lead out their human potential, examine it, refine it, and search for ways to use it. The only sane way of judging how adept he is in his work is to ask the people he is trying to help. Evaluation of his competence could not be established once and for all. He would need continual feedback from his clients all the days of his professional life. A permanent license would be impossible.

THE HGP EDUCATION OF THE FUTURE

My guess is that we are seeing the beginning of the end of schools. The development of growth centers across the nation probably represents a new kind of education that is on its way. In another 30 years, our imposing school building may house a different kind of education. Information accumulation and skill acquisition may be handled efficiently and pleasantly with the aid of highly sophisticated computer-assisted information, thereby freeing much time for the leading out and refinement of human potential.

We will probably still be training physicians and lawyers, but there will be time to help them develop as human beings in addition, rather than simply training them as technicians. The secret of pleasant computer-assisted instruction is the opportunity to learn from your own experience (provided by the computer with unfailing enthusiasm and freshness). People will still learn to spell and read, but they can acquire these skills at their own individual pace and as part of their own individual pattern of interests. No single human teacher could be so flexible (or have such a good memory) in serving the individualistic appetites of a dozen or a hundred students, but this is one realm in which our machine servants have been constructed to serve us well. They can be programmed to satisfy instructional needs pleasantly and leave plenty of time for encounter groups, meditation, massage, alpha-wave sessions, and any number of other delightful and enriching (but as-of-now unheard-of and unlabeled) experiences. It may be a dream but it is not an impossible one.

Formal education was once the domain of the church, but this placed a limit on the freedom of inquiry that became intolerable and secular education gained in stature because it did a better job of permitting human growth. Religious learning centers reluctantly found themselves following the path established by secular education. Times had changed.

Times have changed again. No one can deny the increased cultural permission for personal freedom today. Some of the seemingly established taboos are falling as individuals "do their own thing," make their personal statement, or pursue their own path of inquiry. Our established educational institutions do not seem able to keep up. Many major universities have sprouted unorthodox unofficial appendages that do not offer grades or degrees. They are "experimental colleges" or "free universities," often organized and partly staffed by the university's students. In these new institutions the line between teacher and student blurs or disappears altogether. There is a willingness to break the usual rules, discuss anything, touch one another, and otherwise experiment with experiences in ways considered imprudent or improper in an established educational institution.

The growth centers often carry the "free-university" trend one step further. Some are now branching out from the experiential workshop and adding offerings of ongoing seminars that combine the free experiential inquiry with reading, lectures, and discussions. It may be that we are seeing the birth of tomorrow's educational centers. It is not too far-fetched to see today's respectable universities diminishing in importance because of the irrelevance of their offerings. It is not too hard to imagine these same universities one day following in the footsteps of prestigious growth centers.

School Links Between Today and the Future

The day when universities follow in the footsteps of prestigious growth centers is still off in the fantasied future. If you look around today's schools, however, you can see the beginnings of change. HGP techniques are being used by instructors from nursery to graduate schools. Encounter groups are increasingly popular on the college campus. New kinds of courses are being offered. Keep an eye on these courses because they represent the primitive links between the education of today and the education of tomorrow.

I should like to cite the example with which I am most familiar. Since 1969, Herbert H. Lehman College of the City University of New York has offered a new introductory course in its teacher education program. It is listed as EDU 207: Human Relations. Here is the description in the 1970–71 school bulletin:

> Study of the attitudes and behavior patterns affecting human relations in the schools. The emphasis will be on the development of the personal awareness of future teachers with respect to racial, cultural, and social conflicts and interactions in urban centers. Group dynamics techniques such as sensitivity training and role playing will be used.

This course does not offer genuine HGP education. It could not possibly do so because it is offered in a school setting. It is surrounded by an aura produced during hundreds and hundreds of years of the traditional "putting-in" instruction rather than "leading-out" education. It is a simple, rough first link between education and school training.

All that this course can hope to do is prod its customers to question some of their basic assumptions. HGP techniques can be used well in such a course though. During a class meeting a young man says that he cannot concentrate on the intense emotional interaction building between him and one of the other students because "I'm high."

"On what?" asks the other student.

"Grass. I didn't know it would last this long. I thought I'd be down before class."

Another young man says, "I'm mad, man. I like to smoke too but I wouldn't come here stoned. Your head may be in a good place right now but it's not together enough to get anything done here."

The instructor asks some provocative questions about how the other students feel about Joe being high and what they think about using marijuana. He can do this only because an air of mutual trust has already been established through the use of HGP techniques. If this group had not gone through some hours of feeling one another out and exchanging confidences, the instructor's questions would simply be seen as the condescending curiosity of someone over 30 and would be met with appropriate resistance.

But if a group is at a point where there is minimal trust established, the instructor can use such an opportunity to pull the rug out from under time-honored assumptions. A girl primly states that some of her best friends smoke but she does not have the need for artificial assistance in getting high. The instructor asks if she has tried it. She says, "No." He asks how she can be so sure that she can get there without pot if she has never tried it. She does not know where "there" is; so she is making hollow statements, he says. There follows a discussion of why and how different people use different intoxicants.

For another example, we might look in on a class that has been meeting three hours a week for seven weeks. The group has gone through a number of verbal and nonverbal exercises, designed to facilitate the building of trust and encourage the risk of honesty. A girl says that she knows she is the most quiet member of the group and it bothers her but that she has always been shy and just does not know what to do about it. The instructor asks if she wants to try out some new behavior today or if she simply wants the group to know how she is feeling right now. She says that she wants to try being different. He suggests that she go around the group and tell each person quite frankly what she thinks of him while keeping eye contact and establishing some kind of body contact. She is dressed in a knit suit and wearing jewelry. She comes to a young man with long hair, beard, and torn, faded jeans. She holds his upper arms in her hands and stares into his eyes, but no words come. The instructor encourages her to take a plunge and let her body express what she is feeling nonverbally if she cannot get the words out. She takes her hand away, startled it seems, and says, "You're sexy. I can't believe this is me talking and I know that I'm engaged and that my boy friend is everything I've ever wanted and that I shouldn't be talking this way, but you're sexy." She giggles. "My God, if my mother could hear me now."

The instructor suggests she re-establish contact and get out whatever she has to say to the young man in jeans. She blurts out, "I want to go to bed with you but I know it's wrong. I mean you're not the kind of guy I would want to marry and I know I only want to have sex with the man I marry but there it is."

Again the instructor's questions can provoke expression from others in the group of their prejudices and assumptions about sex. Must it be only with the person to whom you are married? What is the use of getting married at all? Can't sex simply be enjoyed whenever and wherever one pleases?

In this setting an individual can begin to question his basic assumptions. His boat can get rocked. He can afford to be more honest than in the usual class where he is expected to come up with "right" answers. Here he is expected to search and he is rewarded by the instructor and the group if he appears to be searching, no matter how his transitional answers match up with the "rights" and "wrongs" of our culture's mores.

It is a beginning attempt to "lead out" the self that is hidden inside the trained "normal person." But of course it takes place in a setting where students are accustomed to doing schoolwork, being forced to read and regurgitate, being tested and punished, being laughed at and ridiculed for "wrong answers," and seducing the teacher into believing that each of them is the kind of person they think he wants them to be. There is a limit in such a setting to how far out the self dares venture. There is a limit to how much genuine trust can be established in the group. Certain limits still exist. Certain lines must not be crossed. Certain taboos must not be violated.

Let us look at an example of something that happened in an HGP group of college-age people when the group was not connected in any way to a school. A young man is saying that it is hard to believe that the other people in the group have positive feelings for him. He has always felt like an inferior person. He feels dumb and unattractive. His body has always been the bane of his existence. His penis is too small and he is fat and ugly.

One of his peers says, "Look, I believe that that's how you really feel but I have to tell you that you don't look that bad, man. I mean, your body looks okay to me even though you may feel like it's pretty bad."

"I've learned how to dress to cover it up so that people don't notice right away, but sooner or later the clothes don't hide me anymore."

"Why don't you take your clothes off, man, and show us who you really are now. I mean, I'll be honest. I'll tell you what I think your body looks like. I don't think it has much to do with what's bugging you, but if you think a lot of the hang-up is your body, get your ass bare and start from there with us."

After some encouragement from the other group members, the young man strips. He gets feedback from each person on how his body looks. He asks to be touched, and several members of the group willingly give him a massage. He cries. The tears last a long time. He has gotten some negative feedback. Some people think he ought to lose some weight or do some exercises to build up his muscles. No one thinks his penis too small, but some people think his posture is ungainly and that this probably comes from trying to hide his penis in his clothes. He was crying, he says, because it was the first time in his life that he was feeling that it was possible that his body was not repulsive and that he might have a better chance of getting close to people than he ever thought he had.

This episode leads into some few other members of the group shedding their clothes and talking about their needs for more skin contact with other people. The discussion begins to focus on what kind of skin contact each person wants and is not permitting himself to have. Then there is some discussion of the needs that go along with the skin contact for each person.

This example is not chosen for its shock value. Almost any example of the difference between training in a school class and HGP education of the "leading-out" variety is likely to shock if one thinks of it taking place in a classroom because we are so accustomed to the lines that must not be crossed and the taboos that must not be violated. Voltaire and statistics still come up in discussions, but the focus is on the relevance to the student rather than on Voltaire's exact words or the formula for analysis of variance.

A course such as the one in human relations at Lehman College can poke and provoke a student to re-examine his assumptions about "right" and "wrong." Its more truthful format can show him that there are facets to humans that are not usually shown in public. He can see that he has more in common with other humans than he has previously suspected. He can learn that we are all troubled and searching and that we are all capable of finding better answers for our questions. And that is, of course, quite a lot for a college course when we are accustomed to being offered forced-feeding from books and lectures. But it is a far cry from the "no-holds-barred," "let's toss habit and prejudice to the wind and find out what kind of self is hiding in you and who it wants to be" kind of education that is offered in growth centers and will hopefully one day be a standard facet of public *education.*

EDU 207 at Lehman College may frighten too many people, and for pious reasons it may disappear from the bulletin in some not-too-distant year but that is of little importance. It is a symptom of the wave of change that is sweeping the country. It is an example of the kind of course that may not disappear but may be refined and developed into a sizable portion of the curriculum. It is the rudimentary form of the growing link between school and growth center.

Courses like it are being offered in universities all over the country. Some will disappear only to reappear in another form in later years. The change is here. It is beginning. It is growing. Our culture is facing an encounter between the past and the future that makes such past encounters in our history look insignificant. As a part of the giant encounter, we humans are beginning to voice our dissatisfactions with educational experiences that are not personally relevant. We are no longer satisfied with our culture's training schools.

What do we want? Education. When do we want it? NOW!

Bibliography

Alschuler, Alfred S. Psychological Education. *Achievement Motivation Development Project Working Paper No. 1,* Harvard University, 1968.

A.S.C.D. 1962 Yearbook Committee. *Perceiving, Behaving, Becoming.* Washington, D.C.: Association for Supervision and Curriculum Development, National Education Association, 1962.

Batchelder, Richard L., and Hardy, James M. *Using Sensitivity Training and the Laboratory Method.* New York: Association Press, Y.M.C.A., 1968.

Borton, Terry. Reach, Touch, Teach. New York: McGraw-Hill, 1970.

Borton, Terry. What Turns Kids on. *Saturday Rev.,* **50**:72–74, April 15, 1967.

Brown, George Isaac. *Now: The Human Dimension.* Big Sur, Calif.: Esalen Monograph #1, Esalen Institute, 1968.

Bugental, James F. L. *Challenges of Humanistic Psychology.* New York: McGraw-Hill, 1967.

deMille, Richard. *Put Your Mother on the Ceiling.* New York: Walker & Co., 1967.

Duberman, Martin. An Experiment in Education. *Daedalus,* **97**:318–41, Winter, 1968.

Gideonse, Hendrik D. Projecting Alternative Futures: Implications for Educational Goals. *Achievements and Challenges,* The New Forum

Papers, Second Series 1968–69, U.S. Dept. of Health, Education, and Welfare.

Grossman, L., and Clark, D. Sensitivity Training for Teachers: A Small Group Approach. *Psychol. in the Schools*, 4:267–71, 1967.

Gunther, Bernard. *Sense Relaxation Below Your Mind*. New York: Collier Books, 1968.

Gustaitis, Rasa. *Turning On*. Toronto: Macmillan, 1969.

Hall, Mary Harrington. A Conversation with Carl Rogers. *Psychol. Today*, 1:19–69, 1967.

Howard, Jane. Inhibitions Thrown to the Gentle Winds. *Life*, 65:48–65, July 12, 1968.

Huxley, A. Education on the Non-verbal Level. *Daedalus*, 91:279–93, Spring, 1962.

Jones, Richard M. *Fantasy and Feeling in Education*. New York: New York University Press, 1968.

Lederman, Janet. *Anger and the Rocking Chair*. New York: McGraw-Hill, 1969.

Leonard, George B. *Education and Ecstasy*. New York: Delacorte Press, 1968.

Litwak, Leo E. Joy Is the Prize, a Trip to Esalen Institute. *New York Times Sunday Magazine*, 8–31, Dec. 31, 1967.

McKean, William J. Encounter: How Kids Turn off Drugs. *Look*, 33:40–42, April 15, 1969.

Malamud, Daniel I., and Machover, Solomon. *Toward Self Understanding*. Springfield, Ill.: Charles C Thomas, 1965.

Maslow, Abraham. *Goals of Humanistic Education*. Big Sur, Calif.: Esalen Institute, 1968.

Murphy, Michael. Esalen, Where It's At. *Psychol. Today*, 1:34–39, 1967.

Naranjo, Claudio. *The Unfolding of Man*. Research Memorandum EPRC-6747-3. Educational Policy Research Center, Stanford Research Institute, Menlo Park, Calif. 94025, March, 1969.

O'Hare, Mary Rita. Sensitivity Training in Teacher Education. *Teacher Educ. News & Notes*, 19:8–15, 1968.

Otto, Herbert A., and Mann, John. *Ways of Growth: Approaches to Expanding Awareness*. New York: Grossman, 1968.

Rogers, Carl R. *Freedom to Learn*. Columbus, Ohio: Charles E. Merrill, 1969.

Rogers, Carl. The Group Comes of Age. *Psychol. Today*, 3:27–61, 1969.

Schutz, William C. *Joy, Expanding Human Awareness*. New York: Grove Press, 1967.

Simon, D., and Sarkotich, D. Sensitivity Training in the Classroom. *Nat. Educ. Assoc. J.*, 56:12–13, 1967.

Thomas, Hobart F. Sensitivity Training and the Educator. *Bulletin of National Association of Secondary School Principals*, 51:76–88, 1967.

Watson, Goodwin. *Change in School Systems*. Cooperative Project for Educational Development. National Training Laboratories, 1201 Sixteenth St., N.W., Washington, D.C., 1967.

JOURNALS

This Magazine Is About Schools. P.O. Box 876, Terminal "A," Toronto 1, Ont.

Journal of Applied Behavioral Science. National Training Laboratories, National Education Association, 1201 16th St., N.W., Washington, D.C., 20036.

Journal of Humanistic Psychology. Association of Humanistic Psychology, 2637 Marshall Drive, Palo Alto, Calif.

Psychology Today. 1330 Camino del Mar, Del Mar, Calif., 92014.

William Gellermann

〉〉〉17〈〈〈 Encounter and Organization Development*

COMMENTARY

Encounter in industry and its most exciting and comprehensive form, organization development, are described by William Gellermann. He considers the implications for a variety of approaches and presents detailed illustration for specific techniques.

BIOGRAPHY

William Gellermann, Ph.D., consultant in management and organization development, has designed numerous workshops, seminars, and training sessions for use in both short-range and long-range programs. He is presently implementing long-range development programs for large and small organizations: manufacturing, service, educational, community, governmental, and religious. His consultations include Maxwell House Division of General Foods Corporation, Insurance Company of North America, Alliance Brokerage Corporation, American Telephone and Telegraph, International Business Machines, New York State agencies, and others. He was

---

* Printed by permission of the author.

formerly a faculty member of Cornell University, State University of New York at Buffalo, and University of California at Los Angeles. He is the author of teaching materials, articles, and papers on communication, motivation, leadership, group processes, management, and organization development.

ORGANIZATION DEVELOPMENT

In order to maximize the motivation of the people whose work he supervises, a manager must face squarely the organization dilemma of how to coordinate all their available energies and his own in some common direction. Whether he realizes it or not, every manager has this dilemma to deal with, and his behavior contributes either to increasing the coordination of their energy or to decreasing it. If we measure effective organization in part by the degree to which people's motivation is moving them in the same direction, the process of their working together either contributes to organization development or works against it.

Expressed in a different way, everything that is going on within and among people who are working together can be identified as being either organization-developing or organization-defeating.

ENCOUNTER GROUPS AND ORGANIZATION DEVELOPMENT

The organization-developing function of encounter groups is to provide people with an opportunity to become increasingly aware of what is going on both within them and between them and others with whom they are working. These groups can also provide participants with an opportunity to try out in a "laboratory" situation, where the risks of failure are relatively small, new ways of behaving toward fellow-workers both on the job and socially. After having perceived a possible new way, and taken the "risk" of acting it out in the group, a person can then receive feedback from others about how they were affected by him and his new behavior. He can then practice and maintain the new way or modify it as he chooses.

The terms "encounter groups," "laboratory programs," "T groups," "sensitivity training," and "encounter" are often used synonymously. For some purposes, more precise definition is necessary. As I use the terms, *laboratory program* is the most general concept, because it refers to any limited or controlled experience that is designed to help people learn. *T groups* are group experiences designed to train their members in any aspect of group functioning by helping them learn directly from their experience in the group. *Sensitivity training* and *encounter groups* both use a T group to serve the specific purpose of increasing a person's awareness of his own behavior, his effect on others, the effect others have on him, and the effect people have on each other. It also provides an opportunity to experiment with new behavior and discover its effects. *Encounter* refers to one class of experience that many people have during T groups, particularly groups with an explicit "sensitivity training" or "encounter" purpose, in which two people experience themselves in direct, honest communication with each other. This experience has a special quality to it that is different from the usual communication experience. *Encounter* is on the same order as the experience of talking about something important with a trusted friend, an experience that can happen in a lot of places other than T groups.

EARLY USE OF ENCOUNTER GROUPS

The assumption many of us made during the early years of learning how to use T groups was that if only we could learn how to develop and maintain the encounter experience, we would have reached the ultimate. Because the T group was the setting in which we had discovered the "turned-on" feeling of the encounter experience, we then set out to turn on everybody else with T groups. But it didn't work— and I'll explain why later.

Another assumption made during the early sixties was that changing one person was enough. If we could provide each trainee with an encounter experience, he would then be able to return from his training more sensitive to what was going on in his relations with others and more flexible in responding to others so that their cooperation would be increased. But this did not seem to work very well either.

I remember in particular one man, a plant production manager, who had been away from the plant for a two-week training session, including some encounter groups. His enthusiasm about the experience excited me as I heard him describe what had happened during a management meeting after he returned. But the reaction of his fellow managers was to kid him, laugh at him, and in other ways ridicule him— and he began to close up. I was able to help him by describing to the group what I saw going on—but he had already learned that the climate was not warm enough for him to be open about his enthusiasm and so he kept those good feelings to himself.

SYSTEMIC BALANCE

The problem with training that focuses on changing one person's behavior or attitudes is that the change does not stop with him. Change in one extends in one way or another to all with whom he interacts and from them to those with whom they interact, and so on. This action-reaction process has been well described by Lederer and Jackson:

> The poet John Donne said, "No man is an island." We now know that nothing in the universe is an island. There are no self-contained actions. Every action has an influence on everything else, although the influence may be so minor that it is unnoticeable and immeasurable. . . . There is a constant action-reaction between associated things. The closer the association, the more obvious is the action-reaction. If an influence upsets the balance between the associated entities, then a compensating factor is provided *by the system*, to regain balance. This is known as "feedback."[1]

And with the posttraining "feedback" comes pressure for one who has learned a new way of behaving during a training session to move back to the old ways of behaving with which the system from which he came has been maintaining its balance. Thus, the function of the kidding, laughing, and ridicule at the enthusiasm of the production manager referred to above was to maintain systemic balance.

CHANGING SYSTEMS

Although it looked as if many of our trainees did not experience much change back on their jobs, when we talked with their wives we found that the wives did notice a difference. In talking with trainees during follow-up sessions, many shared the experience of the man who said, "The training doesn't seem to have made much difference at work, but the place that I do notice it is at home with my wife and kids. We have talked about things that we would never have talked about before—and I like what's happening."

One reason the changes in behavior are more noticeable at home than at work is that marriage, being a two-person system, is more re-

---

[1] Lederer, W. J., and Jackson, D. D. *The Mirages of Marriage.* New York: W. W. Norton, 1968, pp. 88–89.

sponsive to change in one of its members. From this it followed that we could tap into some of these two-person system effects by encouraging people to come to our training sessions in teams of at least two. By changing the relationship of *two* people who work together, we develop a two-person system that can be mutually supporting and mutually evaluating as it comes up against the pressure of feedback from the larger work system to conform to the old ways of behaving. Thus, when one trainee feels pressure from others in the system, he has someone who can evaluate and support or modify his belief that his new ways are better than the old, and someone who can consult with him on how to be more responsive to others without at the same time compromising his own wants unnecessarily or causing unnecessary problems.

One difficulty with two people from the same system coming to the same training program stems from the fact that the risk of failure in trying new ways of behaving is greater in the presence of a colleague. For this reason, some programs make it possible for men from the same system to participate in separate encounter groups and then come together at other times to talk about how they can translate their learnings during the program into more effective back-home action.

As a result of thinking about how to increase the effectiveness of individual managers, it became clear that changing *abilities of single persons* was a less effective training objective than changing *relationships between persons*. From this awareness, it was a short step to thinking about changing the whole network of interdependent relationships among persons who work together, that is, the total organizational system. This systemic network of relations ranges from things going on within a single person (intrapersonal) to things going on within the total system and includes all the levels in between (interpersonal, group, intergroup, department, division, and other subsystem levels). This is a short step conceptually, but when we try to apply this concept to being aware of what really goes on in an organization with hundreds or thousands of members, the immensity and complexity of the phenomena seem overwhelming.

SYSTEMIC CHANGE AS PERSONAL RESPONSIBILITY

The human effect of seeing one's self as personally responsible for the immensity and complexity of a total system can be put into perspective by referring to a training exercise that has been widely used in laboratory programs. The exercise is based on a conceptual model developed by Joe Luft and Harry Ingham, which because it looks like a window, has been given the name "Johari window." (See Table 17-1.)

Table 17-1 The Johari Window

		A PERSON'S AWARENESS OF WHAT IS GOING ON WITHIN HIM	
		Aware	*Not aware*
Other people's awareness of what is going on within him	Aware	1. Free	2. Blind
	Not aware	3. Hidden	4. Unknown

Panel 1 of the window represents the area of an interpersonal relationship about which a person feels free to be open with others, like the production manager's initial feeling about sharing his enthusiasm with his colleagues. Things a person is not aware of but that others can make inferences about are represented in panel 2, such as a person's feelings of anger—shown in his tone of voice, flushed face, and clenched fist—which he is not aware of himself. Things a person knows about himself but feels he must keep hidden from others, like the production manager's feelings of enthusiasm and excitement after he found that he would be kidded about such feelings, are in panel 3. And panel 4 refers to the things sufficiently controlled by the person's unconscious that neither he nor others are aware of them.

In the exercise, participants are asked to write on a slip of paper, without putting their name on it, the one or two most important things about themselves that they generally keep hidden from other people. The slips are collected and then read back to the group. In all the experience I know of with this exercise, there is a highly consistent pattern of answers. In more than two thirds of the cases, people are hiding feelings of inadequacy, insecurity, lack of self-confidence, fear of failure, and anxiety. The fact that such feelings are widely shared and widely hidden comes, I think, from the fact that such feelings are widely assumed to be "bad" and "wrong" because of society's norms about masculine self-confidence and not talking about feelings.

This brings us back to considering the human effect of the overwhelming immensity and complexity of human organizations with hundreds, thousands, and hundreds of thousands of members. The fact is that any person who sees himself as personally responsible for what is going on around him in the midst of such immense complexity *is inadequate,* and, as he moves to higher levels of management responsibility, he becomes increasingly inadequate. Inadequacy is a fact of responsible organizational life. The relief of managers who realize that it is alright to be inadequate after they have been hiding it for many years is gratifying to observe.

Beyond the recognition that one is necessarily inadequate and that such feelings are neither "bad" nor "wrong" comes an increased willingness to talk about *real* inadequacies with other people. When those others also accept inadequacy as a fact, one finds it easier to face real inadequacies. As one's capacity for tolerating feelings of personal inadequacy increases, one's capacity for sensing real opportunities for personal response and influence on what goes on within one's organization also increases. So, too, do one's capacities for: being aware of what is going on (awareness); reflecting on the complexity of what is going on (learning); thinking about one's reaction or proaction possibilities (planning); and then acting with the awareness that one can and does influence the total system (behaving). Some effects of increased tolerance for feelings of inadequacy are shown in Table 17-2.

Table 17-2

————————————————→ Working, living process ————————————————→
Experiencing ————→ Awareness ————→ Thinking ————→ Behaving
                   (perceiving)

	TOLERATION FOR FEELINGS OF INADEQUACY (ANXIETY)	
	Decreased	*Increased*
Awareness (perception)	Inhibition Distortion Blocking Ignorance Closedness	Perceptual accuracy of events in time and space Expansiveness Sensitivity Openness
Thinking	Defensiveness Restricted Rigidity Inflexibility	Modification Expansion Complication Anticipation
Behaving	Habit Resistance to new behavior Dominating Being submissive	Testing assumptions Experimentation Spontaneity Flexibility Risk-taking

RISK IN ACCEPTING PERSONAL RESPONSIBILITY

The problem in accepting *personal* responsibility is that if one sees one's self in relation to the total system, the burden of acting in the most responsible way and then feeling the potential guilt from the consequences of what one does or does not do can be overwhelming. Bugental has described this well.

> Man finds himself thrown into a world of infinite possibilities where each moment is a choice point, each act gives life (actuality) to some possibilities and condemns others to oblivion. From each such choice branch unimaginable consequences. It is, of course, this very unimaginable quality which is at the base of man's living in contingency. Contingency here means, any act has an infinite array of possible outcomes, and that we can, man can, at any point only recognize some finite part of this infinite array. Man organizes his choices, his adaptations in terms of his estimation of the probability of various outcomes and tries in the process to increase his chances of actualizing that which he wants in his life, while diminishing the probabilities of that which he does not want. The impossibility of insuring the outcomes of one's actions, the consequences of one's choices, means that always there exists the possibility of tragedy ensuing from any choice which one makes. This is a possibility against which we can never be completely insured.[2]

And from the tragedy that we can each identify as our personal responsibility also comes guilt. Not the guilt that comes from accusation and blame, but rather the guilt that comes from regret at facing candidly the injury that one has done to the lives of others. Bugental elaborates on this concept of experienced guilt.

> . . . This existential guilt is always latently present when our actions are founded, as they must be, on insufficient knowledge to prevent the undesired outcome. It is regrettable, but real that many, many of the crucial decisions of our lives, whether they are recognized as such at the time that we make them, are founded on less knowledge, less awareness than is potentially available to us at such times. In such choices we bear the load of responsibility even though we have the best of excuses as to why we did not know more when we made the decision. Therein lies existential

---

[2] Bugental, J. F. T. *The Search for Authenticity: An Existential Approach to Therapy.* New York: Holt, Rinehart and Winston, 1965, pp. 152–53.

guilt, it is the product of our limitedness in an unlimited world; a product of our finiteness in an infinite universe. Existential guilt is a part of man's condition. It is neither a matter for dismay nor for an inert acceptance. It needs to be recognized as a given of our situation.[3]

Existential tragedy and existential guilt are not the only aspects of the human condition, however. There is joy, too, because, as Bugental describes,

. . . Whenever we know all that we need to know to make a decision, we make no decision, but are determined by what we know. Our joy arises from facing the unknown and affirming ourselves. Fulfillment is the flower of accepting our finiteness and yet partaking of the infinite.[4]

The self that is affirmed by the act of choice is a free self. And one's joy comes from experiencing one's self as free.

But if one experiences one's self as free, he lives with risk. At every moment one is conscious of his freedom, he risks feeling responsible for the consequences implicit in the choices he makes as he exercises his freedom. And with those consequences come the feelings of existential joy or existential guilt. Thus, learning to live with freedom also requires learning to live with feeling the existential joy or guilt implicit in that freedom.

To be free involves taking the risk of accepting personal responsibility and this requires courage.

LEARNING TO WORK AND LIVE WITH FREEDOM AND RESPONSIBILITY

A primary objective of laboratory programs, including encounter groups, is to help people learn to work with, live with, and affirm the reality of their freedom and responsibility. We have learned, however, that although the small group (or "laboratory") experiences can be meaningful to an individual, it can create problems when that individual returns to things as they are in his work organization and seeks to relate to those things in a new way. For example, the *Wall Street Journal* describes an instance:

3 *Ibid.*, p. 164.
4 *Ibid.*, p. 165.

Last year a big New York consumer products company sent Mrs. D., a product manager, to a week long sensitivity training program. She got so sensitive she quit the company.

That isn't what's supposed to happen, of course. Ideally, sensitivity training produces better bosses and better employees. Meeting in group discussions with no planned agenda participants are encouraged to respond to each other with brutal candor and on intensely personal levels. Through analysis of their behavior by the rest of the group, participants are supposed to gain a deeper understanding of themselves and others.

Mrs. D. loved that part. "It was a whole week of truth serum, all openness," she recalls. "But then I came back to work and found it shrouded in the usual unnecessary tactfulness and diplomacy. I discovered that the training had so opened me up that I was tired of the Mickey Mouse." When her superiors wanted to delay a decision on a new product development program she had been working on for more than a year, she told them she was tired of their procrastination and quit to take a comparable job elsewhere, where she has more latitude. Her old employer dropped the sensitivity training program in which she participated.[5]

The challenge, then, is to discover ways in which laboratory programs can encourage organization development in a manager consistent with individual freedom and responsibility.

In the case of Mrs. D., there may have been more effective and rewarding ways than quitting for her to deal with the frustration of her goals within the company, which, conceivably, could have benefited both of them. But the fact that the organization had managed to frustrate her to the point of desperate exasperation suggests that perhaps the company was resisting development and change more than was good for its organization, and suffering from clogged channels of communication from lower levels in the hierarchy to higher ones. Apparently someone who could have benefited from knowledge about Mrs. D.'s frustration either did not know the depth and intensity of the feeling that had built up within her or, if he did, failed to deal with it effectively.

People in situations like that of Mrs. D. must find ways of making their feelings known and their inputs effective within one organization or another. We cannot tell from the article whether her company was really a hopeless case for her or not. And organizations that really want to develop and progress must find ways to accept change and to communicate with, relate to, and benefit from creative people like Mrs. D.

[5] Calame, Byron E. The Truth Hurts: Some Companies See More Harm Than Good in Sensitivity Training. *Wall Street J.*, 174:1, July 14, 1969.

No organization can realistically afford to lose very many people like Mrs. D. If they leave, its ability for effective change leaves with them, and those responsible for the future of the organization would do well to wonder why they are leaving.

Mrs. D.'s group experience did not cause her departure. It did help her to become painfully aware of her accumulated frustration. But it may have failed to help her anticipate the difficulty of effectively and constructively using those emotions and her awareness of them to benefit both herself and the company.

An encounter group or laboratory program has the potential for helping people who work and live together talk about and explore what they really want from each other and from the organization in which they participate. For such a program to be effective, however, it must be related to the participants' wants and the organization's needs. This is why many companies have turned away from the free-swinging, brutal candor nurtured in some T groups and have moved toward carefully planned sessions focusing on solving immediate problems of working together, developing structures, procedures, and processes for solving future conflicts and problems, and developing coordinated goals and plans so that future conflicts and problems can be minimized.

AN EXERCISE FOR LEARNING ABOUT FREEDOM, RESPONSIBILITY, AND ORGANIZATION DEVELOPMENT

I have stated that we can measure or evaluate the difference between a well-organized company and one that is less effectively organized by examining *the degree to which the motivation of the individuals in that company is moving them in the same direction.* Also, any act, event, structure, procedure, or process can be identified as either organization-developing or organization-defeating by means of such analysis. Thus each individual in an organization has the power (to one degree or another) to develop and enhance or to defeat and frustrate the effectiveness of the organization in performing its function and its *development* toward more effective organization. Therefore, all participants in a well-organized company should, ideally, be aware of how their thinking and feeling affect the way they use that power.

To develop increased awareness of the degree to which people are motivated in the same or different directions within an organization, I have devised a laboratory exercise in which participants are given an opportunity to experience the reality of their freedom and their personal responsibility in a situation that simulates the complexity of life in an organization and their individual roles in it.

I call the exercise "decision."[6]

The potency of the experience is difficult to describe, just as a T group or encounter experience is difficult to describe to someone who has not had such an experience. Nevertheless, I will describe the experience and will leave the reader to imagine, if he can, the peaks of emotional involvement that are (or may be) reached as participants begin to make decisions and are then surprised, shocked, joyful, and angry as they discover the consequences of their decisions, both individual and collective. The exercise encompasses a wide range of phenomena that affects organizational decision-making, including leadership, influence, power, goal-setting, conflict within and between groups, trust, freedom, suspicion, betrayal, money motivation, communication chains, attitudes, perceptions, wants, values, and responsibility.

In the relatively brief space of two to three hours, the exercise can bring home to a participant the impact his awareness, thinking, assumptions, and values have on his behavior and how, *if he wants to do so,* he can affect the movement of a social system with 60 members. The thought each is left with is, "If I can influence a system with 60 members, maybe I can influence the larger system within which I work."

INTRODUCTION TO THE EXERCISE

In the exercise, each person finds himself as one member of one of six ten-man teams. He is told that he will be participating in an exercise that simulates the process of making decisions in large groups and that the object of the exercise is to "win as much as you can." He then receives three sheets from the timekeeper (reproduced in Tables 17-3, 17-4, and 17-5) and is told that he has ten minutes to read them, discuss them with the other members of his team, and be sure everyone in his team understands the exercise. (The reader who wishes to experience some of what the exercise is like should study Tables 17-3, 17-4, and 17-5 before reading further. If you do this, as you read, ask yourself, "How would I react to these sheets if I were participating in the exercise?")

The first sheet (Table 17-3) describes the procedure of the exercise. It tells each participant that the exercise is like a game in that it has ten rounds. In each round his team will decide to vote either X or Y, marking their vote on a slip of paper. At the end of each round, all of

---

6 The exercise is based on "the prisoner's dilemma," a two-person exercise originally described by Anatole Rapaport. The large-group version I am describing here was developed originally by N. Margulies, L. Stafford, and myself. The present form is my own, after numerous revisions over the five years since 1965.

the team votes will be collected, and the amount each team wins or loses will be announced. The amount won or lost by each team is based on the second sheet he receives, called the payoff sheet (as set forth in Table 17-4).

The pattern by which these payoffs were developed for the payoff sheet is central to the concept underlying the exercise. The reader can see the pattern by looking at Table 17-4, namely:

When all teams vote X (the all-X condition), all *lose* $100.

When all teams vote Y (the all-Y condition), all *win* $100.

When some teams vote X and others vote Y (the X-Y condition), the X's win and the Y's lose.

From the perspective of the whole group, the whole wins $600 under the all-Y condition, loses $600 under the all-X condition, and neither wins nor loses under the X-Y condition (because the total won by the X's equals the total lost by the Y's).

The way the participant approaches the exercise, his fellow team members, and the group as a whole will be determined by how he reacts to this payoff sheet, as I will describe later.

As described in the procedure sheet, each participant also reads that rounds 5, 7, and 10 are bonus rounds, with payoffs multiplied by 2, 3, and 10, respectively. On each of those rounds his team chooses two representatives, who meet for six minutes with other team representatives and then return to their teams for a final vote decisions by each team.

The last point on the participants' procedure sheet is a list of "three key rules": He is not to talk to or signal other teams; all members of his team must agree with the team's vote or at least be willing to go along with it; and his team's vote must be reported on a slip when it is called for at the end of each round.

After his team has had ten minutes to help its members clarify their understanding, the timekeeper asks, "Does anyone have any questions about the exercise?" Most of the questions asked are clarified by restating the procedure in other words. Someone asks, "Does 'win as much as you can' mean win for the teams or everybody?" and the timekeeper's answer is, "It means whatever you want it to mean."

PLAYING THE EXERCISE

When all questions are answered, play begins. The timekeeper announces, "Begin round 1. You have three minutes to mark your vote."

There are a variety of things that can happen during the playing phase of the exercise. All the possibilities cannot be described in detail, but some of the main guidelines for the timekeeper can be stated.

1. He calls time and encourages the teams to turn their slips in with their votes recorded. He does not force any individual or any team to turn in a slip. If any person accepts responsibility for saying, "I cannot go along with my team's choice," he allows them additional time to develop a team choice. If they do not produce a marked slip by the end of five minutes, he stops the process and asks the teams to pick two representatives who will meet with other representatives to decide what the whole group will do. He does not make the group's decision for it, no matter how big the majority against the person who accepts responsibility for saying, "I cannot go along." If necessary, he asks the minority person or persons, "Is there some other way you can get what you want?" The final possibility is that everyone will agree that they have no alternative other than stopping the exercise. If everyone agreed to that, the exercise would be over. Keeping this in mind helps the timekeeper to avoid making the whole group's decision for it.

2. He does not make decisions about the rules of the exercise. If people ask about rules or procedures or in any other way attempt to involve him in decision, he refers them to the procedures, by saying something like, "The procedures say so-and-so." But he does not accept the responsibility for setting limits. The procedures are there for the participants to test. If they go outside the procedures, he does not stop them, although he may point out the deviation from the procedures. The general guideline he follows is that the group as a whole is its own authority, and if it wishes to change the rules, it may. But he does not say this explicitly. If a participant is open to awareness of such a possibility, he can help the group discover it.

Just before the seventh round, the announcement is made that on the tenth round each team's vote will be made by secret ballot of all team members. If any member marks his ballot "X," the team's vote will be treated as X. After the tenth round, final scores are determined.

LEARNING FROM THE EXERCISE

After round 10, participants discuss the following questions: "What happened?" "What did you want to happen?" "Why did things happen as they did?" and "What might you personally have done differently to influence what happened so that it would have been closer to what you wanted?" The discussion begins with the teams, then moves to discussion among representatives in a fishbowl,[7] and then moves to total-group discussion.

If the group's discussion does not develop them on its own, I make the following points:

1. In the procedure, the purpose of the exercise is described as "win as much as you can." In that statement, the word "you" can mean the person, his team, or the group as a whole of which the team is a part. The way one interprets that word and what he wants it to mean will affect the way in which he plays.

2. There is no "right" way to play "decision."

   a. If one wants to play in an exclusively team-centered way, without regard to the group, he has a chance of winning big, but at the expense of loss by others. He can increase the possibilities of winning big if he can get others to believe that everyone will choose Y and then his team chooses X. On the tenth play, when there is no opportunity for anyone to get even, the opportunities for winning big in this way are especially great because the payoffs are multiplied by ten.

   b. If one wants to play in a way that assumes that Y is the "good" choice and X is the "bad" choice, he may influence his team to choose Y without regard to the consequences of choosing Y. (The consequence is that his team's Y rewards other teams for choosing X and, in effect, can encourage them to continue choosing X.)

   c. If one wants to play in a team-centered way, but *does* consider the group as a whole, he can play for maximizing the number of rounds in which everyone chooses Y. Under this condition, everyone wins and no one loses, if he is successful. To accomplish this he *must be* aware of the fact that some others are likely to be playing in the ways described in a and b and he *must be able* to influence their choice.

3. "Decision" has been used with nearly one hundred groups, and less than one out of five groups plays an all-Y condition by the tenth round. The all-Y condition in the tenth round is of most

[7] In the fishbowl technique, the representatives meet in a small circle while all others gather around them in a larger circle to observe the inner group's process and discussion. Because the relationship is much like that of observers of fish in a bowl, the technique is called "fishbowling."

significance to the discussion of organization development because it provides a moment when the wants of all 60 members are
coordinated in the same direction. The ability of a single person
to register his disagreement, by choosing X without anyone knowing he did it, makes this exercise a particularly sensitive test of
any failure in organizational coordination. The processes by
which an all-Y condition can be achieved on the tenth round provide an operational way of talking about the vastly more complex
processes of moving toward organizational coordination in industry, education, government, community, and so on.

4. A person who orients himself to "decision" in a way that is
   stimultaneously self-centered, team-centered, and whole-group-
   centered takes the greatest risk of failure, accepts the largest
   amount of responsibility, and most fully uses his freedom to influence the process of the exercise. One person who wants an all-Y
   exercise and who cares deeply about getting what he wants has
   the power to bring that about. Success cannot be guaranteed, but
   if he accepts personal responsibility for the outcome, he will be
   open to discovering the ways by which he can get what he wants
   and his mind will seek them actively. At worst he can take responsibility for calling the exercise off. To the degree a person experiences himself as responsible for the whole group, he simultaneously experiences the degree of his freedom within the context
   of the exercise.

DEVELOPING INTERPERSONAL RESPONSIBILITY

Against the background of the "decision" exercise, we can conceive
of organization development as the on-going process within which one
person contributes to a multipersonal process in the direction of an
organizational "life" for all that is consistent with what each wants for
himself. He must begin with awareness of people's wants as they are,
including some whose wants are exclusively self-centered and others
whose "wants" are conditioned by absolute concepts of goodness. Then
he must learn to live in the present in such a way that he most fully
contributes to movement toward a "world" in the organization in which
all are fulfilling their wants and no one's fulfillment requires another's
deprivation.

This is an idealistic "world" view. But to keep it realistic, we must
think in terms of people as they are presently able to conceive their
lives. And for most people, this means their families, their social-group
memberships, and their work organizations. In a narrower sense,
organization development refers to coordinating the wants of people
who are working together on a common task. And, more specifically, it

refers to what a manager does on Monday morning at nine o'clock.

For the manager who is able to see himself as personally responsible for the total system, the first step in moving toward coordinating his own and others' energies in a common direction is to examine his own wants. In brief, he needs to ask himself, "What do I want and what am I willing to do to get what I want?" On Monday morning at nine o'clock any member of an organization can do this—alone at first and then involving others. A brief outline of the process includes:

1. List what you most want to achieve:
   a. Over the next year.
   b. Over the next three months.
   c. Over the next one month.
   d. In the next week.
   (In doing this limit yourself to four or five major goals and four or five subgoals for each major goal.)
2. If the statements on your list do not include a specific description of how you will know you are being successful in achieving what you want, revise your statements so that they include specific measures of achievement. For example: "List my major goals and subgoals, including specific descriptions of how I will measure my achievement," is more specific than "Plan my job better." The measure of achievement is a written list.
3. Outline the specific things *you* must do in order to accomplish what you want, including specific target dates and specific requests for action by others.
4. Review your list with at least one other person who is in a position to help you consider the realism of your plans and goals. Such persons can include your wife or husband, your work supervisor, or a trusted friend. (In doing this ask your "consultant" to limit himself to helping you develop what *you* want and not what he wants you to want. This means asking only clarifying questions, such as: "What target date do you want to set for yourself?" "What specific kinds of help do you need to ask from others in order to accomplish what you want?" "If you do thus-and-so, what kinds of things are likely to happen—and in what specific ways do you plan to relate to those consequences of your actions?" "Are there any important barriers to accomplishing what you want that you have not planned for?")
5. Identify the two or three persons whose collaboration is most important to your accomplishing what you want and describe your tentative goals and plans to them, limiting yourself to the portion they need to know in order to collaborate with you. Then ask them if they will do what you want them to do. As much as

possible, make your request in terms of a *quid pro quo;* "If I do this and you do that, we can accomplish thus-and-so. Will you do it?" Be prepared to maintain dialogue with them if their wants are not immediately responsive to yours. Your orientation should be, "What does the other want and in what ways can I help him without compromising my own wants unnecessarily?"

6. In case of conflict between what you want and the other wants:

    a. Be sure that you understand what the other wants; the conflict may be more apparent than real.

    b. Look for a superordinate goal that would coordinate your wants. For example, two men who want to become department heads must face what that goal means to them. If the meaning is higher status, greater power, and higher pay, their wants are necessarily in conflict; one can succeed only at the expense of the other's lesser status, lesser power, and lesser pay. (Like an X-over-Y win in the "decision" exercise.) If they are open to an organization-developing choice, they can both value team achievements and team rewards and agree on a division of decision-making authority and income on the basis of their different abilities to contribute to team achievement.

    c. Be sure that you understand what you really want; you may change your goals or your priorities in the process of clarifying what you want. For example, the goal of achieving higher status, power, and pay can become the goal of maximizing the expression of one's potential (self-actualization), if one examines what one really wants. To come to this realization, however, he may have to begin by facing that at one level he *does* want higher status, power, and pay, and then, after tracing out the consequences of getting them, conclude that he wants something else more.

As one shares responsibility with others by entering into interdependent relationships of this kind, his feelings of personal inadequacy will decrease and his feelings of interpersonal adequacy will increase. This comes because the process is an experience in moving away from deficiency motivation and toward being motivation, away from self-denial and toward self-realization.

The Manager's Role, Systemic Change, and Developing Interpersonal Responsibility

The process described in the preceding section can be followed by all the members of an organization. The manager's role in coordinating his own energies and the energies of all the people whose work he supervises can now be viewed more specifically as involving:

1. Personal development through clarifying personal goals, wants, and plans for achieving them, including the manager's own.
2. Team development through helping subordinates.

   a. Resolve conflicts in their wants and plans, including their conflicts with the manager's wants and plans.
   b. Clarify goals and plans that require the active contribution of several members, including those that cannot even be conceived until members begin asking themselves, "What do *we* want and what are *we* willing to do to get it?"

3. Organization development through helping subordinates, other managers, and other teams.

   a. Resolve conflicts in their wants and plans, including conflicts with the wants and plans of the team's members.
   b. Clarify goals and plans that require active contribution by the members of more than one team, including those that require the we concept.

4. Interorganizational and community development by extending the above kinds of thinking to relations with other organizations and the whole of the organization's environment, including the natural universe.

Exploring relations with the natural universe is central to the current concern with ecology, environment, and fundamental questions of whether or not man can survive because of what he is doing to nature. Moreover, from an existential point of view, we can say that a person's ability to conceive of himself in total interdependent relationship with the universe is a necessary condition of self-realization.

The ultimate goal upon which both person and organization coordinate their energies is suggested by Le Comte du Nuoy:

Until man appeared, evolution strove only, from an observer's point of view, to manufacture an organ, the brain, in a body capable of assuring its protection. All the ancestors of man were but irresponsible actors playing an imposed part in a play which they did not understand, or try to understand. Man continues to play his part but wants to comprehend the play. He becomes capable of perfecting himself, and he is even the only one capable of doing this. But in order to improve himself he must be free, since his contribution to evolution will depend on the use he makes of his liberty. . . . The highest duty of every man is to contribute, to the best of his ability, to this new phase of evolution. No man need worry about the results of his efforts, nor about the importance of his contribution, as long as he is sincere and devotes his attention to improving himself, since it is the effort in itself that counts. His life thus takes on a universal significance; he becomes a link in the chain; he is no longer an irresponsible toy, a cork on the water, blindly obeying uncontrollable impulses, but a conscious, autonomous element, at all times free to regress and disappear or to progress and contribute to the divine task. The whole nobility of man is derived from this liberty which has been refused to the animals. Of that alone could he be excusably proud, but he prides himself on all the rest. . . .[8]

Thus the efficient production of goods and services wanted by man can be coordinated in relation to an organization-developing process in which individual human beings grow toward increasing freedom to develop their potential in their own ways.

I know of no such fully functioning organization. I am convinced that organizations can approach this ideal state. I am committed to this conviction and am engaged in doing things to bring it about. I am also convinced that a manager who does not share this belief will not be able to create a fully functioning organization, because his belief will function like a self-fulfilling prophecy. Namely, if he prophesies that something is impossible, he is likely to behave *as if* his prophecy *were* true—and his behavior is likely to bring about responses and conditions that tend to make his prophecy come true. I believe that people are capable of learning and changing and that they can exercise a greater influence on themselves, their organizations, and their environment than they presently believe is possible.

ENCOUNTER AND ORGANIZATION DEVELOPMENT

In order to know whether or not his company, division, or department is well organized, a manager must be able to evaluate the degree to which the motivation of people who work for him is coordinated in the same direction. His evaluation must be based on something more objective than his personal opinion, however.

I have observed that subordinates do not tell their supervisors about their personal desires, plans, and goals. Even if a supervisor asks for them, his subordinates are likely to tell him either what they think he

[8] Le Comte du Nuoy. *Human Doctrine.* New York: Longman's, Green, 1947, pp. 226, 227.

expects or what they think the company requires. As a consequence, managers generally lack precisely the kind of information about the thoughts and ambitions of their subordinates that is absolutely essential to an informed evaluation of whether their functioning organizational units are well organized, i.e., effectively coordinated, or are not.

Effective management, in the sense of efficient organization and coordination of individual efforts, cannot exist without effective orchestration of personal goals and company purposes, provided that orchestration and the information necessary to achieve it are what organization development is all about. Encounter as one tool of organization development, can be used as an effective means of gathering the diagnostic data about personal motivations that are so often lacking. And it can be used to gather such information in a manner that does not unduly disrupt the everyday functioning of the organization by generating hostility through the stimulation of destructive and unnecessary venting of "brutal candor."

As the *Wall Street Journal* article, quoted above, suggests by its title, truth *can* hurt. Unless candid confrontations serve some useful purpose for the individuals involved and their ability to work together, they should not, in my judgment, be encouraged. Indeed, in the work I do, I prefer actively to discourage such pointless encounters. Unfortunately, during the early experience with encounter groups, there was a tendency to encourage candid confrontation without regard to potential harmful consequences. The assumption was that openness, honesty, and encounters of all kinds would be beneficial. Experience has taught me that this is just not true.

There are still some inexperienced and, I think, misguided trainers who conduct groups based on the old, unqualified assumptions. The negative consequences that come from such groups cannot fairly or accurately be attributed to groups conducted within the limits of what is relevant to and useful for the company and the individuals within it.

A recent experience of mine provides an illustration of how encounter techniques can be used to provide diagnostic information not generally available to a manager. I was conducting a goal-setting and planning interview with a man who interrupted our conversation to say, "You have found out more about me in 15 minutes than anyone in this company knows, and they have worked with me for many years." Prior to our interview, he had spent less than two hours with me in group meetings, and yet he trusted me enough to reveal his personal hopes and plans, including specific major income-generating contributions to his company. His supervisors did not know about his plans; others in the organization were planning for him to do things that could undermine his ability to achieve his goals and to garner their benefits for the company. He was telling me about how he might even have to leave the company if he could not continue to work on things he had begun to develop.

When diagnosis reveals that the motivations of individuals within the system are in conflict or are working at cross-purposes, more extensive dialogue can be developed using encounter groups. Such dialogue can help and resolve differences.

The illustration above presents a problem that deserves serious considerations, namely, whether (or under what circumstances) organization development efforts can be more usefully conducted by outside consultants than by consultants within the company.

In my opinion, after an organization development program has begun and has been in operation for a substantial period of time, it should be possible for internal consultants, present from the beginning, to phase into full responsibility for the program and carry it on along whatever paths it has set for itself. However, during the early phases, my experience has been that an external consultant can gather diagnostic information more easily, conceive alternative change programs more creatively (because he has no involvement with past practices), and generally present the result of his efforts more effectively. He can do so because he is relatively free from vulnerability to the internal frictions and dynamic tensions indigenous to all organizations and that usually serve the function of maintaining the existing structure and processes without regard to whether they serve well or badly the purposes of the organization.

When properly used, encounter groups can provide support for changing an organization-defeating system into an organization-developing system in the service of improving the quality of life for everyone affected by the organization's existence.

Table 17-3 Procedure

---

1. This is a learning exercise. It is like a game in that there are ten rounds and there are other teams with which you are playing—but it is *not* a game.
2. The purpose of the exercise is to win as much as you can.
3. When the timekeeper says, "Begin round 1," your team will decide on its vote for the first round. Your vote may be either X or Y. The payoff for the first round will be determined by how your team's vote is related to the votes of all the other teams. The payoff possibilities are shown on the payoff sheet. (See Table 17-4.) When all votes are collected, the timekeeper will announce how the teams voted and how much each won or lost.
4. As shown on the score sheet (see Table 17-5), you will have three minutes to cast your vote for the first round. For all the other rounds you will have two minutes to cast your vote, except for rounds 5, 7, and 10,

which are bonus rounds. During each bonus round, your team will have two minutes to choose and instruct two representatives. The representatives from all teams will then meet separately for six minutes to talk about whatever they want to talk about. After the representatives have met, your team will then have two minutes to make its final decision about your vote. At the end of each round, when all votes are in, you will be told how much the teams voted and how much each won or lost.

5. There are three key rules to keep in mind:

   a. You are not to talk to other teams or signal them in any way. You may communicate with them, but only through your representative during rounds 5, 7, and 10.
   b. All members of your team must agree on your team's vote or at least be willing to go along with it.
   c. Your team's vote must be reported on the slips provided when it is called for at the end of each round.

Table 17-4 Payoff Sheet

VOTES	PAYOFFS
All teams vote X	All teams lose $100
Five teams vote X;	X's win $100;
one team votes Y	Y loses $500
Four teams vote X;	X's win $150;
two teams vote Y	Y's lose $300
Three teams vote X;	X's win $200;
three teams vote Y	Y's lose $200
Two teams vote X;	X's win $300;
four teams vote Y	Y's lose $150
One team votes X;	X wins $500;
five teams vote Y	Y's lose $100
All teams vote Y	All teams win $100

Rounds 5, 7, and 10 are bonus rounds; for them the payoffs are multiplied by 2, 3, and 10, respectively.

Table 17-5 Score Sheet

ROUND	TIME ALLOWED (MIN.)	COMMUNICATION ALLOWED	X OR Y VOTE	$'s WON	$'s LOST	ACCUMULATED $ BALANCE
1	3	Within team only				
2	2	Within team only				
3	2	Within team only				

Table 17-5

Round	Time Allowed (min.)	Communication Allowed	X or Y Vote	$'s Won	$'s Lost	Accumulated $ Balance
4	2	Within team only				
5	2	Within team only	Bonus round: Payoffs are mutliplied by 2			
	6	Among teams through representatives only				
	2	Within team only				
6	2	Within team only				
7	2	Within team only	Bonus round: Payoffs are multiplied by 3			
	6	Among teams through representatives only				
	2	Within team only				
8	2	Within team only				
9	2	Within team only				
10	2	Within team only	Bonus round: Payoffs are multiplied by 10			
	6	Among teams through representatives only				
	2	Within team only				

BIBLIOGRAPHY

Bugental, J. F. T. *The Search for Authenticity: An Existential Approach to Therapy.* New York: Holt, Rinehart and Winston, 1965, pp. 152–53.

Calame, Byron E. The Truth Hurts: Some Companies See More Harm Than Good in Sensitivity Training. *Wall St. J.,* **174**:1, July 14, 1969.

Le Comte du Nuoy. *Human Doctrine.* New York: Longman's, Green, 1947.

Lederer, W. J., and Jackson, D. D. *The Mirages of Marriage.* New York: W. W. Norton, 1968.

Leonard Blank

 **Encounter Techniques in Education, School-Community, and Industry**

COMMENTARY

In this chapter, the rationale and examples of the application of encounter techniques in various areas are described. In education, a workshop designed to explore the relevance of curriculum in a context of youth-adult and black-white encounter is presented. A task-centered interactional program for school and community is cited together with the results that followed. An industry program for effectively absorbing unemployed and underemployed men completes the chapter.

BIOGRAPHY

Leonard Blank received his Ph.D. in clinical psychology from New York University, a certificate in psychoanalysis and psychotherapy from the N.Y.U. postdoctoral program, and worked in sensitivity training and organizational development with the N.T.L. Institute of Applied Behavioral Science. He has taught at Stanford University, San Francisco State College, and Rutgers University. In private practice in Princeton, he is the president of Princeton Associates for Human Resources, Inc., adjunct associate professor of clinical psychology at Rutgers University, and the author of various articles, chapters, and books, including *Sourcebook for Training in Clinical Psychology* and *Psychological Evaluations in Psychotherapy.*

In this chapter, we shall examine examples of the application of behavioral science, in the form of encounter techniques, to educational, school-community, and industrial organizations. The possibilities and need for these applications seem limitless, for any organization of people requires an awareness of their communicative processes and an exploration of vehicles with which to encounter and work with each other. The examples cited are the actual cases worked on by PAHR, an organization of behavioral scientists utilizing primarily group techniques addressed to people problems.

EDUCATION

Major issues currently raised in education are the relevance of the curriculum to students of differing backgrounds, sensitivity of faculty and administration to student needs, racial problems, and communication among the various school components and with the community.

The high-school students of a large city complained that their curriculum was not relevant to their needs and especially to those of minority students. The relevance of their course work to both the vocational and adult roles they hoped to assume were seriously called to question. Not only did communication seem impeded between faculty and the student body, but new teachers fed in by the nearby training college appeared to be as insensitive to the issues as did their senior colleagues.

A faculty committee from the high school and college invited high-school and college education department faculty and students from both schools who had expressed an interest in the problem to participate in a workshop. The final group consisted of these four groups of whom half were black and half white. Black and white staff then conducted a five-day curriculum relevancy workshop with these participants at a facility removed from their everyday surroundings.

Although the theme of the workshop was a critical evaluation of the curriculum with recommendations for change, the basic objective was to explore how the people involved with the curriculum related and communicated to each other.

OBJECTIVES

The primary purpose of the program was to develop a critical re-examination of the effective "relevance" of the curriculum substance and instructional methodology at the junior-high, senior-high, and college level in preparing the student:

1. For a continuity of education at successively higher levels.
2. For a vocational career.
3. And as a significant contributor to the society of which he is a part.

It was agreed among the workshop planners that a detailed substantive examination and critique of curriculum and instructional methodology could not be effectively accomplished without free and open communication between and among the various segments represented by the participants.

Underlying the stated purposes of the workshop, therefore, was the constant effort to provide an atmosphere that would encourage and foster free and verbal interaction between teacher-student, youth-adult, black-white, and all other points of view represented in the workshop. Constructive confrontation was encouraged and developed. The objective was to avoid the typical conference-type intellectual verbalizations but rather to enable participants to gain a better understanding of the behavior, thoughts, feelings, and attitudes of themselves and other people. This newly gained knowledge and insight could then provide a functional basis for positively modified behavior toward individuals "back home" (Blank, 1969; Bidwell, 1966).

PROGRAM APPROACH

A. PROGRAM ELEMENTS
   The program elements were designed to:
   1. Maximize participant interaction with as many different people as possible.
   2. Encourage the participant's awareness and understanding of *his own* feelings, needs, values and attitudes—and those of *others*.
   3. Develop awareness of how feelings and attitudes affect behavior and the impact of behavior on others.
   4. Demonstrate the meaning and effect of nonverbal (as well as verbal) communications.

5. Encourage honest dialogue.
6. Effect constructive confrontation.
7. Help the participant relate his experiences in the workshop to life "back home" in school, on the job, in the community.
8. Assess possible modifications and innovations "back home" in school, on the job, in the community.
9. Increase participant awareness of the factors involved in planning and instituting change, and especially those changes in curriculum and instructional approach that might develop as a result of the workshop.

B. Schedule

Each participant received an orientation kit, which included a detailed workshop schedule.

C. Sessions

The following is a description of the principal interactional group activities that took place at various sessions.

1. *Communication Exercises.* A series of nonverbal activities (e.g., milling, trust walk, trust fall) designed to facilitate the development of mutual trust between individuals.

2. *T Group.* A small group, each with an assigned group leader, consisting of a heterogeneous mix by age, sex, color, and allowed to function in an unstructured manner designed to initiate each member's awareness of his interpersonal style and its effect on the behavior of others, and awareness of the interpersonal style of others and the effect of the behavior of others. The leader's principal role was to create an atmosphere in which the group stressed feelings rather than words (although feelings were expected to be verbalized), honesty rather than social amenities, and an examination of what was occurring in the "here-and-now" of the group's experiences (by stressing verbal rechanneling) rather than in the "there-and-then" of other past experiences. The members related to each other as individuals rather than in the roles of "teacher," "black man," "group leader," and so on.

3. *Logs.* Confidential written expression of feelings and reactions to the happenings in each T-group meeting. These logs, which were added to at various points throughout the workshop, offered the participants an opportunity, in the process of writing, to explore feelings (their own and others) encountered during group meetings.

4. *Pairing.* Each member of a T group chose another member (different ones at different times) for the purpose of sharing (and thus comparing) feelings and thoughts about each other ("myself" and "you").

5. *S Group.* A small homogeneous group (e.g., high-school student groups, college student groups, junior- and senior-high-school teachers, and college faculty) conducted by a group leader who sought to maintain the environment of free expression of feelings. The emphasis here, however, was in dealing with the "back-home" relevance of what was going on in the workshop. The interchange among S group members dealt more with practical applications and solutions and placed less emphasis on feelings, values, and attitudes per se. Typical S groups explored such problems as drug use, student-teacher-parental conflicts, school grievances, sex, and racism in the schools.

6. *Community Exercise in Conflict Resolution.* Each participant selected another with whom he had perceived some personal or ideological conflict, or with whom he had encountered difficulty in communicating. These participants were then involved in a series of exercises (verbal and nonverbal) designed to clarify the source of conflict and to diminish or resolve it.

7. *Gaming.* Groups (different from the S and T groups) were given a variety of materials and asked to construct a project. Each project was judged by a staff member based on three criteria:
   a. How easily the meaning of the project was communicable to others.
   b. Creativity.
   c. Utilization of materials.
   Although the ostensible purpose of this gaming was to stress the importance of communication of meaning, the underlying objective was to demonstrate how each individual could make a constructive and creative contribution as a member of a group where the atmosphere was unstructured and where the interpersonal relationships were free from hidden prejudice. There was clear evidence of informal leaders arising within each group and efforts made by the groups to involve members who at first seemed either reluctant to participate or "left out." Although each group worked independently, all the themes dealt with various facets of peace, the dignity and equality of man, and harmonious living.

8. *Community Exercise (Note-Passing)*. This activity, at the very end of the workshop, constituted a form of feedback for staff members and group leaders. It consisted of all the participants exchanging written messages stating how each perceived the appearance, attitudes, behavior, and expressions of the others or making any comment whatsoever. It was evident in the reading of the messages (by the recipient) that some participants were generally freer in their written expressions than they had been previously within their groups or on a verbal basis.

9. *Planning Session*. Midway through the workshop a planning session was held involving all participants. The session was presented as an exercise of community self-government. The leaders yielded to the group the right to plan and implement the activities for the remainder of the workshop, with the understanding that—except for planned data collection on the last day—the entire program could be discarded or modified, provided that the entire "community" agreed. Participants in S groups then negotiated with other groups.

The changes in program reflected a desire to utilize the free-communications environment and improved interpersonal relations atmosphere to deal with more specific back-home problems from the viewpoint of homogeneity of interest. The result was a series of meetings between rationally and creatively structured groups of teachers-students of the high school, teachers-students of the college, college and high-school students, and college and high-school teachers. These new groupings, created by the participants, seemed more effective in meeting emerging needs. The staff acted as process observers only. Teacher-student dialogue at all levels was pointed and productive. There was little evidence of teacher defensiveness or teacher domination.

Both student and teacher groups delved into such problems as the black student in white schools, the incompetence of teachers, the different values emphasized by teachers and students, the extent and use of personal and group power, and how changes in the system could be realistically initiated and maintained. There was expressed desire on the part of student groups and teacher groups to cooperate in achieving specific educational goals. There was a strong sense of agreement on certain school policy critiques and institutional problems. The college group set a date for their own meeting to develop a possible course of action for seeking to initiate constructive changes.

FEEDBACK AND FINDINGS

For the purpose of providing feedback to the sponsoring agencies of the workshop, replies to a questionnaire administered at the beginning and end of the workshop are summarized below.

The following themes were found to recur frequently during T groups, S groups, and the various community exercises:

1. Vacillation between reacting to an issue as "me, an individual" or as "me, a black."
2. Clarification and questioning of personal values.
3. The effect of parental conduct and relationships on one's behavior and personality.
4. The difficulty, and gratification, of understanding and accepting others.
5. Dissatisfaction with the teacher-pupil relationship.
6. The difficulty of understanding—and communication—between blacks and whites with emphasis on the need for whites to take initiative in this direction.
7. Lack of agreement as to the needs, values, and goals of "blacks" by blacks.
8. The difficulty of communication between young and old, with the greatest difficulty being experienced by the young.
9. Student grievances against the schools.
10. "Black" charges against a racist society.
11. Feelings of being dehumanized by others, and by the society as a whole.
12. Evidence of disagreement among blacks being as great as between whites and blacks as to defining basic "back-home" applications of the group's experiences. This black-black dichotomy was seen as one of the problems "back home" (i.e., in the school and community).

SUMMARY

The workshop seemed to achieve the basic, first-step objective of opening up communications between student and teacher at high-school and college levels, between teacher and teacher at different levels in the educational system, between administrative and faculty functions, between youth and adult and black and white.

Within this resultant environment, the consideration of the various aspects of curriculum and instructional relevance appeared to provide a more constructive dialogue and candid critique and a more open expression of feelings and attitudes than could have otherwise been achieved in the didactic atmosphere of a conventional meeting.

SCHOOL-COMMUNITY

There are many community problems that cry out for attention to the human issues involved where encounter techniques appear most valuable. Examples are police-community relations, drug abuse, relations among varying ethnic groups, and so on. Perhaps the most expeditious entry into the community arena is via the school-community vector. This is what occurred in the Willingboro program.

The approach used was a *task-centered interactional workshop*. In such a workshop, both the *process* of participant interaction and a defined task calling for specific, *pragmatic* recommendations are emphasized. In some ways, this resembles the theme-centered workshop described by Ruth Cohn elsewhere in this book. However, here it is not only focus on themes that is stressed but a requirement that participants both develop and apply their problem-solving and conflict-resolution skills to produce an actual and implementable program.

The school district of Willingboro experienced phenomenal growth in the 13 years between 1957 (the birth of a Levitt community) and 1970. From a student population of 85, housed in one building and serviced by a professional staff of four, the district has expanded to a student population of approximately 14,000, housed in 12 buildings and serviced by a professional staff of over 700.

The impact of this growth and the accompanying changes within the community contributed to the development of problems in communication and interaction among various levels within the school organization (school board, administration, teaching staff, students) and between the school system and community agencies of government.

The superintendent of schools in Willingboro, Dr. Gabriel Reuben, explored outside professional assistance in initiating approaches to (1) improved communications within the school system, (2) more effective interrelationships between school and community systems, and (3) the development of a coordinated school-community effort to deal with the problems of growth and change in Willingboro.

The result was acceptance of a task-centered interactional workshop designed by Princeton Associates for Human Resources as the first step in achieving coordinated movement toward common school-community objectives.

PARTICIPANTS

Invitations to attend the workshop were extended to school board members, administrators, and teachers. The final list of 38 participants included:

  2 Willingboro township officials (the mayor and the police chief)
  5 members of the school board
  3 central school administrators
11 school building administrators
  4 high-school department chairmen
  3 guidance counselors
10 teachers

OBJECTIVES

Preprogram. Needs and objectives emerged from a series of interviews conducted by group leaders with each member of the school board, the superintendent of schools, and the director of special services.

Program. The laboratory workshop was designed to be a task-oriented workshop within an interactional framework. It was considered of primary importance to facilitate a concrete plan of action coming out of the workshop that represented the thoughts, feelings, desires, and determination of the participants concerning an ongoing human relations program for the school system and community. Hence the workshop included two features:

1. The interactional process. This involves facilitating the participants' awareness of how they deal with each other, handle conflict, solve problems, plan, and make decisions and of the influence of their feelings and attitudes in these activities.
2. The creative task. This task was geared toward the objective of the workshop, that is, the designing of an ongoing, comprehensive human relations program for the Willingboro school system and community. It is the attention to the interactional process that permits an effective approach to the task of coming up with a pragmatic, negotiated, and implementable proposal created and "owned" by the participants.

Elements of the program were sequentially designed to:

1. Provide an atmosphere that would encourage and foster free, honest, verbal communication among board members, administrators, and teachers on any issue of concern.
2. Develop a sense of trust among the participants.
3. Maximize participant interaction with as many different people as possible.

4. Provide the opportunity for participants to gain a better awareness and understanding of feelings, needs, values, and attitudes.
5. Develop an awareness of how feelings and attitudes affect one's behavior and the impact of that behavior on others.

Many of the procedures utilized in this task-centered workshop were employed in the curriculum relevance project. There was, however, more emphasis on strengths and weaknesses and focus on cognitive and communication exercises.

As a result of the continuous feedback throughout the workshop, the following themes were found to recur frequently during T groups, S groups, and various exercises:

1. Dissatisfaction with student-teacher-administrator relationships.
2. Feelings of lack of support and direction for middle-administration management (principals, assistant principals, and so on) by upper-level administration.
3. Teachers feeling ignored, and without satisfactory status or recourse.
4. The difficulty of understanding—and communication—between blacks and whites.
5. Indications of insensitivity to the needs of minority-group members in the schools and community.
6. Concern for improved student-police relationships.
7. Clarification and questioning of personal values and attitudes.
8. The need to further enhance human relations in the schools and in the community.

SUMMARY

There seemed to be an over-all sense of "community," in which each individual was valued and with common objectives to which individual commitment was high. Despite mixed expectancies, various components of the school-community developed a productive working relationship and produced workable suggestions and plans to which they were committed. The board of education, administrators, and faculty, in unprecedented fashion, were able to communicate and agree, or agree to disagree. This was true as well for the city administrators, who were both open to and contributing of innovations in programs. Therefore, not only were programs suggested, but those in positions of influence were committed to their implementation.

Industry

The task-centered interactional workshop, of course, can be applied in appropriate form to industrial as well as other organizational entities. In business, it is necessary to indicate that the objective is productivity, and when the goal is human productivity, this must be related to the process—not the other way around. That is to say, it is unreasonable to expect the businessman (or any administrator for that matter) to appreciate that dealing with communicative processes maximizes the productive use of the human resource. It isn't even always true. But if there are defined problem areas, participants can address themselves to practical and creative solutions when they set themselves this task. At the same time they are helped to become aware of their processes and vehicles of communications, problem-solving, conflict resolution, and decision-making. The comprehensive attention to these processes and relationships of systems to each other in an organization is called organizational development (OD).

Blake and Mouton (1970) define OD as a systematic way of inducing change, progressing in a programmatic sequence of steps from individual learning to organization application. There is an emphasis on confronting and resolving conflict as a prerequisite to valid problem-solving and employment of a variety of techniques of organizational study and self-learning to bring about needed change. I shall not cite OD examples here because they are similar to the Willingboro program and because they are described elsewhere in this book by William Gellermann.

A pressing need for society in general and business in particular is the integration of the disadvantaged—the unemployed and underemployed, often minority—worker into the work force.

The National Alliance of Businessmen has reported varying statistics, but 75 to 80 per cent is the figure usually quoted for the turnover of such employees who do get a chance for employment. Their attitudes about work, money, and time and their very self-image are all blurred, and if such workers are not dealt with patiently and creatively, the odds are heavily against their retention (National Association of Manufacturers, 1968).

PAHR has been involved in a number of projects associated with the National Alliance of Businessmen. One such project was for a moderate-sized rubber products plant in Trenton. Over-all turnover for the plant had been about 58 percent, and there was a 78 percent turnover for employees who might be considered disadvantaged (previously unemployed or sporadically employed). The training consultants were engaged to design and implement a human-relations program for one hundred newly hired disadvantaged employees.

An orientation was instituted for all components of the company: executive management, foremen, "buddy" coaches, and new employees. In this way, everyone from the president of the firm to the entering new employee was familiarized with the over-all program and involved in its implementation.

An outline of this program is presented below.

PROGRAM DESCRIPTION

ORIENTATION
A. *Executive management orientation*
   1. In order to ensure the success of the company's new hiring program, company's "top" executive management was involved with and committed to the objectives of the program. This was the primary purpose of the one-day executive management orientation.
   2. This orientation included a review of the entire program and an explanation of its implications for the company and the extent and importance of executive involvement.
B. *Supervisory orientation*
   1. The success of the company program was greatly determined by the extent to which the company's staff and line supervisory management and union representatives were prepared to contribute to the successful integration of the new JOBS-program employees into the work environment and work force of the company.
   2. With this purpose in mind, the supervisory sessions were designed to:
      a. Review the over-all program, its objectives, the potential problem areas, the role of the participants in the program phases, and their understanding of the human relations implications.
      b. Prepare supervisors for the difference in values that the new JOBS-program employees may have as compared with other members of the work force.
      c. Develop an awareness of the needs, attitudes, and feelings the new employees will bring to their jobs.
      d. Apprise supervisors of the kinds of problems they may have to cope with to establish acceptance of regulations by the new employees.
C. *Orientation of job coaches ("buddies")*
   1. The purpose of any job coach is to train a new employee in

how to do his job. In many cases, this is the responsibility of
the foreman; the idea of the job coach is to pay attention to
more of the details than the foreman may have time to do,
especially if the foreman also has to be a productive worker.
In the case of the JOBS program, the company wished to
be sure not only that all of the new employees to be hired under the program understood their job and learned how to do it
as quickly and efficiently as possible, but also that if any new
employee had any personal problems *that might affect his job
performance,* the job coach would be able to help the new employee resolve the problem.

The company designated ten of its regular employees from
various manufacturing operational departments to serve as
"buddies." Each of the ten "buddies" was responsible for
10 new employees as they were hired under this JOBS program.

D. *New employee orientation*

The purposes in devising the particular kind of orientation for
the employees to be hired under this program were:

1. To demonstrate a genuine interest in and concern for providing a meaningful employment opportunity with possibilities
   for growth.
2. To convince the new employees that the company is interested
   in their needs, is aware of and sensitive to their attitudes and
   feelings about the requirements of working in an industrial
   setting.
3. To establish a relationship based on genuineness, acceptance,
   and understanding of the new employees by the company.
4. To provide a sense of belonging to a team, by the assignment
   of "buddies" and by regular group meetings as part of
   human-relations training involving not only the new employees but regular employees and supervisors.

The company hoped to determine the beneficial effect of this
kind of orientation for new employees so that some form of
orientation could be adopted for regular use in the hiring of
employees in the future, after this program had been completed.
As each group of new employees (20 the first time and 10 every
two weeks thereafter) reported on the payroll the first day, they
participated in a three-day orientation conducted jointly by the
company and the training consultants.

HUMAN RELATIONS TRAINING SESSIONS

A. *Purpose*

The company wanted to ensure that during the first few months of employment the new employees hired under the JOBS program were given every opportunity to adjust to the work environment and the requirements of their jobs. To facilitate this, all the new employees attended weekly human-relations training sessions conducted by a professional group leader/trainer.

It was the purpose of these sessions to determine how the new employees were getting along in terms of job performance and relationships with their supervisors (foremen) and with fellow-workers, how they felt about the requirements of their jobs, whether they felt they were making progress toward personal goals, and how they felt about the company.

B. *Composition*

In order to maximize the desired results of these human-relations sessions, the composition of each group was as follows:

10 new employees
1 job coach buddy
2 supervisors (foremen)

C. *Feedback*

It was intended that work-related problems that arose during the week would be fed into the weekly human-relations session by the employees, the job coach, the supervisory job coach buddy, or the participating supervisors. This not only enabled the group leader to develop an open discussion of problem areas but provided feedback to company management for the purpose of improving its relationships with all employees for long-term benefit after the JOBS program was concluded.

CONCLUSION

One tangible result of this program was an increase in retention of employees from only 22 percent to almost 80 percent. Another consequence was an examination and rehauling of the over-all company orientation, training, supervisory, and management practices.

BIBLIOGRAPHY

Bidwell, C. E. The School as a Formal Organization. In J. G. March (ed.). *Handbook of Administration and Organization Theory*. Chicago: Rand McNally, 1966.

Blake, R. R., *et al.* Breakthrough in Organizational Development. *Harvard Bus. Rev.*, **42**:133–53, 1964.

Blake, R. R., and Mouton, J. S.   OD.—Fad or Fundamental. *Training &
Devel. J.*, **24**:9–17, 1970.

Blank, L. Group Techniques in the Schools. In G. Gottsegen and M. Gottsegen. *Professional School Psychology III*. New York: Grune & Stratton,
1969, pp. 51–72.

Effectively Employing the Hard-Core. National Association of Manufacturers, 277 Park Ave., New York, N.Y., 1968.

Ferdinand Jones
Myron W. Harris

 The Development of
Interracial Awareness
in Small Groups

COMMENTARY

This is a report on the use of small groups to study racial attitudes of individual blacks and whites trying to communicate and to reduce the barriers to that communication. A predictable pattern of approach, resistance, avoidance, and contact has been observed and described in detail. Implications for understanding communication difficulties of large interracial groups in American communities are discussed.

BIOGRAPHIES

Ferdinand Jones is on the faculty of Sarah Lawrence College where he offers courses in psychology and in black studies/social change. He is dedicated to the more extensive contribution of social scientists to the movements to correct social ills. He and Myron Harris started their work with groups in 1965. This is one of several projects concerning white racism that they are engaged in together or separately.

Dr. Jones was born and raised in New York City, where he attended public schools. He received his A.B. degree from Drew University in 1953 and his Ph.D. in psychology from the University of Vienna in 1959. He is a member of numerous professional organizations and maintains a private practice in Hartsdale, New York.

Myron Harris, Ph.D., trained as a clinical psychologist at New York University and Bellevue Hospital. He has been school psychologist at Bronxville, N.Y., has taught at Hunter College and Columbia University, has been psychologist with New York Hospital, educational counselor with Urban League of Westchester, and consultant with community agencies, and is currently in private practice with young people and families. He is coauthor of the textbook *The School Psychologist*. He has been white coleader of black-white discussion groups for five years, part of the effort to free himself of the distortions and misconceptions resultant from growing up in a white-dominated society that insisted on its being considered as a democracy for all.

We shall be describing a method directed toward reduction of barriers in understanding between black and white individuals. We shall also be indicating a philosophy from which the method derives.

Two clinical psychologists, one black and one white, were appointed by their local psychological association to study ways in which psychologists could more actively serve their community with their professional skills. Meeting together, they agreed that the field of choice was very wide. Most of the apparent alternatives did not seem to utilize the special abilities and qualifications of psychologists. The two psychologists then embarked on a series of dyadic meetings of several hours' length in which they discussed their own experiences—as the white suburban Jew growing up, seeing, experiencing, but never closely knowing blacks, and as the urban black living under the ghetto restrictions and seeing himself reflected in the eyes and attitudes of a white majority. The experience was planned as an effort to inform each other, and to resolve the differences of observation, attitude, and prejudice that would prevent the two psychologists from working together. For the white, the most striking knowledge gained was the degree to which his experience and his viewpoint (and he was a liberal thinker who had been peripherally concerned with and even at times working in the field) had blinded him from understanding many of the judgments, the nuances of communication, the jokes, the "soul," and the motives of his black counterpart. As for the black, the comprehensive quality of his guarded stances vis-à-vis whites became articulate in a way that it had never been for him, and the accompanying anger and hurt were allowed new, direct, and unqualified expression. He could experience himself with greater objectivity and with a sense of relief.

Out of this ferment of exchanging and changing views came the decision that for this pair of clinical psychologists their contribution could be that of helping other individuals—black and white—to examine and clarify their attitudes and to deepen their emotional/ intellectual understanding of one another.

The implementation of the decision for action was then established on certain basic postulates:

1. Without exception, Americans have grown up in a country whose ingrained, thoroughly established racism has held an integral and cherished place in American culture.

2. The principle that the black race is inferior to the white race is the essential element of American racism. The incompatibility between the established belief (and consequent practices) and that which many of us have wished to believe that we believe is the area to which these efforts would be directed.

3. The processes of therapeutic interchange can assist in resolution of the inter- and intrapersonal conflicts over racism, thus diminishing cognitive dissonance and hopefully leading to more rational behavior. It may be necessary to stress here that the numeric majority of victims suffering from the intrapsychic conflict over racism are, of course, white.

THE METHOD

The procedure was to hold workshops of varying duration as experimentation with the method determined. None had been less than four sessions and less than one hour in length. The customary schedule has emerged to be six to eight weekly, hour-and-a-half sessions followed by a long (six-hour) session. The number of participants has ranged from 5 or 6 to 25; 10 to 15 is considered optimal. From the beginning and in all instances the leaders have been invited by individuals interested in this kind of experience for themselves or their staffs. The racial composition of the groups has also varied. Most frequently the majority are white; in some instances the only black was one of the coleaders. The black-white leadership is essential in these experiences. It provides an example of an interracial team working in the manner in which we want the group members to work; it allows the members to observe the leaders in frank discussions of their feelings toward one another and toward the many issues involved in black-white interrelationships.

We have generally been asked to provide services by individuals who have concern about some setting where black and white people must relate to one another. Characteristic problems prompting such invitations were:

1. A school system that had been newly integrated through the merger of two formerly segregated districts was prompted by its local citizen task force on integrated education to look into methods for helping teachers understand the needs of the black community.

2. The staff of a large metropolitan hospital had long been severely divided. A strike of nonprofessional workers of which 90 per cent are black brought previously submerged racial tensions to the surface. Although the labor and union issues involved traditional strategies and familiar labor-management divisions, the racial differences remained highlighted after the strikers returned to work. The psychiatrist in charge of one ward on which resident psychiatrists and other mental health teamworkers are trained wanted to confront and resolve the differences.

3. Professionals who wished to work in interracial settings—as consultants to agencies, as teachers, as psychologists in poverty programs, and so on—or individually sought opportunities for improving their communication with other-race individuals and pursued a better understanding of the dimension of the problems in themselves.

4. A mental hygiene clinic with a predominantly white staff working in a community that has an increasing black population recognized its inadequacy in providing services that meet the black population needs. The clinic was concerned that white therapists could not find themselves in meaningful communication with black clients of a generally lower socioeconomic class.

5. The specifics were generally unclear to another group requesting these experiences, although the problems were felt to be quite definitely within the black-white relationships. They were phrased in such general terms as "to understand more how to work with the community," to "get along better, to understand black people better," "I want to learn how to help the black children in my class who seem to have trouble learning," "I don't like raising my children in an atmosphere of this much suspicion and hatred —I want to know what my hang-ups are."

THE BEGINNING

We begin by explaining the basic tenet, on which we base our approach: that in tone, practice, law, and custom we have all grown up in this racist society and have been influenced and shaped by it. Most of our influencing has taken place without our being aware of the learning steps, inasmuch as we have been part of a society that has struggled to deny the racism that has been specifically written into law and engraved into practice. We operate on the postulate that the more each of us can understand that which we have been through in growing up, what our experiences have been, then the clearer each of us can be about thinking and acting in honest, unstereotyped, nonracist ways.

The process, we explain, involves forced examinations of one's own attitudes, beliefs, and reactions; it is a procedure for self-examination. There are certain ground rules we go by: the focus of our discussion, although therapeutic in its general framework, centers on black-white relationships and the background of our feelings about them. This is not group therapy in the conventional sense, for there is a definite limit on the range of topics discussed. If we seem to be getting away from that central focus, the leaders of the group point this out and attempt to return to the black-white core. Openness of communication is a highly valued goal—it is better to speak openly of our hatreds, prejudices, or fears than to attempt to mouth the platitudes of brotherhood.

How It Works

Because the fundamental theory behind having a black and white leadership is to present a representative relationship in which the expression and the interrelating of the two leaders can act as a model for stimulation and guidance for others in the group, we begin by discussing our relationship, how we began to explore in this area, and the manner in which we spent several long, dyadic sessions together attempting to understand each other's experiences as black and white. This leads into a frank statement of prejudices, distortions, and apprehensions that one or the other of us has experienced or has continued to experience, e.g., Harris's (the white) childhood belief that somehow all blacks knew each other, his later conviction that being nice to blacks meant freedom from prejudice, and one of his more recent discoveries such as the awareness that his attitude had really been one of trying to make sure that these foreigners or Negroes were treated as fairly as any whites in this country—followed by his realization that most blacks' ancestry in this country dated back two to three hundred years, although his went back only two generations. Jones has referred to some such recent experience as that of explaining to a group of white teachers (after a meeting in which he and other blacks and whites had addressed them) the frustration and anger he could feel at the anonymity or invisibility of individual differences that most whites impose

upon blacks—and the polite disavowal of such attitudes on the part of
the teachers with the intimation that perhaps Jones was not seeing
things clearly. At this point the white teacher-hostess had come up and
addressed Jones most politely as "Mr. Parks (one of the other black
speakers), wouldn't you like some tea?"[1] With this lubrication, or encouragement toward self-expression, people began to talk, speaking of
their own experiences, their reasons for being at the workshop, and so
on. Generally, the first discussants tend to be white.

INTRODUCTORY PHASE (MAY EXTEND OVER ONE OR MORE MEETINGS)

The whites begin by talking about their own attitudes and beliefs, often
using specific experiences to demonstrate. The main theme of these
introductory remarks generally can be summarized as whites making
"I'm a good guy" statements, calling on such evidences as the following:

> I had a friend in college who was black and we got along very
> well together. There was never any trouble between us; we used to
> go out drinking together and for one year even roomed together.
> We never ran into any difficulties at all.
>
> When I was a kid we grew up in a neighborhood that was inte-
> grated and my best friend was a black kid. We used to fight other
> kids a lot, we used to visit in each other's homes, and we never
> even talked about black and white relationships.
>
> I have a very good friend who works in the same office I do and
> there are lots of times when we talk about things that are happen-
> ing—like the violence in the streets, Martin Luther King's as-
> sassination, the savagery of southern politicians . . .
>
> I never had any prejudice because there were no blacks at all
> where I grew up. I went all the way through school and college
> before I even met a black. It was obvious that I never formed any
> prejudices. And then after I got married, I moved to Scarsdale.
> My cleaning woman and I were the best of friends; when she came
> in, we would sit down and talk over coffee for a good period and
> we shared many experiences and dealings together. I felt about
> her as I would feel about any other of my friends.

[1] Those readers who have reacted to this description of Jones with the thought that
he is being "oversensitive" or that such circumstances could happen to anybody, black
or white, are referred to a later section of this paper headed "Secondary Phase" re
whites' initial reaction to blacks telling it like it is.

I'm very confused as to why the blacks are so angry. All of them that I have known seem to be making a good start for themselves, have jobs, and really are quite respectable and responsible people. It seems to me that instead of talking about black-white conflicts these people are going to be helped by education and chances to get jobs.

Several years ago I didn't believe I was prejudiced; I wouldn't even have thought about it; I just believed that I looked upon everyone in the same way. Then recently I began to question myself with some of the things my teen-age daughter kept telling me about what she thinks of my attitude.

These initial movements under later reflection appear to elaborate quite specific white efforts, i.e., the struggle to gain black approval by being seen as free of guilt and responsibility for the racism that both parties know to be taking place in our society, and the effort to maintain an acceptable nonprejudiced self-image.

One black group member described this as the white seeking for his "report card," a process that he encountered frequently, not just in these groups. Another member described it as whites looking for "the black housekeeping seal of approval." It has the goal of finding one black who will say "You're okay" and then the white can settle back with evidence that he shares no prejudice or responsibility for racism. It is so frequent a process as to find almost inevitable occurrence in white group members—either in their reporting of prior experience or in their searches for acceptance in the group.

Our interpretation of what is taking place during this introductory phase is that the whites are struggling to counteract the opening statements of the white coleader who has described the omnipresence of American racism in our society and has strongly implied that no whites have escaped being infected with this. They use the methods described above or they remain silent. It is an interesting manifestation of the effort to subdue distress or discomfort, because essentially what many whites are saying is that they have already reached the end goal for which they have enlisted in the workshop.

The blacks are generally silent for quite a while, apparently waiting to see how the whites express themselves. Soon, however, one of the black members begins to talk about his or her experiences of being black—the struggles with whites, the struggles with oneself, with the setting of goals, and to protect one's children from the ego-damaging experiences that one has had. This is a matter of "telling it like it is," of informing and teaching whites. If there has been some delineation of specific experiences with whites, and the black feelings about these,

Figure 19-1. Telling it like it is. (Photo by Zev Guber.)

we move directly into the next phase, the white counterreaction.

The whites have been silent while listening to the blacks' expressions, acting as though they are in a learning situation and being patiently interested in the process. There is an almost intangible emanation of strong sympathy as if to say, "Oh, I really feel how it is," or "How terrible that was!" This is not always put into words, but sympathetic sounds or facial expressions are brought forth. At this point the white apparently has been trying to express his concern for the black and to somehow dissociate himself from any responsibility for the existence of conditions that have caused such pain to his fellow group members.

The next step—characterized by the need to further separate oneself from the oppressing or undemocratic factions—then emerges as the whites begin their efforts to demonstrate that they too have experienced discrimination, minorityship, or persecution. There may be a German-Jewish refugee in the group; in our experience in the New York area this takes place frequently. This individual announces that fact and thereby, in intention, announces his unanimity with the blacks, his freedom from prejudice, via the logic of "How could I possibly practice prejudice or discrimination when I have suffered it myself and I know what it feels like?" The point is developed in many different ways—the Catholic who grew up in a predominantly white Anglo-Saxon Protestant community, the white child chased out of a neigh-

borhood by the blacks, the Jewish boy who couldn't go with his friends
to church and was at one point physically attacked by them, or the
proclamation of freedom from prejudice through such bona fides as
membership in left-wing political movements or engagement in dangerous left-wing political activities. These expressions are seen not only as
being efforts to dissociate oneself from the unwanted prejudice, but
also as the intragroup search for common ground on which to speak
and understand the basic problems.

THE BARRIER

What impedes this kind of group communication, however, is the
impossibility of finding that common ground. Analogies of a fundamentally absurd nature come forth; i.e., to be a member of a white
society in America, and to find oneself temporarily in a subminority
of that grouping, does not constitute the same thing as being a member
of a minority that has been restricted, oppressed, and, to one degree
or another, enslaved by law, tradition, economics, and massive white-
power Establishment control. Indeed, to be the well-accepted member
of a community—a member succeeding economically, educationally,
and in all other ranges of individual accomplishment—and to then
have the controllers of the society turn upon one with primitive savagery and genocide is terrifying, tragic, and inhuman. But it differs
fundamentally from the experience of life-long degradation, of programmed emasculation and hidden restrictions, that have been the lot
of the black in this society. The fundamental point, it becomes clear, is
that whites cannot find a common group identity with blacks because
blacks have an experience with whites that whites have never had with
each other and do not even realize.

The whites in themselves have learned and practiced the customs of
their society in such a way that each white individual is a part of what
the blacks are talking about as they tell it like it is. A white member of
one group, well after the introductory phase was over, reflected on
this dilemma with what we have come to call "Simon's parable."

It is as if a group of lions had walked into the sheep meadow
and sat down with the sheep, saying, "I know what it's like to be a
sheep and attacked by lions." The lions come in with warmth and
friendship, sheathing their claws and their strength and smiling
warmly. And then they're dismayed, shocked, and hurt to discover
that the sheep don't trust them! They say things like: "Some of
my best friends are sheep. When I was a kid I palled around with
sheep. I never ate any sheep. My family did and all the lions I
grew up with did but I never did. Of course, when we grew up and

started in with our jobs—you sheep doing your job of lying around and grazing, and us lions getting to our work of chasing animals and killing them for food (after all, we are meat-eaters) —then my sheep friends and I tended to grow apart. But I still have the greatest respect for all the sheep that I see, and I tell my kids that they should always be nice to any sheep that they see and never kill any of them except if they have to feed their kids or protect property values or things like that."

The lions are astonished when they find out that the friendly sheep have always been mad at being kept in the meadows and being chewed up on occasion. They always thought that the sheep liked the way it was, and that the sheep understood that all the lions were trying to do was to keep their children well-behaved and well-educated at school, that all they cared about was that their young cubs should grow up to be outstanding and upstanding Lion Club members.

And it is with real horror and anguish, soon turning to fear, that the lions discover that many of the sheep have actually turned into Panthers.

Secondary Phase

Because it has been demonstrated that getting together is as yet impossible, there ensues a struggle on both sides to somehow establish a means of communicating with each other. It is evident that the group still wishes to stay together, to try to establish some means of reaching the goal toward which they have all enlisted themselves.

The black members of the group take up with greater vigor the job of telling it like it is. They do so with largely rational approaches, unimpassioned other than with a somewhat missionary or zealot's effort to explain precisely what life as a black has meant in this country. This is the struggle to reach a mutual understanding that seems to have, from the black point of view, the hope that "if I let you know about my experiences, you will understand what it has been like." As one articulate black professional youth worker expressed it, "If you want to relate to me, this is what you have to recognize and realize and what you have to accept." The statement is meaningful, for at this point in the group development, the whites have most persistently focused on their wish to know the blacks better and to have the blacks relate back to them.

The whites, however, fight accepting this black definition of the black experience in this society. They do so with such statements of doubt, denial, and disagreement as are expressed in the following characteristic phrases or paraphrases:

That *is* terrible, but you know I didn't do it, I'm not responsible . . .

You don't really look at these experiences accurately; you're not seeing them properly.

They didn't mean that when they called you "boy" or "you people."

You're oversensitive . . . you've got a chip on your shoulder . . . all you people do.

One interpretation of this white reaction is that for the whites to accept the validity of the black statements means facing the enormity and pervasiveness of white-over-black and their inescapable part in it as white citizens reaping the benefits of a society in which racism is intrinsic.

With the blacks having opened up somewhat in the presence of whites and having committed themselves to this struggle to inform whites, and with the whites having listened but rejected, there follows a period of frustration and immobilization. On occasion, in later phases of greater frankness, blacks have referred back to their anger toward whites at this period, for once again they hear the white man telling the black how to think, telling him that his perceptions of the world are wrong, and that only whites can tell him how things really are. However, at this point, there is seldom such direct hostility expressed. Instead, feelings of immobility are spoken of or generally set in as the consequence of this failure to establish mutual understanding. The two groups are still on different wave lengths.

Certain reactions then tend to take place as resistance to moving into the real depths of feeling mounts. Blacks may drop out of the group after expressing (or even without stating) such judgments as, "It's useless . . . all whites are the same . . . I've been through this before, it's no different. . . ," "I'm tired of spending my evenings trying to help educate whites. . . ," "I've too many more important things to do than to sit down in a room and help whites get over feeling guilty. . . ," or "It's just the same old jazz all over again; whites aren't going to change."

The whites feel and express a sense of disappointment in the group's progress. They claim, "Nothing's happening," "I got so disgusted with everybody last time I didn't want to come back," "We don't seem to be talking about anything—we're just going round and round and I haven't gotten any feeling out of this at all." Or whites may retreat to earlier defenses such as, "I really think everyone should get along without fighting—look, we're doing it," "Other people are too sensitive," or "I think protest is fine but what I don't think makes sense is all that burning and looting . . . people ought to be able to sit down sensibly and talk things over like we're doing."

Many blacks, as well as whites, stay on in efforts to try to establish some basis for relationship. Apparently this drive to continue and strengthen the intragroup ties that are forming remains strong, and both blacks and whites bypass the frustration by seeking subsidiary levels of relating. Superficial communication, reaching into diversionary places for the attainment of a sense of mutuality, of oneness, of understanding, takes place. A black member and a white member discover with great pleasure that "we're both interested in hunting" and proceed to talk for some moments about that until one of the group members suggests what seems to be happening. Others divert their emotions into pledges of loyalty to the group: "We all realize that this group is really important to us and we want to stick to it." There is a poignant search for something to talk about that is not contaminated by the disturbing reality of the black-white noncommunication and the sprouting shoots of terrible distress and anger that all are beginning to realize lurk there.

It is during this phase that the patience of all members is tried. Often the leaders may experience a sense of discouragement and doubt that they will ever get to the necessary engagement. The leaders have consequently tended to become more aggressive at such a point; for example, the white—whose role as provocateur of feelings provides many opportunities to stimulate anger, hurt, warmth, or distress—on one occasion asked of a half-Caucasian, half-Oriental member who had been expressing strongly "liberal" views how he felt when he was mistaken "for being a Negro." The discomfort that this individual clearly experienced at this question helped him and others to reach down to a more intimate level of feeling. Or the black leader may frankly express his feeling of discontent and impatience with the "chatter" that is going on. It should be noted that the personalities of the two leaders have been in these groups such as to present a relatively calm and friendly personal image. The whites have come to know their black group leader as sympathetic, humane toward them, and not given to those kinds of frightening militant attacks that have driven them into guilty confusion and resistance. Thus it is that when this black reports the same attitudes of distrust, anger, and profound discomfort with whites (until proved otherwise), the group is shocked into a greater realization of the universality of the black experience, but this may not be lasting.

The white, expressing the point of view that attributes the primary cause of trouble to white racism—albeit unconscious and inculcated in the preindependence years most susceptible to imposed learning— is usually criticized strongly at some point by other whites: "I resent your acting as though you can speak for all whites," "You don't know what my experiences have been—how can you say that?" "I've been turned off by him all the way through. From the first day it was clear that he was on the other side."

The group, wanting to stay together, often attempts to start talking about other forms of interpersonal problems. There frequently begins a forceful attack on some group member for being unpleasant, arrogant, or prejudiced. This seems to be a procedure of scapegoating, in which, for the most part, the whites join together to attack as the villain some individual who has left himself open for the accusation of prejudice that all others are trying to find not present in themselves. There is certainly a basis for the observation that prejudice is being expressed, but the struggle of each group member to defensively avoid looking into his own feelings seems to contribute to this effort to cast stones at that individual who has made himself susceptible. It is at this point that whites talk about their reactions to other whites in generally interpersonal rather than specifically black-white terms; e.g., "Claire always makes me angry when she starts talking," "I was thinking about what you were saying about your experiences last week and I don't think you had to be so angry and fearful about things. That was really some kind of prejudice," "I think you should begin to look at some of the things you've been saying. You'd see that you really have a lot more hang-ups than you realize." These are white-to-white efforts to therapeutically give solutions to another white as to how to think. We have come to see this whole phase as somewhat of a latency period in which people seem to have to cast about for some period of time until an emergence of truth occurs: a black speaks out and somehow is listened to with intensity and acceptance.

THE MOMENT OF TRUTH

This has been a most significant occurrence and has impressed us as the necessary ingredient to kick the discussion off into more therapeutic growth directions. It is a moment in which a black individual's anger becomes *unequivocally* expressed. It is not tempered by the need to question oneself, to placate other group members; it is not diluted or distorted by black doubt as to adequacy or other feelings of inferiority; it is an ultimate explosive statement. It may not always emerge with raging anger; the tone in which it is presented is not the critical point, but rather that a black's feelings have led him to finally say what it is like without fear of retaliation, shame, or doubt hinder-

Figure 19-2. The moment of truth. (Photo by Gary Madderom.)

ing his statements. Such assertions as these are taken from moments in different groups:

> I don't give a damn who likes me; I don't give a shit what they think about me. I'm going to tell it like it is at this point and they're going to hear it.
>
> I was away from the group last week; I was down in the islands on my vacation and I thought a lot about what's been going on and I decided I was going to come back in here and blast their asses off.
>
> I'm tired of all this damned talking—I hate every white I've ever seen. I can't trust any one of you here. I'm tired of having to act like a good nigger.

The essential element here seems to be that the feeling is brought out so strongly and so honestly as to dominate over expressions or emotions of lesser intensity. The domination may be through rage, or it may be through a calm, systematic, and comprehensive statement. For example, in one group a new member appeared for the final session, which was of several hours' duration. This man, a black psychiatrist, was known to the group (the staff of a clinic) and was obviously in a position that held prestige and commanded respect. He explained the problems he encountered as a black in the community, doing so in a quiet but unhesitant manner, even smiling at times as he portrayed circumstances and feelings, telling it with most restrained certainty. It was in fact not clear to the white coleader that this was "the moment of truth," and he could not understand what had mobilized the group to greater depths of expression until later when the black coleader told him that this black psychiatrist, on leaving an hour before the meeting had ended, said to him privately, "I'm sorry I have to leave —I wanted to give it to a few more of them."

There are times when this role of bringing the truth out with passion and direct shock has to be carried by the black leader. The essential of it seems to be the turning of an individual generally seen as quiet and congenial into one revealed as furiously angry; this is no longer a matter that can be rationalized or denied by the whites as happening to some wild-eyed ghetto dweller or to some unreasonable blacks "out there." It is an unquestionably valid emotional-intellectual expression by a member of the group whom they well know. Thus, when the black leader expresses his own unanimity with militant black attitudes, when he explains that he too enjoys attacks on whites, there is general disbelief and astonishment, e.g., "But you're not really black, you're white," or "But you don't seem like other blacks; I can't believe what you're saying."

The moment of truth introduces a new and deeper form of black-white relationship, a period in which the real probing work of self-examination begins. The black who has been participating for this long period, with hope, cannot be seen as alien. He is known and felt as a member of the group, he is one of us, and he says, "I've tried it; I've tried to make it with you whites on a friendly basis and it doesn't work!" His exasperation forces the whites to look and to listen. These are words from someone who has been a coworker, someone who has been a positive and hopeful member, who has stayed with the group rather than drop out—and he has reached the end of his rope! In one group there was a black member who had been seen as conciliatory and unassertive, had been accused of "Uncle Tomism" by other blacks. When he broke loose and told how he felt, the group could not help but listen. There is some reason to believe that if this had come from another black member of the group, one who had been more overtly expressive of his distrust of and anger toward whites and had been already identified as provocative, there would be significant doubt as to whether any expressions of force that he would have made could have provided this moment of truth, because the group's defenses already had been constructed against him. Further, at such a moment, the group is not able to use customary analytic defenses against the person's statements; there are brief efforts to say, "That's his problem," "That's his personality . . . he's just an angry person," and so on, but this does not suppress what has been said as it might have at an earlier time.

The whites usually try not to hear it for a brief period, by means of withdrawal, silence, brief protests, or rationalizations—all of which seem to be efforts to calm down the anxiety they have begun to feel. But soon the whites do listen.

Often at this point the blacks have a conflict among themselves about whether to support this forceful statement, to deny it, or to avoid it. If they, the blacks, can come out in support of this statement, the group begins to move. If the blacks are hesitant to endorse such a statement, it takes longer to reach this point of accelerated movement. The role of the leaders is important here; if only one black member is present and he has made this statement, or if the speaker remains largely unsupported by other blacks, the black leader helps by authoritatively endorsing the statement. If there is only the black leader present, he must carry the ball, provide the moment of truth, and follow through.

The whites generally sit quietly and listen to the interchange of black attitudes and to the blacks' evaluations of one another. Many of the whites tend to feel stunned as they seem to realize that there is a vast difference between how they thought things were (from the liberal, "I'm trying my best to do all I can" viewpoint) and what they are suddenly beginning to realize is the reality of how things are in the stark clarity of black expression. The contrast between sympathetic understanding, warm-hearted liberalism, and the real awareness of the black experience is etched out. As one white psychiatrist commented after the moment of truth was initiated by a black psychiatrist colleague, "I'm just realizing that there really is something different— it's not like being a Jew." In another group a vigorously articulate white member, who had, several sessions earlier, been part of a violently angry exchange with an equally volcanic black member in which accusations of racism and prejudice were thrown back and forth, expressed his sudden awareness that a "pocket of distrust" had to be there in all blacks: "They know what's been taught to the whites; they know what the whites have been thinking about them all the time . . . and even if they find that it's not there with some whites, with white friends of theirs, they can't help but be on guard for the insults or the patronizing showing up when they least expect it. Blacks just always have to be careful."

Insight is gained into more of the facts of the matter and also into the awareness that no white has ever had the totally degrading, unyielding presence of American racism settling on him. Identification takes place, a matter of significant moment, as the whites recognize

the difference between sympathetic awareness and actual identification. Even if it be a fleeting glimpse, enough has been established to
considerably restrict the limits of later attempts at denial.

But the whites also recognize what it is the blacks are hating, that
the whites are the objects of the hatred and the blacks are the bene-
ficiaries of white exploitation and false superiority. This may lead to
the white's realization of his own part in the American society's
process that has generated this hatred—and at that point the white
group members may begin to question all the activity in which they
have been involved in support of civil-rights activities, all the liberal
protest, movements, parades, and so on. It is with a distressing wrench
of awareness that the white notes that he has been in a different dimension, that in fact he has been playing in a different ball park, living
in a different world, and often seeing things from an opposing viewpoint. Sometimes this is expressed in a sense of despair; at other
times there may be a response such as that of the head of a hospital
ward who was brave enough to expose himself to the judgment of his
staff and who ended up with their respect and acceptance after a few
weeks. One woman similarly could not understand why the group was
hostile to her description of how she had fought back bravely against
a racist dinner partner until later dawning insight helped her to see
that brave liberal positions were considerably different from valid
identification with black refusal to accept degradation.

There ensues a self-forced review of white experiences in the past
with blacks, or of situations relating to blacks. The whites tend to think
over these circumstances in light of the new insight, the new, closer
awareness of what it means to be black. The whites begin to develop a
much clearer, frightening inkling of how things are; they begin to
view themselves and their lives through newly focused glasses. Such
expressions as the following characterize this:

> I've been sitting here listening to what Bill has been saying and
> thinking about myself. I've been realizing that I have a feeling of
> superiority in me toward Bill and toward Ferd (the leader), but I
> haven't been able to figure out why. I thought maybe it's because
> I have a doctorate and not everyone else does—but that doesn't
> seem right; I've really gone through that. Maybe it's because I
> think I can talk better, but I haven't been doing very much talking
> in this group and I've been impressed with what people have said.
> I get down to the fact that I think I'm superior because I'm white
> —that upsets me but that's it and I don't know what to do about
> it.
>
> I'm beginning to realize that the statement I made at the end
> of the last session when I said I would treat a white client and a

black client exactly the same way—when I said that without even
a minute of thinking about it—was wrong! I know now that I
couldn't be thinking the same about both of them. I know that
I've got some things to work on and we've got to do a lot of
talking about it.

Well, I'm scared of those kids. They come in and they talk to
me about black protest movements and black anger. I'm here to
teach them and I really want to give them the chance to learn well
so that they can go on to college and do the things that they want
to get done. Why don't they leave their anger at home?! The thing
is that I know that they are not going to learn from me as long as
I'm feeling scared about them that way, and I know that they can't
stop being enraged as long as things are as they are in this community or, I guess, in this country.

However, not all the whites in the group go through this process of
insight and beginning self-examination. Some seem to be unchangeable; this seems the only conclusion one can make from the rigidity
of their voiced expressions, from their implacable insistence that
everything is fine in their thinking, that perhaps there is this one little
quirk such as not wanting one's daughter to marry a black, but that's
easily avoided and implies nothing of any other prejudice that could be
disruptive in a black-white relationship. Those individuals who tend
to have developed their personalities around the repression of impulses
and awareness are likely to resist what opportunities for insight are
available to them in this intensity of group experience, and thus come
out of the workshop with little apparent change.

Another category of unlikely-to-change whites we have termed "the
polite-lady syndrome"; these are individuals, not always female, who
immediately express their wish to be understanding and friendly, their
eagerness to be of help in the antiracism struggle, and who frequently
turn out to be eager to protect anyone against whom some aggression
seems to be pointed. They are likely to apologize for those individuals
in the group who make overt prejudicial statements or those who
openly come forth and state that this is a problem with them. The
"polite lady" is afraid to look into her own feelings of fear and aggression, and her anxiety leads her also to attempt to prevent others from
looking into these upsetting areas. The role is palliative in general and
specifically obscurant of revelations of reality.

Some examples of whites' attitudes in this category are as follows:

Sally was a young mother who identified herself with the current younger generation and expressed liberal ideas that had
moved rapidly to the radical thinking epitomized by the Students

for a Democratic Society. But as she experienced the shock of the moment of truth, she seemed to find nowhere to go; she expressed bewilderment as to what she really felt, asked, "Tell me what I should feel," and remained in a state of indecision as she found the process of moving from general liberal/radical thinking into specific identification with black action-directed attitudes too unsettling.

Harry, a psychologist, reported in the first session that he was eager to see the black revolution succeed and that his only concern was that things were not moving rapidly enough or with enough wisdom and therefore the blacks might defeat themselves. As the sessions continued, however, it became clear that he had never really been able to allow himself to look at black attitudes from a black viewpoint, that in dealing with patients who were black he had never initiated any discussion of their feelings about working with a white therapist. He was hesitant to invite black colleagues to his home lest they be insulted by the attitudes of neighbors who would be patronizing or not understanding. Although he certainly wanted to feel identity with the right way of thinking, Harry could not understand the difference between the right words and a true identity with black attitudes.

As has been stated above, the process that seems to take place in whites at this stage is one of self-examination and self-evaluation, leading them to choose either to resist the process and maintain themselves in the earlier posture or to become so aware of the black reality of American racism that their identification with black feelings, black anger, and black insistence on change becomes strengthened. The conclusions suggest that the procedure is a self-expanding experience, but not for all individuals—that some people do not respond to the method we have been describing for emotional/attitudinal changes.

During this same period in the group's progress, the blacks have been generally participating to help the whites understand or have been largely silent. However, a process of self-examination and understanding parallel to that which the whites have experienced has been taking place, and the blacks begin to be much more open in their expression of attitudes toward one another. It seems as though they are feeling in a manner later expressed by one participant as: "Listen to that! Maybe we can really get something across this time!" There seem to be relief and surprised delight that this group of whites are really listening and struggling to understand, struggling to see what the black experience is like and to correct their earlier misconceptions. It has been striking to recognize that many of the black participants have been impressed and, to some extent, encouraging

Figure 19-3. Maybe we can really get something across this time. (Photo by Zev Guber.)

and supportive as they observe that the whites are at least beginning to question themselves and are really immersed in the effort to change what they have grown up with. At such moments the black members have often been far more patient with expressions of white conflict, awareness of prejudicial attitudes, and so on than have been the other whites.

The struggle for blacks at this point seems to be that of freeing themselves of any taint of fear-driven accommodation in attitude and of trying to grow strong enough to express their anger at having to live with inferior status. The fact that these discussions can be held openly in this black-white group is seen as a clear statement by the blacks that they feel themselves in an atmosphere of trust among these whites. The setting at this point seems to be one in which the individual is openly working on his internal problems, with a feeling of trying to grope and grow that was not there earlier. Blacks and whites are freer to make statements of a prejudiced or frightened nature that they never were able to say earlier, and to help each other with resolution of the problems. For example:

Irene, a black woman, reached out to help Irving, a white, in his conflict over the problem of asserting his right to choose his own woman rather than being dependent on his parents' approval.

Irving, Jewish, said that he could never bring a black woman home to his parents, that this would so alienate him from them that he would have to sever all connections—this despite the fact that he could conceive of himself as being strongly attracted to or in love with a black woman. Irene expressed with the warmth and affection that she felt for Irving that he had to know that he was a man, that he had to let himself find his woman and be with her, and that if he denied himself this in order to keep peace with his parents, he would never be either adult or happy.

Another exchange took place between two black women, one expressing her anger at the other's denial of ever having experienced significant prejudice or discrimination. She claimed that the second woman, lighter in skin, was struggling to act white and was thereby denying herself and failing to feel pride and satisfaction within herself.

Two black professional mental health workers tossed accusations of Uncle Tomism at each other as one accused the other of being scared of the whites and needing to try for the boss's friendship. Even as they argued, however, it was clear that a kinship of understanding bound them together, and each knew that the goal was that of growing into a courageous independence.

The whites' understanding of what is taking place in black-black confrontations deepens their awareness of the internal black struggle; they can comprehend the strivings for emancipation from self-hatred, self-denial, and self-destroying fears. Often the whites, beginning to feel more comfortable with their attitudes, are able to participate and help resolve some of these conflicts by expressing their view of what is taking place. It should be emphasized, however, that many of the whites, those of the "polite lady-syndrome" or those who have not been able to engage in the self-examination procedure, do not find it possible to be of value in this person-to-person interchange.

In general, however, a climate of openness has been achieved, and the condition for relating without much of the distortion and superficiality engendered by black-white emotional distance has been accomplished.

CONCLUDING PHASE

In the climate of increased openness the most striking features are two: the demonstrations of mutual trust, and the indications of awareness that change must take place immediately rather than in some idealized future. Blacks seem to strengthen their convictions and attitudes about their own self-worth. Whites seem to have turned the corner of awareness and have begun to re-examine and restructure their thinking and perceptions. This is not to say that all participants in the workshop experience these changes or that there is a uniform pace. We are impressed, however, by distinct attitudinal shifts on the part of the majority of group members at this point in most of our workshops.

We have judged, at the current stage in our experience, that the goal we strive for in ending is the initiation of a process. Sometimes it is called "thinking black." This refers not to skin color but to the release from, or continued subjection to, the tight cords of the racist-bred anguish in self-concept, and dissonance in relationships that were formerly present. The white has been able to begin the process of freeing himself from the distortions, closed-mindedness, and inculcated ignorance that have helped him deny his mutual humanity with the black. And the black begins to find release from the self-hatred, the doubts, the fear, and the distrust that have forced defensiveness and separation on him.

Evaluation

Clearly, measurement standards need to be established in a more objective manner. However, we find the following circumstances to be indicators of change:

1. Both black and white members of our various groups report that they have experienced changes in attitude and climate within the group itself.
2. We observe a shifting of topics from the generally defensive or protective to the far more personal and intimate, and that the communication on these lines is done on a cross-racial basis.
3. Individuals become more direct in asking for help in dealing with problems and conflicts in interracial communication and action. Help is asked for and given in sensitive areas without the customary restrictions and closed-mindedness induced by racially stereotyped preconceptions of one another.

Conclusions

1. Effective evaluation of the procedure will rest on the development of appropriate research methods to measure the nature, duration,

and effect of attitudinal and emotional changes taking place in the groups.

2. Many individuals report that they have been able to operate with greater freedom from stereotyped thinking after the group experience, and therefore that they felt themselves able to deal with reality issues with greater practical objectivity.

3. Because the therapeutic direction of these encounters has been to free the participants of distortions in thought and emotion (with the ramifications into self-concept, confidence in self-assertiveness, methods of handling fear and anger, and so on), we would conclude from the therapeutic hypothesis in general that release from distortions leads to increased productivity.

IMPLICATIONS

On the hypothesis that some positive change has occurred, we must then consider the implications for broader fields of application:

1. There is evidence that people sharing a problem, i.e., the distance existing between individuals of different races, and then brought together with the encouragement of open and frank discussions on this topic, are able to significantly lessen the social and emotional distance between them. There is therefore reason to believe that this leads to increased effectiveness in their subsequent work problem activities together.

2. Groups of individuals responsible for the administering of working out of problems that involve black and white persons, e.g., boards of education, hospital staffs, city councils, police departments, church leaders, human rights commissions, and teachers, are in key positions of influence. These positions should require a more comprehensive understanding of the black-white relationships in this society than is generally the knowledge of most blacks or whites. The opportunity for developing this understanding would further the opportunities for such influential community leaders to effectively serve their total communities.

3. We are discussing individuals who are engaged in sensitive and responsible positions vis-à-vis other citizens. We are not here speaking of institutionalized racism with the vested interests and economic value that stem from and support the maintenance of these institutions. We are aware that there are many strong and hostile dissident forces that are vigorously seeking to impose their extreme views as the solution of racial difficulties. Unless there

is in these groups some consideration of interracial cooperation toward mutual goals, there seems little likelihood that such humanistic approaches as are represented by these workshops would be useful.

4. The parallel between the claims of many blacks that only violence awakens white concern and movement toward change (e.g., Watts, Detroit, Newark) and our evidence that it takes an explosion of unexpected black anger to awaken deep white concern and movement toward change is striking. Is it possible that we are seeing in the workshops a microcosm of the workings of American society as a whole?

Although we remain optimistic about this work with individuals, our findings provide little ground for optimism in believing that reason next time will replace the fire that seems to be the customary mechanism for initiating significant social change.

BIBLIOGRAPHY

Fanon, Frantz. *Black Skin, White Masks.* New York: Grove Press, 1967.

Jordan, Winthrop D. *White over Black: American Attitudes Toward the Negro.* Chapel Hill: University of North Carolina Press, 1968.

Kovel, Joel. *White Racism: A Psychohistory.* New York: Pantheon, 1970.

Lester, Julius. *Look Out Whitey! Black Power's Gon' Get Your Mama!* New York: Dial Press, 1968.

Stringfellow, William. *My People Is the Enemy: An Autobiographical Polemic.* New York: Harcourt, Brace & World, 1964.

Part E

Theory and Research

Bernard G. Rosenthal

20 The Nature and Development of the Encounter Group Movement

COMMENTARY

Bernard Rosenthal offers a subtle, far-reaching psychosocial and philosophical analysis of encounter phenomena. He concedes the immense potential value and importance of this movement and takes into consideration the possibility that the sensitivity approach is a phenomenon akin to a manifestation of a declining Western capitalistic civilization.

BIOGRAPHY

Bernard G. Rosenthal has been professor of social psychology at the Illinois Institute of Technology since 1964. Prior to that, he served on the faculties of Princeton, Harvard, and the University of Chicago. He did his undergraduate work at Northwestern and received the M.A. and Ph.D. degrees at Princeton. He is the author of over 30 papers in psychology, and his book *The Images of Man* has been published by Basic Books this year. He has been an officer of SPSSI and of the Association of Humanistic Psychology and has also served as cochairman of the Greater Boston Committee for a Sane Nuclear Policy and as chairman of the Greater Illinois

Faculty Committee on Vietnam. He is currently coeditor of the journal *The Human Context.*

The encounter group movement is one of those extraordinary phenomena of the times that both has a significant and encouraging character and, at the same moment, is symptomatic of deeper forces in contemporary society and possibly, as well, of all complex societies undergoing the stresses of conflict and change. Thus, it deserves the most searching psychologic, sociologic, and historical analysis, not only for its particular content and significance for mental health, personal growth, and actualization of human potential, but also for the characteristics it may have in common with similar movements at other historical periods, for its connection with eruptive forces in an unpredictably changing world, and for its possible function in diverting concern from more fundamental social and personal issues.

The thrust of this chapter, then, will be to address itself proximately to this analysis and these issues. Therefore, little or no attempt will be made to make a taxonomic analysis of the types of encounter group experiences[1] and their distinctive properties; the numbers, demographic features, and varieties in orientation of its growth centers; the social and psychologic characteristics of seminar leaders, speakers, and sensitivity trainers; the socioeconomic and other important attributes of the clients who attend these centers and the governing boards who direct their policies; the fee schedules for participants and the compensation rates for seminar leaders; and, finally, the generalized or particular content of the seminars, group sessions, and self-actualizing experiences. In the absence of a comprehensive collection and analysis of such data, which, it goes without saying, should be carried out, the following essay will be based on whatever summary materials and evidence are presently available. Thus the presumption will be made here that a general picture, if quite impressionistic, has emerged of the materials and experiences of the encounter group movement, of its professional practitioners, and of the constituency of its paid participants.

At the outset it must be emphasized that nothing said in the course of the following analysis should detract from those salutary qualities that mark the encounter group movement. These include an open and unimpeded orientation to sensation and feeling; the search and affirmation of genuine personal identity; the effort to achieve interpersonal understanding through the acceptance of the feelings of one's self and others as well as through the dissolution of interpersonal ritual and

---

[1] See other chapters of this book on these points.

hypocrisy; the elimination of intellectual defensiveness as a barrier to emotional insight and mutual understanding; the liberation of affirmative sexual impulse and other positive feelings; the achievement of a richer awareness of one's affective potentialities, inner experiences, and diversity of esthetic, sensory, and proprioceptive impulses; the extension of empathic sensitivities to the responses and deep personal experiences of others; and the enrichment of compassion and warm, generous feeling toward particular individuals and to the world in general.

This, then, is a kind of renaissance of man—the feeling, generous, spontaneous, authentic man—that the encounter movement through its various procedures and techniques presumes to abet. If so, surely no humanistically oriented person can deny it is not only a reaffirmation of some of the most fundamental qualities of man—qualities that have accounted for his great historic contributions and biologic persistence —but a restoration of these fundamental attributes to proper and proportioned recognition both in the scheme of experience and in the field of psychology. Further, it is an exhilarating affirmation in the sense that it is opposed to the prevailing disregard or antagonism of middle-class, materialistic, organizational-bound culture toward these qualities and related human patterns.

Nor would anyone concerned with advances in the nature of psychologic science or further explorations in human consciousness deny the value of the various sensory, meditative, introspective, and interpersonal methods or techniques that, in general, the encounter group movement and its allied orientations have contributed to American experience. The opening of the sense modalities to awareness of heretofore latent experience and feeling, the exploitation of numerous previously untouched areas of consciousness and unconsciousness, the investigation of various mystic and spiritual conditions, and the incitement to awareness and intensive exploration of interpersonal mutual experience are all substantive matters of great importance. Thus, in issues and topics to be acknowledged and scientifically investigated and in areas of experience that have richly added to our awareness of man's resources and potential, the encounter movement has made significant contributions.

But one may look at the movement in another perspective, concerned with, as previously implied, its relation to the present human condition, its reflection of a particular state of human desperation, its one-sided emphasis on sensationalism and excitements, its lack of a broad human philosophy or a social and moral direction—in short its deficiency of informed and enlightened humanistic perspective, its significance in repeating a particular stage in the cycle of human history—notably one of decline—its lack of a broad-based view of man including his social functions and fully spectrumed capacities, and, till now, its arrant anti-intellectualism as expressed not only in its aversion to theory and conceptualization but also in its indifference to an integration of such "humanistic" areas of experience into the broad field of psychologic science and into balance with issues of ethics, social values, human goals, and philosophies of life. Let us consider these issues in order.

SENSATIONALISM AND EXCITEMENT

Another view of the encounter group movement would see it, in broad canvas, as an expression of the disintegration of the coherence of a society, of the decline of its ruling spirit and ethos, and as the frenzied search for individual indulgence and pleasure inasmuch as its binding ties and organic value orientations have deteriorated. As a consequence, there is no longer a substantial human purpose, a cohesive value system, or a meaning that gives direction and significance to life and that provides a medium and goal in accord with which human beings can orient their work, the upbringing of their children, and the fabric of their lives. Because of this dissolution of the vital spirit and thrust of the society, humans are left without purpose, direction, personal meaning, and social or existential identity. As a consequence, personal alienation increases, authentic and meaningful personal relations are fragmented, the texture of group coherence and community commitment is undermined, and a sense of personal loneliness, abandonment, and isolation grows apace. The growth in feelings of suspicion, conflict, anxiety, and lack of trust or intimacy as well as a decrease of warm, accepting altruistic human relations, in this view, is a direct result of the lack of purpose and the undermining of collective and valuative ties that, whether evident or not, guide the unity, coherence, identity, well-being, and future hopes and purposes of a society.

The sources for this deterioration may vary. According to Spengler (Spengler, 1926) and Geddes (Geddes, 1915), all great cultures go through a cycle of birth and decay; according to Toynbee (Toynbee, 1947–1957), there are similar stages with, however, the proviso that there may be rebirth, whereas to Spengler decay is inevitable. According to other cultural or economic historians (Borkenau, 1934; Gerschenkron, 1968; Lukacs, 1962; Marcuse, 1964; Mumford, 1964; Rostovtzeff, 1957; Schumpeter, 1939 and 1947; Strachey, 1935; Usher, 1937; Weber, 1968), however, contemporary anxiety, loneliness, and fragmentation are a result of a particular economic system in an accelerated process of deterioration, of an excess of mechanization without human consideration, and of the exploitation of human beings as things and objects rather than their generous and empathic treatment.

In addition to these causes for personal alienation and group fragmentation, there is also the dissociation of work activity from interest and satisfaction in it, the discrepant and often incompatible compartmentalization of the various social roles that one plays in life, the sense of anonymity due to immersion in mass society, the profit- and success-oriented values of the marketplace and indeed of most social life, and the sense of personal impotence in the face of an implacable bureaucracy and mass governmental power. All these factors, too, add to the sense of dehumanization, lack of personal authenticity and identity, and deficiency in the fulfilment of one's genuine humanness and of one's distinctive human capacities.

To these conditions, contemporary men—as did those in comparable stages of past historical cycles—react by an intensity of sensation-seeking, a thirst for excitement, and a drive for extremes of pleasure and violence. Such indulgences have the function of compensating for their spiritual and existential death, for their social fragmentation, and for their occupational mechanization. It is from such a broad perspective that one must see the frantic urgency for all sorts of thrills, for intense visual, auditory, or muscular stimulations, and for novelties of taste, whether they be of interpersonal, physical, sensory, sexual, or other varieties. It is from despair and pessimism that such excitements are bred in order to make men feel human and "alive" again. Nor are these conditions unique to contemporary times. They have occurred, historically, say Spengler and Toynbee, at each period when, like today, the ethos of society has been fractured and man has lost his spiritual courage and has suffered a failure of moral and human nerve. Thus, as Roman power waned, such sensationalism grew rampant, marking the impending decline of society as was the case in Byzantium in the eleventh century and in Paris at the end of the *ancien régime*.

Indeed, in an analysis of the same historical conditions but from the perspective of city development, Patrick Geddes has contended that we are in goodly measure now living at the fourth stage of historical development, or that of megalopolis, whose characteristics Mumford describes as follows:

> Beginning of the decline. The city under the influence of a capitalistic mythos concentrates upon bigness and power. The owners of the instruments of production and distribution subordinate every other fact in life to the achievement of riches and the display of wealth. Physical conquest by military means: financial domination by trade and legal process: loans, mortgages, speculative enterprises. The agricultural base extends: the lines of supply

become more tenuous: the impulse to aggressive enterprise and enterprising aggression grows as the lust for power diminishes the attraction of all other attributes of life: as the moral sense becomes more callous and the will-to-culture increasingly impotent. Standardization, largely in pecuniary terms, of the cultural products themselves in art, literature, architecture, and language. Mechanical reproduction takes the place of original art: bigness takes the place of form: voluminousness takes the place of significance. Triumph of mechanism in every department: passivity: manual helplessness: bureaucratism: failure of direct action.

Megalopolis ushers in an age of cultural aggrandizement: scholarship and science by tabulation: sterile research, elaborate fact-finding apparatus and refined technic with no reference to rational intellectual purpose or ultimate possibilities of social use: Alexandrianism. Belief in abstract quantity in every department of life: the biggest monuments, the highest buildings, the most expensive materials, the largest food supply, the greatest number of worshipers, the biggest population. Education becomes quantitative: domination of the cram-machine and the encyclopedia, and domination of megalopolis as concrete encyclopedia: all-containing. Knowledge divorced from life: industry divorced from life-utility: life itself compartmentalized, finally disorganized and enfeebled. Representatives: Alexandria, third century B.C.; Rome, second century A.D.; Paris, eighteenth century; New York early twentieth century.

Over-investment in the material apparatus of bigness. Diversion of energy from the biological and social ends of life to the preparatory physical means.

The city as a means of association, as a haven of culture, becomes a means of dissociation and a growing threat to real culture. Smaller cities are drawn into the megalopolitan networks: they practice imitatively the megalopolitan vices, and even sink to lower levels because of lack of higher institutions of learning and culture that still persist in bigger centers. The threat of widespread barbarism arises. Now follow, with cumulative force and increasing volume, the remaining downward movement of the cycle.[2]

Megalopolis is succeeded by the fifth stage, tyrannopolis, many of whose features are prevalent today.

---

[2] From *The Culture of Cities* by Lewis Mumford, copyright 1938, by Harcourt Brace Jovanovich, Inc.; renewed 1966 by Lewis Mumford. Reprinted by permission of the publishers.

Extensions of parasitism throughout the economic and social scene. Politics becomes competition for the exploitation of the municipal and state exchequer by this or that class or group. Extirpation of organs of communal and civic life other than "state." Caesarism. Development of predatory means as a substitute for trade and give-and-take: intensification of the cycles of commercial depression, following overexpansion of industry and dubious speculative enterprise, heightened by wars and war-preparations. Failure of the economic and political rulers to maintain the bare decencies of administration: place-hunting, privilege-seeking, bonus-collecting, favor-currying, nepotism, grafting, tribute-exacting become rife both in government and business. Widespread moral apathy and failure of civic responsibility: each group, each individual, takes what it can get away with. Widening of the gap between producing classes and spending classes. Multiplication of a *Lumpenproletariat* demanding its share of bread and shows. Overstress of mass-sports. Parasitic love of sinecures in every department of life. Demand for "protection money" made by armed thugs and debased soldiery: organized looting, organized blackmail are "normal" accompaniments of business and municipal enterprise. Domination of respectable people who behave like criminals and of criminals whose activities do not debar them from respectability. Imperialistic wars, internal and external, result in starvation, epidemics of disease, demoralization of life: uncertainty hangs over every prospect of the future: armed protection increases all the hazards of life. Municipal and state bankruptcy. Drain of local taxes to service increasing load of local debt. Necessity to appeal to the state for further aid in periods of economic disorganization: loss of autonomy. Drain of national taxes to support the growing military establishment of the state. General loss of nerve. Attempt to create order by external military means: rise of gangster-dictators (Hitler, Mussolini) with active consent of the bourgeoisie and systematic terrorism by pretorian guards. Recrudescence of superstition and deliberate cult of savagery.[3]

Such, then, is the condition of modern men according to these cultural historians. In their view, the present portents of decadence—reflected in the spirit of *la dolce vita*—may have, if in a more respectable and cultivated way, certain parallels in the encounter group movement. Not completely, of course, for there are many affirmative dimen-

[3] *Ibid.*

sions and prospective signs of renewal in that process if they are given force and positive direction. But surely, the exploration of every experience for its own sake, the unstructured indulgence in each and every sensory stimulation, the promiscuous titillation of interpersonal sensuality and inner spiritual experience—all without a value orientation, balance, broader social purpose and context, or reasoned direction, and despite a patina of credible ritual, humanistic language, sophisticated procedure, and appropriate appeals to the humanistic and psychologic ideals in whose name they are produced—may well reflect the conditions of *la dolce vita* and sensationalism characteristic of the times.

ESCAPISM OR OPIATISM

From another view, the encounter group movement may represent an escape or diversion from the authentic humanistic challenge of the day-to-day world—the true arena of depersonalization and alienation —by allowing its practitioners to get their humanistic fulfilments in those week ends or seminars at which there is no serious threat to their everyday mode of life, no immediate challenge to their daily vested commitments or economic and materialistic interests, and no serious jeopardy to their social positions in the established society of which they are a part. In this view, the sensory explorations, inner experience, and the like of the encounter movement permit the luxury of humanistic-like indulgence, of liberated affect and sensation for an interval of time, and, possibly, of temporary renewal in order to return afterward to the depersonalization, interpersonal manipulation, and materialism of the "real" world that nurtured the alienation and, as a result, the fragmented rebellion against it. Thus, the division between the encounter group movement and life reflects, in part, the very dissociation between genuine interest and conformist activity, between authentic humanistic experience and ritualized counterfeit behavior, that the encounter group was designed to resolve.

In these respects, the encounter movement represents an escape from the fundamental issues that a more genuine and courageous humanism would face in the world of everyday life, bringing whatever wisdom and power it could summon to bear on the realistic human issues it confronted and on the political and social world that would be the legitimate arena for its activity. By diverting this active humanism to disassociated-from-real life issues, it never comes to gauge its real power, test its effectiveness as compared with other values in the crucible of life, and plumb its root meaning and capacity for yielding human gratification in the face of other competing needs (materialistic, power, survival, status) and satisfactions (family, friends, work, career), but rather becomes an abstract, escapist, indeed a rather precious quality by virtue of its isolation from all the other realistic human and social issues that, simultaneously, it disingenuously trumpets it should confront.

In a sense, then, this form of encounter group orientation and its satellite experiences (sensory awakening, inner meditation, affective excitement, and so on) is really a middle-class recreation, a diversion, a relief from the mechanization, dehumanization, and ennui that it was developed to confront and rectify. As such, the question must be raised whether it is different from any other middle-class recreation or diversion—a week end in the country, a *la dolce vita* interlude, a trip to Europe, a wild party, and the like—in its capacity for evoking authentic human feeling and experience. Is its function, then, in these respects no more than that of affluent middle-class "kicks" with a patina of sophisticated ideology and of avant-garde, esoteric delight? Of course, it gives its participants a sense of being liberated, enlightened, and sophisticated, in tune with the advanced themes of the day and the movements of the young (the hippies, the yippies), and to that extent gives them a sense of renewed youth and freshness—a brief diet of uninhibitedness that doubtless middle-class life sorely needs. But the issue still remains whether this is any more than personal release or indulgent recreation with a facade of sophisticated "advanced" ideology or myth to give it sanction and respectability.

Indeed, some of these recreations or entertainments have a markedly sexual component: one sympathetic observer has called certain encounter week ends nothing more than expensive bawdy houses with a serving up of intellectual dessert. They are, at times, a curious world—ecstatic, pleasure-seeking, with just the right recipe of a Ph.D. psychologist or consciousness-widening practitioner disseminating wisdom and insight either to explain what is being "experienced" or to calvinistically expiate any residual guilt from the pleasures enjoyed by the acquisition of knowledge or by spiritual elevation.

It is not inconsistent with this appraisal that the fees of these encounter week ends or occasional seminars are high, and the constituency who pay them are rather affluent middle-class Americans seeking relief from the ennui, dreariness, oppression, and even desperation of their commercial, conformist, flat lives. Where, better, can they revitalize their jaded and jejune orientations, excite their dulled sensibilities, reinvigorate their oppressed sexual appetites, reawaken their interest in a life beveled by the mechanization, shrewdness, cunning, artifice, and control of the workaday world they are compelled to inhabit than at these spas of esthetic, sexual, and sensory delight, which, at the same time, satisfy their middle-class desire for respectability, status, and values received by giving them a goodly dose of knowledge, spiritual elevation, and intellectual enlightenment to make up for any guilt suffered or profitless time spent during the periods of pleasure-seeking they have engaged in.

For some, the world of encounter groups is not unlike Viennese society between World War I and the coming of Hitler: a society of hopelessness, desperation, and pretense. On their comparable week ends, the Viennese middle class of the day—affluent and directionless —would put on masks emulating the various roles of the persons they would have liked to be: lover, hero, pleasure-seeker, adventurer, explorer, and the like—all the roles and functions in which they could not participate in everyday life—and on these week ends, like children in a make-believe pantomime, would achieve the fantasied satisfaction to sufficiently buoy them up to return with less ennui or asperity to their dreary everyday lives. Nor is the nature of these week ends and seminar encounters, in the large historical view, substantially different from that of the pleasure-seekers of Rome at the decline of the Empire, the court of Charles II marking the end of the Restoration, the *après moi le déluge* and *fin-de-siècle* excitements of the Bourbons before the Revolution, and the ecstatic delights of Byzantium before the end of its world. What did all these experiences amount to: a last ecstatic and pleasurable gasp to hide the wounds of despair and purposelessness; a frenzied excitement of sensation and thrills to mask the failure to confront the overwhelming issues of the real world—a world in which there seemed no avenue for satisfaction of affirmative and vital human impulse or in which the options for an authentic human renewal and for purposeful and fulfilling resolution of the deepest problems of human frustration, meaninglessness, and corruption appeared not likely to emerge.

OPIATISM AND THE UNWITTING MAINTENANCE OF THE STATUS QUO

As a result of these factors, it is not remarkable that many have claimed that the encounter group movement has unwittingly sustained the very forces that called it into being, i.e., the status quo. By diverting the desperation and resentment engendered by the prevailing sociocultural system to innocuous transient satisfactions, it has prevented the confrontation and attack on the very issues that have spurred dehumanization. By encouraging temporary self-actualization at episodic seminars and on week ends, it has artificially and falsely transformed the humanistic impulse and value orientation into a nonauthentic process in a closed-chamber environment and thus given a rather illusory view of its nature and power. In so doing it has asymmetrically dealt with the humanistic dimension, overweighting it disproportionately and not correctly assessing its magnitude or influence in conjunction with the realities of life and the power of other functions. Thus it has established an illusory world—an Eden as it were—for many of man's oppressed humanistic urges and faculties but, by the same token, it may have simultaneously served as a release valve for them and accordingly have funneled them off from the obligation of tackling the hard issues of the real world that a genuine humanism must face. In so doing, it has weakened, where most needed, its real quality, power, and capacity for integration with nonhumanistic factors and where, too, this might have a reconstructing effect of greatest significance in daily life.

Indeed, if an examination were to be made of the participants in these encounter experiences, it might be found that a very large portion of their constituency were those middle-class persons who are essential for the maintenance of established society but who, also, are rather disenchanted with the psychologic gratifications it offers. Committed as they are through tradition and training to the day-to-day roles they play, to the status positions they enjoy, to the substantial incomes they receive, and, in general, to the materialist gratifications and related establishment attitudes they acquire, it is extremely difficult for them to directly confront worldly activities with genuine humanistic orientations or to analyze them in terms of the humane and generous values they pursue in the encounter experience, isolated as it is from the authentically realistic world. For to do so might evoke doubts about the means and ends of their income-pursuing methods; raise skepticism about their support of or silence on so many established institutions and status quo practices that are antihumanistic, ritualized, and repressive of the very values they say they wish to be realized; call into question their day-to-day relationships with their colleagues, business associates, or family; and, in general, raise disconcerting questions about their conformity, materialism, acquisitiveness, overpracticality, cunning, repression of free impulse, lack of interpersonal openness, and deficiency of inner spiritual experience.

No wonder that these humanistic satisfactions, interpersonal delights, and sensory explorations are sought not in the real world but rather out of it in the seminars, week ends, and discussion groups where the hard, practical urgencies, status demands, and materialistic regards of authentic day-to-day life are not operative. Here, one can indulge in all these diverted and repressed delights without fear of jeopardizing one's status, job, income, and, often enough, related establishment attitudes. Thus, one may have one's cake and eat it too:

the frustration and depersonalization bred in the real world whose earthy gratifications and material rewards one does not wish to renounce are satisfied in quite another world with quite another group of experiences that do not threaten the patterns that one follows in day-to-day life. Indeed, the very dissociation between these two worlds serves to sustain the viability of the practices followed in the real one while giving the impression, by virtue of engaging in the diversionary encounter experiences, that one is genuinely humanistic or has dipped deeply into the wellsprings of being a real human being. Thus one feels one is humanistic, i.e., has an opening on the humanistic view, but, at the same time, is protected from applying this humanism too deeply, too genuinely, or too perceptively to the institutions that subvert it. In this way one may rationalize one's compliant if not unquestioning participation in the nonhumanistic world because one is engaged in a kind of pseudohumanistic life as it transpires in a particular diversionary week end or escapist world. In this way one may not only obtain some gratification for the frustrated human and sensory needs of the real world but may also feel that one's humanistic obligations have been discharged, or, at least, that one has the proper "in" humanistic attitude.

It should be noted here, as preliminary to a more extended discussion, that the issue of whether the experiences, behaviors, and insights engendered in encounter groups and their satellite agencies are extended into the real world, generalized to others in everyday contacts, and embodied in deep-lasting attitude or behavior changes has been but little investigated. But surely this is a significant factor in whatever impact the encounter group experience may have.

Yet, willy-nilly, we know little about it as if, from a cultist or parochial view, it is not terribly important to know how humanistic experiences have an effect on one's outside life so long as they are satisfying in the "encounter world" itself. If this is true, it would be clearly consistent with the contention that there is a deep chasm between the encounter group and "real" life and that the former is a diversionary experience or bromide whose value—and possibly purpose—is to distill and symbolize a separate dimension of life and not one of genuine alliance with a realistic humanism confronting the world of everyday existence.

DISSOCIATION OF FEELING FROM COGNITION

Though there can be no quarrels with the encounter group movement and its allied satellite experiences in terms of the enhancement and liberation of sensory freedom, interpersonal relations, and emotional enrichment, a nagging question nevertheless remains whether this is at the expense of rational purpose, the role of discrimination and logic, the place of moral and ethical value, and the nature of economic and social reality, or, in short, at the expense of the functions of intellect and knowledge of human experience.

The emphasis on feeling, elementary sensory experience, interpersonal spontaneity, spiritual elevation, and esthetic delight is all understandable and valuable in the encounter movement. These are precisely the qualities and themes denied in the workaday world of mechanization, bureaucratization, and materialism. What is not so clear is the tenacious outcry against intellectualism, against historical knowledge of the issues that the encounter movement wrestles with, against putting "feeling" into a context of judgment and reason, against a rational consideration of the emergent forms and values of the emotional experiences that are aroused in encounter sessions, against consideration of the role and priorities that reason, morality, social goals, philosophy, and even expediency should have in the direction of and relation with emotion, and against a detailed and balanced consideration of how feeling may contribute to human wisdom and happiness and how it may not. Related, also, is the resistance against the consideration of its optimal integration with a philosophy of life and salutary social ends, its intelligent use to achieve thoughtfully or deeply valued goals rather than to exclusively serve as a vehicle for promiscuous expression, and its wise and proportionate outlay with which to obtain optimal pleasure over a maximal interval of time rather than its release in transitory, intensive, and often jading indulgence.

The concern with feeling for itself without reference to purpose, direction, values enhanced, public policy sustained, social organizations supported, way of life abetted, and image of man subserved is one of the characteristics of this movement. Without question, it can be a healthy antidote to the ritualization and ennui of the role-playing of the day-to-day world except if these feelings, themselves, become ritualized, the encounters, themselves, become affective role-playing games, and the procedures of inducing spontaneity and richer interpersonal relations become a product of a mechanistic mold. Beyond this, what must be remembered is that feeling qua feeling may lead to excesses of self-indulgence without reference to other values, human resources, or concern for others. This indulgence in feeling, by itself, without reference to human or social consequence may not, in principle, be different from the social psychologic matrix out of which emerge collective frenzies, hate manias, and other varieties of social or political fanaticisms. Such emotional indulgence can lead to vast collective delusions whether of persecutory, messianic, benign, or barbaric nature and to systematized escapist patterns and rituals. At the personal level, they may appear as impulse-ridden, excessively sensate, sensation-seeking, and yet other asymmetric forms of uninhibited affect.

Though such unmodulated expressions have a symbolic significance for the protest against the dehumanization and ritualization of present times, in and of themselves they reflect no direction, no ethical end or value, no prescription for a wise or even fulfilling human condition, no social goal or context of societal values, no broader philosophy of life, no defined view of what potentialities of men have prior or lesser importance for their achievement of happy self-actualization, and, in general, no view of what constitutes the conditions of human happiness and the hierarchy of feelings, sensations, and cognitions necessary to achieve it.

To the contrary, the practice seems to be that any feeling, sensation, or spiritual experience is an end in itself provided it be either intense, broad, exciting, diverting, or delightful enough as well as resistant to the ennui of repetition. The end, then, to put it crudely, is escalated self-indulgence, whether masking under sensory delight, interpersonal stimulation, or spiritual intensity.

It is in this sense that there exists a dissociation of feeling from cognition and in this sense, too, that the encounter group movement can be said to be anti-intellectual. For no question is consistently raised about the value of such experience in yielding insight relative to the ends of a salutary existence or to its role in the whole catalogue of personal and collective human expression. Nor are the further questions raised as to whether these experiences are genuinely healthy, infantile, cathartic, or unequivocally sensual, reflect a wish for an earlier childlike state, and the like. Thus, affect, however paramount it is in the human condition, is not examined—in the encounter movement—for the authentic and vital functions it plays in actualized human life or for the goals it purports to subserve, nor analyzed for the content and quality of its constituent properties, but rather is uncritically accepted as sufficient unto itself. This is, in part, a child's view of affect and may represent, too, a wish to return to a child's world.

In a more historic sense, and as Spengler and Geddes speak of it, these trends represent a search for a fulfilment and identity in a type of experience and feeling that no longer genuinely marks the spirit of our times. It is quite roughly what Spengler called "second religiousness," i.e., exciting sensation and other intense experience to drown the actual present-day temper of purposelessness and despair. In this sense, not only the motive of the movement but also its nature is evangelical in character, calling for the redemption and higher dedication of man through the myth and themes of feeling, spirituality, intimacy, mysticism, communion and collectivity, and ecstatic religiousness.

LACK OF A PHILOSOPHY OF MAN AND SOCIETY, AND OF AN ETHIC

One of the manifestations of the dissociation between feeling and intellect in the encounter movement and its satellite activities is the lack of a well-defined humanistic philosophy, image of man, view of society, or coherent morality. As previously indicated, it is not clear what purposes the liberation of feeling serve: is it to augment manipulation of others, for a therapeutic goal, to satisfy a hunger for contact, to fulfill a need to love or to be loved, to be an end in itself, or to rapidly establish interpersonal closeness and obtain its fruits without undergoing the traditional process of extended acquaintance and myriad mutual experiences usually presumed necessary to test the character and responses of one's associates?

Moreover, there is no consideration of the broader social context into which the encounter group experience fits. Are these liberated feelings and interactions calculated only for personal relief and for establishing dyadic and small-group interpersonal relationships, and then only under conditions of relaxed exploration such as mark the encounter group environment? What functions can these modalities of "openness" of perception and response play in the makings of society, in the creation of functional social organizations in the real world, and in the formation of viable political structures? Are their effects limited to their own particular settings beyond which there is no extension to the outside world, thus leaving intact the social and economic attitudes that prevail in everyday life and, by implication, sustaining the social structure and the cultural atmosphere that, in part, nurtures these attitudes? Finally, how are the insights and sensitivities gained in the encounter environment to be applied in the real world to fundamental ethical and moral problems involving love, power, competition, kindness, and the commitment of one's energies to social causes, to the alleviation of distress in others, or to intervention when social or personal cruelties occur? Whatever the goals of the encounter group movement may be for personal liberation and awareness, there are surely no indications that they should and will be carried out in the world one faces every day. It is here that the real meaning, the values, and the upshot of all the training, sensitivity, and augmented awareness occur—and if the insights and sensitivities gained in encounter experiences are only to be used to subserve the traditional, mechanized, materialistic, egotistic ends of contemporary life or as deceptive ploys and "humanistic masks" to abet the values of the very world whose oppressions instigated the desperate search for self-actualization that mark the humanistic revival, the growth that is presumed to accrue from such practices must surely be questioned.

If the lack of examination of these other crucial human values and conditions is a result of a lack of social or historical awareness and a general anti-intellectualism stemming from an absence of genuine direction or philosophy, the encounter group movement may be afflicted with the same meaninglessness and purposelessness it was designed to remedy and with a comparable dissociation from vital reality, authentic earthy feeling, and deep human interest that it was generated to counteract. If this is true, it would be as atomistic, meaningless, and counterfeit—though in the realms of emotion, spirituality, and sensation—as the mechanized, ritualized life it presumes to confront.

Further, if the cause of this dissociation is, indeed, a lack of valuative direction, then it is not clear which image of man or philosophy of life these liberated feelings and sensations should be directed to subserve. Surely there are as many humanistic images of man and as many diverse philosophies of life as there are sensations and affects to explore, as many types of self-actualization as there are human resources, and as many social organizations and ideal societies as there are varieties of interpersonal relations.

But here the encounter movement leaves us in limbo, as full of puzzled doubt and uncertainty as it claims is the condition of contemporary man in his struggles with the modern mechanized world. For surely with each different image of man, philosophy of life, or system of ethics, quite different types of sensation, feeling and interpersonal experiences would ensue. For example, if justice were conceived to be an all-consuming end of life as well as a directing philosophy of the encounter movement, there possibly would be less tendency to encourage certain types of interpersonal behavior and more to encourage and explore others; viz., there might be a less tolerant view of personal excitements and pleasures—particularly at the expense of others—and possibly more concern with experiences that fuse others in sympathy and compassion or with those that generate attitudes of fair and just treatment of them. To apply such specific humanistic values or goals to the encounter movement itself, there would be, for example, more concern with the scale of fees charged for seminars and group meetings, more concern for soliciting lower-class and minority-group clients, more awareness and possibly dismay about the profit motive of various of the growth centers, and more concern, too, with the economic motives and self-aggrandizement of various of the seminar leaders.

Indeed, in my book *The Images of Man* (Rosenthal, 1971) I specifically deal with such concepts or models of self-actualization as configurations of qualities each of which would require quite particular types of emotional training and awareness to be incorporated or even understood. Of these, the encounter group movement at its present time and focus presents a promiscuous plethora of options that are often either fragments of more coherent images and philosophies or of isolated components taken out of context from dissimilar value systems and mixed together without cohesion; indeed, on occasion, more asymmetric particles or atoms are isolated from a particular philosophic model and then exaggerated beyond genuine proportion and balance. By contrast, what I have dealt with in my study are three quite dissimilar but integrated images or philosophies of man originating at the time of Periclean Greece, the high Middle Ages, and the Renaissance, and each, though involving humanistic orientations, emphasizing quite different segments of the humanistic spectra of qualities and values. In the Greek image, for example, excellence and versatility of mind, high integrity, purity of feeling, and splendid courage were among the paramount features. In the Middle Ages, the image was, in part, made of inner beatitude, compassion, tranquility, and benign feelings. And in the Renaissance, the ideal model was of a robust and earthy life, an incessant empiric quest, uninhibited sensuality, unremitting competitiveness, and a worldly, sensory, and exhilarating conception of art and beauty. With each of these images went different interpersonal values, ways of treating people, and conceptions of happiness, differently esteemed and depreciated emotions and feelings, separate approaches to morality, and, in short, distinct philosophies of life.

Now into which of these three images or philosophies would the experiences of the encounter group fit? Which should it tailor its practices to and which exclude? Or should it, despite the resulting confusion, choose whatever elements it wishes from each image and so produce a sort of humanistic cafeteria or potluck view of man? Or should it add aspects of still other images: a stoic one, for example, an epicurean one, a poetic one, a romantic one, a commercial one, or even a socialist one? Each of these has its unique human values, configuration of desired and derogated traits, approved interpersonal relationships and practices, schedule of esteemed pleasures and delights, and the like. Perhaps the encounter movement should combine all of these in one large encyclopedia or index of humanistic man. Or would it be better to successively run through each image or combinations of them, till all had been systematically explored in an extensive series of encounter sessions? Surely the latter expedient would have the merit of avoiding the anarchy of present practice but, on the other hand, would not be as open or protean. But is not this latter condition—and without the advantage of a systematic exploration and assessment—precisely that of the nebulousness and confusion in which the movement finds itself today?

Surely the encounter movement ought to differentiate for each ethical or value system and for its generally desired quality and texture of experience the correlated types of sensations, feelings, interpersonal practices, and the like that should be cultivated. It is here that the encounter movement reveals its affective promiscuity and valuative limbo—or possibly nihilism. For it is ready for all experience, all states of being, and all explorations of sensation. It is like Prospero's Ariel in *The Tempest* shouting, "Freedom, heigh day," but the question is what will become of Ariel when he grows up. It is like a desperately hungry man who will eat anything, a thirsty child who will drink brackish water as well as champagne not knowing how to judge them, or a sex-starved human who will sleep with any member of the opposite or the same sex. There is much humanism—and humanness—in this, of course, but it is not clear whether it is an animal humanism, an infantile humanism, a humanism of emotional desperation and starvation, a humanism of recreation, a humanism of escapism, or a humanism of deliberate dissociated and thoughtless indulgence. Is it, then, a humanism that refuses to grow up, to see itself as part of life and society, as devoid of an ethic and a morality, and as one that must be related to the everyday economic and social realities of the world in which we live? Is it possible that it is really a movement of despair—or sensate nihilism—as Spengler and Geddes would submit, or is it the authentic beginnings of a new organic human hope, if but in a desperate or primitive form?

Alternatively, it has been argued that the encounter experience should be used as the basis for finding the direction to what specific form social groups, society, social organizations, and a general value system ought to take. And on the presumption that when vast psychologic and interpersonal experience is accumulated and reflected on, a more variegated, reasonable and humane orientation of life may come from it, this is true. There are issues remaining, of course, for with a vast diversity of potential emotional and sensory experience, numerous enlightened and richly satisfying options are available as witnessed by various cultures that have chosen quite dissimilar experiential paths. Too, there is no certainty that there will be a detached view of these experiences and that their practitioners will not become prisoners of them, thereby prejudicing the outcomes. Nor that a capsule of a viable humanistic society, morality, or even an everyday humanistic group process can be established in or extracted from the encounter group procedure itself; nor, indeed, that its practitioners are not more concerned with particular types of personal problems or have not been already self-selected to respond to certain experiences and solutions, or, indeed, are capable of finding only a specified few of them.

For these and other reasons and because all perception and response are related to an implicit or explicit value context or system of societal norms, there can be, it appears, no way of eliminating moral, social, and collective issues from the very conception and onset of the encounter group experience. Otherwise, anarchy, unreflected bias, and a blooming, buzzing confusion of experience would result. Thus, though there must be no discounting of the great salutary importance of the liberation of affect and sensation and the opening to new experience that the encounter group provides, this must be placed simultaneously in context with issues such as: To what end is it directed? For what group? To what image or vision of man does it speak? For what society will it be beneficial? What particular ethic or morality will it subserve?

These issues must be faced wisely and courageously, and questions must be asked such as: What is the psychologic meaning and effect of these so-brief encounter group contacts? What is the nature of the morality involved in superficial and transient emotional relationships precipitously induced for a short interlude? What type of emotional training is being given in encounter groups for a bureaucratic, mechanized society where sensory and affective openness and humanistic values ought to be brought into every sector of life in a way that takes full account of the complexities and obstacles that the present cultural system, with its materialistic preoccupations and intense competitions, presents to their full realization and whose socioeconomic structure, therefore, may have to be modified or transformed before the humanistic ethos can be genuinely implemented? Only when the question is squarely raised as to whether those practices and experiences enable men to be more humanistic, gentle, and liberated in their everyday existence, only when the ends of awareness, sensitivity, compassion, appreciation of beauty, and the like are related to the life of the real world and to our present social system can the experiences of the encounter group and its allied activities be put fully into balance and assessed.

SOME ISSUES OF ENCOUNTER EXPERIENCES THEMSELVES

All the above considerations are of the greatest relevance when one examines the encounter experience itself. It goes without saying that many of the encounter practices engaged in are salutary, giving augmented sensitivity and richness of interpersonal experience and liberating overrestricted affect. Though, of course, there is much diversity in encounter group practices, there surely can be no quarrel in human beings constructively exploring and becoming more aware of one another, facilitating their empathic relationships, and generally acquiring heightened sensitivity.

One problem of these groups, however, is whether their leaders and clients are able to impart and accept these experiences with salutary effect or whether they frequently result in excesses, superficialities, and distortions on the part of the leaders and unnecessary distress, confusion, and precipitated disturbances on the part of clients. Is it possible that in many instances (particularly in those of superficial contact) the encounter experience serves to stimulate sexual interest, intimacy, personal revelation, and the like without an enlightened basis being present for these interactions or without the emergence of a significant understanding essential to making them meaningful and constructive? Do not these types of contact often result in excitements without purpose or fulfilment: superficial sensations or titillations that are often mistaken for a significant and full-bodied experience but that, too frequently, are only provocations without genuine satisfaction? Nor do these excitements or temptations often fit into a larger humanistic orientation of genuine personal, cognitive, and ethical interest in one's partners and associates or into a humanely differentiated and evaluative basis for a relationship in response to their character, intellect, and deep-lying interests. Sometimes these encounters seem stripped of all but atomistic, unintegrated, and primitive instinctual or affective process as if all the humanistic issues of morality, values, social goals, and a philosophy of life had virtually little significance. It is as if the crucial factors were blocked instinctual, affective, or sensory impulses that should be liberated in these encounter contacts and a hunger for elemental emotional fulfilment that could be speeded up, packaged (or ritualized), and almost instantly gratified. How reminiscent this is of the other productive, marketing, and advertising practices of our society that are also directed to the ends of quick exploitation of economic opportunities and quick profits. But this is surely not the full-bodied perspective, morality, and value context of a genuine humanism.

These tendencies are evident in the quite large size of encounter groups and seminars, which often means that the seminarian or leader cannot pay sufficiently close attention to the individual participants. But because most encounter procedures, if not all, involve personal experience and relationships in some depth, touching on various buried or unacknowledged complexes, themes, energies, or fixations, they surely require the most acute sophistication and skill, for there can always be a risk of a damaging outcome with participants who are too ill or immature or in states of incipient breakdown.[4] How can the professional leader observe and empathize with the intricate process of encounter group experience as it affects all his clients if he has little chance to carefully observe any particular one at all? How can he maintain a protective and therapeutic concern for those, particularly, who have quite serious problems and for whom the encounter might be hazardous? Even if he were to have the most sophisticated training in psychiatry and clinical psychology, even if he acutely knew all the prognostic signs of breakdown and distress, could he, in such large groups, detect them for each individual participant with acute attention and loving care? Of course not, and the consequence may be that many may grow more ill, confused, or desperate in these groups while others further develop or exaggerate illusions they already harbor, stimulate frantic excitements or fragmented sensations, generate dissociated or frenzied affects, or intensify immature wishes. The result may not be humanistic growth in the fully balanced and spectrumed sense of that term but rather an asymmetric stimulation of certain affects and sensations and a superficial, precipitous, or distorted view of the nature of rich and healthy human interrelationships.

All this means is that the lack of a cogent philosophy of what constitutes salutary experiences and human happiness and the lack of a fastidious concern for its richly balanced emergence may be reflected in the absence of clear moral and intellectual responsibility for the clinical dynamics of the encounter process, a deficiency in the deeply grounded understanding of the nature of emotional growth, and may also reveal the lack of a clear conception of an image of man that these experiences should subserve. Indeed, if these experiences are valued only for themselves—without a benevolent concern for each person participating in them—and if their effects cannot be followed up with medicant concern, it may appear that significant issues of morality, solicitous consideration for participants, compassion, and other hu-

---

[4] In their paper "Sensitivity Training: Interpersonal 'Overkill' and other Problems" (Kuehn and Crinella, 1969), John L. Kuehn and Francis M. Crinella contend that at least four groups should be excluded from T groups: psychotics, characterologic neurotics, hysterics, and individuals in crisis.

mane preoccupations are substantially missing in the nurturing of these experiences, as they are in other aspects of them.

For there can be no doubt that unless such fastidious concern is shown with such intense, intimate, and prospectively crucial experiences, though much good may come to some, much damage may also be done to others in spite of slogans of awareness, sensitivity, and human growth.

THE ENCOUNTER MOVEMENT AS REFLECTING THE CULTURAL SYSTEM OF RITUAL AND PROFIT

Not inconsistent with the neglect of these humanistic orientations are other trends that seem to mark the encounter group movement. One is a ritualization of affect, sensitivity, and expansion of consciousness in and of themselves as well as of the practices and procedures that give rise to them, and the other is a rather substantial commitment to relatively high fees for participants and goodly emoluments for seminar leaders.

This ritualization, as I call it, is designed to achieve an opening or heightening of consciousness. It is ritualistic in the sense that the same proximate or possibly stereotyped procedures are almost always used to obtain desired ends but rarely with reference to the particular personal needs of the participants or to the philosophic, valuative, cognitive, and other issues previously discussed. Moreover, it is as if the awareness and feelings desired must fit largely into the same mold of liberated, spiritual, mystic, or sensually exciting affect and sensation, and profound deviations from these modes of response or the fusion of cognitive and valuative functions with them, though not discouraged, are not given much latitude to emerge. The result, deriving from these set techniques, is a ritualization of rather elemental feeling, primary sensation, and interpersonal stimulation, or, in short, an enshrinement of experiences and sensitivities that are different from those of everyday life and that are separated from its context of reality, cognition, and value.

Enshrinement inevitably ritualizes and sanctifies desired experience, and the encounter movement does so too. There is a procedure for its evocation and a language for its incantation and description. As part of the mysterious and possibly magical practice necessary to achieve these particular precious, ineffable, and exotic feelings, a particular series of rituals must be exercised (touching, seeing, kinesthetic activities, chanting, interpersonal gambits and ploys, and so on) that distinguish these presumable humanistic experiences from those of everyday life both in the methods of evocation and in the ends to be

achieved. These particular exotic and semireligious techniques are implemented for particular psychologic effects in much the same way as
any system of rituals, be they those of religion or of the mechanized
role-playing relationships of everyday business and social life that the
encounter experience was designed to remedy. Indeed, the emphasis on
feelings of a certain kind and awareness of a particular variety have in
form, sanctity, and repetitiousness much the same character as the
rituals of the everyday world, whose content, however, is materialistic
and status matters, whereas that of the encounter group involves man-
ufactured spontaneity, codified awareness, instant warm feelings, and
elementary varieties of sensory and affective experience.

A not unrelated issue focuses on one of the foundations of the behavioral system that the encounter movement proclaims it wishes to
dethrone, i.e., preoccupation with money and profiteering. Surely,
there can be no question that the fees charged for enrolment in the
seminars and meetings designed to demonstrate the emptiness of material and monetary pursuits are often rather elevated, so elevated,
indeed, that frequently those who are in eminent need of these experiences lack the funds to gain admission into these antimaterialistic
seminar sessions.

If there is further evidence required for the contention that the encounter experience is, in part at least, diversionary, recreational,
exotic, and not immediately concerned with confronting head on the
materialistic issues of the real world, it would be found in the high
fees demanded and received by the peregrinating practitioners of the
movement as well as in the highly developed business orientations of
the various executive boards of the humanistic growth centers who
employ them. It is not necessary to go into the carefully calculated
profit-and-loss estimates of each seminar offered in terms of fees, travel
expenses, and the like, the increasingly large public relations and
advertising outlays to attract larger and possibly more affluent audiences, the glossy brochures, the dissemination of esoteric tidbits, and,
indeed, what sometimes almost approaches commercial advertising in
newspapers and television. Such an orientation would be expected in
business enterprises and in those whose goals are of the materialistic,
exploitative, deceptive world the encounter group is presumably opposed to. What, then, are these established practices of the dehumanized business world doing in the company of those who wish to reform
it or, at least, attenuate its power?

One possible answer to these contradictions, as suggested previously,
is that lacking an authentic and well-formulated humanistic and
philosophic perspective, the encounter movement falls, if only by
inertia, into the prevailing values of the day; i.e., it tacitly assents to
these values by failing to counterpose a clear and detailed adversary

position. A second possible reason is that since its *stated* purposes are
not to conform to the affluent status quo and the values associated with
it, it unwittingly or disingenuously uses the diversionary escapist orientation with its accompanying recreational and *la dolce vita* values
as a device to maintain the very accommodation to the status quo that
it so vehemently decries. For this diversion and escape—which is not
the same as an authentic humanism—the encounter group leader exacts
the same charge for his services as would any other expert practitioner
of a craft, profession, or other entertainment committed to the values
of the material world. This, too, is consistent with the ritualization and
esotericism of highly specialized professions or crafts, for they are not
designed to deal directly with the general humanistic issues of life in
the everyday world. Rather, their techniques are comparable to the
social or occupational rituals (efficient or expedient methods and
procedures abstracted from the total human process) of the role-
playing, manipulative business society whose pre-eminent values are
money and status. Similarly, the skill of the encounter group practitioners is in providing a diversion or release valve for their clients and
in persuading them that they are or can be spontaneous, genuinely
human, and compassionate. In so doing, they permit them to be more
sanguine about the real world and the harsh effects it has on them
because they can affirm (after the encounter "treatment") that they
are not irreparably damaged by it and, indeed, can always find a remedy for it in the encounter experience. Hence, the disciples can endure,
indeed can support, life in the dehumanized, harsh everyday world
more easily because by following this regimen they would not be involved in the turmoil of confronting it, and possibly rebelling against
it, nor in the equally unpleasant prospect of sacrificing its monetary
rewards, which, in fact, not only assure them of its materialistic fruits
but also provides the high entrance fees needed to obtain the remedial
humanistic experiences that the encounter movement dispenses.

For these and other reasons, the high fees demanded and received
are part of the releasing, diversionary, and tranquilizing aspects of the
present social system, and for this service affluent persons—and especially those ridden with purposelessness or ennui—are prepared to
happily contribute for the soothing balm of experiencing some spontaneous and humane feelings and for the privilege of thinking of
themselves as genuinely human. Thereupon they can better sustain the
deadly and depersonalizing effects of the real world, indeed often
believing that the behavior they evince in it—manipulative hard,
opportunistic, callous—is not really so bad or serious because their
real selves, or substantial segments of them, are so basically benign
that their day-to-day acts do not genuinely characterize their true
nature. Indeed, even when engaging in these acts, they do so—if they

have learned their lessons well in the encounter sessions—with a smile and a graciousness and sensitivity that make them seem more human to themselves, and possibly deceives others in the same way. If this is true, what may be happening as a side effect of these encounters is a vast escalation of guile, double talk, double think, and circuses of sham and deception calculated to hide and mitigate the impact of the harsh everyday world that encounter group clients are convinced will have no substantial deleterious effect on them—or they on others—if they proficiently practice the encounter arts. Is it possible that what issues from these experiences, then, is a new trickiness, a new salesmanship, a new hypocrisy, or a new set of contrived masks? Is it possible that the encounter group movement does not vitally evoke in its clients the genuineness and courage to face the obstacles to humanism in the real world and to resolve them with compassion, insight, and sensitivity? Rather it may be that it offers them the illusion—or the ruse—that they are resolving these humanistic issues (particularly when they do so on week ends and in seminars away from realistic confrontation with them) or that they *think* they are now more courageously humanistic than they were before they became encounter participants. Or do these sessions teach them the gambits and techniques of appearing to be humane, warm, and benevolent to others—as in the manner of good politicians and salesmen—while, in fact, disingenuously not precluding them from engaging in the same order and spirit of behavior as before, though now with a greater sense of diplomacy, sensitivity to interpersonal relations, and awareness of how to sweeten their hard purposes and actions and, indeed, of how to deceive others (and possibly also themselves) as to their genuine intent?

If the above appraisal has more than a grain of truth, it may testify to the broad historical vision of Spengler, Toynbee, and Geddes. Particularly is this so in the case of Spengler who, in a number of cultures, examined the nature and rituals of comparable sensations and feelings, their exotic character, their religious-mystic and intensely personal quality, their cultist attractiveness, their ornamental and hyperintense excitements, their evangelical zeal, their dissociation and often alienation from the root issues of the ongoing world, and the esoteric charisma of many of their recondite leaders, who, like Dionysian priests or peripatetic medicine men, moved from place to place, dispensing their aphrodisiacs of sensation and spirit, evoking pleasure, excitement, or inspiration, and disseminating abstruse and earth-moving insights and wisdom. And these experiences are, in many respects, as distinct from confrontation with the salient problems of a society as are the psychic remedies, palliatives, and placebos they dispense. Faith healers and magic doctors are found in numerous cultures to heal the despairing, the weak, or the grievously wounded, to bind up injuries of the strong, and to give inspiration and fortitude to all others for the hard and exhausting struggles for life. Indeed, both Toynbee and Spengler point out that such movements have often appeared in other Western societies when there has been a malaise of spirit, a deterioration of social institutions and collective purpose, an eruption of internal conflict and social violence, a compensated excitement to despair, and, in general, a decay of vital forces. Whether the encounter movement is a modern symptom of this decline or is an omen of a general renewal, only the long run of the future will tell.

THE RESEARCH ISSUE

Related to all the foregoing issues is the question of research on the encounter group, particularly that dealing with the extension to the outside world of feelings and attitudes induced while engaging in its practices. There are also questions of the extent, duration, and quality of change that may result from encounter participation.

Despite the fact that these encounter practices have abounded for some time, there has been remarkably little research performed on them (Berzon and Solomon, 1966; Cohen and Carrera, 1967; Crawshaw, 1969; Feather, 1963; Glueck, 1968; Gottschalk and Pattison, 1969; Greening, 1964; Grossman and Clark, 1967; Kaplan, 1967; Karsarjian, 1965; Keuhn and Crinella, 1969; Lakin and Carson, 1964; Lundgren, 1969; Malamud and Machover, 1965; Tannenbaum and Bugental, 1963; Tannenbaum et al., 1961), for surely the encounter group's effects should be measured not only by the experiences it evokes during its immediate duration but also by the influence it has in other situations.

The absence of extensive research in this area may have several causes. The encounter movement has had a relatively short history and there has not been an abundance of time in which research could actually have been carried out. Also, many of the phenomena appear so striking or novel that formulating appropriate research to study them has been more difficult and time-consuming than in the case of more prosaic phenomena. Further, no conceptual system of any magnitude with clear and specified theorems and hypotheses has been worked out to give general direction to research, to focus on particular issues or experiences, and to instigate development of fertile research designs.

Granted all this, there may be still another reason why research has not emerged in this area. And as outrageous a suggestion as it may appear, it has the merit, if only that, of being consistent with the tenor of previous discussion. Thus, although it would indeed hold that dispassionate research would clarify whether the encounter group does have any substantial effect on behavior in day-to-day life, it would also be true that if the movement does not have this purpose—i.e., if its intent is recreational, diversionary, and, in the last analysis, to make the real world more acceptable or bearable to despairing, jaded, or anomic human beings—dispassionate research would not, in fact, be its primary concern. Indeed, if its purpose is as just stated, there might be some apprehension or, at least, disinterest in determining whether its experiences have their purported effect in heightening sensitivity and expending humanism in the everyday world. For if this were not found to be the case, it would put into question the movement's claimed purpose and ostensible validity, thereby revealing its own particular manipulative and commercialized use of the materialistic world it is so intent on transforming. For inasmuch as the movement appears under the sanction of professional and clinical values and is practiced by professionals who espouse, in tune with current ideology, the values of science, humanism, growth, or therapy, its image would grievously suffer from research results that questioned these presumed humanistic and therapeutic effects. Thus, if one contends that the implicit purpose of the encounter group movement is recreational and that, in the end, it affords a reconciliation with the social and economic realities of the everyday world, it is understandable why a strong and viable research commitment should not yet have emerged. For this might run the risk of raising doubts about the movement's authentic humanistic or therapeutic direction and, therefore, not be in tune with experiences that may not foster a courageous and realistic humanism to confront the social, economic, and personal issues of everyday life.

SUMMARY

From the perspective followed here, the encounter movement must be seen as a reaction to the dehumanization, mechanization, and materialistic pre-eminence of contemporary industrial society. These trends produce a loss of personal identity, warm human relations, spontaneous individual feelings, and deep social cohesion. The encounter group, as in the case of various forms of religion, the new communes, yippie and hippie culture, and other current efforts to re-establish fellow feeling and personal concern, is in part a reaction to these trends. In part, too, it may be a reaction to what Spengler and Geddes called the decline of Western culture, the growth of Caesarism, and the early signs of necropolis. Such tendencies have been repeated numerous times in the past history of both the West and the East, and at the stage of development represented by contemporary society, they are characterized by sensationalisms, evangelicisms, and frantic searches for collective fellow feeling or imperative community.

The encounter group, as in the case of some of these other movements, is dissociated from the day-to-day experience of life and serves, to some degree, as an opiate, a release valve, or an agency for reconciliation with the very world that bred the ennui it was designed to remedy. In effect, therefore, it may become a device for preservation of the status quo and for appeasement of resentment to the trends of modern society. This is especially so because it does not immediately and directly confront the issues of the real world and the fundamental causes of the dehumanization in it. Rather its thrust is to build psychologic and cultural atmospheres that escape from or deny such confrontations and such consciousness. As a result, it cannot admit numerous issues of sophisticated adult dimensions of experiences to enter into its compass—hence the relatively superficial dealing with feeling and interpersonal relationships, i.e., the role-playing or ritualization of them in accordance with an unacknowledged theme of avoidance of genuinely involved, fully spectrumed interpersonal relationships and confrontations. In part, then, the encounter experience may be a game and not a deep, extended experience that could refine and enrich organic and integrated feelings and sensations of everyday life. All this, too, is abetted by the short-term nature of the encounter meetings, by a lack of concern with the well-being of individual participants, which is a departure from the sacred obligation of the medicant to care for his client, and by a lack of real knowledge of the character and interest of the person(s) one shares these experiences with or of authentic contact with them as differentiated personalities. It is as if these experiences were shared with a disembodied person, i.e., an anonymous figure who acts out or role-plays, if candidly, these emotionally pure or idealized experiences, which, though genuine, nevertheless appear to be in vacuo. (In this sense, the encounter group experiences are quite as anonymous, ritualized, and depersonalized as those of business except that the nature of their commerce or transaction is in intimate or exciting emotion and that the "negotiators"—in feelings and emotions —have fuller contact, if not unimpededly so, with the persons they are dealing with.)

It is in this sense that the encounter group nurtures superficial experience and sensation, however differently they may appear to an observer or feel to those undergoing them and however infrequently they occur in the everyday world. Indeed, it is this infrequency that helps give the impression that these experiences are deep, unusual, and of rich significance. Also significant is their charade-like quality—as if undergoing them were like being in a dream or hypnagogic state or as if one were dissociated from reality and were playing a role with only part of one's self involved, and as if, though knowing this experience was illusory or make-believe—like a movie—yet taking it to be real. In effect, there is not often in these encounters the full commitment of self—cognitively, emotionally, and executively—that one has in a significant and extended experience of everyday life that would have repercussions for one's welfare, aspirations, and general well-being as well as, perhaps, for that of one's family or friends. In this sense, these encounter charades are often representations of illusory selves—or perhaps silhouette selves would be a better expression—and so are analogous to the superficial charades and roles of business or of everyday interpersonal manipulation and maneuver. However, in the latter case, the fragmentation (or dissociation) is of the shrewd, the acquisitive, and the exploitative dimensions (or selves) from the full human matrix of genuine affect, sensation, and experience. So, too, is the encounter experience often similarly fragmented except that in its case the functions that are extracted from the human matrix are exactly those that are pushed aside in the everyday materialistic world, i.e., the sensory, the affective, and the spiritual.

In effect, then, both crucibles of experience (the business world and the encounter world) are, in their separate ways, superficial and fragmented and agree in not acknowledging the total matrix of human experience including that of a broad philosophy of life, a full integration of feeling and intellect, or, in sum, a humanistic cognition. What the one emphasizes, the other de-emphasizes as if the stress on the shrewd, materialistic, and manipulative components of experience had to be compensated for by an equivalent stress on the affective, sensory, and spiritual components. Thus, in a wider context, both point to the main currents of dissociation of the times and to the lack of integration of basic and complementary sectors of experience with each other as well as into a fuller human matrix whether through hyperdevelopment or exclusion.

Consistent with this hyperdeveloped emphasis on separate and dissociated sectors of behavior is the fact that the pleasure or excitement of encounter experiences is often their primary goal: a feasting on them due possibly to their previous deprivation and a sort of childlike indulgence in their most elementary forms, which are devoid both of differentiated development and of the cognitive components with which they could be integrated. Rather like those of a child, these experiences have a quality of self-indulgence, of excitement for its own sake, of lack of concern with more extensive and deeper issues, and of unwillingness to confront certain aspects of external reality. In addition, because they do not often occur in everyday life, they appear as titillating and intriguing as children's new toys.

But it is also true that these experiences have the character of a ritual or of game-playing and, in effect, often transpose the anonymous role-playing of real life into that of instant role-playing emotion and instant personal relationships. By this charade or fragmented recipe of and flirtation with feeling—or a carbon of feeling (actually a dissociated sector or advertisement of it)—these encounters avoid what may be too disturbing and onerous to face: a confrontation with authentic emotions in the realistic context of day-to-day life as they are affected by values, cognition, and the nature of one's job, status, family, and friends as well as by the character and interests of the person(s) with whom they are shared. In effect, this means the most searching examination of one's daily behavior and feelings in terms of these espoused humanistic sentiments as well as of the social and cultural institutions that shape them. Such an awareness, however, may be too disturbing to face, for it might put into question the claims and values not only of the encounter movement but, more importantly, of the texture, practices, and values of one's day-to-day life.

Are these encounter group interactions, then, in some respects like the superficial business contacts one makes in everyday life except for a patina of friendliness and graciousness? Surely, the varnishing or advertising of self by such warmth and congeniality is an established practice in politics, salesmanship, and advertising and in the life of a business society, as a whole. Is it not possible that the encounter movement, in part, is an exercise in massive selling of the idea that humanistic, warm, spontaneous, and salutary interpersonal experiences are within reach of almost everybody and that the encounter process is the instrument for their attainment? If true, such a traffic in pseudo-feeling and pseudohumanistic experience not only may reflect the general spirit of our advertising, selling, role-playing culture but also may protect one from the distress of deep self-probing and unvarnished confrontation with reality. Thus, the picture partially emerges of a cult of ritualized feeling and sensation, perhaps fragmentary, perhaps conjuring up humanistic images to themselves and others to make up for the emptiness and depersonalization of life, perhaps ardently trying to wrest some measure of genuine humanism from their constant emulation and play-acting at it, or perhaps anxiously attempting to convince themselves and others that they are undergoing a depth of humanistic experience. In overview, there is a confusion between illusion and reality, between the advertisement of a wished-for self and the real self, between the need for emulating the humanistic image and one's real image.

Again, this is not to exclude the possibility that these fronts or presentations of humanism do play an important personal role in a world of mechanization and exploitation. People need to be accepted, loved, and warmed and will positively respond to the expression of those sentiments by others. It also enhances their economic position, professional status, and interpersonal relations if they can exhibit these feelings. Indeed, the salesman is an integral part of contemporary society whether as a particular person or as a symbol of prevailing norms. In a world of depersonalization and conflict, what helps to effectively sell one's self or one's product is a humane and warm image. This is the thrust in advertising, politics, and packaging: instant kindness, instant genuineness, and instant personal concern. It is no accident that such selling goes on in the encounter process in quick interpersonal relations, rarely deep or probing. It is a contact, a chimera, or a token of a real experience in much the same way that an attractive new product seems to be of genuine and enduring quality but, in fact, quickly becomes obsolescent and can be easily replaced.

In this sense, the encounter group is an arena for training in good contact, in facile acceptance of others and oneself, and in the techniques of compatible interaction. But these are precisely the urgencies and values of the contemporary business and professional marketplace: to get along with others, sell one's self quickly, and thereby be approved. Simultaneously, participants can experience some measure of sensory and emotional openness and fulfill other humanistic impulses as well. Thus does the encounter group movement equip its clients with those techniques of understanding, openness, and spontaneity that will ensure the greatest ease of accommodation and selling-of-self while also providing them with some degree of emotional and interpersonal fulfillment.

Many aspects of these encounter group phenomena, as previously indicated, represent what Spengler took to be the earmarks of a society in process of decay. In his view, the accompanying despair and alienation reveal themselves not only in more magnified and decadent displays of ritual and sensationalism but in more desperate and indiscriminate searches for community, collectivity, and love, as well.

In a sense, the urgency for warmth, acceptance, and understanding that marks the encounter movement symbolizes this search for community and inclusiveness, for such a search is a reaction to the fragmentation and isolation of contemporary life and a frantic effort to relieve this condition by acquiring the personal qualifications and human techniques (warmth, spontaneity, sensitivity, and so on) necessary for the development of and participation in such a humanistic community. But in its desperate effort to remedy a condition inherent in the nature of present society, this search often takes diffuse and indiscriminate forms whether these be week-end encounter sessions or training in a sensitivity that it is contended—possibly more in terms of utopian wishful thinking than in realistic assessment—will ensure the emergence of community, if only an amorphous and play-fantasied one or if only one confined to a few transient, undifferentiated, or charadelike relationships. By engaging in such encounter activities, however much self-actualization, benevolence, and liberation of feelings they may provide, the mood of unthinking desperation that originally gave rise to them—and that may defensively conceal their more fundamental causes including those of vested self-interest and commitment (economic, social, and psychologic)—is revealed. For how else can we explain that these practices take no account of the realities of personal interest and temperament, or of the social and economic nature of the everyday world in which such a community must be established, or of the authentic humanistic components (cognition, values) that are often more honored by neglect than by observance. What does seem to passionately matter is the urgency to satisfy the desire for human fellowship and community; indeed, it is from this passionate desperation that there comes the unwillingness to ask the central and courageous question as to how such a humanistic community can be established in the real world, which is its worst enemy and, indeed, the root cause for its frantic search. When this question has been carefully posed and answered, a substantial advance will have been made in the conception of the humanistic community, and the schism between its search in the encounter group and in the real world will have been more closely bridged.

Finally, there is no question in what has preceded of the rich potential of the encounter group movement for liberating feeling, heightening consciousness, and abetting interpersonal relations. These prospective contributions have been stressed over and over in this essay. Improved sensitivity, awareness of the inner life, and open-hearted spontaneity are immensely salutary qualities, and if the encounter movement can genuinely enhance these processes, this is in itself a large achievement. The question is whether it can put them into a larger context of values and life, give them a broad and realistic social direction and meaning, and relate them to everyday experience so they do not become a luxury, an escape, or an opiate. When and if the encounter movement consciously directs its energies to resolving these problems, it will have reduced its current dissociation and one-sided emphasis and it will have taken a long step to making its contributions a significant part of a humanism that is authentically integrated with life.

BIBLIOGRAPHY

Berzon, B., and Solomon, L. N. The Self-directed Therapeutic Group: Three Studies. *J. Counsel. Psychol.*, **13**:221–27, 1966.

Borkenau, Franz. *Ubergang vom Feudalen zum Burgerlichen Weltbild (The Transition from the Feudalistic to the Bourgeois World View)*. Paris: F. Alcan, 1934.

Cohen, Arthur M., and Carrera, Richard M. Changes in the Judgments of Sensitizers and Repressers in Response to Failure and Success Evaluations of Group Performance. *J. Social Psychol.*, **72**:217–21, 1967.

Crawshaw, Ralph. How Sensitive Is Sensitivity Training? *Amer. J. Psychiat.*, **126**:868–74, 1969.

Feather, Norman T. Cognitive Dissonance, Sensitivity and Evaluation. *J. Abnorm. Soc. Psychol.*, **66**:157–63, 1963.

Geddes, Patrick. *Cities in Evolution*. London: Williams and Worgate, 1915.

Gerschenkron, Alexander. *Continuity in History and Other Essays*. Cambridge, Mass.: Harvard University Press, 1968.

Glueck, William F. Reflections on a T-Group Experience. *Personnel J.*, **47**:500–4, 1968.

Gottschalk, A. Louis, and Pattison, E. Mansell. Psychiatric Perspectives on T-Groups and the Laboratory Movement: An Overview. *Amer. J. Psychiat.*, **126**:823–40, 1969.

Greening, T. C. Sensitivity Training: Cult or Contribution? *Personnel J.*, **41**:18–25, 1964.

Grossman, Len, and Clark, Donald H. Sensitivity Training for Teachers: A Small Group Approach. *Psychol. in the Schools*, **4**:267–71, 1967.

Kaplan, S. R. Therapy Groups and Training Groups: Similarities and Differences, *Inter. J. Group Psychother.*, **17**:473–504, 1967.

Karsarjian, Harold H. Social Character and Sensitivity Training. *J. Appl. Behav. Sci.*, **1**:433–40, 1965.

Keuhn, John L., and Crinella, Francis M. Sensitivity Training: Interpersonal "Overkill" and Other Problems. *Amer. J. Psychiat.*, **126**:840–45, 1969.

Lakin, Martin, and Carson, Robert C. Participant Perception of Group Process in Group Sensitivity Training. *Inter. J. Psychother.*, **14**:116–22, 1964.

Lukacs, Gyorgy. *Die Zerstorung der Vernunft (The Decline of Reason)*. Neuwied-Am-Rhein: Luchterland, 1962.

Lundgren, David C. Interaction Process and Identity Change in T-Groups. *Dissertation Abstr.*, **29**:961–62, 1969.

Malamud, D. I., and Machover, S. *Toward Self-Understanding: Group Techniques in Self-Confrontation*. Springfield, Ill.: Charles C Thomas, 1965.

Marcuse, Herbert. *One-dimensional Man*. Boston: Beacon Press, 1964.

Mumford, Lewis. *The Culture of Cities*. New York: Harcourt, Brace, 1938, pp. 289–91.

Mumford, Lewis. *The Condition of Man*. London: Secker and Warburg, 1964.

Rosenthal, Bernard G. *The Images of Man*. New York: Basic Books, 1970.

Rostovtzeff, Mikhail. *Social and Economic History of the Roman Empire*. New York: Oxford University Press, 1957.

Schumpeter, Joseph A. *Business Cycles: A Theoretical Historical and Statistical Analysis of the Capitalist Process.* New York: McGraw-Hill, 1939.

Schumpeter, Joseph A. *Capitalism, Socialism, and Democracy,* 2nd ed. New York: Harper & Brothers, 1947.

Spengler, Oswald. *The Decline of the West.* New York: Alfred A. Knopf, 1926.

Strachey, John. *The Coming Struggle for Power.* New York: Modern Library, 1935.

Tannenbaum, Robert, and Bugental, J. F. T. Dyands, Clans, and Tribe: A New Design for Sensitivity Training. *Human Relations Training News,* 7:1–3, 1963.

Tannenbaum, Robert J., Weschler, Irving R., and Massarick, Fred. *Leadership and Organization: A Behavioral Science Approach.* New York: McGraw-Hill, 1961.

Toynbee, Arnold. *A Study of History.* Abridgement of Vol. I–X by D. C. Somervell. New York: Oxford University Press, 1947–57.

Usher, Abbot. *Economic History of Europe Since 1750.* New York: American Book Co., 1937.

Weber, Max. *Economy and Society.* Totowa, N.J.: Bedminster, 1968.

Morton A. Lieberman
Irvin D. Yalom
Matthew B. Miles

∭21∭ The Group Experience Project: A Comparison of Ten Encounter Technologies*

COMMENTARY

The contributors present one of the few research evaluations of a comparison of the most widely used encounter techniques. Although the report is preliminary, with limited conclusions at this point, the reader has an opportunity to sense both how these techniques may be compared and the directions these comparisons may take.

BIOGRAPHIES

Morton A. Lieberman, Ph.D., writes of himself:
I have been associated with the University of Chicago since 1961, first as a student then as a faculty member in the Committee on Human Development and the Department of Psychiatry. My interests during this period have alternated between investigations into the influence of small groups on personal change and developmental issues in adult personality. The first interest has been expressed through active involvement as a fellow in the National Training Laboratories, where my initial research efforts were on

* With the collaboration of Peggy Golde, Ph.D., Stanford University Medical Center. Printed by permission of the authors.

469

T groups, a series of clinical explorations on group psychotherapy that led to the publication with Dorothy Stock Whitaker of *Psychotherapy Through the Group Process* (1964). I have been active in the training of clinicians in the use of groups for personal change as well as approaches to changing social systems in mental health. My interests in adult personality have been expressed during the past seven years in a series of studies on adaptation and survival under stress and as the codirector at the University of Chicago of the Adult Development and Aging training program. Current publications include: "Issues in the Training of Group Therapists" (*International Journal of Group Psychotherapy*, 1969); "Distance from Death as a Variable in the Study of Aging" (*Developmental Psychology*, 1970); and "Institutionalization of the Aged: Effects on Behavior" (*Journal of Gerontology*, 1969).

Irvin Yalom, M.D., is an associate professor of psychiatry at Stanford University. He has been actively engaged in the group therapy and sensitivity-training field for a number of years and has contributed a number of research and theoretical articles to the literature on these subjects. Recently he was chairman of an American Psychiatric Association task force on recent developments in small groups and has published a text on group therapy: *The Theory and Practice of Group Psychotherapy* (Basic Books, 1970).

Matthew B. Miles, Ed.D., describes himself as follows:
My core interest as a social psychologist over the past 15 years has been problems in the induction of change—in persons, groups, and organizations. My active involvement as a fellow of National Training Laboratories led to the publication of *Learning to Work in Groups* (1959) and to evaluation research on the effects of T groups (*Journal of Applied Behavioral Science*). Educational systems have always seemed an interesting site to me for the testing and application of social psychologic theory; this generated *Innovation in Education* (1964) and a series of studies on organizational development projects in schools.

Currently, I am most interested in exploring the data base described in this chapter, with special interest in the processes by which group norms are formed and in turn affect individual learning. The speculative question that interests me most is: Why should focusing on the "here-and-now" have such striking, magical effects on persons and groups?

Current publications include *Learning in Social Settings* (1970, with W. W. Charters) and *Organizational Development in Schools* (1971, with R. A. Schmuck).

The misgivings attendant on reporting research not yet at midpoint need not be elaborated. Despite them, we agreed to the editors' request to describe the whats and whys of our current research on encounter groups in the hope of making known some efforts to plow what has been a wasteland of inquiry. The central interest of our study is in the specific effects of the encounter group experience on the lives of participants. We are endeavoring to determine whether such experience leads to meaningful change or growth (or is psychologically harmful) and to identify the factors in the experience that induce growth or are harmful.[1]

Our interest in assessing the effects of encounter groups evolved from two sources: We experienced a growing uneasiness, a researcher's equivalent to therapeutic despair, over the widening chasm we felt between ourselves as doers and inquirers in the group psychotherapeutic and training enterprise. A similar influence was an oscillating excitement and concern about developments that increasingly bore the earmarks of a major social movement. Each of us had participated intensively in these developments, had helped to encourage the expansion we were witnessing; yet, what was emerging caused us some discomfort.

Limitations of Current Theory

Most theories of group therapy or personal growth have been developed by expert practitioners largely on the basis of their own experience. Although these theories frequently reflect the artfulness and perspicacity of their originators, we came to believe they might be severely limited by the theorist's own experience—and in some cases by his unusual talent. Frequently they operate as self-fulfilling prophecies, shaping the phenomena being theorized about.

A less common foundation for theory has been the intensive clinical observation of a small number of groups. Although this approach has provided an important source of information for beginning the development of group-based theories of therapy or personal growth, it severely restricts the variables available for study. Most investigations of this type have subjected only a few groups to intensive study and have, for the most part, been confined to a single type of therapy group

[1] We should like to acknowledge the contributions of the Ford Foundation Special Education Fund at Stanford University and the Mary Reynolds Babcock Foundation and the Division of the Biological Sciences of the University of Chicago in providing encouragement and financial support. The authors are heavily indebted to Mr. Herb Wong, who lent considerable research management skills and computer sophistication to our numerous complex operations; to Mrs. Leah Freedman for her research assistance; and to the many others who played key roles as observers and group leaders.

or training group. This restriction on the types of groups studied increases the chance that salient group or leader dimensions might vary too little for measurement. Indeed, some carefully designed process studies have not been able to "discover" measurable variations in such variables as therapeutic style and group norms. Although lawful relationships may be established through such process studies, they may represent only fragments of more general relationships. For example, although this style of investigation may uncover a lawful relationship between therapists' interventions and outcome, it can never answer the prior question of *how* much influence the therapist has on the treatment processes.

Experimental manipulation, on the other hand, given the existing lack of conceptual precision about therapeutic change and personal growth processes, appears limited to the production of rather broad-gauge results. A recent study of the outcome effects of trained and untrained group therapists (Poser, 1966), for example, although provocative, could not specify the relevant variables associated with the effects found. The conceptual tools currently available can, we believe, only produce findings akin to those from the early studies in group dynamics such as the classic Lewin, Lippitt, and White study of leadership styles—overly broad and poorly articulated generalizations. The use of nontherapeutic experimental groups is dogged by our inability to determine their degree of isomorphism with personal change or therapy groups. Although this problem is general to experimental social psychology, it seems particularly relevant for groups directed toward therapy or personal growth. A massive assault using experimental strategies waits upon its resolution.

These characteristics of the current state of knowledge about (Lieberman *et al.*, 1969) and methods of inquiry into group treatment suggest that reliable theory requires data from a wide variety of growth-oriented groups—a condition fortunately made available in the current group scene by the mushrooming of diverse endeavors described by a potpourri of labels. These run the gamut from the older ones of T and sensitivity training to the more recent designations such as encounter groups, Synanon games, transactional analysis groups, and so on, which are directed toward personal change.

Despite highly varied formats and nomenclature, these efforts share many common features: they attempt to provide an intensive group experience; they are generally small enough (6 to 20 members) to permit considerable face-to-face interaction; they focus on the here-and-now (the behavior of the members as it unfolds in the group); they encourage openness, honesty, interpersonal confrontation, and self-disclosure; they encourage strong emotional expression; the participants are usually not labeled "patients"; the experience is not ordinarily labeled "therapy," though the groups strive to increase awareness and to change behavior. The specific goals of the groups may vary. Occasionally they seek only to entertain, to "turn on," to give experience in joy, and so on—but the over-all goals in each case typically involve some type of personal *change*—of behavior, of values, of life-style. At the same time, they are sufficiently heterogeneous with respect to particularities of goal, population, and method to permit comparative analysis. Such an analysis, methodologically akin to cross-cultural research, offered the possibility of generating the taxonomy needed to develop a general theory of group change.

Encounter Groups as a Social Movement

The second force propelling us to the present inquiry was the explosive expansion of such groups, which may literally be involving tens of thousands of people each year. The growth of the encounter group movement seemed to promise too much potential for testing of hypotheses about broad-scale social developments to be left unstudied. What are encounter groups? Why are they "catching on"? What do they do for participants? How does the movement relate to other social processes and other dimensions of social change? To mental health professionals, further questions of whether and in what ways this group movement offers a new system of service, and how it relates to other service forms, are more than academic.

Throughout history small groups have flourished in times of rapid social change when old values and behavior patterns were no longer working and individuals were forced to re-examine and redefine their value systems. Such groups have always served as important healing agents. From the beginning of history, groups have been used to inspire hope, increase morale, offer emotional support, induce serenity, renew confidence in the benevolence of the universe, and thus counteract psychic and many bodily ills. Religious healers have always relied heavily on group forces, but when healing passed from the priesthood to the secular professions, the conscious use of group forces fell into a decline concomitant with the increasing reverence of the doctor-patient relationship. The encounter movement exists outside of the traditional help-giving institutions of society. Its strong egalitarian overtones may represent a reaction against many of the traditional institutional forms of help-giving.

The encounter movement also has potent recreational aspects. Encounter groups are the verbal equivalent of sky diving—they are high-risk, high-contact endeavors. Encounter groups are partially controlled, semiregulated surprises; all participants share some image of what will unfold, but there is sufficient mystery about details to give a quality of danger or excitement.

The rapid growth of encounter groups, the bewildering variations in form and function, the infusion into a variety of established institutions, as well as the development of new institutions such as growth centers and "living-room groups," add up to a picture of a vigorous social movement touching many facets of human endeavor. We suspect that they may be a response to a pressing need in our culture. The California milieu, the most potent incubator of encounter groups, exaggerates certain characteristics of contemporary American society. Many Californians have few roots in the community, institutional or personal. Geographic and social mobility are the rule rather than the exception. The extended family is rarely represented; the stable primary family is uncommon (one of two California marriages ends in divorce); the neighborhood or work group has diminished importance because the average Californian has arrived recently and is expected to leave soon. The neighborhood merchant and the family doctor are rapidly disappearing, and organized religion has become irrelevant to many young people. In short, the cultural institutions that have provided stability and intimacy are atrophying, without, of course, a concomitant decrease in human needs for these elements.

In the fall of 1968, we discovered at least 200 encounter groups operating in the Palo Alto area. Many of these groups have no institutional backing and recruit participants only by word of mouth. Teachers were leading encounter groups in the classroom; housewives were leading encounter groups in their homes for their friends or the friends of their adolescent offspring. Some groups had loose institutional affiliations: one free university offered an assortment of approximately 50 encounter groups every quarter; one highly structured institution, Synanon, offered an astonishing number of groups known as "square games" for nonaddicts (the Oakland Synanon branch alone had 1,500 individuals participating weekly in groups and another 1,000 on a waiting list).

A very visible index of the encounter group movement is the rapid proliferation of "growth centers." Some 75 growth centers, many of them spin-offs modeled on the Esalen design, have arisen around the country. Many churches, particularly on the West Coast, have been almost "swamped" with encounter activities to the extent that some professional churchmen have expressed serious concern[2] about the

---

[2] Perhaps of even greater concern is the potential of encounter groups (unlike the bowling leagues) as direct competition with traditional church functions, insofar as both meet needs for communion.

number of ministers who have thrown off their ministerial robes to become full-time encounter leaders.

The encounter group may be viewed as a social oasis in which societal norms are explicitly shed. No longer must facades of adequacy, competence, self-sufficiency be borne. In fact, the group norms encourage the opposite behavior: members are rewarded for expressing self-doubts and unfulfilled longings for intimacy and nurturance. The encounter group offers a unique form of intimacy—one that has no commitment to permanence.

Members attend encounter groups not only for affective supplies but for "self-validation": they are intrigued by an opportunity that permits adults to expose themselves, to be examined, and to be approved. A great majority of individuals, though functioning competently, have deep concerns about their adequacy: few other institutions offer an occasion for what appears to be a comprehensive examination of one's status as a human being; many individuals attend encounter groups with the hidden agenda of finding out: Am I acceptable? Am I lovable? Do I match up to others?

THE RESEARCH CONTEXT

The style of inquiry was shaped by general methodologic and practical considerations. Our initial intention was to undertake a field study, traveling to various loci of group activity to participate in, observe, and interview ongoing groups in their natural settings. Preliminary probes suggested serious limitations to such a strategy. The encounter group movement has a strong anti-intellectual flavor—a bias that might make leaders and participants less than ideal research subjects. More important, however, was likely to be the selective influence of population differences across different types of encounter groups. Critical to usable outcome research was sample randomization to the various group forms.

The need to control population created the dilemma of how to accomplish this goal while minimizing the effects of "being researched" so that both participants and leaders could have a genuine experience.

This dilemma was resolved by a fortunate happenstance. The instructors of an experimental course at Stanford, "Racism and Prejudice," approached us with questions of how to make the course more relevant to the students' lives. In the previous quarter it had been conducted as a lecture course with auxiliary weekly "laboratory" sessions, some of which had appeared to turn into racial encounter groups led by inexperienced group leaders (teaching assistants) with disappointing results. This situation meant that some of our research interests could be combined with the university's interest in evaluating such educational experiences. Highly experienced encounter group leaders, both black and white, were recruited to offer personal-growth programs to interested students from the course, as well as other undergraduates interested in personal-growth experiences. The contract with the students was open: they were offered the opportunity to participate in groups composed of all white or all black as well as mixed black-white groups; thus, they could use the group experience to explore both racial and other areas. The encounter leaders were informed of our general research interests, as well as our intention to evaluate the effects of encounter groups on racial attitudes.

Despite protracted negotiations with many student groups, we could not recruit a sufficient number of blacks to make racial encounter the major emphasis. Occurring in the winter of 1968, the recruitment process took place at a time when most black Stanford undergraduates perceived other political concerns as more pressing. Mistrust of white researchers (despite the participation at that time of a black psychologist in the research team) also made it difficult for many black students to accept the research endeavors. The final research design, therefore, involved only four white-black groups (two led by black leaders and two by white leaders) within the context of the over-all research. The major emphasis of the research was geared to issues of personal learning and growth rather than the issues of racism. The present report omits discussions of the research on black-white variables, though the four black-white groups are included.

RESEARCH DESIGN

Our goal of generating data for comparative analysis required the inclusion of groups representing different technologies and divergent theories of human growth and change. In the interest of representing major approaches to the encounter experience, as well as of maximizing differences that might be masked by the generic term "encounter," ten examples of group types used widely in California (and elsewhere) were selected. Included in the study were 18 groups representing: (1) T groups following the early approach of the National Training Laboratories (NTL), (2) groups reflecting an amalgam of NTL and rogerian orientations, (3) Synanon groups, (4) transactional-analysis groups, (5) Gestalt therapy groups, (6) "nonverbal" groups patterened after those developed at Esalen, (7) psychodrama groups, (8) psychoanalytically oriented groups, (9) marathon groups, and (10) leaderless tape groups (Berzon's Bell-and-Howell program).

Considerable care was given to the selection of group leaders. All too often inquiry into group psychotherapy or other growth-oriented group experiences has been based on the work of inexperienced leaders. On the basis of our own knowledge and that of others who knew the encounter area well, we compiled a list of 60 experienced leaders representing the ten approaches just outlined. For each of the ten approaches we then asked professionals familiar with the specific type of approach, "Who are the two best leaders in the Bay Area?" The leaders selected represented several disciplines (most were psychologists or psychiatrists), but were uniformly highly experienced, many with over ten years of experience in encounter group leadership. A number have national reputations and all are well known in the Bay Area.

Each leader was offered a generous professional fee for his time. A time limit (30 hours) was set on the total duration of the group. The only other restriction on format was that only those leaders selected to conduct marathons could utilize their total time in a continuous manner if they chose. To encourage the leaders to feel unrestricted in fully utilizing their skills, we exercised flexibility wherever possible. Some leaders preferred to meet twice a week for ten weeks; others began with a six-hour session followed by weekly sessions and a six-hour terminal session. The leaders were informed that the research was an outgrowth of the racism-and-prejudice course. We emphasized, however, that we were engaging them to "do their things," to conduct the groups in the same manner they normally would to enhance the possibility of their group members' experiencing personal growth. What was unusual about the experience, of course, for most of the leaders was the heavy load of research tasks involved. Each leader was asked to fill out a number of questionnaires before, during, and after the research experience, as well as to permit tape recording and ongoing observation of his group.

Participant recruitment proved even more complex than the recruitment of the leaders. Course credit was offered for participation in the groups to legitimize (for the students) the educational functions of the endeavor and to provide a mechanism for establishing a realistic research contract with them.

Students were recruited through a course listing in the time schedules of the university, articles in the student newspaper, and posters placed around campus. Of 251 students who registered for the course, 29 per cent came through the racism-and-prejudice course and the rest through the other recruitment procedures. Students who expressed interest in the course were invited to a series of meetings in which the research staff discussed the purposes of the inquiry and the nature of the experience to be offered. A microlab technique was employed at these meetings to illustrate the "feel" of encounter groups. The students were asked to break into small groups of four and five, and various exercises were given to demonstrate here-and-now communication, feedback techniques, and fantasy and personal revelation techniques. The students were told that the learning experience offered the opportunity to explore racial issues, but that individuals were free to pursue any personal learning goals. We indicated that the experience might be emotionally taxing and occasionally upsetting. Students were also informed of the concerns of the university about the potentially harmful effects of encounter group experience, and we described mental-health facilities available to participants if the experience did become emotionally stressful. Students were also told that one member of the research team was available to anyone who wishes to discuss his feelings or to seek help because of events related to participation in the group. Students were randomly assigned to groups based on stratified random sampling of sex, class year, and previous encounter group experience. Table 21-1 shows the population characteristics.

Table 21-1 Population Characteristics*

	% MEN			
Experimental	71			
Control	66			
Drop	57			

CLASS	FRESHMAN (percent)	SOPHOMORE (percent)	JUNIOR (percent)	SENIOR (percent)
Experimental	32	20	18	30
Control	35	25	19	21
Drop	29	29	17	25

PREVIOUS ENCOUNTER GROUP EXPERIENCE				
Experimental	49%			
Control	54%			
Drop	48%			

* N = Experimental 174
      Control 69
      Drop 40

CONTROL GROUPS

Some students who registered for the course could not be accommodated in the groups because of schedule problems. Others decided to take a different course; a few "changed their mind." (Groups met all days of the week, making it unlikely that a systematic bias was associated with students who could not be accommodated.) A control group (CGI) of 37 students was developed from this population. In addition, all students who indicated interest in the course were asked to list names of other students they knew to be interested in such an experience, but who were unable to participate in the group experience that quarter. A random sample of these individuals was invited to participate as control subjects. Thirty-two matched controls (CGII) were obtained through this procedure. The purpose of the research was described to these students, and they were asked to participate in the testing sessions. They were paid $5 for each testing session (approximately two and one-half to three hours).

The control groups offered a comparative population through which to assess the over-all effects of the experience on the participants. It should be emphasized, however, that a much more powerful method of control was inherent in the research design. If the several groups could be shown to possess different properties, comparison among groups would provide a much more meaningful and specific basis for comparison. Although at pretesting CGI controls did not know that they would not be participants and thus their expectational sets were identical to the participants', the same cannot be said for the CGII controls.

By the time the groups ended, a third sample (CGIII) of 40 individuals who dropped out of the groups was available for comparative purposes.

OUTCOME MEASURES

Any careful reading of outcome research in either the group psychotherapy or T-group literature will easily convince the prospective researcher of the difficulties and frustrations incumbent in such research. Problems of what to measure and when and how to measure it are chronic sources of consternation. These problems were magnified in the present study because the variety of orientations meant leaders would differ in their goals for participants and in their assumptions about what learning experiences were crucial. We approached the outcome question in terms of the role of encounter experience in the lives of participants, in order to acknowledge that individuals may enter such experiences with varied expectations and goals (as well as at different points in their life cycle, although this condition did not prevail in these groups). Given these individual and group differences, our strategy was designed to test a multiplicity of conceivable learning outcomes. Wherever possible, we used instruments that have been used by other investigators, but we nevertheless found it necessary to develop many new outcome measures.

All S's were tested on all outcome measures at three points in time: several weeks before group assignment, within a week or two after the groups terminated (about three months after the pretest), and six months after termination. Some of the questionnaires were administered several times during the life of the groups. No prior assumptions could be made about the interrelationship of outcome measures, and it was possible that some individuals could have a meaningful experience that would be reflected in only one dimension. Nor could we assume a priori that change in many dimensions would reflect greater significance.

Areas of Outcome Assessment

Religious Experience. For some participants the central importance of what is taken from the encounter group may be reflected in "oceanic, enthusiastic, conversion-like" feelings. Such individuals may not be able to report specific inner or behavioral changes. Nor would observers be able to pinpoint specific aspects that have changed. Yet such individuals may have a deep conviction that the experience was important and significant in their lives—a "peak experience" that the individual views as a landmark having long-term implications, an anchor point, a goad to further experience, or determinant in life-planning. Although a peak experience can be assessed only through self-report, entailing all the known problems of this method, such a report may signal specific subsequent changes. Peak experiences were identified by providing participants with a paragraph-long description of "peak-experience." They were asked whether they had ever had such an experience and under what conditions it occurred.

Interpersonal Construct System. For others the central import of the encounter experience may be a change in the way they view other people, their category system for persons. As a consequence of the encounter experience a person may become more or less critical of others, more or less tolerant; he may come to view people as more complex, less detailed. He may increase or decrease his belief that interpersonal difficulties can be worked out. The device used to measure this dimension (personal-description questionnaire) was an adaptation of Roger Harrison's adaptation of Kelly's REP test (Harrison, 1962). The S was asked to describe four close friends on 35 adjective scales, yielding a measure of how the S perceives significant others in his world as well as how many constructs he uses to differentiate people.

Self Issues. Three procedures were employed to assess issues related to self: (1) self-ideal discrepancy was measured on the same scales used to measure interpersonal constructs, (2) the Rosenberg (Rosenberg, 1965) scales and the self-description ratings on the personal-description questionnaire provided two measures of self-esteem, and (3) the congruence between self-perception in a specified context (the group situation) with others' views of self was assessed during the early, middle, and late meetings of the group by means of a 21-item sociometric (members of this group) covering various group roles and statuses.

Value Reorientation. The meaningfulness of encounter experience may be reflected in a reordering or reorientation of perceptions of what is personally important. Two realms of values were sampled: (1) *Personal behavior,* such as spontaneity and expression of feelings. Participants were asked to indicate how important such behaviors were for them (personal anticipations, part C). Seven test items were keyed to those areas stressed in encounter group theory. (2) *Abstract life goals.* Participants were asked to indicate on the life space questionnaire their most important life goals as well as to project seven years into the future and imagine their goals at that point in time.

Life Decisions. People often join encounter groups when they are facing life crises, such as the breakup of a marriage or career change, that require them to make major decisions. For such people the most salient aspect of the group experience may be the work done in resolving such dilemmas. To track these changes, S's were asked to indicate on the life space questionnaire whether they were contemplating any change in life space related to salient goals—altering a direction, making a new choice, entering into new activities, or giving up old activities or relationships.

Metalearning (Learning to Learn). The encounter group experience may also open up new ways of dealing with personal dilemmas. For example, a person may learn that paying attention to his inner life aids coping; he may utilize the world of feelings more frequently; or he may find that establishing symmetric feedback relationships aids problem-solving. Learning new modalities or broadening one's problem-solving approach to personal issues may be the prime learning carried away from the experience. The personal-dilemma questionnaire was developed to assess this area. Part I asks each participant to describe three actual dilemmas and how he coped with them. Part II presented a series of seven-point scales representing 19 strategies; S's were asked to indicate the likelihood of using each strategy if faced with these dilemmas tomorrow.

Interpersonal Changes. Three approaches were employed to assess this area: (1) A series of 15 scales (personal anticipations, part A and B) was presented prior to participation on which participants rated "where they were now" and "where they hoped to be at the end of the group," with respect to expression of affection and anger, spontaneity, and similar issues. At the end of the experience each participant was given his own form and asked to indicate where he was now. A similar format describing situational opportunities for such behavior —expression of feeling, spontaneity, and so on—was also administered before and after the experience. (2) The FIRO-B (Schutz, 1966), which has been used in a number of studies of T groups, provided a measure of preferred interpersonal style (wanted and expressed control, wanted and expressed affection). (Scales for inclusion were omitted because several previous studies have shown that they correlate with affection measures.) The test has also been used to measure discrepancies between behavior expressed by the self and that wanted from others, the implication being that encounter group experience may alter this "reward" score (discrepancy between wanted and expressed behavior) (Pollack, 1966; Smith, 1964). (3) The friendship questionnaire was administered to assess both the extensiveness and intensity of friendship behavior outside of the group.

Other Self-Report Indices. (1) An index of attitudes toward encounter groups consisted of 24 scales measuring the degree to which the individual perceived the encounter group experience as dangerous/safe, genuine/phony, and socially relevant/irrelevant. (2) Participants were asked to evaluate the personal relevance of the experience by means of open-ended questions as well as scales.

EXTERNAL CRITERIA OF CHANGE

All these measures rely on the participant's self-report. Three other perspectives for measuring the impact of the encounter group were employed, recognizing that the elaborate array of changes suggested in the self-report material could not be duplicated.

Leader Ratings. Many psychotherapy and T-group reports suggest that despite the potential biases of the therapist or trainer, professional judgments of change have proved to be a useful, valid source of information. In the present study group leaders were asked to rate every member on a nine-item self-anchoring scale. The items covered many of the same areas described in the members' rating of change (personal-anticipation questionnaire) and reflected the major dimensions the various leaders saw as important change areas. Self-anchoring was accomplished by asking leaders to recall all previous groups they had led and to think of someone who had greatly benefited, someone who was an "average changer," and a person who did not benefit. Using these anchors as reference points, the leader rated each participant for change.

Social Network Ratings of Change. Following a method developed by Miles (Miles, 1965), participants (both experimental and control) were asked at the onset of the study for the names of five to seven individuals who knew them quite well. At the six-month follow-up, letters were sent to each participant's "social network" asking whether the person had changed over the past six months. If the respondent indicated "yes," he was asked to describe the nature of the changes. Although deceptively simple, this procedure offers the researcher an external checkpoint on whether changes reported by leaders, coparticipants, or self are of sufficient magnitude to be perceived by an individual's relevant social network (Bunker, 1965).

Group Members. Coparticipants in the group provided another perspective for assessing member change. Several times during the course of the group experience, participants filled out a sociometric questionnaire (the members of this group) rank-ordering each group member relative to the amount of learning achieved as well as for specific group behaviors. Although this measure can be used relative to only a single group, it provides an additional view of change during the life of the group.

PSYCHOLOGIC RISK

Although it may be somewhat misleading to label the dimension of psychologic risk an outcome measure, the issue of whether encounter group experience is psychologically dangerous for participants is one of the most compelling problems facing the encounter field. The evidence is distressingly limited, but there is no dearth of emotional reaction to the issue. On the one hand, there is a tendency to see only the hazards of the encounter group techniques. Some mental-health specialists who have seen psychiatric casualties from encounter groups have responded by labeling the entire human relations field as dangerous and irresponsible. At the other extreme, there is a tendency to ignore or to disregard rather compelling evidence of adverse consequences of the encounter group experience. Many group leaders and growth centers are hardly aware of their casualties. Their contact with their clients is intense but brief; generally the format of the group does not include follow-up, and knowledge of untoward responses to the experience is therefore unavailable. Furthermore, some group leaders reject the medical or psychiatric definition of adverse effects. They assert that stressing of members to the point of such extreme discomfort that they require professional help is an accomplishment, not a danger, of the encounter group. These leaders believe that such individuals, although temporarily appearing worse, have in fact undergone a growth experience that will in the long run help them to be more fully integrated individuals.

The evidence supporting either of these positions is meager. The data relating to encounter group casualties are in a chaotic state and extraordinarily difficult to evaluate (*News and Reports*, 1969; Sata, 1967; Rogers, in press; Gottschalk and Pattison, 1969; Jaffe and Sherl, 1969). Systematic follow-up studies are scarce. Much of the material is anecdotal, and a large number of participants in a group or a laboratory increases the likelihood of multiple reporting; if 50 laboratory participants report the same single negative event, it soon takes on massive proportions.

The social relevance of the issue of casualties in encounter groups and the dearth of systematic studies led us to make a concerted effort to identify all individuals who might have been psychologically harmed by the experience. These people were then interviewed to assess their actual psychologic status. Five sources were used to identify potential casualties:

1. *Students who required emergency psychiatric aid* for distress encountered during the actual course of the group. Of the 209 students who participated in at least one session of the encounter group, three serious events occurred: one student committed suicide; a second had a manic psychotic attack and required hospitalization; a third needed emergency service for severe anxiety as a consequence of an incident that occurred in the encounter group. The case history of the student who committed suicide reflects the general difficulties in assessing the danger risk of the encounter group. Because the student killed himself two days after the third meeting of the encounter group, hasty reasoning would have impugned the encounter group as the responsible agent. However, the psychologic post-mortem revealed that the student had been severely disturbed for many months, had reached out for help from a number of sources, and had been in individual psychotherapy and in group therapy. Such a complex chain of events points out the difficulties of pinpointing the degree of danger in encounter groups.

2. All students from both the experimental and control groups who entered *psychotherapy* during the encounter experience or within six

months after the groups terminated. Obviously, without further examination, such a sample could not be labeled a casualty list. Some of these students may have been highly successful participants whose entrance into psychotherapy was part of a growth or exploratory stream begun in the encounter group. Preliminary data show that 10 per cent of students who participated in the encounter group entered psychotherapy during or subsequent to the encounter group as compared to 3 per cent of the control group.

3. *Coparticipants* in each encounter group were asked to identify for interview individuals in the group who might have been psychologically injured by the encounter experience.

4. Casualties were also identified through certain outcome scores such as sharp decreases in *self-esteem levels* or *major negative changes noted by the group leaders*. The lists of names generated by these four methods were compiled into one master list for study purposes.

5. Participants who *dropped out* of their groups were also considered as possible casualties. During the course of the three-month group experience, 40 participants dropped out of their groups prior to termination, most during the first two or three meetings. The format of drop-out interviews differed somewhat from that used for other potential casualty groups, because we wished to understand the dynamics of drop-out and some of the events that led up to the student's decision as well as to identify casualties. Drop-outs were asked to listen to a tape of part of the last session they attended and were then interviewed about their feelings and recollections regarding the encounter group, reasons for leaving, and so on. A preliminary analysis suggests that few, if any, of the drop-outs had experienced psychologic harm via their participation. It is possible that their self-terminations were preventive, because the outcome data on the drop-outs reflect high psychologic denial and exceedingly high positive change in some areas. This was particularly true of self-esteem, even for those students who had attended only one meeting. The reasons given for dropping out support a preventive hypothesis. Although varied, a recurring theme was the danger they perceived in the encounter group; they left for fear that they would be attacked or that they would lose control of their own anger.

STUDY OF GROUP PROCESSES

Even a reasonably clear answer to the question of how much and what kinds of impact encounter groups have on their participants would have only partially satisfied the perhaps overly ambitious goals each of us brought to the project. The stimulus for constructing the elaborate study design stemmed from our collective interests in developing a meaningful model for describing characteristics of groups and leader inputs that would be relevant to participant learning. Each of the investigators came to the study with overlapping and yet somewhat separate "favorite variables." Through our interaction still other questions and dimensions were developed. As the project grew, we began to describe this part of the study as the construction of a data bank that would permit us to answer a number of specific questions about the characteristics of group and leader behavior, in part as a potential resource for other investigators—a plan that has, even at this early date, been put into practice.

Some Questions. The following are some examples of our questions. Are some groups more effective than others, and if so, what are the characteristics of effective groups? Specifically, how much does a group leader contribute to the success of a group, and what are his specific techniques or interventions that result in successful experiences for the participants? To what extent do the personal qualities of the leader have an impact on participants, as contrasted with the particular technology he employs? What are useful ways of describing leader intervention styles, and are these styles similar to those used by therapists? To what extent can successful or unsuccessful learning in an encounter group be accounted for by the goals, expectations, and anticipations the learner brings to the group? To what extent do participants' personality characteristics affect their chance of outcome success or failure? Are there interactions between personality characteristics of individuals and particular kinds of groups so that person-group interaction is associated with degree of benefit derived from encounter groups?

Many theories about "self-analytic" groups of the sort we are studying make assumptions about group development; yet few empiric studies exist to support the theoretic formulations. The variety of leader styles represented in the study provided an unusual opportunity to test out some prevailing ideas about group development. Are there reliable sequences over time?[3] Do groups that go through particular sequences have different characteristics and different impact from those who do not?

Of particular interest was the role of group norms. What are the important norms in encounter groups? What impact do they have on the characteristics of the group and on the members' experience? What influences the establishment of norms? Do leaders have the major impact on the development of group norms, or do they develop

---

[3] As in B. Tuckman's review, Developmental Sequence in Small Groups. *Psychol. Bull.*, **63**:384–99, 1965.

primarily out of the interaction of the members in solving crucial issues inherent in group life? And are the effects of norms mediated or strengthened by group cohesion?

Other Considerations Influencing the Design. The most important effect on the measurement of group characteristics was our desire to discover "new dimensions" or ways of looking at groups. Achievement of this goal required that information be gathered about numerous qualities of group life. Other considerations were to include in the design as many dimensions as possible that prior researches on group therapy and T groups have demonstrated to influence the participants' experience. We were guided in the selection of these variables by the goal of creating a data bank. There were certain types of information collected, e.g., group climate rating, that did not have special interest to any of the investigators; yet such dimensions matched other studies in the area. Data about the characteristics of the group or leader behavior that could help determine the points of similarities and differences between group therapy and encounter groups were also gathered whenever possible. These data were, for the most part, gathered by observers, in order to add as little as possible to the heavy demands placed on participants to complete the outcome research forms.

Observations. The lead time for launching the study was unfortunately limited. There were only three months from inception to beginning the groups. This restricted the possibility of lengthy observer training.[4] To overcome some of the problems set by restrictions in training time, we composed the observer team of individuals who had participated in and, in several cases, led encounter groups[5] and had the observers work in pairs to increase the reliability of judgments about group characteristics and leader behavior.

The large number of group hours required a methodology for making the data gathered by the observers directly translatable for computer processing. The observation tasks were therefore cast at a macroscopic level. Observers made no ratings during the meeting; a log sheet was used to make notes during the meeting. Immediately

---

[4] Total training time was approximately 15 hours—12 hours prior to first observation and three hours after the third observation. Training consisted of orientation to the study; microlab techniques for team building; practice use of instruments on the data produced in the microlabs, and systematic practice of observation skills using encounter group films.

[5] Twenty-nine observers (including the research staff) were recruited from pre- and postdoctoral clinical psychologists in a local VA hospital, graduate students in clinical psychology with particular interest in groups, and psychiatric residents who had participated in a group psychotherapy training program.

after the end of a three-hour observation period (our standard period) each observer reviewed his notes and filled out a set of rating forms. The departure of our observation techniques from more conventional ones may be illustrated by the process we employed to assess group themes of covert emotional issues in the group, modeled after focal conflict theory (Whitaker and Lieberman, 1965). The usual procedures for this analysis require judgments based on a transcript, a detailed and obviously time-consuming procedure. For the present study, a form was constructed that presented the observer with an ordered sequence of possible conflicts. The observer indicated his relatively complex judgments in codable form. Thus, our observer data represent midlevel abstractions, rather than microscopic ratings, of the interaction in the group. The use of such procedures was based on the assumption that relatively sophisticated clinicians can process complex group events and make reasonable and reliable judgments upon reflection.

This design placed a high demand on the energies and skills of the observer and posed bias problems as well as problems of adaptation to particular groups. A further risk was that the compelling quality of encountering might draw the observers into the emotional drama and cause them to lose their objectivity. To circumvent such influences, a large number of observers (29 in all) were recruited so that two observers could be present to make independent judgments for all meetings. Furthermore, observers and observer pairs were systematically rotated among the groups and from one session to another. In most cases, observer pairs never met more than once for a period of observation, and most observers only saw the same group once or twice in its lifetime. These systematic rotations, although losing some of the quality of information gained as an observer "gets to know a group," did correct for personal biases and provide relative uniformity of information across groups. After making their independent ratings of each observer period, the observers met, discussed their ratings, and attempted to resolve any differences in their judgments. Thus for each meeting we had two independent observations plus a third rating based on observer discussions. Table 21-2 describes in summary form the areas rated by observers.

Other Measures of Group Characteristics. Certain group characteristics could only be assessed by having the participants report on the group experience. Measurements of the following parameters were made at the end of an early, middle, and late session.

Group norms. A 48-item questionnaire asked the participant to take the role of "orienting a new member" by indicating whether particular behaviors (covering areas such as intimacy, aggression, boundaries

Table 21-2 Observer Ratings

1. Topic of discussion—inside-outside
2. Content of discussion for (a) outside, (b) inside
3. Predominant work pattern
4. Indications of nonverbal procedures
5. Degree and extent (number of people) of revelation
6. Rank order of participation (amount)
7. Group climate (12 Osgood semantic differential scales)
8. Dominant group themes—a 32-item questionnaire directed toward coding the underlying themes or issues confronting the group during the entire meeting—themes of goal direction, movement, power, influence, status, characteristics of relationship, expressivity, emotional affects, and characteristic group ways of handling problems were included in this questionnaire
9. Potential norm violation—a series of 48 items identical with the norm questionnaire given to participants (do's or don'ts). Observer task was to indicate whether such forms of behavior occurred and what the typical response to this behavior was
10. A 12-item checklist directed toward determining the sanctioning and rewarding behavior of the group. Ratings were made of the mode of discouragement and mode of the encouragement used by the group, for example, ridicule, ostracization, praise, solidarity
11. Checklist of leader behavior—series of leader intervention styles (28 in all) covering five basic areas of leader behavior—evocative (inviting, challenging, calling on), coherence-making (comparing, contrasting, clarifying, summarizing), support, management (suggesting or setting rules, limits, norms, stopping, blocking, interceding, managing time sequences), use of self
12. Focus of leader's attention—group, interpersonal, intrapersonal
13. Global observer judgment of leader style—nine global categories of leader style. Observer is asked to indicate the degree to which the leader's over-all behavior was characteristic of this style. Styles such as releaser of emotions, personal leader, teacher, challenger
14. Personal reactions of observer to leader. The feelings the observer had toward the leader. Eight Osgood differential scales. (These personal reactions were not made into one rating, but were treated separately for each observer)

between inside and outside, confidentiality) described in the items would be appropriate or inappropriate in his group at the present time.

Cohesiveness Questionnaire. A 13-item test measured the degree of felt attraction to the group (Yalom et al., 1967) by asking participants to rate such items as, "Since the last session I have thought about the group all the time . . . not at all," on a seven-point scale.

Charisma Questionnaire. A ten-item test asked the participant to choose among four words for each item that best described his group leader. Each of the ten questions contained four words keyed to four styles of leadership—charisma-oriented, love-oriented, peer-oriented, and skill-oriented.

Personal Experience. Each participant's "personal" experience was assessed in two ways. (1) A one-page questionnaire (personal-incident questionnaire) was administered at the end of every other meeting, which asked: "Of the events that occurred in the meeting today, which one do you feel was the most significant to you personally and why was this experience significant to you?" (2) At the last group meeting participants filled out a 14-item questionnaire (curative factors) in which they were asked to check those aspects of the group experience that were personally helpful in growth or learning. Items included such dimensions as expressing feelings, using others as models, understanding own impact on others, and so on.

Critical Group Events. At the close of alternate meetings, participants identified important or significant events that had occurred in the group and gave their personal reactions and feelings.

A MODEL OF THE PROCESSES ASSOCIATED WITH CHANGE

The theoretic relationships examined by the project are represented schematically in Figure 21-1, which charts the possible sequence of events leading to and influencing individual learning or change. The diagram is not meant to imply that all changes are equivalent, or that the same relationships are invariant for all changes; these are matters for empiric examination. What is implied is a causal sequence of events associated with outcome.

Starting at the bottom, G presents a scheme for representing outcome as to (1) amount, (2) type, (3) stability of change (does the individual maintain time I–time II changes at time III?), (4) casualty or psychologic harm, and (5) drop-out status. The events most proximally associated with outcomes are the participants' experiences in the encounter group (F)—revelation, receiving feedback, a critical emotional experience, "insightful experience," and so on.

What conditions bring about such experiences? Why do some participants have them and not others? The focus here is on characteristics of the group. Because the research design aimed at maximizing general differences among the groups, the assumption here was that differences in such group characteristics as norms and levels of cohesiveness would also be maximized. Relationships between differences in group characteristics and the participants' experience (E) are illustrated by such questions as: What is the relationship between amount of revelation

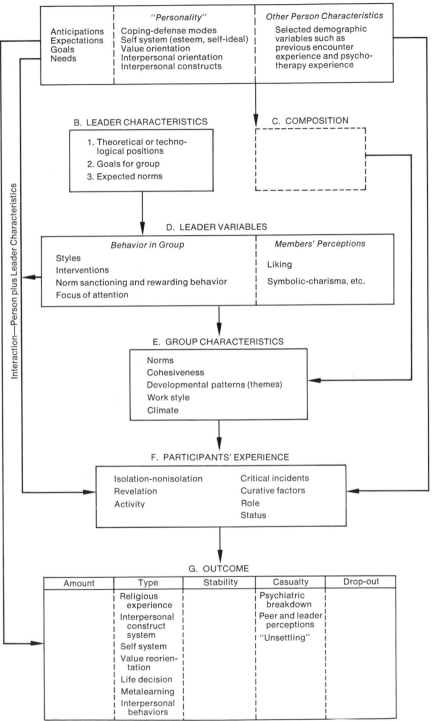

Figure 21-1.

491

and cohesiveness? What is the relationship between receiving useful feedback and the existence of certain group norms?

The critical "experimental variable," which was assumed to make the differences among the groups, was, of course, the behavior of the leader. The hypothesized sequence relates leader variables (D) to group characteristics. Leader variables have been divided into two general areas—actual behavior of the leader in the group and perception of the leader by the participants (charisma, warmth, and so on). Also of interest was what relationships might exist between theoretic or technologic orientations and leader behavior (B).

The dotted box (C), composition, is intended to take into account (as other studies have shown [Yalom and Rand, 1966; Harrison, 1965; Lieberman, 1958]) that member composition affects group characteristics. Although the research strategy of random assignment to groups minimizes some of the influence of composition, personality data may reveal some composition influence, especially in groups that exhibit similar leader behavior but different group characteristics.

The uppermost square (A) lists personal characteristics of the individual members. A number of possible relationships exist. For example, if we ask questions about the encounter group experience (and ignore differences among the groups) outcome may be highly related to personality variables. Several psychotherapy studies (Goldstein and Shipman, 1961; Friedman, 1963) indicate that the degree of anticipation of potential change and the amount of valuation (expectation) toward the psychotherapeutic relationship relates to the amount of change. The line AG in Figure 21-1 represents this possibility. This relationship may be more complex; person characteristics, such as anticipations and expectations or coping and defense modes, may interact with group type. Or, the relationship may be mediated through the participant's experience (line AF) in which degree of revelation, for example, may depend more on person characteristics than on particular group conditions. Yet another set of relationships for "explaining change" may be found in the interrelationships between participant and leader; the interaction between specific person variables and leader variables may account for much of the quality of the participant's experience and his subsequent change. This relationship is shown by the line ADF.

This schematic representation shows only classes of expected relationships. In practice, tests of these relationships will be carried out both on *classes* of variables (boxes as shown in the diagram) as well as on *individual parameters* shown in each box. Thus it is possible, using multivariate statistics, to assess the relative contribution of composition variables as a class as compared to leader variables as a class. It is possible to test out the influence of specific leader variables on specific group characteristics asking such questions as to what degree the leader's intervention style affects the norms of the group.

ILLUSTRATIVE FINDINGS

Considerable caution must be used in interpreting the incomplete findings presented in this section. Our analysis of time I and time II differences is incomplete; time III is as yet unavailable. The illustrative findings are addressed to questions of: Over-all, does an encounter group experience have an impact on those who participate? Are there different effects of various "types" of encounter groups? If so, what are the important differences among leaders that may be associated with these differences in effects? Do the group characteristics themselves differ? and What about the participant's phenomenal experience—do these differ from group to group?

An overwhelming majority of participants saw the group as a constructive experience. Seventy-five per cent reported immediately afterward that the group had resulted in positive change in themselves, and of these, 75 per cent expected the changes to be lasting. Approximately 95 per cent of the students stated they would like to see the encounter group experience become a regular elective part of the university curriculum. This uniformly enthusiastic response, as one would anticipate, did not match the degree of change in the participants exemplified in measures of time I–time II differences. Over-all, although there were measurable differences between the experimental population and the control subjects, the magnitude of these differences was not impressive. The Rosenberg Self-Esteem Scales, for example, showed some of the largest experimental-control differences. Twice as many of the experimentals compared to control S's increased their self-esteem; and, at about the same ratio, those participants who entered the study with high self-esteem (and because of "topping" the scale could show no further "improvement") were more likely to maintain this high level than were the control subjects. The number of individuals, however, showing such changes was only about 35 per cent of the experimental population.

More striking were the extensive differences among the groups—over-all, some groups had almost no impact on their participants whereas other groups affected nearly every member of the group. Again self-esteem scores are illustrative. In one group 100 per cent of the members showed a rise in self-esteem, whereas in another group only

15 per cent showed a similar rise.[6] An alternative statistic measuring impact on self-esteem showed a marked improvement or sharp decline in self-esteem among 60 per cent of the members of one group, while demonstrating neither a high rise nor sharp decline in self-esteem in any member of another group. In other words, some groups seemed to have high impact, in both positive and negative directions, whereas other groups left the members relatively untouched at the end of the experience. Still other measures of time I–time II differences show the same patterns. There are groups that, across a number of measures, seem to have high impact; there are other groups that show very little change in either direction; still others are skewed in a negative direction.

The groups differed markedly in the number of drop-outs. The drop-out rate ranged from a high of 40 per cent to a low of 0 per cent. Group characteristics associated with drop-out were those that emphasized attack, challenge, and confrontation with few visible means of support. High drop-out rates, however, also occurred in groups that had very little stimulative input by leaders—leader characteristics that were also associated with few marked time I–time II differences. Such discrepancies among the groups would suggest that the leaders and the groups did indeed differ in their characteristics. Two analyses of leader behavior and group characteristics are illustrative of these differences.

Leader Behavior. A factor analysis of observer ratings of leader behavior (see Table 21-2, "checklist") yielded seven interpretable factors. Three of these describe the stimulation function of the group leader. We have provisionally titled these factors intrusive modeling (factor 1), which includes behavior such as challenging, confronting, exhorting, revealing self, revealing values, focusing on self, and behaving as a participant; command response (factor 3), which involves such behaviors as inviting, eliciting, questioning, suggesting procedures, and facing the group with a decision task; and stimulation by drawing attention (factor 5), which includes behavior such as reflecting, calling on, comparing and contrasting, and focusing. Leaders differed vastly in the style of stimulation as well as total amount of such behavior. For those accustomed to psychotherapist behavior heavy utilization of such stimulative behaviors may seem strange, but it will be less so to those experienced in encounter group work. Leaders who tended not to be "high stimulators" all turned out to be leaders whose primary day-to-

---

[6] We are pointedly not identifying *which* groups showed these changes. Until our analyses are complete, to do so would be irresponsible. In any case, it seems clear from our work so far that high or low outcomes are not as strongly associated with a particular group "label" (Gestalt, nonverbal, T group), as much as they are with particular leader or group *behavior*, regardless of the official label.

day responsibilities were treating patients and who came into the encounter group movement subsequent to becoming psychotherapists.

Preliminary inspection of the data suggests, then, that the encounter leaders differ widely in how they conducted their groups, a departure from the common finding in psychotherapy research that experienced therapists behave pretty much alike. The four other factors that came out of this analysis were: cognitive inputs (factor 2)—explaining, interpreting, providing frameworks, and providing concepts; setting limits (factor 4)—behaviors grouped around some aspect of group management; factor 6, a noninput-type factor we have provisionally termed "mirroring," which includes behavior such as reflecting and summarizing; and, lastly, support (factor 7)—protecting, showing love and affection, exhibiting support and encouragement, and inviting feedback.

Other data suggesting that the groups did, in fact, differ radically in their characteristics were drawn from an instrument—do's and dont's—that was administered to all participants in the early, middle, and late life of the groups. The questionnaire, composed of 48 items, asked each individual to judge the appropriateness/inappropriateness of specific behaviors such as joking, expressing anger, appealing to the leader for support, and being absent. A factor analysis of the second administration of this instrument yielded five interpretable factors that account for 41 of the 48 items. The first factor, composed of 14 items, was tentatively labeled "the expression of intimate authentic feelings;" it contained such items as "warmly touched another member," "cried," "asked for reactions or feedback," "frankly showed sexual attraction to another person in the group," and so on. Some groups had a uniform commitment, namely, a large proportion of the group endorsed many such behaviors as being appropriate in their group, and in other groups members were much less inclined to agree that such behavior was appropriate in their group. (It should be said, though, that 6 of the 14 items in this cluster were endorsed by 15 of the 17 groups—thus it is a kind of basic "encounter group culture" factor.)

Tentatively entitled boundaries, the second factor contains such items as joking, talking about the details of sex life, refusing to be bound by group decisions, bringing up problems that the person had with others who weren't in the group, and so on. These items seem to refer to the degree to which flight from the here-and-now was appropriate in the group, as well as the degree of permeability of the group's boundaries by outsiders. Wide differences are evident among the groups on how appropriate or inappropriate such behavior is considered by most of the group members. (For example, "frequently joked" is seen as appropriate by a majority of one group's members and inappropriate in another group and is regarded with mixed feeling in the remaining 15 groups.)

At this point in time, we cannot provide material on the meaning of such norms relative to outcome. The fact that the groups differ widely in the amount of change and perhaps even the type of change, as well as in both leader behavior and such a central group characteristic as norms, heightens the probability that meaningful relationships can be established between such characteristics and outcome.

Our analysis to date strongly suggests that a view of encounter groups as a uniform activity is incorrect. It thus appears that the generic title "encounter groups" covers a wide range of operations by leaders that lead to many kinds of group experiences, and perhaps to many types of learnings.

Perhaps the most appropriate way of illustrating findings is to reflect on some of the differences among groups as seen by the participants. At the end of the encounter group experience each participant was asked to indicate on a 14-item questionnaire what sorts of experiences he saw as critical to his learning or change. Members' responses differed, in part, according to the group they were in. In some groups, participants felt that what was important in the group was that they were accepted and involved or that they were able to express their feelings fully; in other groups participants felt that they were helped by receiving advice or learning that other people had the same types of problems they had; in yet other groups participants focused on more intellectual factors such as that they felt they were helped by understanding the sources and causes of their problems.

Group membership, however, does not explain the total variance; students who appeared to have learned a great deal (as measured by their own testimony) tended to value certain factors such as group cohesion, cognitive understanding, and revealing embarrassing aspects of themselves while still being accepted; those who appeared to be "low learners" tended to value such factors as receiving advice, expressing feelings, and helping others.

It thus appears that in studying encounter groups we are in essence studying a range of leader styles and group characteristics, and perhaps not one learning experience, but several types, at least as perceived by the participants.

BIBLIOGRAPHY

Bunker, D. Individual Applications of Laboratory Training. *J. Appl. Behav. Sci.*, **1**:131–48, 1965.

Friedman, H. F. Patient-Expectancy and Symptom Reduction. *Arch. Gen. Psychiat.*, **8**:61–67, 1963.

Goldstein, A. P., and Shipman, W. C. Patient Expectancies, Symptom Reduction and Aspects of the Initial Psychotherapeutic Interview. *J. Clin. Psychol.*, **17**:129–33, 1961.

Gottschalk, L. A., and Pattison, E. M. Psychiatric Perspectives on T-Groups and the Laboratory Movement: An Overview. *Amer. J. Psychiat.*, **126**:823–39, 1969.

Harrison, Roger. The Impact of the Laboratory on Perception of Others by the Experimental Group. In C. Argyris. *Interpersonal Competence and Organizational Effectiveness.* Homewood, Ill.: Irwin Press, 1962.

Harrison, Roger. Group Composition Models for Laboratory Design. *J. Appl. Behav. Sci.*, **1**:409–32, 1965.

Jaffe, S. J., and Sherl, D. J. Acute Psychosis Precipitated by T-Group Experience. *Arch. Gen. Psychiat.*, **21**:443–49, 1969.

Lieberman, M. A. Relationship Between Emotional Cultures of Groups and Individual Change. Unpublished doctoral dissertation. University of Chicago, 1958.

Lieberman, M. A., Lakin, M., and Whitaker, D. S. Problems and Potential of Psychoanalytic and Group-dynamic Theories for Group Psychotherapy. *Internat. J. Group. Psychother.*, **19**:131–41, 1969.

Miles, M. B. Changes During and Following Laboratory Training: A Clinical-experimental Study. *J. Appl. Behav. Sci.*, **1**:215–42, 1965.

News and Reports. NTL Institute, **3**:Nov., 1969.

Pollack, H. Change in Homogeneous and Heterogenous Sensitivity Groups. Unpublished doctoral dissertation. University of California, Berkeley, 1966.

Poser, E. G. The Effects of Therapists' Training on Group Therapeutic Outcome. *J. Consult. Psychol.*, **30**:283–89, 1966.

Rogers, Carl. Cited by M. Parloff. Group Therapy and the Small Group Field: An Encounter. *Internat. J. Group Psychother.*, **20**:267–304, 1970.

Rosenberg, M. *Society and the Adolescent Self Image.* Princeton, N.J.: University of Princeton Press, 1965.

Sata, L. Unpublished study, 1967.

Schutz, W. *The Interpersonal Underworld.* Palo Alto, Calif.: Science and Behavior Books, 1966.

Smith, P. B. Attitude Changes Associated with Training in Human Relations. *Brit. J. Soc. & Clin. Psychol.*, **2**:104–12, 1964.

Tuckman, B. Developmental Sequence in Small Groups. *Psychol. Bull.*, **63**:384–99, 1965.

Whitaker, D. S., and Lieberman, M. A. *Psychotherapy Through Group Process.* New York: Atherton Press, 1965.

Yalom, I., Houts, P., Newell, G., and Rand, K. Preparation of Patients for Group Therapy. *Arch. Gen. Psychiat.*, **12**:416–27, 1967.

Yalom, I., and Rand, K. Compatibility and Cohesiveness in Therapy Groups. *Arch. Gen. Psychiat.*, **13**:267–76, 1966.

Leonard Blank

 **Confrontation Techniques—
A Two-Sided Coin**

COMMENTARY

In this concluding chapter, some negative as well as positive features
of confrontation programs and encounter techniques are examined.
Theoretic rationales for, and social implications of, these programs
and techniques are explored.

Recently, there was a cartoon of two ladies sitting under hair driers.
One remarked to the other, "I don't know what I'm getting out of my
group but I certainly have got the goods on a lot of people." In other
words, group techniques may have their disadvantages as well as advantages.

Basic encounters, marathons, and sensitivity or interactional training are confrontation techniques that are capable of mobilizing powerful inter- and intrapersonal forces in a most constructive manner.
Moreover, these techniques are not restricted to patients or even clients
but are available to any segment of the population—to people and
people issues.

THE NEGATIVE SIDE OF THE COIN

There is, however, another side to the coin. That side reflects the misuse and abuse of interactional processes. We shall consider the equivocal training of many group leaders; the questionable objectives of participants, as well as those who guide them; the problems of cultism and the buckshot application of group techniques; and the misapplication of these techniques.

There is a vast and hungry demand for human interaction nowadays in education, government, industry, religion, and other organizations, not to mention legions of "unaffiliated" persons. Where there is marked demand, supply usually rises to meet it—even if the quality suffers. So we witness the phenomenon of large numbers of newly self-anointed group leaders, trainers, and encounter facilitators or guides. These "experts" often may have been baptized by participating in a one- or two-week training laboratory, having a week-end encounter experience, visiting Esalen, or reading *Joy* or the writings of Perls, Rogers, Maslow, *et al.* And they have decided that this work is more fulfilling and humanizing than accounting, personnel work, ministerial duties, or experimental psychology. They have seen the light and tasted the joys and poignancies of human interaction; so why shouldn't they lead and inspire others along these routes?

Perhaps more sophisticated is the diverse and amorphous group lumped together under the rubric of behavioral scientist and the helping professions. This includes, but does not exhaust, such occupations as sociologists, social psychologists, physicians, nurses, speech pathologists, rehabilitation workers, industrial relations managers, and management consultants. It is questionable whether the expertise of these specialists, which ranges from study of laboratory group process to enhancing increased business production, is suitable for the clinical and interpersonal and intrapersonal phenomena that are stimulated in encounter and interactional groups. More about this when we consider objectives.

There is question, as well, about the efficacy of the clinician who thinks in terms of a traditional medical model—the psychiatrist, clinical psychologist, social worker, psychiatric nurse, counselor, individual therapist, or even group therapist. One is reminded of the psychiatrist who accounted for an extremely large number of diagnoses of schizophrenia in the mental hospital at which he worked. The incidence of this diagnosis decreased sharply when he left for a position as a school psychiatrist. Schizophrenia, however, became a quite popular diagnosis at this school. The clinician is rather prone to stress psychopathology and therapy even though this may not be critically indicated or desired. And he will therapize or encourage group participants to therapize because this is what he knows and what gratifies him. The participants will also be gratified because "personal growth" is so desired. Then all will rationalize that great good has been achieved despite forgotten objectives (such as knowledge of group dynamics and interpersonal skills) and uncertain evidence of more-than-transient gains. One thinks of those psychology or sociology books we read to learn something; we soon get seduced by sexual material, intriguing gambits, and exotic case material. They are certainly worth reading for the fun of it, and we might learn a thing or two. But we have been cheated out of our objective of mastering specific knowledge.

In other words, unqualified or irrelevant training for group leaders may waste group effort or aggravate conflict. Now, this is not a brief for training versus perceptiveness, interpersonal skill, and humaneness, which are certainly not the restricted possession of the professional. But relevant training geared toward specific objectives is at least a minimal guarantee that the leader is not working out merely his own needs of filling his loneliness or satisfying his voyeurism, exhibitionism, or desire for power—that he at least recognizes these needs and is channeling them constructively in the service of the individuals who make up the group. Humanists tend to be antibureaucratic (or so it would logically seem), but some form of certification seems in order so as to provide protection for the public and the "science-art" of group leadership. I must hastily add that accreditation also has its drawbacks—certifying bodies or training centers may also become parochial, so that innovativeness is lost. I should think that a multidisciplined, varied-theory approach requires contribution from professional associations, universities, agencies, and impartial consultants.

What are the objectives of the myriad numbers of people who seek group or interactional experience? Some seek to learn about their style of interaction with others and the interpersonal techniques of others. Some want to learn about group process so they can function better in groups or utilize the productive learning and problem-solving powers that groups manifest. Others want to improve their communication or human side of themselves—they look for better human relations, race relations, or very generally personal growth. Many really want psychotherapy whether they appreciate this need or not. (Wise people seek personal growth—patients and sick people seek psychotherapy.) Some are looking for a spiritual, religious, or sensual if not orgiastic experience. A rather large number of people, I think, are searching to fill a void in their lives and many settle for going from one turning-on experience to another with nothing in between. The last group includes many persons who have tried or are still trying drugs,

ESP, spiritualism, yoga, Eastern religion, mysticism, and what not.

I personally, believe that any of these objectives is legitimate and respectable. The only trouble is they are not clarified for the seeker or in the group facilitator's mind. Often, the rationale is that the group will work out its objectives once it forms, no matter what the group composition, the training skills, and the tactics of the trainer. It seems to me that the particular chemistry of a group and who and what the leader is and why he wishes to work with a particular group are extremely important. It also seems to me that different objectives require different techniques.

Therefore, screening procedures geared toward specific objectives can prove to be of crucial importance. They are insufficiently employed and what are substituted in some instances are pious rationales, silent prayers that psychotic episodes will be avoided, and the hope that more people will benefit than not. Incidentally, the danger of precipitating a psychotic manifestation tends to be overrated by critics of encounter groups. Nonclinicians, including many behavioral scientists, tend to view raw expression of emotion or vital expression of irrationality as uncontrolled madness. A cohesive group with a skilled leader provides control for these emotional storms to the vast benefit of the individual and the group. There are many ambulatory psychotics who, however, in their quest for human contact, find a group in order to "experience" with people. There is some doubt whether the group's objectives are most furthered by the discrepant needs of these individuals. There are many others who really are very threatened by human interaction or any type of personality uncovering but desperately seek help. Here again, more formal psychotherapy or a more homogeneous group seems indicated. Advertising for participants for training laboratories or encounters led by "Esalen-trained" or "NTL-experienced" leaders in newspapers and indiscriminately distributed brochures seems to be foolish as well as unethical for the very reason of disregard of screening.

The objectives of the newer, less experienced leaders in the encounter fields may also be confounded and contaminated. They know they have hold of a powerful vehicle and, therefore, looking for any substantial theory, believe they can apply interactional techniques to anyone, anywhere, for any reason. So the T group that worked so well for a group of educators or a marathon that clicked for students or patients is transferred lock, stock, and barrel to middle management in a medium company, black-white dialogues and confrontations, clergy, a P-TA meeting, or an American Legion convention. This is a buckshot approach—whoever is hit, fine; whoever doesn't bleed or emote has not responded because he remained out of the line of fire.

Smacks of rationalization, doesn't it? (Campbell and Dunnette [1968] in their extensive review of sensitivity training conclude that there is little evidence to support the contention that T groups alter work behavior.)

More dangerously, faddism, cultism, and fanaticism seem to be creeping on the scene. "If you haven't experienced sensitivity training, you'll never know what we are talking about." "You need to enter a marathon to really be able to relate to people or know yourself." "If you don't take an annual trip to Mecca, that is, Bethel or Esalen, you are not really alive." "People will get along together only if they all participate in T groups." I have heard all these statements and even more extreme ones. We know that religion can be very helpful for people but we also know that religiosity fans conflict, rivalry, and hatred. The same is true of cultism. And a beautiful and powerful experiment—the interactional approach—may be vitiated by breeding irrationalism, unquestioned faith, conflict, and suspicion—the very processes it seeks to counteract.

THE POSITIVE SIDE OF THE COIN

There is considerable interest matched with as much confusion about a variety of group phenomena—encounters, marathons, and sensitivity training, to name several.

Sensitivity training, or T groups, are the most commonly known and most unfortunately named. The term suggests to many an indoctrination or conditioning. In fact, the opposite is intended, for the objective of sensitivity training is the enhancement of self-awareness and awareness of one's relationships to others—the opening up of more options for communication. T groups originated with Kurt Lewin and his fellow social psychologists in New England who were concerned with the democratic process in small groups (Bradford, 1964). It was in New England, of course, that the town meeting became an essential ingredient of our budding democracy. This progenitor of the T group encouraged the frank and free interchange of opinion and attitudes among people concerned with and involved in the democratic process.

Nevertheless, there is a vocal segment of the populace who link sensitivity training and encounter techniques with brainwashing, communism, immoral experimentation, and such. To analyze why there is such polarized interest and criticism, let us consider the context or the psychosocial climate.

Fromm (1945) has discussed the increasing sense of alienation of people in highly industrialized societies. What seems to take place is a clash between two intense human needs—the need for individuation and freedom versus the quest for security. The latter apparently is prevailing for most people.

The mobility in our industrial society and the decline of the working family as a unit have attenuated that social unit and the security associated with it. Job specialization and fierce competition undermine security at work, and complexity of community and national affairs combined with international tensions generates insecurity with respect to one's place in society. When one adds, to the already steaming cauldron, differing and conflicting roles of youth and adult, male and female, white and black, white collar and blue collar, the entire issue of identity becomes shaky (Erikson, 1968).

Therefore, Fromm postulates, people attempt to escape from individuality and freedom because they need reference points and want to be protected and guided. One way to accomplish this is to search for strong leaders, whether benign father figures or stern authoritarians. Another, usually complementary choice is that of concrete symbols. These are oversimplified, distorted versions of flag, church, institutions, politics, cults, and fraternal organizations, but they do provide a sense of unification and belonging. Unfortunately, what is often sacrificed is the meaningful participation of, and respect for, the individual as well as team and group interaction. Yet another, and most pervasive, way of escaping from the threats and *responsibilities* of freedom is to assume rigid roles and insulate oneself from the needs (perceived as demands) of one's fellow man.

It feels dangerous to be too human. Roles must be chosen that minimize this danger by such techniques as:

Keep contacts minimal or at least shallow.
Don't really look at the other (or at least don't see him).
Never touch—unless for sex, to hurt, or to control.
Avoid listening, certainly do not hear (Rollo May, 1969).

Situations or interactions that do not permit such insulating tactics are threatening to people seeking to maintain security. Human relations, group programs, confrontation experiences, and so on are perceived, therefore, by the threatened as ominous, unpatriotic, irreligious, and whatever other label can be scared up. The result is weak or superficial communication and stereotypic relationships.

A number of influences, however, have emerged to contribute to reaction against personal isolation or, more positively, as a stirring for interpersonal and group closeness.

Ego Psychology

The preponderance of personality theory, from such diverse sources as learning and behavior theory and traditional psychoanalysis, has explained personality as being fixed relatively early in life. The individual, these theories postulate, is conditioned and essentially reacts to his environment (Hilgard and Marquis, 1961). In the last decade or so, however, ego psychology has offered conceptualization and research data to indicate that man is more than reactive. He is adaptive, curious, interested in shaping his environment, and prone to experimentation (White, 1964; McClelland et al., 1953).

Existential Theory

The popularity of another theory, the existential approach, with youth and intellectuals is also focussed on experimentation. As with ego psychologists, existentialists are concerned with the investigation and opening up of options for enhanced dimensions for living. The emphasis is on the present and the implications of future possibilities rather than on the limitations of the past on one's life (May, 1958).

Gestalt Theory

Adding to the dimensions of adaptability, experimentation and existential reality, the Gestalt approach emphasizes the whole person, including the significance of the body and "gut" reactions (Perls, 1969). Gestalt concepts have been utilized in academic psychology for many years, but their application in psychotherapy and interpersonal interactions, particularly in combination with such therapeutic theories as Reich's (Reich, 1949), is much more recent. Stress on the body and its language and gestures, *ipso facto*, emphasizes the immediacy of the moment and validates the merit or distortion of verbal communication.

Youth Expression

Only a few of our youth are acquainted with the theoretic inputs just cited. Nevertheless, the psychosocial climate that seems to be nurturing the interest in these theories appears also to be stimulating the expression of youth in analogous claims: "I want to be me, to experiment in living, to be a person and a whole person—body and mind—and to live in the present." Apparently, there is a revulsion by youth against the impersonalization and dehumanization of huge populations, computerization, automation, and constant threats of bombs, radiation, pollution, and throttling in our own wastes. So a thrust for life and individuality and identity results (Fromm, 1945; May, 1969; Erikson, 1968).

MINORITY PROTEST

Although springing from different sources, the minority and civil-rights movement also is voicing its claim for identity and individuality. There is a commonality of goals and, even in the extreme forms of protest and militancy, shared objectives.

The concatenation of theoretic influences such as ego psychology, existential approach, and Gestalt theory and the struggle of youth and minorities to assert themselves is part of a social ferment. There is an increasing search for contact, communion, and engagement. This search for personal and interpersonal awareness is called *humanism* (Maslow, 1963; Bugental, 1967). The humanistic orientation has appealed to a spectrum of individuals as well as to educational, religious, and industrial organizations.

There has been a proliferation of groups and encounter phenomena to meet this appeal. Some of these situations are wild experimentation and others smack of cultism or fadism. Behavioral science, on the other hand, studies and applies knowledge of interpersonal dynamics and group processes to communication and personal growth. If we designate this area of interest as interactional processes (what the editors of this book have described as encounters in self and interpersonal awareness), the objectives are enhanced interaction and communication, especially sensitization to see, hear, and understand the other fellow in relationship to oneself.

BIBLIOGRAPHY

Bradford, L., Gibb, J., and Benne, K. (eds.) *T-Group Theory and Laboratory Method: Innovation in Re-education.* New York: Wiley, 1964.

Bugental, J. (ed.) *Challenges of Humanistic Psychology.* New York: McGraw-Hill, 1967.

Campbell, J., and Dunnette, M. Effectiveness of T-Group Experiences in Managerial Training and Development. *Psychol. Bull.,* **70:**73–92, 1968.

Erikson, E. *Identity: Youth and Crisis.* New York: W. W. Norton, 1968.

Fromm, E. *Escape from Freedom.* New York: Farrar & Rinehart, 1945.

Hilgard, E. R., and Marquis, D. G. *Conditioning and Learning.* New York: Appleton-Century-Crofts, 1961.

Hull, C., and Lindsey, G. *Theories of Personality.* New York: Wiley, 1970.

McCelland, D., *et al. The Achievement Motive.* New York: Appleton-Century-Crofts, 1953.

Maslow, A. Fusion of Facts and Values. *Amer. J. Psychoanal.,* **23**:117–31, 1963.

May, R. *Existence.* New York: Basic Books, 1958.

May, R. *Love and Will.* New York: W. W. Norton, 1969.

Perls, F. *Gestalt Therapy Verbatim.* Lafayette, Calif.: Real People Press, 1969.

Reich, W. *Character Analysis.* New York: Orgone Institute Press, 1949.

Schutz, W. *Joy.* New York: Grove Press, 1967.

White, R. *The Abnormal Personality,* 3rd ed. New York: Ronald Press, 1964.

Index